GLOBAL
MINI-NATIONALISMS

Global Mini-Nationalisms is the second volume in a sub-series to CONTRIBUTIONS IN POLITICAL SCIENCE entitled GLOBAL PERSPECTIVES IN HISTORY AND POLITICS, edited by George Schwab.

GLOBAL
MINI-NATIONALISMS
Autonomy or
Independence

LOUIS L. SNYDER

CONTRIBUTIONS IN POLITICAL SCIENCE, NUMBER 71
GLOBAL PERSPECTIVES IN HISTORY AND POLITICS

Greenwood Press
Westport, Connecticut . London, England

Library of Congress Cataloging in Publication Data

Snyder, Louis Leo, 1907-
    Global mini-nationalisms.

    (Contributions in political science, ISSN 0147-1066
no. 71. Global perspectives in history and politics)
    Bibliography: p.
    Includes index.
    1. Nationalism. 2. Autonomy. 3. Regionalism.
I. Title. II. Series: Contributions in political
science; no. 71. III. Series: Contributions in political
science. Global perspectives in history and politics.
JC311.S549   320.5'4   81-6950
ISBN 0-313-23192-3 (lib. bdg.)   AACR2

Library of Congress Catalog Card Number: 81-6950
ISBN: 0-313-23192-3
ISSN: 0147-1066

First published in 1982

Greenwood Press
A division of Congressional Information Service, Inc.
88 Post Road West
Westport, Connecticut 06881

Printed in the United States of America

10 9 8 7 6 5 4 3 2 1

To

Leslie Adams; Alice and Rudolph Binion; Yvonne and
Joseph Blotner; David Van Deusen Edwards; Adrian
and Elsa de Groot; Allesandra Lippuci; Robert Bernard
Martin; Ruth and Walter Meserve; Aileen and David
Morley; and May and William Walsh—with affection
and a bow to the magic of Bellagio

CONTENTS ————————————————

PREFACE _____

This study owes its completion to the help and encouragement of the Rockefeller Foundation and the Alexander von Humbolt Foundation, both of which share the author's belief that nationalism is one of the most important historical forces of the contemporary era. Just preceding the outbreak of World War I, the British publicist Norman Angell wrote: "Political nationalism has become for the European of our age the most important thing in the world, more important than humanity, decency, kindness, pity; more important than life itself."

Allowing for journalistic hyperbole, there is still more than a grain of truth in Angell's comment. The people of the world have learned that nationalism is a critical historical force which literally means life and death for all of us. Clarification of nationalism in all its phases is a matter of high priority for historians and for scholars of related disciplines.

Much attention has been paid to nationalism itself in the pioneer work of Carlton J. H. Hayes, Hans Kohn, Boyd C. Shafer, and their colleagues, but there has been relatively little work done on two corollaries existing on its peripheries—macro-nationalism and mini-nationalism. Macro-nationalisms are the broader pan-national movements which represent attempts to combine similar nationalisms in a larger movement. The mini-nationalisms are the so-called liberating movements by which minorities inside centralized states seek either more local autonomy as part of the state structure or outright independence. These mini-nationalisms exist in varying forms throughout the world. Some present moderate demands; others turn to terrorism to achieve their goal.

The original intention of this study was to produce a comparative analysis of the macro-nationalisms and the mini-nationalisms in one volume, but it soon became evident that there was far too much material for a single book. It was decided to limit this volume to the mini-nationalisms and reserve the macro-nationalisms for a later comparative study.

The aims of this work are fourfold: (1) to define the meaning of mini-nationalism and the terms closely associated with it; (2) to place each form in historical context; (3) to compare the moderate and extreme forms of unsatisfied nationalisms; and (4) to indicate the global nature of the mini-nationalisms. There is no pretense here of final

xiii

judgment, but an attempt is made to find such common denominators as territory, language, politics, economics, and culture—in short, the common historical motivations.

It is a pleasure to express my thanks to John J. McKelvey, Jr., of the Rockefeller Foundation; Dr. Heinrich Pfeiffer, General Secretary, and Dr. Dietrich Pappenfuss of the Alexander von Humboldt Foundation; and Dr. Arnold Ebel, Director of the New York office of the Deutscher Akademischer Austauschdienst (DAAD). I am also indebted to Prof. Dr. Erich Angermann, Director of the Anglo-Amerikanische Abteilung of the Historisches Seminar of the University of Cologne; his colleagues Dr. Hermann Wellenreuther and Dr. Marie-Luise Frings; and to Franz-Wilhelm and Irmgard Koch.

I am grateful to the staff of the Firestone Library at Princeton University, who allowed me access to the stacks of the library and considerably eased the task of research. A similar word of thanks should be added for the librarians at the New York Public Library, the City College of New York, the City University of New York, and the Universities of Cologne and Bonn.

A special word should be added about the Rockefeller Foundation's Study and Conference Center at the Villa Serbelloni in the Italian Alps overlooking Bellagio and Lake Como. Here, in ideal surroundings, at a spot where Pliny the Younger, Charlemagne, Napoleon, and Mark Twain, among others, enjoyed the magnificent Italian scenery, a succession of scholars in many disciplines have been able to work on specialized projects. Under the expert guidance of Roberto Celli, the Administrator, and his assistant, the charming Josephine Ardovino, the scholars-in-residence and their wives are able to make excellent progress on their varied projects.

For Ida Mae Brown Snyder, my lifetime companion, a special paragraph of appreciation and gratitude is required, An admirable research scholar and a superb stylist, she is responsible not only for the polishing of this work but also for much of its content. Without her talent for research and editing, this work would have encountered far too many pitfalls.

Princeton, New Jersey   Louis L. Snyder
May 1982

INTRODUCTION: A MATTER OF DEFINITION _____

Nationalism and its corollaries are suffused with inconsistencies, contradictions, and paradoxes. Related terms are often used interchangeably although there may be slight variations in meaning. To meet Socratic objections, an effort will be made here to clarify such terms. There are, of course, almost always exceptions to the rule.

Nationalism. A condition of mind, feeling, or sentiment of a group of people living in a well-defined geographic area, speaking a common language, possessing a literature in which their aspirations are expressed, attached to common traditions and customs, venerating their own heroes, and, in some cases, having the same religion.

Nationalitarianism. The idea that, under appropriate conditions, a nation can develop out of a common matrix. It may also indicate a special identity or the sentiment of a proto-nation moving toward nationhood (Zaire).

Diaspora nationalism. The national sentiment of a special group dispersed among another people and resistant to assimilation (Magyars in Czechoslovakia). The term originated with the dispersion of the Jews after the Babylonian exile.

Fissiparous nationalism. A nationalism distinguished by the quality of splitting, or reproducing, or the production of new units by fission. The term was first used in the national context by Prime Minister Jawaharlal Nehru, who warned that "fissiparous tendencies" might one day shatter the Indian union.

Macro-nationalism. The broader pan-national movements, representing attempts to extend nationalism on wider political, economic, cultural, religious, or ethnic grounds. Included are Pan-Slavism, Pan-Germanism, Pan-Americanism, Pan-Arabism, Pan-Islamism, and Pan-Africanism. The macro-nationalisms have been uniformly unsuccessful in achieving their goals.

Mini-nationalism. Term used here in a specific sense: it refers to those smaller nationalisms, or regionalisms, absorbed into a larger centralized state. Believing themselves to be a distinct people, mini-nationalists demand either greater autonomy or outright independence.

Ethno-nationalism. Nationalism linked with ethnicity, a sense of belonging due to common descent. An elusive, confusing term often tied to discredited racial theories.

Regionalism. Often used interchangeably with mini-nationalism, regionalism refers specifically to a people living in a homogeneous area who have characteristics differing from peoples in neighboring territory. They have a consciousness of differing historical traditions which separate them from the rest of the country.

There are several subsidiary meanings. Regionalism may denote a separate administrative system or a social movement. It may refer to the characteristics of a certain area, such as the nature of its speech pattern. It may signify the devotion of an individual to his own region. In the literary sense it denotes the practice of emphasizing regional characteristics, locale, or setting.

Sectionalism. Sometimes used as a synonym for regionalism, sectionalism refers to a disproportionate or excessive regard for local interests. It is stressed in the United States, where the national census combines certain states into statistical groups.

Localism. Used to indicate local interests overriding the national. It may also refer to local ideas, customs, or peculiarities of speech.

Tribalism. Term used loosely to describe disparate ethnic communities, especially in Africa.

Communalism. The sense of community among ethnic or linguistic groups. Often used as a synonym for tribalism. It also denotes a system of government in which communes or local communities have autonomy inside a federated state.

Particularism. A political term meaning exclusive attention to one's own interests, party, or sect. In political theory it means the principle of allowing each state in a federation to promote its own interests and retain its own laws inside the nation-state. For example, from 1871 to 1918 Bavaria had its own army and special political powers in the German Second Reich.

Self-determination. In international law, the goal of the population of a territorial unit to decide its own future political status. All mini-nationalisms call for self-determination.

Irredentism. A program or policy for regaining lost territory. The term originated in 1878 when an Italian political party called for *Italia Irredenta* ("Unredeemed Italy").

Autonomy. Specifically, the quality, or right, or state of being of self-government. The aim is political independence inside the centralized nation-state. An autonomous people administers its own government without outside control. Autonomy means a special political status inside the national state.

Semi-autonomy. Partial self-government, especially in internal affairs. Moderate dissenters are often satisfied with the status of semi-autonomy.

Semi-sovereignty. Used interchangeably with semi-autonomy. Sovereignty refers to independent political authority inside a state, while semi-sovereignty means a limited authority, as in the agreement between Denmark and Greenland.

Devolution. Transference from one stage to another of property, qualities, or rights, such as the devolution of a crown. When used in connection with mini-nationalisms, it means the delegation or surrender by a centralized government of its total political authority over details in local government. It indicates a process of decentralization and carries with it a note of moderation (Wales and Scotland).

Separatism. The character, act, principle, or practice designed to withdraw completely from a centralized body. Extreme activists reject autonomy or semi-autonomy as half-way measures and call for withdrawal. Separatists regard themselves as patriotic liberators. For authorities of the centralized state, separatism is regarded as treason.

Secession. The formal act of withdrawal. The term suggests an unnatural and destructive act, while self-determination asserts an allegedly positive and sacred right.

Independence. The goal of complete freedom. When a mini-nationalism wins independence, it is transformed into a full-blown nationalism.

GLOBAL
MINI-NATIONALISMS

CHAPTER 1

NATIONALISM AND ITS PERIPHERIES _____

Surprising though it may be the prophecy of our Vanguard [Marxist-Leninist ideology] that nationalism would fade has not come true. In the age of the atom and cybernetics, it has for some reason blossomed.
                                                    —Aleksandr I. Solzhenitsyn

Persistent Nationalism

In the closing months of the seventh decade of the 20th century, an old man of 79 years, with hooded eyes staring balefully from beneath a black turban, led a revolution which gave the world a frightening taste of the power of xenophobic nationalism. The Ayatollah Ruhollah Khomeini, Imam of Iran's Shi'ite Muslim laity, a religious mystic, revealed an unusual ability to embody the passionate emotions of his people. Ignorant of and indifferent to non-Muslim cultures, he attempted to create a theocratic nation which would expel all foreign influence. He aimed to set up an Islamic republic with its supreme law in the Koran.

Khomeini opted for terrorism as a governmental policy. With surrealistic judgment he allowed the execution, without proper trial, of those he deemed to be enemies of the state. He supported the original seizure by "students" of approximately 75 hostages at the American Embassy in Teheran, a bizarre and unprecedented event in the history of international relations, and defied protests by the United Nations Security Council and the World Court.

This kind of fanatical nationalism had repercussions which Khomeini did not intend—a surge of patriotism among the American people that made them more united than they had been for more than two decades. The spectacle of a giant nation being held at bay by Iranian terrorists was followed by a solidification of the wavering sense of American nationalism. The problem was to find means of diplomatic, economic, and military pressure that could be used to meet this totally unexpected display of hostage blackmail.

1

The events in Iran brought attention once more to the power of nationalism as a historical force in the late 20th century. Historians have devoted their lives to the study of this complicated phenomenon, and new generations seek to unravel its mysteries.[1] Revolutions and wars have been promoted by nationalism; great empires have broken down under its impact; it remains a seminal force for both union and disruption.

Those who advocate a more livable planet see nationalism as a historically artificial phenomenon that has outlived its usefulness and that must be discarded in the advance of civilization. It is based, they say, on "obsolescent sovereignty." They see national sovereignty as the foundation stone of our contemporary international system, an outgrowth of the now-discredited system of the divine right of kings. They believe that no nation, no matter how powerful, is in a position to determine its own destiny. All who inhabit the earth are so closely identified with one another that nationalism has lost its significance. With the resources of the earth being depleted rapidly, it has become increasingly obvious that the land, like the skies and the seas, must be regarded as the common heritage of mankind. No longer can permanent security, it is said, be provided by the alignment and rectification of frontiers. Meticulously drawn national boundaries are futile. Anthems, flags, and slogans—the tools of nationalism—are decrepit and outworn. Wendell Willkie's "One World" is a goal in sight.

Unfortunately, this rosy picture of a new international community of nations has many flaws. Far from retreating, nationalism has become even more powerful as a historical force. Before his death, Walter Lippmann, a lifelong observer of the nation-state, said: "For as long as we can see there will be large nation-states, and they will exist without being able or wanting particularly or needing to dominate other nation-states."[2]

There are many paradoxes associated with this historical ism. Not the least of them is that nationalism is on the rise even at a time when common world interests seemingly can be solved only through the recognition of global interdependence. The spectacle of the weakness of the United Nations in dealing with the explosion of Iranian nationalism indicates the relative strength of nationalism as compared to internationalism.

Communism Swamped by Nationalism

In projecting his set of symbols to explain the course of history, Karl Marx insisted that all human motivations could be reduced to materialist impulses. Nationalism, in his view, was a characteristic of bourgeois society that would disappear in the rising new internationalism of a Communist world society. It was, in Marx's view, an anachronism that had outlived its usefulness—good riddance to an evil historical force.

Marx's "laws" became the gospel of a new religion, promoted with such intensity that all non-believers were dismissed as either fools or knaves. Human beings, however, are perverse animals, and most are not inclined to accept "absolute laws of history." Several aspects of the Marxist theory of society turned out to be erroneous. Predictions failed to be justified by events. The false estimate of nationalism as a despicable bourgeois phenomenon is only one of the major errors of Marxist theory.

Far from disappearing in a world in the process of change, nationalism has triumphed over communism and its ideological base. Marx would have been amazed by the proliferation of different national traditions and interests existing in the new Communist states. His predictions were mocked by events. Neither inside the Soviet Union, home base of the new society, nor outside it did nationalism conform to Marxist theory and wither away. It became stronger.

In the decades since the Bolshevik Revolution of October 1917, Soviet ideology and vocabulary inside the USSR have remained Marxist-Leninist and internationalist, but in practice, nationalism has emerged as dominant over professed internationalism.[3] The Soviet state was set up as a federation of 15 union republics, within which there are further subdivisions. A centralized state was fashioned in which many nationalities were held together by force. The major confrontation with Hitler's Third Reich in 1941 resulted in the strengthening of Russian nationalism in what Stalin called the Great Patriotic War. Since 1945 there has been an added sense of national consciousness.

In recent years the Soviet people have undergone an identity crisis. While Lenin's image still looms large, many of his revolutionary ideas are often forgotten or ignored. Contemporary Russian intellectuals are beginning to show a deep interest in the remaining relics of the Czarist era.[4] Coming after many decades of indoctrination in Marxism and the supposed superiority of the new order over the old, the new fascination with the Russian past implies a certain disillusionment with the present.[5] The new Russian nationalism sees the nation inextricably bound to yesterday's Imperial Russia. More and more Russians seem to feel that they are united with their predecessors of the 18th and 19th centuries. This is a striking departure from the internationalist slogan: "Workers of the world, unite!"

The triumph of nationalism over communism is revealed also in the world situation outside the Soviet Union. After the Bolsheviks won their way to power, they set up a Comintern, a Communist International, under which the Kremlin would be the hub of the wheel of inter-nationalism. But the successors of Lenin worked in vain to maintain Moscow's supremacy as the leader of world communism. Instead of becoming global leaders of a proletarian Communist society, they have had the misfortune of seeing their own nationalism challenged by nationalism in other Communist societies. They have had to contend with a powerful Yugoslav heresy which chose nationalism instead of Kremlin internationalism. In the summer of 1980 they were astonished by a daring workers' revolt in Poland, when workers sang "*Bozecos Polske*" ("God with Poland"), a defiant nationalist hymn dating from Poland's 19th-century Russian occupation. They have also seen the emergence of a giant rival in Communist China, whose rigid sense of nationalism matches their own. Moreover, in recent years they have been made uncomfortable by the rise of what they deem to be a dangerous Eurocommunism, which has no intention of taking orders from Moscow.

Added to its worries about nationalism in Communist states through-out the world, the Kremlin is concerned about proliferating unrest among the more than 100 nationalities inside the Soviet Union. There is always the fear that concessions of autonomy to any one mini-nationalism—be it Ukrainian, Armenian, or any other—will lead to a domino effect and to the dissolution of the centralized state. To meet this threat, current Soviet leadership decrees bullet or banishment, a quick or a lingering death. Such is the triumph of nationalism over communism.

The Urge to Self-Determination

Self-determination in international law concerns the quest of a people of a territorial unit for its future political status. One of the most pervasive and tenacious movements in history, it reflects the aspiration of a people who believe themselves to be united to rule themselves and not to be controlled by others.

In an excellent survey, Dov Ronen, from the Center for International Affairs of Harvard University, sees five types of self-determination as dominant, at successive periods, between the French Revolution and the present: mid-19th-century European national-determination; late 19th-century Marxist class self-determination; post-World War I Wilso-nian minorities' self-determination; post-World War II non-European racial self-determination; and contemporary ethnic self-determination.[6] Until the time of the French Revolution, there were few advocates of the concept that man has a right to be free. Subsequently, the idea of self-determination, strengthened by the modernization process, better com-munication, and the impact of two world wars, has made progress on a global scale.

Self-determination acts both as a force for convergence and a force for divergence. As a force for convergence, national self-determination is characterized by integration and unification. It inspires peoples within the confines of a given territory to create the national state (Germany, Italy). People of varied backgrounds are combined in a unifying sense of community, and the nation is regarded as homogeneous, unique, and indivisible—"we" as opposed to "they." The apparatus of the state is used to administer problems caused by differences among the people who are welded together. This sense of self-determination may be called the "larger nationalism."

Self-determination as a force for divergence is disintegrative and disruptive. Here we see the unwillingness of a people inside the larger nationalism to accept the domination of the centralized state. They may call for more accommodation, more autonomy, or even separation and independence. As the process of national self-determination declined in the 20th century, this "Balkanized" regional self-determination took on added significance. Unsatisfied minorities believed that the centralized authority, the political center, did not respond adequately to their politico-economic and cultural aspirations. They insisted that they had the right to rule themselves. This kind of self-determination may be called the "smaller nationalism."

The term "mini-nationalism" is used here to describe these smaller nationalisms controlled by a larger nationalism in multi-national states. Other terms have been used to describe the phenomenon—"ethno-nationalism," "ethnic pluralism," "ethnic identity," and "ethnic conflict." The word "ethno-nationalism" was used first by Walter Connor in an article describing "internal discord predicated upon ethnic diversity."[7] This was followed by an extensive literature utilizing the same ethnic approach.[8]

Connor describes "ethnic group" as derived from *ethnos*, the Greek word for nation. It is "a basic human category (*i.e.*, not a sub-group) characterized by unity of race and culture." Unfortunately, there are always difficulties connected with the term "race." Undoubtedly, Connor used the word in a broad sense to indicate shared language, traditions, and culture. There is a dangerous complicating semantic factor: in the scientific sense, "race" can be used only to describe a biological base. Here, we run into trouble. By "race" we mean the continuity of a physical type, expressing affinities of blood, representing an essentially natural grouping, which can have nothing to do with the concept of nationality. To extend the term to social groupings means a redefinition leading only to confusion. Georgi Pasquali, an Italian journalist, expressed it this way: "I prefer the word *nation* when I speak of human beings, and the word *races* when I speak of Pekinese, racing horses, chickens, and Yorkshire swine."[9]

The word "ethnic" and its variations continue to be used despite semantic difficulties. Apparently, it is felt that they remove some of the onus attached to indiscriminate use of the word "race." It would seem wise, however, to avoid equating racialism with nationalism.

The intensification of self-determination by mini-nationalisms throughout the world indicates that theories of modernization and nation-building have not worked out as well as had been supposed in the past. It was assumed that national unification in Europe would have an assimilative effect and that the process would extend to other continents. However, as always in history, there was change instead of completion. National self-determination was succeeded by mini-nationalisms moving away from integration.

In both forms of self-determination, power is the deciding element. Both in the formation of larger nation-states and in the aspirations of the mini-nationalisms, power (might, strength, potency, authority) is the ultimate arbiter. It is expressed in the German term *die Macht* and in the words of Otto von Bismarck in 1862: "Not by speeches and majorities will the great questions of the day be decided—that was the mistake of 1848 and 1849—but by iron and blood." The existence or dissolution of contemporary nation-states depends upon the outcome of the power struggle. Where the centralized authority maintains its strength, militarily, politically, and economically, self-determination of its component parts tends to remain relatively quiescent (Soviet Union). Where the fulcrum of power weakens, unsatisfied peoples will seek to break their bonds (Iran). Self-determination is seldom achieved by logical argument.

The Psychology of Disparate Elements

Nationalisms and mini-nationalisms are complex historical forces for which there are varied motivations—political, economic, social, cultural, linguistic, and psychological. These component factors vary in strength, though Marxist-Leninists insist that only economic determinism deserves serious attention. Because nationalism and its corollary are sentiments or feelings expressed by human beings, a word should be added here about its psychological impulses, without denying, of course, the relevance of its other motivations.

Psychologists are not altogether unanimous in their interpretation of the term "normal." It is used generally as a synonym for "standard," "regular," or "natural." It has specific scientific meanings in biology and in analytical, physical, or organic chemistry, but not for the social scientist. For the psychologist it usually indicates average intelligence or development, or freedom from mental disorder (not being insane or neurotic).

This semanticism leads us to several questions about the word "normal" in the psychology of human relations. Is it "normal" for human beings of similar backgrounds to relate to one another? Is it "normal" for people of common culture to fear the stranger? Is it "normal" to equate protection and survival with autonomy or independence? Is it "normal" for disparate elements to look upon the centralized state as a natural enemy?

If by "normal" we mean average reactions, one of the characteristics of human behavior over the course of recorded history has been an urge for freedom. The sentiment has a long historical tradition. In ancient times governmental tyranny was the rule rather than the exception. The Greek democracy pointed the way to freedom, but it, too, was grounded on a sub-structure of slavery. There was little freedom in the closed medieval society, geared as it was to security and self-sustenance.

The concept of human freedom received its most powerful stimulus in the work of 18th-century rationalists. They promoted the idea of individual freedom. They applied the idea of natural law not only to celestial mechanics, religion, and economics but also to government. Baron de Montesquieu denounced despotism: "The despotic state continually grows corrupt because it is depraved in nature."[10] Voltaire fiercely attacked intolerance, bigotry, and superstition: "All of us are formed of frailty and error. Let us mutually pardon each other's folly. That is the first law of nature."[11]

John Locke gave his own version of the social contract: the people are the real rulers, and if a majority of them declare that the contract has been broken, they have the right to rebel and install a new government. Popular sovereignty, in his estimation, was a precious possession of the people.[12] Jean-Jacques Rousseau converted Locke's thesis into a magnificent piece of political propaganda by placing all government on the consent, direct or implied, of the people. Man is born free, he said, but is everywhere in chains.[13] "The social contract, in place of destroying natural liberty, substitutes a moral and legitimate equality for the natural and physical inequality between men. While men may be unequal in strength and talent, they are all equal by convention and right."[14]

Montesquieu, Voltaire, Locke, Rousseau, and other rationalists were the intellectual theorists who stimulated the activism of the French Revolution, a historical watershed of modern times. It was truly a political awakening aimed at the complete recognition both of the human being and of the "normality" of the struggle for freedom.

The French Revolution originally sought individual, not national, self-determination. With the dramatic events of the Revolution, the urge for individual freedom was translated into a demand for collective freedom.[15] This was the essence of modern nationalism—a collective expression of the desire for freedom. Attention was directed not only to the individual but also to the nation as "historically active." The idea of freedom was tied up with that of the Fatherland. The Declaration of the Rights of Man and of the Citizen was transformed into a call for national independence.

Thus a new "normality" was declared for the nationalism of the 19th century and the mini-nationalisms of the 20th century. This belief in collective liberty survived the chaos of two world wars. World War I was supposed to "make the world safe for democracy," but it was followed by the emergence of rigid dictatorships. Despite fire and sword, the urge for freedom survived every attempt to obliterate it; it has become "normal" and "natural" and "standard." The psychological drive for freedom persists in the confrontation between disparate nationalisms and centralized authority. So deep is the emotion that men are willing to sacrifice their lives to achieve the fruits of freedom for their compatriots. Such is the psychological "normality" behind the mini-nationalisms.

The Problem of Clarification

In all probability, the most rewarding way to treat the mini-nationalisms is to use the conventional tools of history in analyzing the phenomenon. This involves: (1) examining the more active mini-nationalisms; (2) searching for common denominators and differences; and (3) placing them in historical context. This was the procedure adopted by Carlton J. H. Hayes, Hans Kohn, and Boyd C. Shafer in their pioneer studies on nationalism. It did much to clarify what is a most complex force in modern times. This same procedure is indicated for the mini-nationalisms.

Social scientists, as well as scholars in all disciplines, are always searching for clarification of historical movements. The study of nationalism, for example, took a new turn in 1953 when a distinguished American scholar, Karl W. Deutsch, wrote a seminal book on *Nationalism and Social Communication*.[16] At the core of the new Deutsch formula was the belief that nationalism deepens as individuals among a people become involved in common enterprises and are able to do this in communication with the others. Deutsch thus assigned major importance to communications in the development of nationalism. Our present knowledge of nationalism, he wrote, has given us a wealth of empirical data as well as techniques to ascertain its character and symptoms.

In directing his attention to social communication—the ability to convey messages and have them understood quickly and accurately— Deutsch recommended applying modern techniques of measurement to the study of nationalism. He was convinced that the recent great advances in statistical methods could be used to clear away much of the confusion as to why economic growth in certain areas led to national unification while, in others, it resulted in greater diversity. He envisioned a social science of nationalism that might even enable the prediction and control of events as well as the prevention of national conflicts with their nefarious results.

These views made a deep impact on younger scholars of nationalism, who found that, at long last, they had the key to understanding how the redoubtable ism worked. Using the Deutsch formula as a base, they began to search for empirical data at the local level. Then they sought to move from the inductive level to the general level by formulating relationships between nationalism and the process of modernization. They were anxious to learn how nationalism is connected with its built-in process of change which all contemporary societies have gone through in the modernization process. Above all, they rejected what they regarded as an outmoded view—that nationalism is an anti-rational ideology designed to seduce the masses.

Younger American scholars of nationalism, and especially their German counterparts, were entranced by the possibilities of the Deutsch formula.[17] Instead of the conventional methods of seeking meaning, characteristics, and historical development, they turned to cybernetics and computerization to "measure" nationalistic instincts.

It would be unfair to attribute this approach to historical faddism, but it would also be unreasonable to accept it without criticism. The Deutsch methodology is certainly important in research on economic nationalism and, to a lesser extent, on its social content. A word of caution must be introduced when it is applied to political, cultural, and psychological aspects of nationalism, which do not lend themselves easily to mathematics and computerization—or to predictability. An assiduous examination of Corsican separatism, including the number of bombs used on Parisian streets, together with other mathematical data thrown into the computer, is not apt to distinguish Corsican from Scottish nationalism.

At the root of this problem is the belief among the new generation of scholars of nationalism that history is more science than social science. It is a mistaken notion. If we have learned anything at all from the study of the past, it is that history does not respond easily to materialistic formulae. There are far too many irrational factors at work that cannot be measured with any degree of accuracy. There is always the danger of overemphasizing measurement, projecting questionable premises, using false analogies, and, worst of all, descending to obscure historical or sociological verbiage. Computerized predictability is fine for the chemical laboratory, for guided missiles, and for the space program. It is less than satisfactory for the task of making sense out of nationalism and the mini-nationalisms.

CHAPTER 2

CHARACTERISTICS OF THE MINI-NATIONALISMS _____

Independence is the fetish, fad and totem of the times. Everybody who can muster a quorum in a colony wants Freedom Now—and such is the temper of the age that they can usually have it.

—*Time*, March 11, 1966, pp. 38–39

Impulses for Freedom

MR. ECEVIT, WE DEMAND REPARATIONS AND RETURN OF OUR TERRITORIES!

Prime Minister Bulent Ecevit of Turkey is visiting the United States as we observe the 60th anniversary of the founding of the Independent Republic of Armenia on May 28, 1918. The Republic was. . . .

—ESTABLISHED during World War I by freedom loving Armenians. . . .

—FOUNDED just three years after the Ottoman Turkish government initiated the first major holocaust of this century against the Armenian people, resulting in the loss of over 1,500,000 lives. . . .

—RECOGNIZED as one of the family of nations by the Paris Peace Conference. . . .

—ATTACKED in September 1920 by Kemalist Turkey and the Soviet Union on two fronts. Despite a valiant defense and unable to resist overwhelming odds, surrendered to Bolshevik Russia. . . .

11

Today, most of Armenia is under Turkish rule, barren and undeveloped. The remaining one quarter of its territory forms one of the republics of the Soviet Union. In either case Armenia is no longer free. . . .

Mr. Ecevit we demand the return of those Armenian territories held by Turkey to their rightful owners as an essential step towards reestablishment of a UNITED, FREE AND INDEPENDENT ARMENIA!

This message from the Armenian National
Committee, 212 Stuart St., Boston, Mass. 02116

All the aspirations of an unsatisfied mini-nationalism—union, freedom, independence—are summarized in this advertisement by an Armenian separatist organization active outside the homeland.[1] "Armenia is unable to determine its own destiny"—this has become the watchword of dissident minorities everywhere. It is the complaint, among others, of Basques in Spain, Corsicans in France, Croats in Yugoslavia, Ukrainians in the Soviet Union, and Kurds in Iran.

The political units we call modern states are held together by the cement of nationalism, a historical phenomenon that wears many faces and is always in flux. In the formation of national states, the drive for unification almost always forced together peoples of diverse backgrounds, of different languages and cultures. They were required to accept the domination of a central authority, and they were subjected to a process of assimilation designed to strengthen the central authority. Added to the compulsion for unity, characteristic of all nationalisms, was a reverse trend toward disruption. Superimposed on the framework of the national state were unsatisfied peoples who had a nationalism of their own. These smaller nationalisms added another dimension to the meaning of contemporary nationalism.

Stated in simple terms, a mini-nationalism is a little nationalism controlled by a larger nationalism. It is the sentiment of a people who feel they are held in bondage against their will. It calls for a separate identity based on historical, geographical, linguistic, cultural, religious, and psychological ties—usually a combination of several of these factors.

Viewed from another angle, a mini-nationalism may be regarded as a nationalism that has not yet come of age. In this sense it may represent a demand for independence by a small or a substantial minority inside an already formed state. It might seek the status of a separate nation. It might claim to possess all the rights and powers of a distinct nation and call for separation from an "alien nationalism."

On the other hand, there are mini-nationalisms that stop short of the goal of independence. Such unsatisfied minorities are willing to settle for greater recognition of their rights. For many of them, the deciding factor is economic: they see a complete break as being to their economic disadvantage. They will accept autonomy or semi-sovereignty and remain inside the borders of the larger nation as long as their demands are satisfied.

Mini-nationalisms come into existence when a small group of local patriots begins to organize the already existing sentiment. Such leaders regard themselves as liberators. They publicize their cause by hammering away at the claim that their legitimate aspirations have been thwarted in an alien society. They want their own nation with a distinctive flag and national anthem. They see varied reactions among their own people: there may be apathy, indifference, mild support, or enthusiastic collaboration. Most often, followers regard their activist leaders as liberators chosen by destiny to lead them to freedom. Where progress is slow, activists may turn to terrorism in the belief that assassinations and bombings are more effective than words in the struggle for independence.

Hegelian thrust and counter-thrust! Freedom fighters must contend with reaction from the central authority. Established governments look upon separatism as treason and treat it as such. They may be willing to use accommodation or appeasement, but to go beyond these moderate solutions may mean dissolution of the state. Semi-autonomy—yes; but outright independence—emphatically no. Authorities of established states point out that national unity was achieved through the clash of arms and the spilling of blood. They have no intention of allowing a domino effect that would lead eventually to disintegration of the nation.

There is no objective outside force able to mediate the difficulties between centralization and decentralization. Any effort by an organization such as the United Nations to help solve the problem would be deemed interference in the internal affairs of a sovereign nation. As in most historical changes, the fate of mini-nationalisms is determined by the power principle.

Common Features

The modern nation-state, at best an imperfect structure, almost always holds within its confines one or more dissident minorities who want autonomy or independence. Such mini-nationalisms may vary in nature but possess, at the same time, common characteristics. Some generalizations may be made, although, as in most matters concerning nationalism, there may be exceptions.

The pressing goal of most mini-nationalisms is an urge for regional freedom. Nationalism in all its forms is concerned with some region. In other words, it seeks a territorial base. Both the larger and smaller nationalisms attempt to consolidate their separateness by the possession of land, territory, or a region. It is a kind of territorial imperative that demands exclusive use of a portion of the earth's surface.[2]

A dominant feature is a sense of unsatisfied aspirations. British historian Hugh Seton-Watson speaks of unsatisfied nationalisms "whether because their claims have been refused or because their national consciousness is still in process of formation, or because their spokesmen are themselves uncertain of their identity."[3] There are always feelings of resentment, unfulfillment, and envy of other peoples who have won their independence.

Cultural affinities are basic. National minorities feel themselves to be set apart by a common cultural pattern. They resent the imposition of what they regard as an alien culture. Their indifference to other cultures is often motivated by xenophobia, fear of the stranger, a sentiment they share in common with the larger nationalisms.

While mini-nationalisms have common characteristics, they may vary in type. National minorities in the older nations feel that they have been left behind in the nation-making process (Scots in Britain, Armenians in the Soviet Union, Basques in Spain). Others may live in nations in the process of formation (Kurds in Iran). There may be unfulfilled communities that see themselves as vestiges of an independence movement (Northern Irish). They may be separatists who earnestly desire the status of another nation (*Québécois* in Canada).

The phenomenon is global and not limited to any one continent. In both old and new nations, minority peoples have been forced into subjugation. Following the collapse of great empires in World Wars I and II, there was a nationalistic upsurge promoted with almost religious fervor. Dozens of new nations appeared. There was no set pattern: new boundaries were fixed with little regard for the rights of minorities inside the new states. Some peoples were left behind in the race for independence.

By no means European in scope, the process spread throughout the world. Africans and Asians who had learned nationalism from their colonial masters began their own form of territorialization. After winning independence, they, like the Europeans, welded together diverse peoples to construct their own national states. It was not diffusion from Europe but actually political parallelism.

Most mini-nationalisms want to be full nationalisms. If by historical circumstance, such as the result of a major war, a regional minority wins its way to freedom, it is no longer a mini-nationalism but develops a full-fledged nationalism of its own. For example, after the three partitions of the late 18th century, Polish mini-nationalism inside Russia, Prussia, and Austria was converted in 1919 by the Treaty of Versailles into a larger Polish nationalism.[4] Similarly, Serbian mini-nationalism in the old Austro-Hungarian Empire emerged as a full-blown nationalism in the newly created Yugoslav state, only to be subjected, in turn, to the appearance of Croatian mini-nationalism.[5] In such cases the centralized authority was opposed by disaffected nationalisms inside its new borders.

The Terrorist Syndrome

Mini-nationalists vary in the intensity of their demands, which range from calls for more autonomy to semi-sovereignty to outright independence. Each mini-nationalism has its own quota of moderate autonomists and extreme separatists. The number of each depends on local conditions.

The moderates may be satisfied by concessions. Often they want nothing more than recognition of their rights. This is true especially in those cases where economic ties are so close that separation would result in severe economic dislocations for the national minority. Jurassic mini-nationalism in Switzerland is French-oriented culturally but is tied tightly to the mighty Swiss franc. Similar economic interests play a role in Welsh or in Scottish nationalisms inside the United Kingdom. Even when a mini-nationalism is successful in winning a status of semi-sovereignty, there are close economic relations with the centralized government, as in the case of Greenland vis-à-vis Denmark. The moderate approach stops short at the boundary of complete independence.

Extremists, on the other hand, settle for nothing less than separation. Here, the activists go beyond mere theory. They protest that they are being held against their will by an alien power and that they must fight their way to freedom. Issuing declarations of independence, they devote their lives to the task of winning their freedom from the centralized power.

Moderates and extremists differ on the means to the end. Moderates who want more political autonomy are willing to settle for recognition of their demands. They will accept the accommodation of devolution because it satisfies their geographical, economic, and cultural wants. The key to their satisfaction is compromise.

Militant separatists have no use for this kind of soft approach. Convinced that only violence can serve their cause, they denounce moderation as weakness and turn to terror as standard operating procedure. They seek a special focus around which they can build their cause. In their view only extreme measures can put flesh on the skeleton of their ideology. They see the manifestation of change only through power.

They accept terror as a specific strategy and a tactical approach shaped to their needs. The bullet and the bomb, they fervently believe, will lead to the blessings of freedom.

Such extremists reject the term "terrorist" as inapplicable and insist that they are "liberationists," heroic fighters against exploitation by a more powerful centralized nationalism. Veiling their lives in mystery, they see themselves as romantic Robin Hoods fighting to redress the injustices of history. If today they are regarded with distaste, tomorrow, they believe, they will be looked upon as heroes. They point to the case of Menachem Begin, Prime Minister of Israel and recipient of the Nobel Peace Prize.[6] Once denounced by his enemies as a terrorist, he became a statesman in power. Militant activists are certain that their own violent deeds would be forgotten in the flush of victory.

Terrorism may be defined as a special form of coercive intimidation.[7] It involves the threat of murder or injury and uses violence systematically as a means of influencing individuals or groups. It employs such weapons as bullets, grenades, and bombs. Because its proponents are unpredictable, terrorism spreads fear and anxiety among prospective victims. It accepts no ethical or humanitarian limits: men, women, and children alike are expendable in the interest of the cause. It recognizes no rules or conventions. It is a license to savagery.

Contemporary terrorism is an outgrowth of the 19th-century cult of the revolutionary fighter, the romantic hero forced into conflict with society or into isolation by a distrusting world. This self-assertive egoism, amoral and anti-intellectual, predated certain aspects of 20th-century existentialism. Martin Heidegger and Jean-Paul Sartre propounded the idea that it is only through our own actions or will that we can escape from despair. This type of thinking, presented by honorable philosophers, was enormously influential in shaping the ideology of terrorists. Under certain circumstances, such a belief could stimulate acts of terrorism.[8]

Terrorist activities by separatists did not necessitate a mass-based following, nor did they require large amounts of funds. Even if terrorists failed to win the support of a large majority of their fellow countrymen, they could feel a sense of triumph in their revolutionary virtue. Harried by the police, unsuccessful in their immediate ends, many had to leave their homelands and settle abroad.

Terrorists displayed little regard for their victims. On occasion, the violence was not only cruel but it was also irrational. PLO guerrillas considered it an act of war when they slaughtered Israeli athletes at the Munich Olympic Games in 1972. When Irish terrorists killed Lord Louis Mountbatten in a remote-controlled boat explosion on August 27, 1979, they justified the murder with the argument that Mountbatten was a member of the British royal establishment and hence a legitimate target in an all-out war. Terrorists dismiss victims as casualties on the road to freedom.

Four major types of terrorist movements emerged in recent years: (1) nationalist, autonomist, or other minority units; (2) ideological sects or secret societies calling for some form of liberation or revolutionary justice; (3) exile groups with separatist, irredentist, or revolutionary aspirations of their country of origin; and (4) transnational gangs using terrorist support from two or more countries in the name of some vague world-revolutionary goal.[9]

With the exception of category 4, in which motivation is indistinct, all these factions or movements are concerned in one way or another with nationalism. Wherever there is a sense of regionalist resentment against alien rule, there is apt to be a small, or sometimes a large, faction which chooses terrorism as its most effective mode of operation. Even miniscule terrorist factions, no matter how dubious their credentials, take on significance when they claim to represent the whole group constituency. They often count on the support of millions of people who think as they do but who are wary of direct action.

Terrorist nationalist organizations may function both inside and outside the country. The Basque Euzkadi Ta Azkatasuna (ETA) and the Corsican National Liberation Front (FLNC) prefer to work inside, withholding cooperation from the incumbent regime and exploiting its political and military weaknesses. Some umbrella organizations, driven from their homelands, such as the Irish Republican Army (IRA) and the Palestine Liberation Organization (PLO), turn to terror outside the country in the struggle to restore national sovereignty. Others, such as Croatian militants, find it more useful to attack ambassadors abroad and hijack planes to win attention to their cause.

A new dimension to the study of contemporary terrorism was added with the publication in 1981 of Claire Sterling's *The Terror Network*. A respected American foreign correspondent who has lived in Europe for three decades, Sterling looked into the causes, actions, and sponsorship of the rash of terrorism that has plagued the West. Her study documents the claim that there has been a deliberate and unified network of terrorism extending from Havana to London to Palestine whose ultimate beneficiary and undercover patrons have been anti-Western. Sterling presents evidence to show how the militant wings of mini-nationalist movements, such as the IRA, the PLO, and the Spanish Basques, look eastward for inspiration, training, and material support.

Following is a summary of the case presented by anti-Soviet observers. More than six decades after the Bolshevik Revolution of 1917, the leaders of the Kremlin still live in deadly fear of the capitalist world, which, they are certain, is hell-bent on their destruction. They prefer to "bury" their enemies. In the process, they welcome terrorist guerrillas as allies in the struggle for control of world society. They see any type of capitalist disruption as a plus factor. By their logic, those terrorists who rob banks, kidnap industrialists or judges, or kill or maim innocent by-standers by bomb assaults are merely "liberators," "freedom fighters," "revolutionary heroes." Those who fall in battle are "martyrs." They reject issues of right or wrong, decency or indecency, as sham morality. The categorical imperative is for weaklings; morale is what advances the cause of communism, what breaks the bonds of decadent capitalism. Defenders of the Soviet system denounce these charges as wildly ex-aggerated and without foundation.

The European Split Nationality

The story of the mini-nationalisms is closely bound up with the history of Europe. The European continent was the scene of a clash between unity and disruption, a confrontation that was to be repeated later on other continents. After the Germanic infiltrations and subsequent invasions across the Rhine and the Danube, the Roman Empire fell in 476 A.D. Moved by the pressure of tribes scrambling out of Asia, Ostrogoths swept westward and down into the Italian peninsula. Visigoths traveled even farther west, driving down into Spain and across to North Africa. Others—Vandals, Lombards, Alemanni, Teutons, and Franks—migrated westward into forests and swamps and moved on only when forced to do so by superior power.

The result of these migrations was a kaleidoscope of different peoples, each with its indigenous culture and each possessing its own characteris-tics. Even with the consequent Roman-Germanic-Christian adjustment, tribal separateness was retained. There followed the formation of me-dieval entities, complicated by dynastic rivalries and religious dif-ferences. Great empires were formed, dissolved, and re-created under other leaderships. Eventually, in the late Middle Ages and in early modern times, tough rulers hammered out their own national states. The course was influenced enormously by the dramatic events of the French Revolution.

The amalgamation of national states was seldom clear-cut and deci-sive. Peoples differing in language, traditions, and historical experience were thrust together in centralized nation-states with little regard for their wishes. The "national interest" was decided by the power of the sword.

Thus, from its beginning, the age of nationalism was tempered by the existence of disruptive tendencies. There were three closely related currents in the 20th century: (1) the maintenance of the *status quo* by the already formed larger nation-states; (2) the appearance of a movement to overcome nationalism and replace it with a continent-wide unity in a proposed United States of Europe; and (3) the drive of the mini-nationalisms for autonomy or independence. European experience in these three forms was to be recapitulated later on other continents.

Following a millenium of conflict and two major wars in the 20th century, Europeans began to see that what they had once regarded as powerful, unified national states were in reality only second-rate nations. Perhaps bigness might be a solution for their troubles—a United States of Europe which would merge the European system of separate nations into a new, more powerful political community. European political integration would be prepared by economic union, and the old tribalistic quarrels of the past would disappear inside a larger administrative unity.[10]

Such was the dream of Jean Monnet, the French theoretician of European unity. In 1957, the Treaty of Rome set up the European Economic Community (EEC), the Common Market, with specific goals: (1) to remove barriers of trade among member nations; (2) to establish a single commercial policy toward non-members; (3) to coordinate eventually transportation and agriculture; (4) to remove private and public measures restricting free enterprise; and (5) to ensure the mobility of labor, capital, and entrepreneurship. Among the achievements of the Common Market were the removal of internal tariffs, the establishment of a common agricultural policy, the removal of restrictions on the movement of labor, and progress toward the integration of capital markets.[11]

Added to the Common Market Inner Six was the European Free Trade Association of the Outer Seven (EFTA).[12] This second economic association was organized to remove trade barriers in industrial goods among the members, but with each nation maintaining its own commercial policy toward countries outside the group. Members were committed to a schedule of tariff reductions and quota liberalizations for industrial goods.

The urge to economic union was stimulated further by the formation in 1952 of the European Coal and Steel Community (ECSC) designed to integrate the coal and steel industries of major European states.[13] The European Atomic Energy Community (Euratom) was organized to form a common market for the development of peaceful use of atomic energy.[14] In July 1967, ECSC, EEC, and Euratom were merged into a single Council of Ministers and a single Commission of the European Communities. All three organizations claimed that they were working for economic unity only, but it is clear that their sponsors hoped that economic unity would be followed by political integration.

Another force for European unity was the formation on May 5, 1949, of the Council of Europe with representatives of 17 western European states.[15] Its goal was continental union, to be achieved within a framework of human rights. With its headquarters distributed in three places—Strasbourg, Brussels, and Luxembourg—it hoped eventually to organize a European Parliament—a Euro-Parliament—elected by direct universal suffrage.

Other plans for European integration were related to the Cold War. The European Defense Community (EDC) was an abortive attempt by the western European powers, with support from the United States, to counterbalance the military might of the Soviet Union by the formation of a supranational European army. The EDC was regarded as a prerequisite for a politically united western Europe. It would not only make German rearmament possible but would also encourage western European nations toward the goal of federation. Charles de Gaulle, who was opposed to the plan, preferred a federation of sovereign states led by France. Britain, too, was reluctant to join. In 1955 a considerably modified plan called the Western European Union was organized, with no mixture of commands at lower levels. Military cooperation was continued primarily inside the North Atlantic Treaty Organization (NATO), to which West Germany was admitted in 1955.

Europolitics gathered momentum when, on June 7–10, 1979, the first European elections were held for a European Parliament. The goal was to stimulate broad, new public interest in a united Europe and give it a direct, democratic flavor. It was hoped that the focus of political activity would be shifted from national parliaments to a European one. In the world's first international parliamentary election, 410 members from nine countries[16] were elected to the European Parliament.[17]

Despite the enthusiastic claims of its adherents, European political unity was not achieved, and the Continent settled down once again to the "Europe of Nations" advocated by Charles de Gaulle. Governments were warier than ever of sacrificing national power for the greater good of Europe.[18] The galvanizing impact for European federation was lacking. Neither pragmatism nor gradualism, projected by Europeanists, seemed to offer any felicitous solution.[19] The Council itself soon degenerated into a body of institutionalized bureaucracy overwhelmed by paperwork, deadly boredom, and frustrating roadblocks. It became an object of international derision.

National consciousness has proved to be stronger than the vision of a united Europe in replacing the rivalry of a thousand years. Europeans want peace, prosperity, social justice, welfare, and a clean environment. They do not see any effective international organ to obtain such goals.

They turn, instead, to the only viable government they have—that of the national state. There may be similar political structures, there may be gains of economic union, but separateness is increasingly asserted. Western Europe remains a kind of customs union of separate nation-states. In June 1979 French President Valéry Giscard d'Estaing, despite his vocal support for a European Parliament, acknowledged that the original post-World War II fervor had drained out of the European idea. "Most Europeans no longer intend to sacrifice their national values, so the original model, a United States of Europe, will not work for us now."[20]

Most European statesmen believe that they reflect the wants of their constituents when they oppose any loss of sovereignty to a European Parliament. Their concern is more with disintegrative separatism inside their own borders, which they see as an immediate challenge to national unity. They regard European integrationists as harmless visionaries but believe militant separatists to be dangerous enemies. They equate unsatisfied nationalisms with treason.

Community Versus Separatism

On the surface, the transnational movements seem to be making great headway in such international organizations as the United Nations, in multi-national economic organizations such as the European Economic Community, and in multi-national enterprises such as International Business Machines (IBM). Statesmen of individual nations speak eloquently of the advantages of international cooperation, but always with the understanding that their own political borders are inviolate. They are considerably more worried about the mini-nationalisms in their midst.

Such statesmen have cause for worry. Mini-nationalisms present an omnipresent danger for them. Separatist factions, far from diminishing in recent years, have increased their activities to a point where central authorities think in terms of a clear and present danger.

Separatist ideologists and activists usually work inside the larger national state, but even here, there has been a tendency to think in terms of a wider international organization. In theory this idea was presented by the French historian Charles Seignobos, who suggested "*un syndicat des petites nations mécontentes*" ("a syndicate of little discontented nations") which would be set up in Paris. The concept received practical expression in 1975 when a number of European mini-nationalists established a small Bureau of Unrepresented European Nations with an embassy in Brussels. Thus far the organization has remained small and ineffective.

Behind it, however, is a strong sentiment of disaffected nationalism, one that must be taken into account not only for European development but for world development as well.

Classification

To describe and analyze these ubiquitous unsatisfied mini-nationalisms is the theme of this book. Attention will be devoted here to the more important mini-nationalisms. The emphasis is on European separatism because of its extensive development on that continent; but there is also treatment of mini-nationalisms elsewhere, especially in Africa and Asia. Latin American examples are notably absent.[21]

Europe

Country	Mini-Nationalisms
Belgium	Flemings
	Walloons
Denmark	Greenlanders
France	Alsatians
	Basques
	Bretons
	Corsicans
	Occitains
Holland	Frisians
Italy	South Tyroleans
Rumania	Germans
Soviet Union	Armenians
	Azerbaijanis
	Estonians
	Georgians
	Latvians
	Ukrainians
Spain	Basques
	Catalans
Switzerland	Jurassics
United Kingdom	Manx
	Northern Irish
	Scots
	Shetland Islanders
	Welsh
Yugoslavia	Croats
	Macedonians

Montenegrins
Serbians

Middle East

Cyprus   Turks
Iran   Arabs
                          Azerbaijanis
                          Bakthiaris
                          Baluchis
                          Kurds
                          Lurs
                          Quasqais
                          Seistanis
Lebanon   Christians
                          Muslims
Turkey   Armenians

Western Hemisphere

Canada   *Québécois*
Latin America   ?
United States   black nationalists
                          Indians
                          Puerto Ricans

Asia

Burma   Kachins
                          Karens
India   Kashmirs
                          Nagas
                          Pakistanis
Indonesia   Moluccans
Malaysia   Sabahs
                          Sarawaks
Pakistan   Bangladeshis

Africa

Angola   North Angolans
                          South Angolans
Burundi   Huttus
Comoros   Maoris
Congo   Katangas
Ethiopia   Eritreans

Ghana	Ewes
Kenya	Luos
Mali	Senegalese
Nigeria	Biafrans
	North Nigerians
Sudan	South Sudanese

CHAPTER 3

BRITISH DEVOLUTION I: SCOTTISH NATIONALISM ———

Bitter experience has taught us the difficulty of resistance to
demands made in the name of nationalism unless we are prepared to take measures which our tender conscience forbids.

—Max Beloff, in the London *Observer*, August 16, 1974

Mini-Nationalisms in Britain

The British have had some success in dealing with mini-nationalisms in
their own island. By a process of accommodation called devolution, they
have been able to appease unsatisfied regionalists and retain them within
the framework of the United Kingdom. There has been friction with
Scots, Welsh, Shetlanders, and Manx, but concessions to local consciousness have bolstered the cause of national unity. Separatism still exists but
it is muted.

The situation is different in the neighboring island. After centuries of
subjugation, the Irish won their independence as a sovereign state, with
the exception of the six counties of Northern Ireland. Here, the majority
of the people, English in sentiment and Protestant in religion, preferred
to retain their ties with the United Kingdom. For the Provisional wing of
the Irish Republican Army (IRA), this was an uncompleted revolution, a
betrayal of aspirations for a united territorial homeland. Failing to win
British acquiescence, the IRA inaugurated a campaign of terror which,
by 1980, cost more than 2,000 lives. Despite the heavy loss of life,
Westminster remained obdurate and refused to "desert" its kinsmen in
Northern Ireland.

Scottish Ambivalence

Devolution, independence, or *status quo*? This is the choice facing the
5.2 million people of Scotland. For centuries the Scots have had their
own territory, their own history, and their own religious, educational,
and legal institutions. Though united with England in 1707, they re-

25

tained a separate identity, with a rugged Highland culture in contrast to that of the English. They hold on to their special accent and mannerisms, qualities of a separate nation, but they do not have the distinction of being a separate state.

Despite close ties, the Scots have an ambivalent attitude toward their neighbor to the south. Should they support the democratic way of devolution, which would involve an increased regional authority against London centralism? Should they heed the call of Scottish nationalism and demand independence?[1] Or should they maintain the union with England?

The Scots have decided not to activate any specific identity in a quest for self-determination.[2] Despite a long history of confrontation, they have preferred to remain inside the boundaries of the United Kingdom. Geographical proximity is a strong motivation: Scotland forms a continuous unity with England and Wales. No large body of water separates them, as is the case with the recalcitrant Irish.

The Scots felt deprived of their rights during the days of empire, but this feeling did not prompt a movement for separation. Even then, there were political slogans for home rule, but they were not effective. Not until the 1960s was there an activation of Scottish identity, resulting from profound politico-economic changes on the European scene.[3] At that time the British economy began to decline, due in part to the loss of colonies and to a drastic reduction in Marshall Plan aid. In that troublesome period, many Scotsmen began to look upon the British Government, not as an intermediate for their aspirations, but as an obstacle. The result was a rising sense of Scottish national consciousness and an augmented interest in home rule. The trend was intensified in 1973 with the discovery of North Sea oil, which Scottish nationalists claimed as the exclusive property of a future independent Scotland.

The Scots, unlike Irish extremists, did not turn to terror. They held strong economic grievances, but at the same time, they recognized that the English, too, were caught in an economic bind. It was difficult to build an anti-British case. Milton J. Esman gauged it correctly: "Despite the efforts of an earlier generation of literary and romantic nationalists, despite the continuing concern of some Scottish Nationalist Party (SNP) activists, the great majority of modern Scotsmen did not define their deprivations in cultural terms and cannot be mobilized emotionally or politically against the English on language or cultural issues. This is true of all classes, regions, and age groups."[4]

Equally important on the issues of union, devolution, or independence for Scotland is the attitude of the English. It is unlikely that the 635-plus lawmakers of the British House of Commons intend to preside over the liquidation of the United Kingdom. They have met the problem with a shrewd combination of economic, political, administrative, and psychological moves which have done much to smooth Scottish sensibilities. They have recognized the depth of Scottish sensibilities, and they have responded with rational measures. The principle is simple and effective—moderation encourages moderation.

Recognizing the decline in Scottish economic life, the English have done what they could to alleviate unemployment and hard times in Scotland. Politically, they assured fair, equitable representation for Scotland in the union; in matters of administration, they have been careful not to overextend centralism. Psychologically, the English have sought to bolster Scottish pride in Great Britain as well as in their own land. The result is a containment of what could have been a strongly separatist mini-nationalism.

The Anglo-Scottish Confrontation

Anglo-Scottish collaboration has been won despite a long history of confrontation. The Scots fiercely resisted aggression by Romans, Anglo-Saxons, and English alike.[5] Failing to conquer Scotland, the Romans after 120 A.D. erected Hadrian's Wall between the Tyne River and Solway Firth, which became the frontier of the Roman Empire in Britain. With the end of Roman occupation, two kingdoms of the Picts and the Scots were formed in the north. During the 11th and 12th centuries, when the Norse hold on English territory was relinquished, Scottish authority was extended. Scottish kings claimed northern counties of England, but aside from minor incidents, there was peace between the two countries.

In 1294, however, a conflict began which was to last for two and a half centuries. When Edward I asserted English superiority, the Scots were goaded into defiance. Edward wanted to construct a united England and Scotland. The Scottish war which raged from 1294 to 1307 was a result of that policy. Edward died in 1307, with the Scots in open rebellion. In 1314 Edward II gathered the largest army which had ever been sent into Scotland to strike at Robert Bruce. The Battle of Bannockburn, fought on June 23–24, 1314, between 100,000 English and 30,000 Scots, was the most humiliating defeat ever inflicted on the English by the Scots.[6] The English renounced all claims to supremacy over Scotland and recognized warrior-king Bruce as ruler of an independent Scotland.

Bannockburn checked English efforts at domination but not English desires. There followed two centuries of sporadic conflicts, leading to the impoverishment of Scotland. During the Hundred Years' War between England and France (1337–1453), Scotland was the ally of France. The wars between England and Scotland came to an end after the Reformation.

In 1603 a succession of events began which led to the union of England and Scotland. On the death of Elizabeth in 1603, James VI, King of Scotland, was recognized as King James I of England. This union of crowns did not bring with it a union of parliaments or administration, but it did strengthen the position of the monarchy.

It was decided at the beginning of the 18th century to join the two kingdoms organically. Although there was little sentiment in Scotland for a merger at the time, the English offered some tempting advantages: should the Scots agree to union, they would be given rights they had wanted for a long time, including a share in the British East India Company, the English colonies, and the English system of Navigation Acts and mercantilism. The result was the creation in 1707 of the United Kingdom of Great Britain. Under the agreement the Scots could retain their own legal system as well as the established Presbyterian Church. The two governments were merged, and the term "British" was now applied to both English and Scots.

The union with England brought Scotland into the mainstream of English commercial life. Scotsmen now had access to the riches of the vast British Empire. Although deprived of their independence, they enjoyed economic equality with the English. Customs barriers between the two countries were eliminated. English colonies were open to Scottish settlers and tradesmen. The fusion was not complete: the Scots were guaranteed their Church, their law courts, and their own legal code, but little more.

The union of 1707 thus did much to alter the century-long tradition of confrontation. Once it was consummated, however, some Scotsmen, recalling the golden days of independence, began to resent the merger, especially the role of Scotland as a junior partner in what was supposed to be a union of equals. One result was a Scottish sense of inferiority, which, as we shall see, Westminster did its best to alleviate. At the same time, the large majority of both Scotsmen and Englishmen began to think of themselves as members of the same British society. As in other mini-nationalisms, a small vocal group called for independence. The separatist cause gained some strength in times of economic discontent, but it never succeeded in winning the support of the majority of Scotsmen. British accommodation discouraged a separatist explosion.

The Language Issue

The linguistic factor is only of minor significance in the Scottish search for identity. Virtually all Scots speak a dialect version of English.[7] There are two Scottish tongues: the vernacular language of the Lowlands (Scottish, Scots, or Lallans), and Gaelic, spoken in the Highlands. Lowland Scottish is a form of English closely related to Middle English. As spoken today, it is no different from standard English than are many other

English dialects. It had its origin in the dialect of the Anglian invaders who pushed into southern Scotland in the 6th and 7th centuries. By the 13th century, Lallans supplanted Gaelic in much of the Lowlands.

Scottish Gaelic, still spoken by a minority in the western Highlands and the islands,[8] was the preferred vernacular tongue until the 15th century, when it gave way to Lowland Scottish. The surviving vernacular was influenced so much by English that it can scarcely be called a distinct language. English is actually the language of Scotland, though it is not quite the same as the English spoken throughout the United Kingdom. There are literally hundreds of dialects in which English tones can be heard—including Scottish.

As a literary language, Lowland Scottish has not been used for prose since the 16th century, but it was revived for use in verse in the 18th century. Scottish writers have a choice of three languages—Lallans, Gaelic, or English—but most novelists, poets, and dramatists prefer English. This does not mean that Lallans and Gaelic have been neglected. There have been sporadic attempts to revive the earlier forms as a means of stimulating Scottish nationalism, but they have not made much progress.

In poetry, fiction, and drama, Scottish writers seek the revival and extension of the Scottish, or Lallans, vernacular. Christopher Murray Grieve ("Hugh Macdiarmid") sought to create a new poetic language by reviving older Scottish words. His enthusiasm won him disciples among younger Scottish poets.

Gaelic-language organizations in Scotland promote the use of Gaelic even though it has been supplanted by English. Two such societies, the *Commun nan Albannach,* modeled on a Welsh example, and the *An Commun Gaidhealach,* compete with each other in promoting the use of Gaelic. Both demand expansion of the Gaelic services of the British Broadcasting Corporation.

Despite the efforts of these small groups of zealots, both Lallans and Gaelic revivals have faded, and English has become the language of most Scottish writers.[9] The connection with English has always been a close one. Early Scots originally called their language English and used the term "Scots" to describe the speech of their Gaelic fellow-subjects from whom they were distinguished not only by speech but by culture and societal structure. It is reasonable to conclude that, unlike the characteristics of mini-nationalisms elsewhere, language is not a compelling factor for Scottish separation.

The Scottishness of Scottish Culture

The Scottish people do possess elements of a distinct culture.[10] On the contemporary scene, despite their union with England, they retain their own national educational system, Church, and legal customs.[11] On the surface there seem to be two different cultural identities—Scottish and English. But rivalry between the two peoples is based on politico-economic and not on cultural factors. Scotsmen seldom think of their deprivations in cultural terms.

There is a flourishing cultural tradition in Scottish society which has branched out in two directions: one was influenced by those who came from Mediterranean lands and the west coast of France; the other, by peoples from the North Sea area and the European mainland. In the process, two differing cultures spread throughout Scotland.

Expressed in another way, the two major cultural influences were Celtic and Teutonic. The Scots divided themselves into Lowlanders, who traced their origin to Teutonic sources, and Highlanders, who believed themselves to be of "pure" Celtic stock. These two traditions coalesced into a distinctive Scottish culture. For some time, a clan system, a remnant of tribalism and feudalism, existed in the Highlands, but today the clan issue may be dismissed as a bogus one. It entertains the false notion that all Scotsmen with the same surname have a common ancestor, and stresses "clans" and "chiefs" and "clan tartans," which are all artificial Lowland inventions.

The Scottishness of Scottish society is revealed in traditional celebrations. Among them are: Bride's Day, featuring handball games in border towns; Baltane, when visits are made to wishing wells; local fairs called Lammas; *Burns nicht* (27 January); and appropriate Halloween and New Year's festivals. These celebrations represent the amalgamation of the two early cultures: one part was contributed by the Highlanders, speaking Gaelic, and dominantly Celtic in culture; the other by the Lowlanders, speaking "Inglis," and Anglo-Saxon in culture but with French connections. For a time the two cultures were mutually hostile before being fused into one form.

Added to the traditional celebrations are special efforts which serve to express Scottish national pride. The Edinburgh Festival of Music and Drama, the Scottish National Orchestra, the Scottish Opera, the Scottish Ballet, all retain a provincial identity. The Scottish Royal Academy has annual exhibitions of painting and sculpture. The Scottish Arts Council supports theaters, concerts, and exhibitions. Eight universities give attention to Scottish history, literature, and politics. The School of Scottish Studies, attached to the University of Edinburgh, collects Scottish folk songs and music. The National Mod, a music festival run annually by *An Communn Gaidhealach,* seeks to keep Gaelic alive by sponsoring competition among poets, soloists singing in Gaelic, and bards composing Gaelic verse. There are special summer sports, including the Highland Games, in which strong men toss the caber (a heavy pole), pipers play, and boys and girls dance Highland steps.

All these intellectual and artistic pursuits give testimony to the Scottishness of Scottish culture. Yet, it is fair to say that British influences transcend the provincial level. Today, most Scotsmen consider their culture to be primarily English. The trend is strengthened by radio, television, and newspapers, all of which tend to portray Scottish culture as more national than regional. Scottish nationalists have not been successful in their goal of separating their own culture from that of the English.

Economics as Leveler

Economic factors may or may not be decisive in setting the tone of a mini-nationalism. Although almost always present, they do not necessarily affect regional self-awareness and may take a secondary role to territorial imperative, language, culture, or religion. In the case of Scotland, an interlocking economic relationship with England had a determining effect on the nature of its mini-nationalism.[12]

With an area of 30,411 square miles, occupying the northeastern 37 percent of the main British island, Scotland is rich in mineral resources and agricultural products. It has a population of 5.2 million people. England, with an area of 50,331 square miles and an estimated population of 42 million, is, after Taiwan and Bangladesh, the most densely populated country in the world. England tends to be economically unbalanced, and a potentially rich Scotland must share her troubles.

Roots of economic ties run deep in the history of both areas. In the Middle Ages, land was held directly by the Scottish Crown or by lay or clerical landowners. Throughout the 17th century, Scotland remained primarily agricultural. The union with England in 1707 brought a change as Scotland was converted from an agricultural to an industrial economy. By the end of the 18th century, the Industrial Revolution was in full swing.[13] After a series of inventions by men such as Richard Arkwright and Samuel Crompton, the spinning and weaving of cotton became a major industry in the west of Scotland. Cotton from abroad flowed into mills around Glasgow. The invention in 1828 of the hot blast for melting iron revolutionized the iron industry in Scotland, which then became an important center for shipbuilding, engineering, and locomotive construction.

Along with the new industrialism came a social upheaval. The rapid growth of towns was accompanied by grave social problems. Industry brought work and wealth for the Scots but also a heritage of slums and public-health problems. In the 20th century, economic decline began, partly due to the distance from important markets and high transportation costs. There was a declining market for Scottish products as other countries became industrialized. The center of British industry shifted southward to English towns. Scotland was left on an industrial fringe, with an unemployment rate twice that of England.

Throughout that period, economic power remained in London; and no economic decision of any importance was made in Edinburgh. Most Scottish entrepreneurs were dependent upon their English counterparts. At one time Scotsmen had shared English colonial glory and profits, but the situation changed with the decline of the British Empire. Many Scotsmen began to have second thoughts about their economic subservience to London. They began to feel economically deprived, and they began to object to British control.

The discovery in 1973 of sulphur-free oil in the Scottish sector of the North Sea introduced a new problem into Scottish-English economic relations. Scottish nationalists regarded oil as a propaganda factor of utmost importance. They believed that new supplies of the precious commodity, with its enormous monetary value, could make Scotland the richest nation per capita in Europe. They pointed out that the English demand would exhaust the rich oil resources in 25 years but that under Scottish control, the supply would last 10 times as long. Whether or not this argument in favor of independence convinces the vast majority of Scots is a matter of debate.[14]

Despite its own problems, Westminster attempted to allay Scottish economic discontent by granting subsidies and incentives to attract foreign capital to Edinburgh. The English were concerned with their own economic difficulties in the Midlands and in southern England, where they had to provide harried industrialists with large-scale rent rebates and payroll subsidies. In the process, Scotland was bound to be the loser.

Political and Psychological Accommodation

To retain Scotland within the United Kingdom, the English were careful to show concern not only for its economic problems but also for its political life and psychological needs. The long-standing process of Anglicization was largely successful, continuing through the 19th and 20th centuries to a point where Scotland and England merged politically into a common state. For the most part, Scottish public opinion accepted this situation as normal and desirable.

The English nurtured a policy of conciliation and accommodation painstakingly designed to retain Scotland inside the mainstream of British life. Scotland was given a generous share in government.[15] In 1707 the Scots had given up their own Parliament. Although they now have no legislature of their own, they are well represented in the House of Commons, with about 71 members out of approximately 635. Since 1634, all Scottish peers have held seats in the House of Lords. Scotland is represented in the British Cabinet by a Secretary of State for Scotland, who is responsible directly to Parliament in the administration of agriculture, health, and education, and who handles home affairs, including the judicial system and the police.[16]

There is a wide range of local government: in the four main cities of Glasgow, Edinburgh, Aberdeen, and Dundee; in the 33 counties (formerly called "shires"); in 198 burghs; and in 197 districts. These local administrations are financed partly by governmental grants and partly by local taxes. This kind of political accommodation does much to satisfy the Scots' desire for political equality. Since the late 19th century, a disproportionately high number of Scotsmen have held the office of Prime Minister, which is a fair indication of the absorption of Scotland into the British political structure.

Added to the political conciliation is a psychological accommodation that has done much to lessen the effectiveness of Scottish nationalism. Even though they accept the political union with England, Scotsmen generally retain the distinctive features of their life. Proud of their past, they point to their great men—Adam Smith, David Hume, John Stuart Mill, Thomas Carlyle, Robert Burns, James Watt, and many others. Their sense of self-confidence has been sapped by long English rule and by the feeling that Scotland has been condemned to a secondary role in British affairs. Many Scotsmen are disturbed by what they regard as a "mentality of dependence," a kind of inferiority *vis-à-vis* their English compatriots.[17] This sentiment, added to practical grievances, gave ammunition to the cause of Scottish nationalists.

Aware of Scottish sensitivity, the English took steps to placate it. From the time of the wars against Napoleon, Scotsmen were welcomed into Britain's armed forces. They fought side by side with the English in Britain's wars and developed a sense of sharing the British cause. Scotsmen took part in the colonial wars of the old British Empire. This sentiment of togetherness was enhanced during the Industrial Revolution, when both Scotsmen and Englishmen found it to their common interest to attack problems on a national and not on a local level.

An additional factor for accommodation is the mutual love of pageantry. The English have a talent for organizing colorful parades with blaring bands, horse-drawn vehicles, and marching soldiers in blazing red tunics. Scotsmen, too, are enthusiastic about their own kilt-clad marchers in plaids and tartans amid the stirring strains of bagpipes. Both Englishmen and Scotsmen delight in such ceremonies as the trooping of colors in London or the exhibitions at Holyrood Castle in Edinburgh. This kind of common interest is further strengthened by royal attention. Members of the royal family make it a point to be photographed in kilts and tartans and take summer holidays at Balmoral Castle in Aberdeenshire on the banks of the River Dee. It is a royal tradition to attend such summer sports festivals as the Braemar Games in Aberdeen County.

The Scottish quest for self-determination must be judged within the framework of the accommodation by which the two "nations," with their own institutions, combined into one state. Distinctive cultures of mini-nationalisms tend to become less important than the memories of a common history. The policy of political accommodation and psychological understanding has done much to weaken the cause of Scottish separatism.

The Scottish National Movement

While most Scotsmen are willing to settle for a Scottish Parliament with adequate legislative authority—in other words, for more autonomy—a new political party emerged to call for more extreme measures.[18] Founded in 1928, the Scottish National Party (SNP) demanded independence for a new Scottish state, with full self-government and control of defense and foreign policy. It opposed mere home rule as an unsatisfactory reform measure.

On December 8, 1946, the SNP issued a statement of aim and policy:[19]

The People of Scotland, as members of one of the oldest nations in Europe, are the inheritors, bearers and transmitters of an historic tradition of liberty. They have in common with the peoples of all other nations an inherent right to determine their own destiny in accordance with the principles of justice accepted by the social conscience of mankind. The aim of the Scottish National Party is therefore "Self-Government for Scotland. The restoration of Scottish National sovereignty by the establishment of a democratic Scottish Government whose authority will be limited only by such agreements as will be freely entered into with other nations in order to further international co-operation and world peace."

The statement then went on to outline SNP goals. On constitutional matters, it called for the establishment of a representative Parliament as indispensable, as well as for a Constituent Assembly to frame a constitution. A healthy interest in local affairs would be encouraged. Jurisdiction within Scotland would be exercised exclusively by Scottish courts. There would be no religious disabilities. Planning would be directed to a better distribution of work and people. In economic matters, "the land and all natural resources and accumulated wealth rightly belong to the people of Scotland from whom they may not be alienated. Every citizen has the right to share in the national inheritance and to own property." Natural resources would be utilized in the interests of the community as a whole. There were additional statements on agriculture, labor, industry, and finance, as well as on such social matters as health, housing, and education. A self-governing Scotland would work closely with other countries in international relations. This program of the SNP summarizes the goals of mini-nationalisms elsewhere. The demands go beyond autonomy to the status of full independence.

SNP leaders, like those of separatists in other countries, regard themselves as patriots, liberators, and the authentic voice of their country. They define their cause as "a struggle for the soul of Scotland." They denounce English control of Scottish steel, fishing, energy, agriculture, and oil. "London and all those fatheads in Whitehall are ruining our lives."[20] They reject loyalty to the British Crown and to the United Kingdom as plainly unsatisfactory.

For several decades, the SNP carried on a lonely and stubborn campaign to win the support of the Scottish people. They canvassed from door to door, distributed leaflets, and electioneered zealously. The argument was always "freedom from English control." Scotland, they said, was a better-balanced country than England, but she had been forced into an inferior status and exploited by absentee landlords and industrialists in London.[21] They pointed to nearby Scandinavian countries, with populations approximating that of Scotland, as thriving while maintaining independence. England was "overcentralized and fossilized," a vessel foundering at sea. Scotsmen, they said, should set out in their own ship.

The SNP used publicity to promote its cause, but unlike extremists elsewhere, it did not resort to terror and violence. On Christmas Day 1950, Scottish nationalists removed the Stone of Scone (otherwise called the Stone of Destiny) from Westminster Abbey in London[22] and deposited it inside the ruins of Arbroath Abbey, several yards from the spot where the signing of the Scottish Declaration of Independence in 1320 was reenacted each year in a summer pageant. For the nationalists, this was something more than a schoolboy prank or frolic; it was a serious attempt to publicize their cause.[23] To place greater emphasis on their goal, they refused to recognize the title "Elizabeth II," and regularly damaged post pillar boxes bearing the Queen's cypher.

From its beginning, the SNP challenged the major political parties—Labour, Conservative, and Liberal.[24] For more than three decades, its drawing power was small and unimportant.[25] Its efforts began to bear fruit when, in the general elections of 1970, it won 11.4 percent of the vote and its first seat in the House of Commons.[26]

The nationalist cause was strengthened in 1973 with the discovery of oil in the Scottish sector of the North Sea at a time when the energy crisis was beginning to deepen. SNP leaders saw in this unexpected development a long-delayed realization of Scotland's economic potential. They demanded that Edinburgh, not London, control this new source of wealth. The argument was effective. The clash on oil resources was followed by a quick upturn in the fortunes of the SNP. In the general elections for the House of Commons, it won 7 seats in February 1974 and 11 seats in October 1974.[27] Scottish nationalists made heavy inroads on traditional Labour constituencies.

There were additional factors in rising SNP prestige, including the dynamism of the movement, a deepening economic crisis, and an admiration for active SNP leaders.[28] But the idea of separatism did not win majority support among the Scots. Conservatives, Labourites, and Liberals all supported home rule or devolution in one form or another.

The Politics of Devolution

Historically, a sense of Scottish nationalism thrived whenever a radical party held power in Westminster. As early as 1908 the Duke of Montrose left the Tories to join the "Kilties" in a call for more autonomy for Scotland. The issue of home rule became more pronounced with the approach of mid-century. On October 28, 1948, a Scottish Convention issued this resolution:

The National Assembly, representative of the people of Scotland, reaffirm the belief that the establishment of a Scottish Parliament with legislative authority over Scottish affairs is necessary for the national interest of Scotland, and in order to give the people an effective means of demonstrating their determination to secure the reform, the Assembly resolves to invite Scots men and women to subscribe to a Covenant in the following terms: "We the people of Scotland who subscribe this Engagement, declare our belief that reform in the constitution of our country is necessary to secure good government in accordance with the spiritual and economic welfare of our nation. . . . With that end in view we solemnly enter into this Covenant whereby we pledge ourselves, in all loyalty to the Crown and within the framework of the United Kingdom, to do everything in our power to secure for Scotland a Parliament with adequate legislative authority in Scottish affairs."

This resolution received 1,250,000 signatures within six months—a large representation of the Scottish population.[29]

The key phrases—"in all loyalty to the Crown and within the framework of the United Kingdom"—revealed a request modest in aim and lukewarm in attitude. It was not accompanied by either-or demands or the turbulence associated with Irish Republican Army tactics.

At the same time, the modestly expressed proposal was a clear warning to Westminster that something had to be done, after 241 years of union, to give partial self-government to Scotland. For the first time, the British Government began to think seriously about satisfying the Scottish quest for self-determination. The key was to relinquish power without permitting separation. Devolution meant partial surrender of authority from central government to regional authority. As a governmental and administrative reform, it proposed a new deal for Scotland.

The issue of devolution came to a head in 1978, when Prime Minister James Callaghan's Labour Government, troubled by nationalist inroads in traditionally Labour strongholds, decided that the people of Scotland would be given an opportunity to express their opinion on home rule through a referendum. They would vote "Yes" or "No" on the creation of a new Scottish Assembly, which would pass laws and control education, health, and medical care. Regional authorities would be established. The opponents of devolution (the Conservatives opposed it because they believed that it meant eventual separation) managed to win an important concession on the voting: it was stipulated that 40 percent of all registered voters had to approve.[30]

Campaigns for and against devolution took place in the fall of 1978 and the spring of 1979. Newspaper opinion polls predicted that devolution would win by a margin of 2 to 1. The voting took place on March 1, 1979, with surprising results. The people of Scotland failed to give unequivocal endorsement to devolution, even though it was approved by a narrow margin. One-third of the voters marked "Yes"; 31 percent voted "No." The proposal was defeated because it did not receive the required 40 percent.[31]

No single factor can explain the result of this referendum. The basic cause was economic: satiated with taxation, the voters were impressed by the argument of Conservative anti-devolutionists that the cost of home rule would be felt quickly in the form of higher taxes. Politically, Westminster's policy of accommodation appealed to moderate Scots. England's way became Scotland's way. The SNP, despite its concern for "the soul of the country," failed to win heavy backing. Voter apathy indicated that most Scotsmen did not consider devolution a burning issue.

Benign Nationalism

The indecisive referendum of March 1979 was an unexpected blow for Scottish nationalists. It revealed Scottish nationalism as dissent with manners, born of irritation and frustration, not of oppression. It was not permeated with the stuff of revolution. Voters were not impressed with extremists who presented themselves as latter-day Mazzinis. There was much sympathy for the cause but no overwhelming sentiment. Ties with the English had become too strong to be broken.

Scottish moderation was matched by English accommodation. Despite the activities of a minority of hot-headed "patriots and liberators," both Scots and English preferred the way of reason and compromise. This does not mean, however, that Scottish nationalism appeared in the solvent of English accommodation. There was still dissension by both moderates and extremists. Moderates claimed that English concessions have been only minor and unimportant. They pointed out that in the last 90 years, 12 bills have been promoted in Parliament to give Scotland a meaningful degree of autonomy. Every one was supported by Scottish public opinion, but every one failed, voted down by the 8-to-1 English majority in Parliament. There was no control, said the dissenters, over taxation, insurance, banking, money, unions, employment, licensing—or oil. They charged the English with "their usual game of switching the rules."

This was the view of Robert MacBeth Shirley, associate professor of finance at Queen Margaret College, Edinburgh:[32]

Scotland is being extinguished. Emigration continues. Unemployment has hit 11 percent. Top jobs in Scotland are going to Englishmen. Oil is being sucked out of Scotland at the rate of 100 million tons a year. Yet, Scotland is also being turned into the most nuclear-dense country in the world by state-controlled utilities in order to supply cheap power in England and no referendum is proposed on the subject.

A small group of dedicated extremists would go even farther. They excoriated the Act of Union of 1707 as imposed by a militaristic, domineering power—grandly called "Great Britain" but which should have been termed "Greater England." They were not averse to the use of terror. On October 15, 1980, seven Scottish extremists were sentenced in Glasgow to prison terms of from 6 to 16 years for an attempt to blow up the National Assembly building in Edinburgh. The High Court judge, Lord McDonald, denounced the conspirators as being prepared "to kill and maim numerous innocent people in a planned terrorist campaign to win Scottish independence."[33] Even in Scotland there were those who preferred violence to moderation.

The Claims of Shetland

It is a curious commentary on the complexities of nationalism that Scotland itself has to contend with a dissatisfied minority inside its own jurisdiction, a kind of mini-nationalism within a mini-nationalism. Situated 105 miles north of the coast of Scotland are the more than 100 Shetland Islands, which have been a part of Scotland for 500 years. The attachment has been loose and fragile. Restive Shetlanders have long resented Scottish lords who appropriated their best lands and subjected them to centuries of control.

The Shetlanders show a decided preference for the English: they prefer the commands of Westminster to those of Edinburgh. When the House of Commons passed a bill in 1978 to set up an Edinburgh Assembly, representatives of the Shetland Islands and the Orkney Islands pushed through an amendment, over the embarrassed opposition of the Scottish nationalists, giving both sets of islands a special constitutional status of more autonomy.[34]

The discovery of oil in the North Sea stimulated not only Scottish nationalism but also that of the Shetlanders. Scottish nationalists called for the English to keep hands off "Scotland's oil," ignoring the fact that much of the newly discovered deposits lay east of the Shetlands. Shetlanders suggested that the Scots "keep their hands off our oil."[35]

Shetlanders oppose the entire principle of devolution because they fear that once limited home rule is established in Edinburgh, the Scots will go on to demand outright independence. In that case, the Shetlanders would prefer attachment to England.[36]

CHAPTER 4

BRITISH DEVOLUTION II: THE
RED DRAGON OF WALES _____

I do know that, tiny a nation as we are, and being no better or
no worse than any other nations, I do know that we are different and that we want to remain so. We don't have to have
that hot rush of blood to the head when someone mistakes us
for British, or thinks that we are one of England's quainter
countries. We want to be uniquely ourselves and we want to
keep our unique language.
                                    —Richard Burton, actor

The Way of Moderation

Scottish and Welsh mini-nationalisms follow the same pattern—
moderation instead of violent extremism. British democratic institutions
have been won on the domestic scene without extensive use of force. By
the 20th century both British and French democracies were operating at
approximately the same level, but there was a difference in the means.
The French achieved their democracy after a series of violent encounters in the revolutions of 1789, 1830, and 1848, and by the annihilation
of thousands of Communards in 1871. The British, on the other hand,
formed their parliamentary society with comparatively little bloodshed.

By no means does this absolve the British of indiscretions on both
domestic and foreign scenes. On the home front many unfortunates
were hanged at Tyburn for criminal acts as minor as the theft of a
handkerchief. In 1649 Charles I was deprived of his head (to this day,
Englishmen sadly apologize for this display of bad manners). Irish peasants found their pitchforks ineffective against Cromwell's avenging
troops, and British workers were killed in the Peterloo Massacre of
1819.[1] On the foreign scene, Clive, in India, and Kitchener, in Africa,
used the power of the sword in affairs of the British Empire.

However, the English chose the way of moderation in dealing with
their unsatisfied nationalisms in Scotland and Wales. They know that
there is a difference among peoples and that there is no more a pure-
blooded Englishman than there is a racially distinct American or Brazil-

ian.[2] They think in democratic terms of devolution—delegation of regional authority. The result has been that both Welsh and Scots remain inside the United Kingdom and share its politico-economic successes and failures. Both peoples have their hotheads and die-hards who are tolerated patiently by Westminster, but the large majority of Welsh and Scots prefer compromise to sawed-off shotguns and plastic bombs.

The Welsh Search for Identity

Wales (called *Cymru* in Welsh and *Pays de Galle* ["Region of Wales"] in French) is one of the four countries which make up the United Kingdom of Great Britain and Ireland. Occupying the western central peninsula of the main island, it is bounded on the east by England, on the north by the Irish Sea, on the south by the Bristol Channel, and on the west by St. George's Channel. The area is 8,016 square miles, with a population of 2,768,200, according to a 1977 estimate.

Wales has a dual heritage affecting its national life, a history and character of its own. It has many characteristics of a small nation but has never won independence. Despite its distinctive environment and landscape, its life has been associated closely with that of adjacent England for seven centuries. This duality is in part an outcome of much diversity. There are traces of Paleolithic occupation in the coastal caves dating back 200,000 years. In the Neolithic Age, Wales received its most important stock, the short, dark-haired Mediterranean type, who settled in the western area.[3] From eastern Lowlands Britain and from the Continent came additional migrations of Anglo-Saxons and Anglo-Normans, who moved into the mountainous districts of Wales and, through a combination of domination and intermarriage, took control of the area.

Throughout the centuries these two peoples have confronted one another in Wales. Many Welshmen still regard themselves as "natives" and the English as "intruders." To the duality may be added a third element—the Anglo-Welsh—who retain their loyalty to the British Crown.

Historical Background

The historical development of Wales reveals reasons for the gap between natives and intruders.[4] During the late Bronze Age, the area was overrun by Celts. When the Romans came to Britain in the 1st century A.D., they built a line of forts along the Welsh border. After the Romans left Britain in the 5th century, Welsh tribesmen began to swarm into the English Midlands. Here, they clashed with Anglo-Saxons who were pushing in from the east. The Welsh were forced back into their mountainous homeland.

Into the shadowy world of the 7th century appeared the legendary figure of King Arthur, who, through the attention of Geoffrey of Monmouth, was made the central hero of medieval romance. The Arthurian legend is often regarded as the greatest Welsh contribution to European literature.

During succeeding centuries, Wales was divided into feudal units, which traditionally fought among themselves or in frontier wars with the English. Rhodri the Great (d. 878) united Wales and defended it against the Normans. Howel the Good (d. 949) also united the country. Normans overran most of South Wales after 1066. Welsh chieftains began to take part in English affairs; a Welsh nobleman signed the Magna Carta in 1215. They worked assiduously to limit the power of the English king, and several of them helped Simon de Montfort in his attempt in 1265 to set up a parliament beyond the monarch's control.

In 1267 Llyelyn ap Gruffydd assumed the title of Prince of Wales, a designation acknowledged by the British Crown. However, the constant struggle with rebellious Welsh nobles led Edward I (r. 1272–1307) to attempt subjugation of the principality. In 1301 Edward named his son Prince of Wales (later Edward II), thereby starting a tradition which has lasted to the present day.[5]

The peace between England and Wales that followed in the next several centuries was an uneven one. The English introduced their own laws throughout the principality and gradually took over control of Welsh towns and villages. They sought to make their own language dominant over Welsh. Unhappy about what they believed to be foreign penetration, Welshmen broke out in sporadic rebellion. In 1399 Owen Glendower led a revolt against Henry IV. In the Wars of the Roses, both the House of York and the House of Lancaster, as claimants to the throne, looked for support in Wales. The Lancastrian claim eventually went to Henry Tudor, who was himself partly Welsh. At the Battle of Bosworth Field in 1485, Henry unveiled the red dragon banner. After his victory, he ascended the throne of England as Henry VII, first king of the House of Tudor.

In 1530 Wales became an integral part of the Tudor kingdom but retained its status as a principality inside the kingdom. By the Act of Union of England and Wales in 1536, promulgated during the reign of Henry VIII, Wales was absorbed into the realm of England. It was divided into 13 shires (counties), each of which was represented in Parliament. Welshmen were guaranteed equality with Englishmen before the law, but all official business in the principality was to be conducted in English.

At this time, Wales was governed by its own gentry, who administered justice as magistrates and who held seats in Parliament. The Welsh gentry preferred the English language to their own and accepted English folkways and customs. There was a clash of classes: the privileged gentry became more and more alienated from the Welsh tenantry, who regarded themselves as loyal natives of Wales and not, as the gentry, "traitors allied with foreigners in London." This strife between squire-archy and peasantry was later merged into the struggle between capital and labor.

Added to the class confrontation was a religious problem which sharpened tensions in the Welsh countryside. The Welsh gentry remained Anglican in religion after the religious revival of the 18th century, while other Welshmen were predominantly Nonconformist. The two groups remained at odds throughout the 19th century, at the end of which the struggle came to a head in a movement to disestablish the Church of England in Wales. The Conservative Party opposed disestablishment, while the Liberal Party, which was strong in Wales, supported it. In 1920 the Liberals won the religious disestablishment they wanted.

A Welsh national sentiment emerged in the 19th century. This national self-consciousness found expression in the establishment of Welsh institutions of learning. Westminster was aware of the feeling and gave Wales a large measure of local control in educational matters. In the last decade of the 19th century, a move for autonomy was organized by Thomas Elkin and David Lloyd George, the latter the famed war leader. But the movement for autonomy lost momentum when its leaders accepted offices in the national government.

In 1925 the Welsh National Party, *Plaid Cymru,* was formed to win dominion status for Wales. It took part in several parliamentary elections without success, but it did manage to bring to public attention the seriousness of the Welsh movement for autonomy.

The Welsh Language

Oxford scholar Sir John Morris Jones called the Welsh language "the sweetest tongue in all the world." Veneration for this ancient, tongue-twisting language accentuated the differences between Welsh insiders and English outsiders. Welsh, or *Cymraeg,* belongs to the wider Indo-European linguistic family, a member of the Brythonic group of Celtic languages related to Gaelic, Manx, Cornish, and Breton.[6]

At the dawn of history, an Iron Age people brought to Wales a Celtic speech that became the basis of modern Welsh. Far older than English, Welsh was spoken before the Roman conquest of Britain. It developed in three forms: Old Welsh (9th–11th centuries); Middle Welsh (11th–14th centuries); and Modern Welsh (14th century on). Welsh survived not only the Roman occupation but also recurrent opposition by English authorities who hoped to bring Wales into the mainstream of British life.

With the Anglicization of Wales in the 19th and 20th centuries came a decline in the use of the Welsh language. There were several contributory factors: the preference of the Welsh gentry for the language spoken by English peers; the exclusive use of English in the law courts; and the influx into Welsh coal fields of English and Irish workers during the Industrial Revolution. Nevertheless, many Welshmen remain attached to their native tongue. Though each succeeding census in the 20th century revealed a decline in the number of Welsh speakers, Welsh is still the preferred language of many Welshmen.[7] Many natives who reside in rural villages speak the old tongue. The language is taught in all Welsh schools and in institutions of higher learning and is also used in church worship. In contemporary Wales most people are familiar with popular Welsh terms.

Those who take regional differences seriously insist that the old language should be retained not only in schools and in administration but also in everyday speech. These traditionalists see the language question as the heart of their national sentiment and use it to bolster the movement for autonomy.[8]

Welsh Culture

The language question is but one facet of Welsh cultural identity. Despite the union with England, Wales has developed its own cultural institutions. Welshmen take great pride in the fact that, next to the Greeks and the Romans, theirs is the oldest extant literature in Europe. They admit an interplay with English culture and even are willing to accept bilingualism, but at the same time, they hold fast to their own culture.

From its earliest days, Welsh culture has been orally oriented, with parents passing on special tales and legends to their children. They maintain a traditional interest in otherworldly matters such as tales of ghosts, fairies, and spirits. Like the Irish, the Welsh take pleasure in nostalgia. They maintain their love for mysticism despite the onslaught of English materialism in literature, radio, and television.

Welsh delight in the spoken word carries over into lyrics, especially choral singing, for which they have won much acclaim. Much of this taste was associated with religion and its 19th-century revival. Both the song and the spoken word support the idea of *cynghanedd,* solicitude for the preservation of the Welsh language.

Nineteenth-century Welsh arts were dominated almost wholly by the English. By the end of the century, however, there was a renascence of Welsh culture, centered at the newly created University of Wales, a federal university with seven constituent institutions. Here, Welsh

scholars studied the ancient texts to preserve them for future generations. At the same time, Welsh poets,[9] novelists, and essayists published
their works in Welsh. This revival went on into the 20th century, with an
additional efflorescence of publications in Welsh. New institutions accented Welsh awareness: the National Library of Wales, supported by
governmental grants, became a repository for old Welsh documents and
manuscripts; the Welsh Arts Council, also government supported, allo-
cated funds for literature, art, music, and drama, both in Welsh and in
English.

By far the most effective institution working for *cynghanedd* is the
National *Eisteddfod,* a competitive festival, which is the most unique of all
Welsh cultural activities. The tradition of an annual social union and arts
competition goes far back into Welsh history. Early *eisteddfods* were held
by local bards to discuss matters concerned with their craft. In the early
19th century, these meetings were transformed into a yearly festival, a
patriotic event devoted to a combination of competitive choral singing,
recitation of the Scriptures, and poetry composition. Men, women, and
children wore colorful native costumes and joined in singing, dancing,
and semi-religious rituals with harp accompaniment. Several customs
arose, including an annual festival held alternately in North Wales and
South Wales: an annual award to the composer of the best alliterative
poem in strict traditional meter; a prize for the best youth diary kept for
a fortnight; floral dances; and ceremonies led by archdruids.

Today the *Eisteddfod* is held for one week in August. The location is
selected from invitations by regions and towns. The festival always takes
place on open ground so that it can be viewed by large numbers of
people. Welsh cultural organizations as well as commercial enterprises
have their own booths. The bardic circle, *orgorsedd,* is generally the
center of attention. The National *Eisteddfod* is looked upon as the meeting place for the Welsh "nation," but local versions are held in towns and
villages throughout the year.

With these competitions, the Welsh give notice to the English-speaking
world that, while they are tied closely to England in political, administrative, and economic matters, they propose to retain their own cultural
identity. They also serve notice on English "foreigners" that bilingualism
may have its pragmatic usage, but recognition must be accorded to and
respect maintained for the special nature of Welsh culture.

The Welsh Economy

Relations between English and Welsh are tempered by economic discontent.[10] Because of its mountainous terrain, rainfall, and nature of the
soil, Wales is not suitable for arable farming. In the past the traditional

occupation was breeding cattle. Welsh drovers herded their cattle over hundreds of miles to the English Midlands to meet the needs of growing industrial towns. Drovers were respected members of the Welsh communities until the coming of the railroads ruined their occupation.

The Welsh economy rests on two extensive coal deposits, one of inferior quality in the northeast, and the other of greater value in South Wales.[11] Rich coal fields in Glamorganshire and Monmouthshire gave Wales a basis for its economy, but they brought many problems as well.

The rapid industrialization of Wales in the 19th century occurred in an area with limited industrial traditions. Discovery of the South Wales coal fields led to a population shift as "foreign" Englishmen and Irishmen, desperate for work in the mines, moved into the area.[12] Almost half the people of Wales had settled in the vicinity of the coal fields.

The consequences were unfortunate for Wales. Miners profited little from the new demand for coal. Wales was transformed into a series of grim coal-mining valleys. Housing conditions were miserable; wages were low; and there were many periods of unemployment. Derelict towns appeared throughout the countryside, reflecting a chronically unstable economic system.[13]

Welshmen resented both English entrepreneurs and imported English and Irish miners. They accused industrialists from Manchester and London of siphoning off profits from coal mines while showing little regard for the suffering of miners' families. They saw their own grinding poverty as the fault of indifferent English landowners and imported workers who took their jobs from them.

This heritage of economic suffering helped promote a sense of Welsh national consciousness. English authorities understood Welsh resentment and made special efforts to improve the Welsh economy. They agreed that, in a politically centralized state, all its component parts were interrelated and that economic difficulties in one would be reflected in the others. Westminster made a series of governmental grants which, in the 1970s, amounted to about one-half the total Welsh income. It encouraged the movement of new industries into depressed Welsh areas in order to provide work for thousands of unemployed. These economic measures were promoted together with the political devolution process by which the Government hoped to satisfy Welsh aspirations.

Political Accommodation

In the British Empire, the classic response to drives for autonomy or independence was a divide-and-rule technique (Hindus and Muslims in India, North and South in Ireland). In Wales, however, this kind of political strategy was not practical. Here, the goal was to grant just enough autonomy to discourage the possibility of dissolution of the United Kingdom.

The process of political devolution developed slowly during the last century and a half. The Reform Act of 1832 extended the franchise in Wales even though squirearchy rule was maintained. In the elections of 1868, after the Second Reform Act, Wales returned a majority of Liberals for the first time. In the elections of 1885, after the Third Reform Act, 30 Liberals and only 3 Conservatives were elected in Wales. The rise of Welsh "radical" sentiment convinced English authorities that a policy of limited devolution was best for the political health of the United Kingdom.

Although the principality of Wales is governed today from London, decentralization of administration has become the accepted goal. This was indicated in 1964 when the post of Secretary of State for Wales was created. The Welsh Office, centered in both Cardiff and London, was given many governing functions previously reserved for London. To ease local administration, existing Welsh counties were abolished in April 1974, and eight new units were created.[14]

The policy of devolution was designed to meet the aspirations of Welsh moderates. It was stimulated in the last decade of the 19th century with the formation of an early movement for autonomy. Its successor, the *Plaid Cymru*, the Welsh National Party, gained one seat in the Parliament of 1965–1970 and, in the general elections of 1970, polled more than 11 percent of the total votes cast in Wales. *Plaid Cymru* defined its goal as the achievement, by democratic and constitutional means, of a measure of autonomy which would give Wales its own Parliament in a federalized United Kingdom. This moderate policy won large support throughout Wales. At the same time, the English regarded it as a fair and reasonable demand in the direction of devolution.

Welsh militants were reluctant to accept the way of moderation supported by *Plaid Cymru*. As in other mini-nationalisms, a small fringe of separatists called for complete independence based on Welsh linguistic and cultural differentiation. Although few in numbers, these extremists made themselves felt in the Welsh valleys, where their argument of "second-rate nation" had some appeal.

Activists of the Welsh Language Society went so far as to call for a program of civil disobedience. They denounced "the friendly stylized dragon of Wales" used by the Welsh Tourist Board in its publicity and insisted that a green and white flag depicting a fire-eating dragon would represent "the true spirit of Wales."[15] They splashed green paint and Welsh letters over English place-names. In the National *Eisteddfod* held in mid-May 1977, they disrupted the cultural calm of the festivities by wrecking the hall of the British Rail Exhibition because it did not use Welsh in its advertising.[16]

Most Welshmen, despite their sense of national consciousness, look upon these tactics as either harmless exuberance by teenagers or the work of lunatics. They are not inclined to promote irrational extremists to the status of national heroes.

Investiture of the Prince of Wales

In addition to the political and economic accommodation, there has been a measure of psychological appeasement. The English have used every possible psychological means of satisfying the people of the regional principality. Not the least effective approach has been to link Wales with the traditions of the monarchy. Whitehall could not promise, as had Edward I, that another royal prince would be "born in Wales and speak no English," but it could point to the Prince of Wales as heir to the throne. He might, on occasion, make an attempt, no matter how stumbling, to say a few words in tongue-twisting Welsh.

The investiture of the current Prince of Wales was an example of drawing the Welsh into the mainstream of British life. On July 10, 1968, a full year before the scheduled investiture, the *Plaid Cymru* in West Flintstone called for cancellation of the ceremony and suggested that the estimated cost of a quarter of a million pounds be given "to help the starving children of Biafra."[17] Whitehall paid no attention and went ahead with the ritual, not only as a symbol of a thousand years of British history, but also to convince the Welsh that they were a valuable part of British society. The ceremony of 1911, when the last Prince of Wales (later King Edward VIII and Duke of Windsor) was invested with the title, would be repeated.

The investiture took place in late June 1969 on the grounds of the Welsh castle of Caernarvon, with all the colorful pageantry well loved by the public. The 20-year-old Charles Philip Arthur George Windsor, clad in satin knee breeches, appeared before an audience of 4,000 loyal lords and ladies, prelates, Members of Parliament, mayors, and a large number of Welshmen. While half a billion people around the world watched on television, the prince knelt on a slab of Welsh slate, placed his hands between those of his mother, Queen Elizabeth II, and swore the medieval oath of fealty: "I, Charles, Prince of Wales, do become your liege man of life and of earthly worship and faith and trust I will bear unto you to live and die against all manner of folks." At the moment of investiture with the title of Prince of Wales, he proclaimed the 600-year-old Teutonic motto: "*Ich dien*" ("I Serve").

To avoid any possible disruption by Welsh extremists, more than 2,000 policemen, including several Scotland Yard officers in bullet-proof vests, joined 2,500 soldiers to patrol the streets in and around Caernarvon. Helicopters swarmed overhead, minesweepers guarded the nearby strait, and frogmen swam around the royal yacht. Nevertheless, there were several uncomfortable minor incidents. As Queen Elizabeth rode to the castle in an open carriage, she became the target of a thrown egg, which missed.[18] The public, both Welsh and English, regarded that as an act of supreme rudeness.

English psychological calculations were correct: the people of Wales were not only impressed but delighted by the attention accorded them in the important ceremony. Welsh dignitaries, clad in ancient bardic costumes, appeared as symbols of loyalty to the Crown. The dark streets of mining valleys were brightened by flowing banners depicting the red dragon of Wales. Welshmen of all classes entered exuberantly into the gala occasion—the living proof of English-Welsh union.[19]

Devolution Is Deferred

Investiture of the Prince of Wales indicated that public demand for more autonomy was weakening. Nevertheless, Westminster was willing to proceed with a policy of devolution. In late 1977 a plan was proposed for a British federation modeled after the pattern of the United States and the Federal Republic of West Germany. Wales would have its own Assembly, without the power to legislate, while London-made laws would be administered in the principality. London would maintain power of taxation. The plan would be considered by the House of Commons, the House of Lords, and by the Welsh people in a referendum.

After a year of discussion, the proposal was finally put to a vote in Wales and Scotland—with surprising results: both peoples turned it down.[20] Welsh voters rejected it by a 4-to-1 margin. Astonished political pundits sought an explanation for the unexpected result. Welsh voters reacted much the same as did the Scots.[21] Many feared that the practical effect of limited self-rule would be the creation of a costly new bureaucracy. Many others believed that the cost of home rule would be the imposition of higher taxes. Still others felt that devolution might be a step toward dissolution of the United Kingdom, which none but the most extreme separatists wanted. The sentiment of cohesion was obviously stronger than provincial regionalism.

The Welsh experience indicates that a mini-nationalism need not go all the way to independence. Welsh nativism seems quite willing to accept accommodation with British "intrusion." Most Welshmen believe that they and the English can retain their separate identities in a union and contribute at the same time to an Anglo-Welsh tradition. The British contributed guidelines for mini-nationalisms elsewhere by demonstrating that a rational solution could be found to the confrontation between centralized governments and their regional components.

Though rebuffed by the humiliating referendum defeat, by no means did Welsh nationalists regard their cause as lost. Remaining as a passionate minority, they were determined that their language would survive and were willing to break the law to make sure that it did.[22] In the first four months of 1980, 32 vacation cottages owned by people who live in England were destroyed or damaged by Welsh arsonists to show the English that they were not welcome. "Sure they're extremists, those people setting the fires," said a Welsh fisherman. "But you can't help but admire the way they're standing up to the English when all that the rest of us do is talk." The so-called Movement for the Defense of Wales, a clandestine group claiming responsibility for the fires, maintained that it was acting on behalf of the poor of the principality: "We believe that there is widespread sympathy in every area of Wales towards the burning of holiday homes, whatever the politicians and the media say. We hope that the present campaign will inspire steelworkers and miners and everyone else in Wales whose jobs and futures are being threatened terribly."[23]

When in mid-July 1980 Prime Minister Margaret Thatcher went on a two-day tour of Welsh factories, her limousine was bombared with eggs by young Welsh nationalists who were protesting the British Government's refusal to set up a Welsh-language television station.[24]

The incidents, similar to those employed by militants elsewhere in expressing their frustrations, reflect a small but growing nationalism in the principality. As a reminder of the ancient struggle of the Welsh against the English, these outbursts reveal that extremists, although actively supported by only a fraction of the people, do not intend to cast aside their own version of what a mini-nationalism is supposed to accomplish.

CHAPTER 5

NORTHERN IRELAND: THE WAY OF TERROR ─────────

These men [Provisional IRA] are not fighting for a united Ireland; they are maintaining the division of Ireland—the fear and bitterness that exist in the north. It is brutal and horrific gangsterism.
> —Former Prime Minister Jack Lynch of Eire

The Irreconcilable Mini-Nationalism

English policies of moderation, appeasement, conciliation, and accommodation were successful in retaining Scotland and Wales within the United Kingdom. The case of Northern Ireland, however, is entirely different. For a decade, a veritable war waged by the Irish Republican Army has cost nearly 2,000 lives, brutalized the national spirit, and left Ulster with a heritage of violence and terror. The confrontation culminated in the assassination in August 1979 of Lord Louis Mountbatten, an event that infuriated the British public.

Discontented Irish in Ulster claim that occupation by English "foreigners" continued after the liberation of Eire. They reject any appeasement or compromise and insist that all Ulster be free to join an independent Ireland. Calling themselves the Provisional wing of the Irish Republican Army (IRA), they want no representation in the British Parliament. They denounce Scotsmen and Welsh as fools who have succumbed to English promises. They point to the American Revolution as a model—the Americans, they say, did not compromise with George III but turned instead to violence to make the necessary break. As additional justification, they cite the case of the Jews in Palestine who won their way to freedom by striking back at the British. They, themselves, choose the way of the bomb, grenade, and machine gun to wage a continuing war against their oppressors. Their goal is all or nothing. The means—violence and terror until the English capitulate.

The Background and Rhetoric of Confrontation

Celtic tribes from Gaul or Galicia conquered Ireland in the 4th century
B.C. and established their distinctive Gaelic culture. Neither the Anglo-
Saxons, who replaced the Celts in England, nor the Romans, who conquered Britain, came to Ireland; the Irish developed their own way of
life. In the 5th century, St. Patrick converted the Irish to Christianity.
Norsemen invaded the island in the 8th century but were defeated by
Irish King Brian (d. 1014), who was recognized as Ard-Ri, or ruler of his
country. For the next century and a half, the Irish were free of foreign
domination. However, the island was torn by bitter clan warfare. Celts
and non-Celts alike were organized into tribes owing allegiance to five
provincial kings.

Antagonism between the Irish and the English began as early as 1172,
when Henry II landed in Ireland, organized the country after the Norman fashion, reduced the people to serfdom, and granted lands to his
favorite barons.[1] Thus began a long struggle that soured relations between the two peoples. For centuries Ireland was to remain a dependency of the British Crown. Stuart King Charles I inaugurated a carrot-
and-stick approach that was to characterize Irish-English relations for
three centuries. In 1627, Charles, while attempting to rule without Parliament, introduced reforms in Ireland as a means of stopping the fighting there. In the process he antagonized English landlords who had
acquired valuable interests in the island. That pattern of reform became
standard operating procedure in handling the obstreperous Irish.

The Irish were further alienated under the Commonwealth when a
devout Puritan decided it was necessary to subdue them by force.
Cromwell spread his Calvinist fury over Ireland, a policy that was to
leave centuries of scars. He unleashed his pious troops to massacre
Irishmen at Drogheda and Wexford.[2] Women, children, and priests
were put to the sword in an orgy which the Irish never forgot or forgave.
Cromwell sent Protestants to settle in Northern Ireland and new landlords to settle over the whole country, recruiting his landed aristocracy
largely from the ranks of military adventurers. Driven underground,
Irish dissenters rebelled repeatedly against the hated foreigners.

Ireland was not a beneficiary of the moderate political and religious
settlement made after the Glorious Revolution of 1688; another rebellion broke out in 1689. In 1690 exiled James II came to Ireland from
France with the aim of leading a combined Franco-Irish army against
William III. After the French fleet defeated the English and the Dutch at
Beachy Head in June 1690, the invaders prepared to attack England
proper. William, with his new throne in danger, defeated James at the

Battle of the Boyne on July 11, 1690.[3] Once again the Irish settled into apathy.

The quiet was short-lived, for in 1798, the Irish rebelled again. In 1800 Parliament passed the Act of Union, abolishing the Irish Legislature and absorbing Ireland into Great Britain. The Irish were given representation in the House of Lords with 28 peers and 4 bishops elected for life by the whole of the Irish peerage. Provision was made for representation of 100 Irish members in the House of Commons. George III refused to hear of it.[4]

The Economic Clash

The three-cornered struggle between the Irish and the English—on economic, religious, and political grounds—continued on into the 19th and 20th centuries. Westminster met Irish rebellion with a series of slow-moving concessions, all of which were designed to retain Ireland inside the British state, but none of which satisfied an increasing sense of Irish national self-consciousness.

Economic differences hinged on control of the land. In the early 19th century, at least six-sevenths of Irish land was held by absentee English landlords. Irish peasants, miserable, wretched, and poverty-stricken, were often evicted from their farms. In 1846 they suffered from a devastating potato famine, which led to a mass migration to the United States.[5]

There was concern in London about the seriousness of the Irish land problem. The first major attempt to ease the lot of Irish peasants came with Gladstone's Reform Bill of 1870, which protected tenants from eviction as long as they paid rent, and which provided for loans to tenants. In 1879 Michael Davitt, son of an evicted tenant, organized the Irish Land League to work for the "three F's"—fair rent, fixed holdings, and freedom of sale. To win concessions from grasping landlords, the Irish resorted to boycott, in which they refrained by concerted action from purchasing English products.[6] Irish members of Parliament used obstructionist tactics to bargain expertly with both Liberals and Conservatives. In 1881 they managed to win a Land Act that virtually conceded the three F's. Later, the Land Purchase Act of 1903[7] set up funds to enable Irish peasants to purchase farms from absentee English landlords.

After the declaration of the Irish Republic in 1948, economic problems persisted in the six counties of Ulster, where economic relations were merged with bitter religious differences. The half million Ulster Catholics charged that they were victims of discrimination by the million Protestants, especially in employment and housing. In some Catholic areas, unemployment reached 30 percent, much higher than among the Protestants. Jobless young Catholics gathered on the street corners of Belfast and became prime targets for IRA conscription. Catholics complained of discrimination in housing and charged that Protestants invariably got first choice in the allocation of new homes. "We are nothing but 'white Negroes,'" complained one angry Catholic.[8] IRA terrorism fed on this kind of despair.

The Role of Religion

There had been religious unity in Ireland until the time of the Reformation. When the Anglican Church became the Established Church of Ireland, most Irishmen, despite their grinding poverty, had to make dual contributions—to the Catholic Church, their preference, and to the Anglican Church, which they detested.

Roman Catholics were unable to sit in the House of Commons until 1829, when the Roman Catholic Emancipation Act lifted the prohibition. Daniel O'Connell, later to be known as the Liberator, was elected to a seat. From 1831 to 1836, the Irish, resenting forced payments to the Anglican Church, rebelled in the so-called Tithe Wars. The slow-moving Parliament of 1860 disestablished the Irish Church, thereby relieving the Irish of the hated tithes.

Religious differences, frozen into tradition, contributed much to unsatisfied Northern Irish nationalism. The fact that the ruling English were Protestant only confirmed the Irish in their attachment to the Roman Catholic Church. Religion played an important role in the clash between Provisional Irish Republic Army extremists and the Ulster Defense Association, the Protestant paramilitary organization. The Reverend Ian Paisley, a fiery Protestant Member of Parliament, spoke for the hard-liners in recommending resistance to IRA violence. Paisley's political strength, spurred by a rise in IRA terrorism, revealed an increasing polarization between Protestants and Catholics. There was no real dialogue between the warring religious communities. The clash of opposing religions continues to lead to tragic consequences.

Political Differences

The confrontation between the English and the Northern Irish is a residue of long-standing political differences. In 1803 Robert Emmet, who planned an insurrection by seizing Dublin Castle, was captured, found guilty, and hanged. The Irish had their hero-martyr. Fanatical patriots who called themselves Young Ireland agitated for independence, only to see their leaders imprisoned or exiled. Irish emigrants in the United States organized the Fenian Brotherhood, *Sinn Fein* ("We Ourselves"). The *Sinn Fein* movement spread to Ireland, where it was suppressed. Another Irish leader, Charles Stewart Parnell, used a policy of legislative obstruction (filibustering) in Parliament to draw attention to Irish grievances.

In an effort to solve the festering Irish question, Prime Minister Gladstone brought forward two Home Rule Bills, one in 1886 and another in 1893, but both were rejected. Conservatives hoped "to kill Home Rule by kindness." A third Home Rule Bill, introduced in the House of Commons in 1912, received royal assent in 1914, but its operation was suspended in 1914 with the outbreak of World War I.

Embittered by Westminster's delay, Irish nationalists accepted German support and rose in rebellion in 1916. In the immediate postwar years, *Sinn Fein* fought an isolated but intensive war against British forces, the "Black and Tans."[9] Westminster was not willing to grant outright independence, but in 1923 it recognized the Irish Free State and granted it the same position as the Dominion of Canada. But there was to be no new status for the six northern counties of Ulster. Presbyterians of Scottish origin who lived there made it plain that they preferred to remain outside the Irish Free State and inside the United Kingdom of Great Britain and Ireland. It was a critical decision which further intensified the Irish problem. On their part, the English indicated that they would not desert the Protestant majority in Ulster.

The last formal ties with the British Crown were broken in 1948 with the Republic of Ireland Act.[10] Most Irish in Eire hoped for eventual union with Northern Ireland,[11] but they differed on the means to be employed in the process. Here, again, there emerged the common dilemma of the mini-nationalisms—moderation or extremism, autonomy or independence. The moderates believed that the English would eventually recognize the justice of their cause. The extremists, on the other hand, chose the way of violence.

The Sentiment of Inferiority

Added to economic, religious, and political differences between the English and the Irish were long-standing psychological motivations dividing the peoples. For centuries the English had been inclined to look upon the Irish as an inferior people distinguished by loutishness and stupidity. In the 19th century, English cartoonists often depicted the Irish as pigs incapable of self-government, while journalists described them as Neanderthal men, uncouth and primitive, who had not yet learned the ways of civilized society. This attitude carried over into the 20th century, when jokes about the Irish became standard in English pubs. The Irish were "funny little green people." Irish workers in British factories were ridiculed for their lack of manners and for their belief in non-existent leprechauns.

The Irish reacted angrily to such stereotypes, canards, and bigotry. Though they disclaimed annoyance at the way the English looked at them, they resented what they believed to be unfair slurs on their character. They denounced the English attitude as a vestige of colonialism, the system that was holding them in bondage. They acquired what amounted to a deep-rooted sense of inferiority, intensified by English ridicule. The result was widespread sympathy for IRA terrorists.

The Path of Violence

The current Provisional IRA, or Provos, the military, political, and propaganda wing of the Irish Republican Army, is different from the IRA of the early 1920s. The present wing is convinced that its mortal enemy, the "Brits," will never grant independence to Northern Ireland, hence the resort to terror as an ultimate weapon. Organized into small, tightly structured cells, they wage veritable civil war not only against the Protestants in Northern Ireland but also against some 30,000 British troops stationed there in the last decade. Lives have been lost and thousands have been injured in the struggle, many of them innocent bystanders. Belfast, the capital of Northern Ireland, has become a bombed-out city of burned buildings, roadblocks, and sloganed walls. A corrugated metal fence separates Protestant and Catholic neighborhoods, and everywhere, both in cities and in rural areas, the people live with fear.

The wave of terror culminated in 1979 with two assassinations that shocked the British public. In March 1979 Alfred Neave, a Conservative Member of Parliament, was killed when his car was blown up outside the House of Commons. He was due to be named Secretary for Northern Ireland. In August 1979 Lord Louis Mountbatten, a member of the royal family and, as Earl Mountbatten of Burma, a British hero of World War II, was killed in an explosion set by IRA terrorists. British reaction was dismay, bitter anger, and a firm resolve not to give in to IRA terrorism.

Much of the support for the IRA came from the United States, where there are about 15 million Americans of Irish descent. Out of a sense of love for the old country and imbued with cold hatred for the English, Irish-Americans collected funds and weapons for the Provos.[12] The New York-based Irish Northern Aid Committee (Noraid) became the largest American source of cash. In addition, machine guns, rifles, pistols, grenades, and ammunition were sent to help the underground fighters.

Although Irish officials deplored this aid to the guerrillas,[13] Irish-Americans justified their assistance on the ground that their sole purpose was to help support families of Irish fighters killed or imprisoned by the British.

The Provos argued that one man's terrorism is another man's patriotism. They insisted that it was unreasonable to be labeled "murderers" while selectively ignoring the brutality of English occupation of sacred Irish soil. They pointed to history: George III, they say, regarded Sam Adams and the Sons of Liberty as terrorists and would have hanged them if he could have caught them. England's occupation of Ireland, they charged, was always based on violence. Why did she refuse to accord to the Irish people the complete unity they wanted without resorting to legal double talk, political casuistry, or moral legerdemain? They labeled the six-county statelet of Northern Ireland a cynical gerrymander, a concession to bigotry and hatred. They insisted that continued English presence in Ulster was itself responsible for a justifiably violent Irish reaction.

According to Provo logic, those who criticized them were moral relativists and obscurantists who refused to recognize Ireland's right to total independence. They asked that their motivation, not their methodology, be understood. They were not terrorists, they insisted, but liberators. Behind them, they said, was the nationalism of Theobald Wolfe Tone (1791), the patriotism of Robert Emmett (1803), the inspiration of Young Irelanders (1848), and the satisfying example of the Easter Rebellion (1916). Far from being mindless murderers, they said that they were within the best tradition of a struggle for liberation.

To the contention that the murder of Lord Mountbatten was an uncivilized act, the Provos replied that he was a representative, not only of English royalty but also of the British Establishment, and hence a legitimate target in war. The root cause, they insisted, was English bigotry that should be counted responsible for Mountbatten's death. They presented a rhetorical question: how does one compare a single life, even if it be royal, with tens of thousands of Irishmen who have been sacrificed to British colonialism?

Irish terrorists urged London to "do the right thing"—just as France had done in Algeria: end the occupation of Northern Ireland and allow the Irish there to select their own national destiny. They rejected the claims of the Protestant majority in Ulster on the ground that Protestants should not have been there in the first place. Because reasonable arguments, no matter how just, have not won independence, the Provos claimed the right to use bombs, grenades, and machine guns as legitimate weapons. It was the familiar view of extremists at trouble spots throughout the world.

The Backlash

This type of IRA violence was met by stern official and unofficial countermeasures. The British sent large contingents of troops into Ulster to maintain order. Assisted by the Royal Ulster Constabulary (RUC), British authorities tried to intercede between Irish guerrillas and Protestant volunteer forces. Several hundred IRA activists were arrested and imprisoned.[14] Provos complained bitterly of brutal and inhuman treatment in prisons.

The attitude of Protestant antagonists was expressed by Samuel Duddy, one of the leaders of the Ulster Defense Organization (also called Ulster Volunteer Defense Force): "The only thing that pays in this country is violence."[15] They indicated deep anger: "Our own youths emigrate, while the Catholics procreate."[16] In saber-rattling marches, members of the militant Orange Order beat the traditional *lambeg* drums, waved swords in the air, and flourished banners reading: "For God and Ulster" and "No Surrender."[17] There was strong support among Protestants for the Reverend Ian Paisley, whom Catholics regarded as a "gutter fighter" and a "negative politician." This most ardent Protestant extremist worried moderates because of his gain of political power.[18]

The sectarian struggle is bitter. Each year Protestants celebrate with parades the defeat of former King James II, a Roman Catholic, at the Battle of the Boyne (July 11, 1690). Protestants see the victory as a triumph for their cause. Irish Catholics have their own parades on the anniversary of a 1971 British military roundup when hundreds of Catholics were jailed without trial. Both sides seethe with hostility and fury.

In England there was a widely held view that the Irish Government in Dublin was less vigorous than it might have been in fighting IRA terrorism. A survey of public opinion in Eire showed that 40 percent of the Irish in the Free State supported at least the motives of the IRA. Delighted by that response, IRA leaders issued a statement "that the politicians are completely out of line with the aspirations of the people."[19]

Despite the crescendo of violence, the British apparently had no intention of leaving Northern Ireland. They hoped to find an acceptable way of allowing the people of Ulster a greater control of their own affairs. British authorities felt that they could not impose any kind of solution without the agreement of both the Catholic and the Protestant communities. In the current situation, that seemed impossible. The British would not withdraw their troops as long as they were necessary to support the Ulster police against the actions of the IRA. It was an extraordinarily difficult task to police the long 300-mile border between Ulster and Eire. The goal was to defeat terrorism through the law by bringing extremists to court.[20]

Governmental authorities in Dublin were appalled by IRA militancy. Eire's Prime Minister Jack Lynch, despite criticism from the left wing of his own *Fianna Fáil* Party, castigated the IRA as "outlaws" bearing no relationship to the IRA of the 1920s.[21] These were men of violence, he said, who were not fighting for a united Ireland, but on the contrary were maintaining an Irish dichotomy. By placing bombs in crowded places, by indiscriminate killing, they were committing acts of violence "which make Irish people ashamed." Lynch said that if British troops were withdrawn from Ulster, there would be civil war between the IRA and the well-armed paramilitary Unionists. He projected these views while at the same time holding that Northern Ireland was not an integral part of Britain and must not be ruled completely from London.

Both British and Irish moderates associated the IRA with international terrorism—the antithesis of democracy. They accused Provos of associating with like-minded terrorists of the Palestine Liberation Organization in the Middle East, the Baader-Meinhof gang in West Germany, and the Red Brigades in Italy.

The Excruciating Dilemma

The case of Northern Ireland was quite different from that of other mini-nationalisms in that it represented the extremism of a partially satisfied nationalism. IRA separatists insisted that the complete freedom of Ireland was violated when Britain retained the six Ulster counties. They were not willing to view Irish unity as a distant dream to be fulfilled in stages progressing from autonomy to independence. They wanted freedom now from all English control. They charged that Britain was dying with an impotent government that was unwilling to recognize the reality of the Irish problem. They admitted that early 20th-century Britain may have been a vital and efficient world power, but now it was hardly able to maintain stability in its own domain, let alone in Ulster. The IRA gave warning that it would continue its struggle and use terror as the clinching argument.

Both British and Irish moderates called for political initiatives to counter IRA violence and to solve the aggravating problem. Moved by continued disturbances, the British Government in November 1979 suggested several possibilities for home rule, for transferring substantial responsibility to local hands. Its proposals included unicameral government but no legislative powers to be exercised by regional authorities. Special attention would be accorded to the minority in Northern Ireland.

The issue was complicated by hard-liners in both the Protestant majority and the Catholic minority in Ulster. The IRA wanted no part of compromise. It was convinced that Westminster did not contemplate any change in the basic constitutional status of the northern counties and that it would not recognize reunification with Eire. Militant extremists were not interested in a transferal of power inside the United Kingdom.

Hard-line Protestants vetoed any concessions to Catholics. Paisley and his followers feared that political appeasement would be followed by even more calls for independence. They were as determined to maintain their supremacy in Ulster as the IRA was to destroy it. There was no dialogue between the contending factions; both lived in a state of permanent tension.

Ulster thus remained a thorn in the side of an already weakened British lion. English authorities insisted that what happened in Ulster was an internal problem, not a colonial one. They would not desert their own people settled in Northern Ireland. They felt that their reputation for fairness had been blemished. They resented the necessity of taking strong measures to thwart IRA terrorism but, at the same time, felt that there was nothing else they could do in a precarious situation. They hoped against hope that concessions, even major ones, might lead to reduced violence. Traditional British diplomacy presented no answers.

It was a desperate plight for uneasy Britain, no longer the world power of better times. She had declined to a point where she was unable to solve her domestic problems, let alone those in Ulster. To an already endangered status was added the chaos stimulated by an embittered mini-nationalism that was dedicated to overthrowing the type of law and order promoted by the creators of the United Kingdom. Here, again, a larger nationalism felt the sting of a dangerous mini-nationalism.

Irish nationalism in a dangerously divided population approached a further stage of polarization with the death by slow suicide in early May 1981 of 27-year-old Bobby Sands after a 66-day hunger strike, the first in an increasing number of others. Together with other guerrillas of the Irish Republican Army who were serving sentences at Maze Prison near Belfast, he began his fast to force the British Government to recognize IRA inmates as political prisoners rather than as common criminals. While in prison he was elected to the British Parliament.

Sands laid claim to the tradition of other Irish nationalists who had driven the British from the 26 counties in 1919 and 1920 and who had become immortalized as national heroes. To their compatriots, MacDonagh, MacBride, Connolly, and Pease were emphatically patriots and liberators, not terrorists, even though they carried illegal firearms and were accused of blowing up buildings.

The emotions built up by Sands's strike dashed any hopes for a long-term solution of the Ulster question. There was an outpouring of grief, outrage, and sullen anger, as well as an additional intensification of IRA activity. In willing his own death, Sands not only took a place alongside Ireland's martyrs but he was said also to have won a victory over the implacable Prime Minister Margaret Thatcher, the "Iron Maiden."

For the British, the situation was a deliberate campaign by the IRA, a calculated and cold-blooded move to create a siege mentality. Thatcher announced coldly that "a crime is a crime is a crime." This rigid attitude undoubtedly misjudged the depth of Irish nationalism and was based on an earlier awkward experience. In 1927 Britain had granted political rights to nationalist prisoners, but as soon as the special status was granted, the IRA went on a rampage in Belfast in what became known as Bloody Friday. The Crown had a century-old presence in Ireland and was not disposed to desert the unyielding Protestant majority in Ulster. The ancient enmity persisted—Northern Ireland became more of a battleground than ever before.

The clash of nationalisms continues in a milieu of bitterness on both sides. Like unsatisfied nationalists elsewhere, IRA extremists see themselves as freedom fighters representing the noblest aspirations of their people, and they are resolved to fight until British rule is driven from all of Ireland. They accuse the British of lacking compassion, prudence, or common sense and of acting with the barbarity of tyrants. On their part, the British, appalled and angered by the terrorist assassination of the national hero Lord Mountbatten, denounce IRA guerrillas as evil monsters unworthy to live in a civilized world. Faced with the choice of continuing direct rule indefinitely or gradual withdrawal with the definite risk of a blood bath, Britain girded for even bloodier battles. It had more than 11,000 troops in Northern Ireland, and a highly trained "spearhead battalion," already used to quell disturbances, stood by for further action.

There was nothing quiescent about the situation in Northern Ireland—it was approaching what one observer called "something like collective hysteria." Hopes for a peaceful political settlement seemed to disappear with the death by fasting of the Maze prisoners. The confrontation of nationalisms, in this case, was moving toward civil war.

CHAPTER 6

REGIONALISM IN FRANCE, SWITZERLAND, AND ITALY ——

Our country, with her tinted sky, her varied contours, her fertile soil, our fields full of fine corn and vines and livestock, our industry, our gifts of initiative, adaptation and self-respect, make us, above all others, a race created for brilliant deeds.
—Charles de Gaulle

France: A Nation of Patriots

In France—from the days of Sun King Louis XIV through the Great Revolution to the contemporary scene—the idea of political centralization has been and is regarded as sacred, as a fact of life to be equated with the Frenchman's right to bury gold in his back garden. France has her share of mini-nationalisms, but they are contained at the boundary of independence. To most Frenchmen the idea of dissolution of their great country is equated with insanity. After all, what citizen would want to relinquish his attachment to the greatest society ever produced in an imperfect world? Why even think in terms of breaking up a magnificent state?

The highly prized watchword of the French Revolution should be revised, perhaps, to read: "Liberty, Equality, and Fraternity inside the Framework of the Centralized State." France has remained a "nation of patriots"[1] with certain fixed beliefs: (1) to be a Frenchman is *ipso facto* a mark of distinction; (2) Paris is the queen city of the globe; (3) French citizens do not accept a secondary role (even in defeat, General Charles de Gaulle, the voice of France, expected to be treated as a proud victor); and (4) nothing will be allowed to challenge the unity of the national state.

These generalizations help explain the attitude of the Quai d'Orsay to its home-grown mini-nationalisms: no matter what the type, whether moderate or extreme, separatism is to be kept within bounds and must never threaten the existence of the centralized state. Frenchmen see their country as the perfect geographical entity. Unlike unfortunate

65

Germany and the Balkan "powder kegs," with their ever-shifting borders, France has mostly natural borders—the Bay of Biscay, the Pyrénées, the Mediterranean, the Alps, the English Channel—and French authorities intend to keep them that way. French dissenters have all the freedom they want to march in demonstrations and shout slogans, but only lunatics and crackpots would want to separate one square inch of hallowed French soil. To Frenchmen, a French mini-nationalism is a contradiction in terms.

From Île-de-France to Centralized National State

The emergence of France, the Gaul of ancient times, as a nation was a long, involved process.[2] It began with the Treaty of Verdun in 842, which parceled out what are today roughly France, Germany, and Italy among Charlemagne's three grandsons. Hugh Capet (940–996), the first Capetian, ruled over a diminutive domain called the Île-de-France, smaller and weaker than many other fiefdoms. The French state, however, eventually grew out of this modest royal principality. In a process much like adding artichoke leaves to a center core, the Capetian realm expanded through a combination of conquest, purchase, marriage, inheritance, and forfeiture. Strong rulers were able to deprive plundering nobles and petty vassals of their lands and reduce them to obedience.

Across the English Channel were the dangerously aggressive English. The struggle to break English power in France was begun by Philip II Augustus (1165–1223) and was continued in the Hundred Years' War (1337–1453). Commencing as a feudal conflict between French monarchs and English Angevins, these encounters ended as a national war as France became a centralized state.[3]

From early modern times French rulers saw centralization as their prime goal. This sense of unbreakable union persisted even through the dramatic events of the French Revolution begun in 1789.[4] At the outbreak of the Revolution, there were relics of medievalism in the Old Regime with its aristocratic monarch and privileged nobility, an outworn society ready to collapse under its own weight. The Old Regime was burdened by economic evils, arbitrary taxation, political scandal, and medieval abuses. Stimulated by reformers of the Enlightenment—Voltaire, Rousseau, Montesquieu—Frenchmen moved to the barricades in a revolution of ten years that shook the world.

This event was the political watershed of European political history. What happened in the streets of Paris affected the Continent from one end to the other. Modern nationalism received much of its impetus from France. The *levée en armes* (armed uprising) accompanied by stirring strains of the *"Marseillaise,"* revealed the inner strength of French nationalism and set an example for other peoples. French revolutionaries put their faith in the permanence of sovereign states and the durability of national interests. These ideas penetrated into every corner of Europe.

Napoleon, heir to the Revolution, gave France a short period of military glory followed by the humiliation of defeat.[5] Despite his concern for self and family, the Corsican adventurer managed to consolidate reforms introduced by the revolutionaries and gave them permanency before reaction set in. He introduced revolutionary gains in conquered Italian and German territory and, at the same time, promoted national sentiment there. German nationalism was born as an antidote to Napoleonic despotism.

Since the days of Napoleonic glory, France has seen many different forms of government, from that of Citizen King Louis Philippe to that of Citizen President Charles de Gaulle. There were many changes in form and structure, but on one subject there was unanimity—national unity is sacred. The idea took on a special spiritual quality compounded of mysticism and romanticism.[6] It was unnecessary to remind Frenchmen that their country was great—that was a simple fact. Charles de Gaulle expressed this sense of grandiloquence:[7]

The emotional side of me tends to imagine France, like the princess in the stories of the Madonnas in the frescoes, as dedicated to an exalted and exceptional destiny. But the positive side of my mind assures me that France is not really herself unless in the front rank; that only vast enterprises are capable of counterbalancing the divine ferments which are inherent in her people. In short, to my mind, France cannot be France without greatness.

Most Frenchmen accepted this idea of national greatness as *automatique* and *légitime*, as a kind of natural law or self-evident truth. They found it unnecessary to organize Pan-French societies in the manner of Pan-Germanism or Pan-Slavism. Let others set up propaganda machines to accentuate national prestige and mission. Parisian intellectuals deemed it a waste of time to assert the superiority of the French language or French culture in general. The peoples of the world could see it for themselves.

For Frenchmen, territorial unity was the essence of their national existence. They wanted no divisive regionalisms, no dissenting separatisms, no clamoring mini-nationalisms to mar the glory of France. Yet, they, even as the English, Spanish, and Russians, had to contend with this powerful centrifugal force.

Breton Pride and Prejudice

The two most dissatisfied peoples in France are the Bretons in Brittany and the French Basques on the borders of the Pyrénées.[8] There are also mini-nationalisms in Alsace, Languedoc, and Corsica, as well as even smaller separatist movements in Réunion Island and in Guadeloupe.

Brittany (French, *Bretagne*; Breton, *Breiz*), a historic old province in the extreme northwestern peninsula of France, lies between the Bay of Biscay, the Atlantic Ocean, and the English Channel. Today it is divided into the *départements* of Finistère, Côtes-du-Nord, Morbihan, Ille-et-Vilaine, and Loire-Inférieure (Loire-Atlantique, or Lower Loire). Brittany falls naturally into two parts—a maritime zone and an island zone. The waterways are of little value because of their torrent-like character. The indented coast is lined with reefs and islets.

Geography has played an important role in the Bretons' way of life; their isolation contributed to their distinctive customs. Separated from the rest of France, they acquired traditions of their own. Brittany is also distinguished from the rest of France by a strong Celtic background. Here, again, language was of major significance. The Breton tongue belongs to the Cymric division of Celtic, which forms one group of the Indo-European family of languages. It is related to various Celtic dialects such as Gaulish; Goidalic (Irish, Scottish, Gaelic, and Manx); and Brythonic (Welsh, Cornish, and Breton). The basic Breton tongue was brought to northwestern France by Celtic refugees driven from England by Anglo-Saxons in the 5th and 6th centuries. Added to Welsh and Cornish dialects were continental elements. Early Breton folk tales included stories about King Arthur and the Round Table.[9]

The historical development of Brittany reveals a persistent trend toward regional independence. The first identifiable inhabitants were Celts, who, in all probability, intermingled with earlier natives and built large menhirs and dolmens (stone monuments) that still stand. Julius Caesar conquered Brittany in 57–56 B.C. and made it a part of the Roman state. Later, it became known as Amorica, the Roman version of the Celtic word for "seaside." The Romans held the region, despite recurrent Breton rebellions, until the 5th century, when Anglo-Saxons moved in to take refuge among their continental kinsmen. At this time the area was known as Brittania Minor. The Celts of Brittany were converted to Christianity by missionaries from the British Isles.

Breton passion for independence continued throughout the Middle Ages. The goal was an independent duchy beholden to no one. Brittany was included in the extreme end of the Carolingian Empire, but not even Charlemagne was able to subdue it completely.[10] From time to time, Bretons sent out pillaging expeditions into Frankish territory, mainly in the direction of Vannes. Under the leadership of a chief named Morvan (Murmannus), to whom they gave the title of king, Bretons refused to pay homage or an annual tribute to the Franks. Charlemagne's grandson, Louis the Pious, sought in vain to negotiate with Breton rebels. He led Frankish troops into Brittany, but there were no regular battles because the Bretons, in accordance with their usual custom, disappeared from sight and harassed the enemy on their flanks. After the death of Morvan in a skirmish, more powerful Breton chiefs accepted the suzerainty of Louis the Pious.

Breton submission did not last long. The Franks went ahead to waste the countryside but could win no permanent Breton submission. In 826 A.D., Louis the Pious recognized the authority of Nomenoe over the Bretons and gave him the title of *missus dominicus* (envoy or messenger of the king). In turn, Nomenoe did homage to Louis and took an oath of fealty.[11] The union of Brittany under a single head gave the Bretons their national hero. In 846 A.D., Nomenoe revolted against Charles the Bald and restored Breton independence. Succeeding Breton rulers repelled Norse invaders and managed to maintain their independence.

In the 10th century, Brittany's ruler took the title of "Duke" and established his capital at Rennes. Subsequent dukes successfully resisted encroachments by neighboring Normans. Breton adventurers fought with William the Conqueror at Hastings on October 14, 1066, but Breton dukes were not inclined to allow him to add Brittany to his roster of conquests. During the Hundred Years' War, Brittany sided alternately with England and France and was often the object of dispute between the two countries.

Brittany became a part of France with the marriage of Anne, heiress of Brittany, to two successive French kings, Charles VIII and Louis XII. The province was guaranteed local privileges in the Treaty of Incorporation in 1532, with the final union coming in 1547. For the next two centuries, Bretons continued to resist the Crown's efforts at centralization.

Bretons supported the French Revolution at the beginning, even assisting in the agitation leading to the call of the Estates-General. Following the abolition of the monarchy and the introduction of new clerical laws, Bretons rose in rebellion in 1792. They reacted violently in 1795 following the tragic massacre of 1,000 disarmed royalists who were seeking to emigrate to Quiberon. Outraged Bretons remained royalists and anti-Jacobin for a long time.

Throughout the 19th and 20th centuries, Bretons held fast to their sense of uniqueness. Conservative in nature, they preferred their own traditional social structure and religious sentiment. In World War I they were loyal to the central government. Breton regiments were considered to be among the most effective of French soldiers. Nevertheless, working in the background was a long tradition of particularism and a sentiment for independence.

Breton Nationalism

The confrontation between Breton regionalists and French centralists was intensified in the mid-20th century by an official French policy on the language question in Brittany. Orders from Paris made it plain that children in Brittany schools were not to use the Breton language in primary and in secondary schools. Older Bretons were angered because most of their compatriots were literate only in French. Intellectuals began to express their dismay about the very survival of the Breton tongue.

Breton separatism took two forms: a literary movement and a militant action. The literary movement, confined to about 10,000 intellectuals both inside and outside Brittany, was concerned primarily with the Government's official policy of gradually eradicating the Breton language. At the same time, the literary movement called for more political autonomy for Brittany. Breton militants, on the other hand, who regarded themselves as patriots and liberators, wanted more direct action. Influenced by Basque nationalists in Spain and taking their cue from the Irish Republican Army, young Breton activists began a campaign against the French state. Organized in 1966, the Breton Liberation Front (FLB) denounced "French imperialism." Their program was in the classic tradition of mini-nationalisms everywhere:

1. The Breton people are oppressed.
2. The land of Brittany is occupied by foreign French military camps.
3. The existence of Breton language and culture is discouraged by French imperial power.
4. Bretons want an end to their humiliating status of submission and they demand full independence.

At first, FLB tactics were on a modest scale, with mimeographed handbills and wall graffiti used to win attention to their cause.[12] Harmless raids gradually accelerated into full-scale guerrilla attacks. From 1966 to 1979, Breton activists attacked more than 200 targets, including state TV and radio installations, military and police barracks, and a nuclear power plant. An assault was made on the City Hall of Rennes in Brittany.

In early July 1978, Breton extremists attracted global attention when they planted a bomb at Versailles. On a warm summer evening, when some 50,000 people came to the magnificent palace grounds to witness a fireworks display to celebrate the arrival of summer, the Bretons struck. A time bomb was secreted in the château's south wing. The blast went off at 2 A.M., leaving a huge hole in the floor of a hall devoted to Napoleonic art, destroying chandeliers, busts of the great men of France, ornamental panelling, and six paintings of the Napoleonic era. Nothing like this had ever happened before.[13]

Consternation and anger surged through the French nation. It was one thing for Bretons to demonstrate in their own territory and take advantage of a free society to present their case, but it was another and more serious matter to strike at the heart of French culture and civilization. These were symbols of greatness. A government official called the bombing "a deplorable injury to an essential part of the French heritage."[14] Not only was Versailles one of the country's main tourist attractions, but for most Frenchmen, it represented the power and glory of France. It was an outrage.

Responsibility for the bombing was claimed immediately by three extremist groups: the Revolutionary Workers Group, the Unemployed International, and the *Front Libération Bretagne*. A letter to the editor of a newspaper, signed *Youenn ar sorn* ("Little Salamander" in Breton), stated that the attack was made because the people of Brittany were oppressed, their land occupied by "foreigners," and their language destroyed by "French imperial power." Two Breton guerrillas were arrested, tried in November 1978, and given jail sentences of 15 years.[15]

Despite such militancy, the Breton separatist movement received little mass support in Brittany, even though there was much sympathy for its aspirations. French authorities made it clear that they would not tolerate such dangerous hot-headed activism. Breton nationalists did not help their own cause by the destruction of Napoleonic symbols. The incident at Versailles brought them the contempt of Corsican separatists, to whom the island's most celebrated son was still a hero.

In the summer of 1980, Breton separatism took the form of energetic protests against the intention of the central government at Paris to build a giant nuclear power plant in Brittany, actually four power plants in one. More and more committed to nuclear power as a source of energy, Paris chose Plogoff, on a peninsula in Brittany jutting out into the Atlantic, as the site for the huge, new facility.

Bretons reacted angrily. Demonstrators spread the site with garbage and broken bottles and blocked access roads with debris and burning tires. Again and again the police had to clear the area with bulldozers. Under a special anti-violence law, a dozen demonstrators were arrested. Breton die-hards insisted that the plant might be built, "but if they do they are going to need a cop behind every construction pole."[16]

For years Bretons had supported, at least nominally, an active independence movement. For them the proposed nuclear plant was an abomination. It was additional indication, they claimed, that the Government had as usual forgotten them, had lied to them, and had allowed them to remain poverty-stricken, compared to the rest of France. Paris, they charged, had violated their right to regional autonomy.

The Basques of France

The twin separatist movements promoted by both French and Spanish Basques reveal how mini-nationalisms may cut through the borders of neighboring countries. The Basques of Spain, the more active of the two mini-nationalists, will be discussed in Chapter 8. Originally, the two peoples were one, but they became separated with the formation of the two national states on either side of the Pyrénées.

The Basques[17] are a linguistic and social group occupying the slopes of the western Pyrénées in both French and Spanish territory. On the northern side, inside France, they live in Labourd (Lapourdi), Basse-Navarre (Benaparroa), and Soule (Zuberos). In Spain they occupy four provinces (Vizcaya, Guipúzcoa, Alava, and Navarra).[18]

Basques settled in the foothills of the western Pyrénées in ancient times, but the question of their origin has never been resolved.[19] There are many theories, one of which is that they were connected with ancient Iberian and Celt-Iberian peoples who were dispersed throughout the Mediterranean area.

Basques are not notably different in physical characteristics from other western European peoples. Their language, however, does not belong to the Indo-European linguistic family. Like Finnish and Magyar, Basque stands out as an incorporative tongue, unrelated, as far as we know, to any other language.[20] Basques still call themselves *Euskaldunak*, those who speak *Euskera*, or *Eskualda*. The origin of "*Euskaldunak*" is not known, but it probably means "speaking plainly."[21]

The Basque language, isolated and with no known linguistic relatives, is a major unifying factor among nationalists on both sides of the border. There are eight modern dialects, but the division is not strong enough to hide a common origin or to preclude Basque preference for political and social affinity.[22]

The history of the Basques is associated with that of both France and Spain.[23] Little is known of their early life, but Roman authors referred to them as living in what is today roughly the region of Navarre. Both French and Spanish Basques resisted inroads by Visigoths, Franks, Normans, and Moors. By the end of the Middle Ages, most Basques were absorbed into Castile and Aragon. They managed, however, to retain a degree of local autonomy, as well as certain privileges in taxation, trade, and military service that were incorporated into laws known as *fueros,* or *fors.* These jealously protected rights later became the basis for a sense of national consciousness. Retention of such rights over a long period of time becomes the guiding principle of most mininationalisms.

The two *Euskera*-speaking regions on either side of the border never formed a single political system. There were, indeed, social and cultural relationships expressed in similar rural customs. Each of the three French provinces had its own judicial structure before being absorbed into the French state. Labourd, the westernmost province, at first owed allegiance to a viscount; Basse-Navarre, the middle province, was a royal domain; and Soule, the easternmost region, was under medieval feudal rule. In the 15th and 16th centuries, all three provinces were incorporated into centralized France. In the 17th century, royal administration from Paris made heavy inroads into the local Basque economy.

Like the Bretons, French Basques at first adopted a passive attitude toward the French Revolution. As had the Bretons, deeply religious Basques reacted angrily against Jacobin revolutionaries in Paris and their anti-clericalism.[24] Eventually, the revolutionary government abolished the *fors,* those traditional laws which determined the rights of Basque popular assemblies and rules of inheritance. The French Government, anxious to discourage calls for regional autonomy, combined the three provinces into the large southwestern *département* of Basse-Pyrénées.

French authorities tightened their hold on their Basques throughout the 19th century. Otherwise, they paid little attention to the people they regarded as a backward conglomeration of farmers, seafarers, and smugglers. While Basques across the border played a prominent role in Spanish affairs, their kinsmen on the other side of the Pyrénées remained inconspicuous in French life.[25]

Signs of Basque resentment against Paris began to appear in the 1890s, but it was not until the early 1930s that calls for regional autonomy began to be made. Vociferous nationalists called for unity of the three French provinces and ultimate confederation of all seven Basque provinces on both sides of the border. They denounced French authorities for "inattention" to Basques. Marc Lagasse, a libertarian nationalist, became the most prominent spokesman for Basque union.[26]

The movement gathered strength from the 1950s to the 1970s. French authorities reacted with increased restrictions on Basque nationalists, arresting leaders for "subversive activities" and discouraging the celebration of Basque festivals. In early 1979, French police made a series of early morning raids on homes of Basque sympathizers, arresting 23 and expelling to Spain 7 members of the Basque guerrilla organization. An official communiqué stated that Spanish Basques would no longer be granted asylum on French soil.[27]

The attitude of Paris was plain: neither French Basque nor any other mini-nationalism would be allowed to threaten the existence of the centralized state. Public opinion throughout France supported this attitude. Basque nationalists won little support, even in Basque territory. Their movement was much weaker than that of the Basques of Spain. Spanish Basques, with the exception of a small number of extremists, showed little inclination to encourage their fellow Basques in the French provinces.[28]

The Alsatian Autonomous Movement

For a thousand years, the French and the Germans have alternatively held Alsace-Lorraine, the provinces on the borderline between the two countries.[29] Both countries consider Alsace of strategic importance and Lorraine as the source of rich iron and coal deposits.

Alsace corresponds today to the modern French *départements* of Haut-Rhin and Bas-Rhin and the territory of Belfort. Occupied by the Romans in the 1st century B.C., it became a Frankish duchy in the 5th century. From the 10th to the 17th century, it was a part of the Holy Roman Empire. The Peace of Westphalia made it an informal protectorate. Full French control was established during the later years of the reign of Louis XIV (r. 1643–1715).

In the 18th century, the French royal house gave Alsace considerable autonomy, thereby setting a tradition of particularism that persisted among Alsatians until the 20th century. Alsatians customarily spoke two languages: the upper classes using French; most others, German. During the French Revolution, the existence of Alsace as a separate province was terminated, and it was incorporated into France.

From then on the administration of Alsace was linked with that of Lorraine. When France was defeated in the Franco-Prussian War of 1870–1871, Alsace and a part of Lorraine were incorporated into the new Second German Empire.[30] The ensuing process of Germanization[31] awakened a spirit of *revanche* lasting from 1871 to 1919.[32] Though most Alsatians spoke German, they felt themselves to be French and protested vehemently against the "mutilation" of their country. After the transfer of Alsace to Germany, many Alsatians left their homeland.

The Germanization of Alsace-Lorraine was complicated by the language problem. Before 1870 French was the language of administration; but under German rule, except in a few communes, all administration, as well as compulsory education, was to be in High German, which was linked closely with the Allemanic dialect of Alsace.[33]

There were other regions in France, notably Brittany and the Basque provinces, where the mother tongue was not French. The case of Alsace was a special one. German was fostered in Alsace for a generation after 1919. Across the Rhine, it was the official language. Denis Brogan gauged it accurately: "More than that. Germany still had in the Reich a patron which saw in the linguistic patriotism of Alsace a way of keeping the 'Alsatian question' open, while southern Alsace was linked, historically and linguistically, with Germany and Switzerland. It was childish to pretend that in such circumstances German could be treated as Basque or Breton."[34]

Alsace-Lorraine was returned to France after World War I by the Treaty of Versailles in 1919. The French immediately began to eliminate the Germanization that had been so painstakingly applied after 1871. French authorities felt a sense of justification: since the time of the Convention, their official doctrine held that the French Republic was one and indivisible and that the French tongue expressed that sense of unity. There would be no other languages—Basque, Breton, or German—with official approval in France. The counter-thrust on behalf of the French language was accompanied by the efficiency generally attributed to the Germans. German could be taught in schools but only for a limited period. All non-linguistic studies had to be in French. There would be no "foreign tongues."

Along with this process of Frenchification came the rise of an Alsatian home-rule movement in the 1920s. The goal was not independence but autonomy inside the French Republic. Alsatian dissidents were moved also by religious sentiment: they opposed the anti-clerical measures taken by the *Cartel des Gauches*, the post-World War I government.[35] They called for a federal state in which Alsace would be an equal member with its own special rights and privileges. To patriotic Frenchmen this kind of appeal was "merely a blind for German-fostered sedition."[36]

Early in World War II, Hitler's Third Reich re-annexed Alsace and began the process of Germanization again. A half million Alsatians, embittered by German aggression, left their homes and were scattered in French cities and villages. With the German defeat in 1945, the seesaw phenomenon began once again with processes of de-Germanization and re-Frenchification.

After 1945, successive French governments took care to modify harsh prewar attitudes toward Alsace, especially by eliminating those anti-clerical measures that had caused much resentment in a strongly Catholic province. The result was a lessening of the separatist sentiment. There remained a few recalcitrant hotheads, but in general, Alsatian separatism was muted in content and in action. Unlike Corsican dissidents, Alsatian liberationists did not resort to bombs to publicize their cause. For most Alsatians, the era of Nazi control was a sobering experience. They now accepted, with feelings varying from indifference to satisfaction, their place in a functioning French democracy. French authorities, on their part, were quite happy to grant Alsatians their due share of the glory of France.

Languedoc Particularism

In southern France, bordering partly on the Mediterranean and at the foot of the Pyrénées, is the former province of Languedoc. Here, too, exists a mini-nationalist sentiment which resents centralized control from Paris. Today, Languedoc is administratively divided into the *départements* of Ardèche, Aude, Gard, Hérault, Lozère, Tarn, and parts of Haute-Garonne, Haute-Loire, and Tarn-et-Garonne. It is the center of a distinctive culture, including a language form which is the basis of Languedoc particularism. The very name "Languedoc" is derived from the traditional language of southern France: the term *oc* means "yes," in contrast with *oïl*, or *oui*, in northern France. Both the medieval *langue d'oc* and *langue d'oïl* dialects (*patois*) persisted in some rural regions.[37]

In the 2nd century B.C., the area which now comprises Languedoc was part of the Roman province of Gallia Narbonesis, which connected the Italian peninsula to Spain. After the fall of the Roman Empire, the region was controlled by Visigoths in the 5th century and partly by Franks in the 6th century. The Toulousain, the area around Toulouse, was organized under the Carolingians and became one of the great fiefs of medieval France.

The people of Languedoc, speaking a tongue closely related to Latin, developed a distinctive culture of their own by the 12th century. At that time, a Manichean sect called the Cathari[38] became a popular religion in both Italy and France and drew much support from the nobles of Languedoc. Because it was believed to have struck at the roots of orthodox Christianity,[39] neo-Manicheanism was declared heretical by the Roman Catholic Church. Pope Innocent III (held office 1198–1216) attempted to force Raymond VI, Count of Toulouse, to join him in throttling the heresy, but he was unsuccessful. In 1208 the papal legate to Languedoc was murdered, probably by an aide of Raymond.

Proclaiming the Albigensian Crusade, Innocent III supported an expedition of French barons led by Simon de Montfort.[40] The army ravaged Toulouse and massacred its inhabitants. The Albigensians and the heresy finally were annihilated.[41] Languedoc was reorganized with institutions insuring local privileges. This was the kind of grant which lies at the root of most mini-nationalisms: it sets the historical pattern of justification which dissidents use to bolster their case for autonomy or independence. With the French Revolution, however, Languedoc, as did other French provinces, lost its distinctive character and was divided into *départements* responsible to the central government at Paris.

Despite this subjugation, Languedocians retained their particularistic conviction. Intellectuals at Toulouse began to call attention to their special regional history and urged the revival of Occitania.[42] There was also a residue of religious dissent: the Cathari never forgot the persecution of their ancestors, which they blamed on foreigners from Paris.

French authorities show little concern for Languedoc particularism. They regard it with studied indifference, as if it is unworthy of comment, as a benign manifestation of harmless local sentiment. Let these people hew to their own cultural and social traditions as long as they understand the great privilege of sharing *la gloire* of a united France.

The Obstreperous Corsicans

The case of Corsican separatism presents a mini-nationalism of a different color and size. The nuisance value of regionalists to a centralized state is not determined by the size of the territory involved. There are French home-rule movements in Brittany (10,495 square miles) as well as in relatively small Corsica (3,352 square miles). Corsica (French, *Corse*) is an island in the Mediterranean west of Italy, north of Sardinia, and south of the French mainland. After four centuries of colonial rule by the Genoese Republic, it became a part of France in 1769. Twenty years later, it was made into a French *département*.

Two factors shaped the development of Corsica: proximity to the mainlands of Italy and France,[43] and a rugged interior which discouraged alien penetration. Strategically located, the island attracted the attention of various maritime powers, but their control was limited invariably to coastal areas, since it was dangerous to risk the displeasure of natives whose political and social institutions were shaped by a strong sense of independence. Corsican social structure accented family and rural community life; in politics, the tendency was toward autonomous local communities.

The history of Corsica reveals a continuing sentiment favoring independence.[44] In modern times Corsicans rebelled against the Genoese, who occupied six coastal fortress towns. Henry II conquered the island for France in 1553. After annexation by France in 1769, Corsican administration, society, and culture were absorbed into centralized France.[45] In 1794 Corsica voted union with the British Crown, a status that lasted only two years. French possession was guaranteed by the Treaty of Vienna in 1815.

The Corsicans' pride in the career of their native-born Napoleon put an end, temporarily, to separatist sentiment in the island and helped consolidate the link with mainland France. In both world wars, Corsicans were highly regarded for their loyalty to France in times of crisis.

Many gifted Corsicans, impelled by bad economic conditions, moved to other areas of France. Intellectuals who remained on the island devoted themselves to the study and conservation of their cultural heritage. As elsewhere, dissenters were divided into two groups—moderates, who requested more autonomy inside the French system, and activists, who demanded outright independence.

Corsican militants, inspired by Basque guerrillas, were unwilling to rely on democratic means to achieve their goal. The Corsican National Liberation Front (FLNC), organized in the mid-1970s, took advantage of several sources of tension on the island. Many Corsicans were angered by the presence of Algerians who had fled their country after it won its independence. They accused Parisian authorities of allowing these Algerians to buy up the best Corsican lands. Moreover, Corsicans were annoyed by the continued presence of 12,000 members of the French Foreign Legion on the island. To Corsicans, stationing these unwelcome troops was a perpetuation of French colonial rule.

Because it had little faith in accommodation from Paris, the FLNC opted for terror to advance its cause. "The violence we use," reported a FLNC communiqué, "is only a necessary and legitimate means to stop colonial aggression in Corsica. We will reply to colonial violence with revolutionary and popular violence."[46] It was the classic response of a mini-nationalism based on the conviction that moderation achieves nothing.

In the late 1970s, a series of "terror-by-bomb" attacks won the guerrillas the name of "wild Corsicans." Activists placed bombs in banks, travel agencies, public buildings, and television and radio stations, with prime attention to the Paris area. In May 1979 they planted a powerful bomb in the 19th-century Palace of Justice in Paris, the city's main courthouse. An anonymous caller informed the Agence France that the bombing was the work of the FLNC.[47] Although there was only damage to glass and plaster, it was enough to alienate French public opinion. At the end of the month, 22 bombs were set off in Paris in protest against the transfer of Corsican political prisoners from the island to Paris to face trial before the State Security Council. Again, a telephone call identified the FLNC as the perpetrators.[48] From January 1978 to July 1979, Corsican terrorists were responsible for 466 bombings.

In late June 1979, 21 terrorists were tried in a heavily guarded Paris courtroom. The prisoners issued a defiant opening statement: "Your justice is not ours. The right to resistance, to armed struggle, is inscribed in the declaration of human rights. We need to give no explanation in court to justify our actions. If we consent to appear before you, do not attempt to interpret it as an attempt to beg for mercy." Sympathizers in the gallery shouted: "*Eviva la nazione!*" ("Long live the nation!") and "*Francesci fuori!*" ("Frenchmen go home!").[49] Corsicans in the audience called out: "You want war! You shall have it!"[50]

The public prosecutor urged the judges: "Show no weakness to the enemies of the Republic, who have always spat upon the outstretched hand of moderation."[51] Three accused leaders were sentenced to 13 years' imprisonment; the rest received sentences of between 4 and 10 years.

A Dialogue of the Deaf

The reaction of French authorities to Corsican extremism was simple—assault on French unity would not be tolerated. French officials who visited Corsica declared, "Not one inch of Corsica will be relinquished."[52] The soil of France, including Corsica, was sacred. French officials pointed to a poll which indicated that 55 percent of 230,000 Corsicans have no quarrel with Paris and that only 5 percent were in favor of independence.[53] The FLNC, they say, includes no more than 200 hardcore militants. They insist that the Corsican national flag, a black Moor's head on a white background, will never supplant the tricolor of France.

Corsican violence also unleashed a backlash in the French community on the island. A group calling itself FRANCIA (Front for New Action Against Autonomy and Independence) began to bomb the homes of FLNC supporters. It denounced FLNC demands as utopian and called for loyalty to France. The clash between FRANCIA and FLNC remained more emotional than economic. Neither side was willing to yield. It was, said one observer, "a dialogue of the deaf."[54]

Most Corsicans opposed the proliferating violence, but virtually all of them wanted a change. They saw their land as exploited by outsiders, resulting in a situation impervious to social and economic change. They retained their pride in language and culture and demanded a stronger hand in ruling themselves.

To cries of "*Corsica Liberta!*" French officials replied with indifference or half-hearted measures, promising much and delivering little. France, they said, was a nation of patriots, not semi-patriots. Democratic dissent—yes; independence—emphatically no! After all, were not Corsicans, as all Frenchmen, tinged with the aura of French glory?

Nevertheless, the summer of 1981 saw the appearance of a devolution plan for Corsica. This was to become a new-style region of France, with its own legislature and assembly, consultative councils, and cultural identity. The new Corsican region would have its own employment agency, credit bank, agricultural development agency, and a regional company devoted to industrial, commercial, and tourist development. Transport would have its own Corsican organization. The Corsican language would be compulsory in schools, with three hours of instruction at the pre-elementary and elementary levels.

Whether or not these concessions would appease Corsican die-hards remains to be seen. For extremists such a solution was unsatisfactory appeasement—a means of retaining unwanted French supremacy.

Guadeloupe Islanders

Still another liberation army, though a tiny one, appeared in the islands of Guadaloupe, 4,200 miles from Paris. A group of islands in the eastern Caribbean Sea southeast of Puerto Rico, Guadeloupe was legally a *département* of mainland France, with its 320,000 people having the same rights and privileges as the French and with representation in the Chamber of Deputies.

Although Guadeloupians voted in large majorities to remain a department of France, the Guadeloupe Liberation Army (GLA) complained that white Frenchmen dominated the government and were favored economically. Demanding an end to "French colonialism" and calling for independence, it turned to acts of terror. In March 1980 gunmen shot and wounded the only white member of the city council of Pointe-à-Pitre. In September 1980, GLA terrorists attached a bomb to an Air France Boeing 727 and killed a French explosives expert. On January 4, 1981, they set off a thunderous explosion that destroyed the Chanel fashion and perfume store in central Paris. An anonymous caller demanded the departure of French forces from the island and said that the GLA would continue to fight at the heart of French prestige in Paris.

On the surface Guadeloupe was a Caribbean tourist paradise. The GLA, however, possibly with some help from Cuba, was convinced that it could win national independence and throw off the close ties with Paris. Its guiding principle was the same as other mini-nationalisms—only through terror, practiced on the streets of Paris, could the dominant centralized state be forced to grant freedom to a people in bondage.

Jurassic Nationalism in Switzerland

Switzerland has solved most of its national problems. Despite student unrest, it has the reputation of being a smoothly run society, a striking example of unity in diversity.[55] With a population of slightly over 6 million, the Swiss Confederation today harmoniously comprises two religions (Protestant, 48 percent; Roman Catholic, 49 percent) and four national languages (German, 72 percent; French, 20 percent; Italian, 4 percent; and Rhaeto-Romansch, derived from Latin, 1 percent).

The small country acquired its present borders in 1815, when European powers proclaimed perpetual neutrality for the Swiss Confederation.[56] The world's most decentralized government was formed, solidly based on 3,050 communes fitting into 23 sovereign cantons, each with its own constitution, legal system, administration, and budget.

In their first federal constitution, the Swiss made certain that no citizen would ever become secondary to a faceless state. Passages in the constitution referred to the descending authority of God, to the ascending authority of "the Swiss nation," to the dual sovereignty of the centralized state and its component parts, and to the residual sovereignty of the cantons.[57] The cantons were given a wide degree of autonomy. Although federal law prevailed over cantonal law in matters of national security, rights of property, and freedom of trade and industry, all residual powers were cantonal.[58] Three cantons were divided into semi-cantons as a recognition of incompatible linguistic or religious differences.

Added to this recognition of diversity was a decisive economic factor which created strong bonds of union. Despite a lack of natural resources and land so rocky and mountainous that it is used primarily for pastures, the Swiss, by thrift and hard work, built a prosperous and stable country. Switzerland currently has the world's hardest currency—the Swiss franc—and has one of the world's lowest inflation rates. Its citizens enjoy the world's highest standard of living.[59] Disparate elements throughout the country see an enormous advantage in maintaining the *status quo*.

Yet, despite this closely bound unity and its advantages, Switzerland has not been altogether free of the discontent disturbing most countries. There are three major regions: the Swiss Plateau, the Alps, and the Jura Mountains. Stretching along the western border, the Jura region consists of bleak limestone folds. The inhabitants of this area, largely of Huguenot persuasion, are known for their austere faith, frugal manners, and preference for the French language.[60]

Jurassic nationalists believe that they have not been given the liberty to which they are entitled. On May 4, 1968, a protesting crowd of 200 appeared before the Federal Parliament in Bern. From their ranks, three young men turned in their rifles, saying that they would not serve in the army as long as they remained unfree.[61] The Federal Government sent in a mechanized battalion "on maneuvers," but it did not move into action. Jurassic nationalists denounced the move as "imitating the Russians."[62] On November 14, 1968, 31 army officers protested the use of federal troops and stated they would not be indifferent to the "drama" that might have occurred "if the Jurassians had not had a great deal more good sense than the federal authorities."[63]

On November 19, 1968, the Cabinet withdrew its order assigning federal troops in the belief that the danger had disappeared. The Jurassic Rally, a separatist organization, announced that the government had capitulated through fear of consequences.[64] On December 11, 1968, 25 young demonstrators broke into a joint session of the Swiss Parliament in Bern to present their demand for a separatist status. Waving Jurassian flags and shouting "A Free Jura!" they halted the proceedings while their leader read a proclamation calling for a separate canton.[65]

Only a few Swiss citizens support the separatists. Most of those living in the Jura Mountain region have no intention of abandoning their Swiss status in favor of a possible French connection. They would certainly be pleased by a grant of more autonomy in the form of a canton of their own. Theirs is a muted mini-nationalism willing to settle for autonomy, not independence. Above all, they want no violence to disturb the tranquillity of Swiss life or to endanger their prosperity. In their case, a mini-nationalism is governed by a powerful economic stimulus—the mighty Swiss franc.

Italy and South Tyrol

Italy, too, has its regional troubles. Rome is concerned with the problem of accommodating the culture and political future of a 250,000 German-speaking minority in a state of 55,810,000 Italians; consequently, South Tyrol has become the source of an extensive polemic between Italians and Austrians. Again, a mini-nationalism disturbs the tranquillity of the centralized state.

In Roman times the region of South Tyrol in the Alps was inhabited by Rhaetians. In 1363 it came into possession of the Hapsburgs as a crown land. The Treaty of Pressburg in 1805 gave all of Tyrol to Bavaria, Napoleon's ally. When war broke out between France and Austria in 1805, Tyrolean peasants, led by Andreas Hofer, defied both invaders and swept them out of the region.[66] In 1810 Napoleon, in defiance of his Bavarian allies, ceded most of South Tyrol to Italy. Both parts were restored to Austria by the Congress of Vienna in 1815.

The debate over South Tyrol was intensified in 1906, when the Italian Alpinist Ettore Tolomei founded the *Achivio dell' Alto Adige,* an annual publication. Tolomei insisted that South Tyrol, by geography, history, and language, belonged to Italy since it formed her natural border.[67] Later, this became the theme *Italia Irredenta* ("Italy Unredeemed").

After World War I, the Treaty of Saint-Germain in 1919 awarded South Tyrol, including the predominantly German-speaking province of Bolzano, as well as the mostly Italian-speaking province of Trentino, to Italy. Subsequently, there followed a ruthless Italianization of the province of South Tyrol by Mussolini's Fascist government.[68] The use of the Italian language was enforced. Austrians and Germans in the area reacted violently. In 1938, Mussolini and Hitler, anxious to remove a source of friction, agreed to force migration of German-speaking South Tyroleans either to the Third Reich or to other parts of Italy, but the unpopular program soon collapsed.

After World War II, the Council of Foreign Ministers, meeting in Paris, decided that South Tyrol should remain Italian despite Austrian protests. Later, the agreement was incorporated into the Italian peace treaty of 1947. South Tyrol was granted a considerable degree of local autonomy in legislation and in administration, as well as full protection of minority rights. German and Italian were both made official languages.

German-speaking South Tyroleans were not appeased. Supported by Vienna, they claimed that they were not given the autonomy promised them by the settlement of 1946–1947.[69] At the request of Austria, the issue was debated in 1960 in the United Nations, which recommended that Austria and Italy enter into direct negotiations. The situation was aggravated the next year by a series of terrorist attacks in South Tyrol. In 1969 both countries accepted a "package deal" with a schedule for improved conditions in the province.

Both Italian and Austrian scholars began to publish studies designed to bolster claims to Alto Adige.[70] Each side appealed to "the European conscience" for support. The scholarly debate was interwoven with the political dispute—the clash between Italian centralism and a vocal mini-nationalism. Italians and Austrians accused each other of atrocities. Italians demanded that the German minority should remain citizens of Italy—it could have minority rights but not the right of secession. The Austrian minority pointed to its corporate legal status and demanded that Rome fulfill its promises. Despite their small numbers, the German-speaking minority demanded the same kind of strong partnership as in federalized Switzerland. Its leaders insisted that they would not sever their ties with the "mother folk" centered in Vienna.[71]

The conflict between *Italianità* and *Deutschtum* presents a good example of the emotional passions governing a mini-nationalism dissatisfied with its place in the social structure of a centralized state. The Tyrolean minority living among Italians feels itself more closely bound to German-speaking people to the north. It is not impressed by the recommendations of the United Nations that the problem of autonomy be settled by direct negotiation. Like mini-nationalisms elsewhere, German-speaking South Tyroleans oppose the centralism they feel holds them in subjugation. They demand self-determination—the recurrent theme of contemporary global mini-nationalisms.

CHAPTER 7

THE LOW COUNTRIES AND DENMARK ―――――――――――

I speak French to you because you are a gentleman.

—A Flemish butcher

Clash of Mini-Nationalisms in Belgium

Mini-nationalisms usually are concerned with minority peoples who, despite their linguistic, cultural, and supposed ethnic affinity, have been forced into subjugation by a larger, more powerful nation-state. Thus, Bretons form only a small minority in France; Basques, similarly, represent a small percentage of the Spanish population.[1] Smallness is associated with the very name mini-nationalism. However, because nationalism is suffused with paradoxes, there are always exceptions to the rule. On occasion, a mini-nationalism may be promoted by a larger element of the population than the term indicates.

In the case of Belgium, two mini-nationalisms, each with its own characteristics, exist side by side. In the late 1970s the Belgian population of 8.5 million was divided into about 5.5 million Flemings and 3 million French-speaking Walloons. Although greater in numbers, the Flemings believe that they are not granted the constitutional rights necessary for their role in Belgian national life.

Flemings live mainly in the north and west; the Walloons, in the south and east. Flemings were subjected to Dutch-Germanic influences; Walloons, to French historical traditions. Over the course of centuries, a rivalry developed between the two peoples which divided the country into hostile factions. Flemings wanted a greater share in political, administrative, and economic life commensurate with their numbers. Walloons, too, sought to retain their dominant position although they were fewer in numbers. The tranquillity of the Belgian nation was disturbed by this ongoing competition.

85

Historical Background of Flemish-Walloon Rivalry

Roots of confrontation ran deep into the background of the two peoples.[2] In Roman times, what is today Belgium was a part of Gaul inhabited by Celts. During the barbarian migrations and invasions, the area was infiltrated by Germanic Goths. In the early 4th century, Salic Franks moved down from the northeast, pushed the Romans back, and settled on a line that roughly approximates the current division between Flemings and Walloons. After the withdrawal of Roman garrisons on the frontier in the 5th century, Franks moved southward and settled in Gaul proper and what is today Belgium.

At that time there was a split that later developed into the Flemish-Walloon rivalry. Those Franks who remained in the north retained a Germanic speech that eventually merged into Dutch and Flemish, while the Franks who moved southward accepted the language of Romanized Gaul. The latter tongue eventually became French. The division between the two peoples persisted. Separated by a natural coal forest, they went on to develop their own customs and traditions.

In the Middle Ages, the territory was not controlled by a single monarch, nor did the people speak the same language. There were common cultural institutions, but the northern people lagged behind their southern neighbors in stages of development, a situation that carried over into modern times. In 1226 the French imposed the humiliating Treaty of Mélun, which solidified Flemish subjugation. French speech, culture, and customs dominated the southern area. The French were able to find many excuses for political intervention in the area.

In the early 14th century, Philip the Fair attempted to annex Flanders to the French Crown, which resulted in an outbreak of Flemish opposition. At that time France was enduring the traumas of the early phases of the Hundred Years' War, and Frenchmen were strongly attracted to the Belgian area. They had already brought their own culture to the nobility of southern Belgium.

In early modern times, the whole of the Low Countries passed to the control of the House of Hapsburg. On February 24, 1500, Charles V, the future Holy Roman Emperor, inherited The Netherlands as part of his domain. At that time the Belgian provinces were by far the richest and most populous in that area of Europe. Charles V and his son Philip presided over an era of great prosperity in the Low Countries. The Spanish regime lasted until 1700, when Charles II, the last Spanish Hapsburg, died.

In 1792 Belgium was conquered by French revolutionaries, who lost it the next year, and in 1794 it was again annexed to France. There was violent resistance to French rule; consequently, most Belgians were delighted by the downfall of Napoleon. French domination, in effect, contributed to Belgian national unity.

The Congress of Vienna in 1815, while seeking to remake the map of Europe without considering national sentiment, combined Belgium and Holland into the Kingdom of the Netherlands. This alliance between two communities separated by linguistic and religious differences was an unfortunate one. Belgians actually prospered under the arrangement, but they nevertheless became increasingly discontented. In 1830, responding to the winds of change from revolutionary Paris, they declared in favor of independence. The European Powers agreed to recognize Belgium as a constitutional monarchy.

The new kingdom united Flemings and Walloons, but hostility continued between the two peoples. Throughout the 19th century and into the 20th, Flemings developed a sense of grievance. Most Flemings remained loyal during World War I, but some extremists gave support to the occupying Germans. On November 11, 1917, a "Council of Flanders" proclaimed the independence of all Flanders. The Allied victory in 1918 put an end to this proposed independent Flemish state. But the seeds of discontent changed into full-grown competitive mininationalisms.

The Unifying Link of Belgian Fascism

Although Flemish-Walloon rivalry continued through the Long Armistice from 1919 to 1939, extremists on both sides joined in a Belgian Fascist movement which was a part of the European-wide phenomenon originating in Mussolini's Italy. In the early 1930s, militant Flemings and rightist Walloons found a common ground in fascism. Flemish activists formed the *Verband van Dietsche Nationalsolidaristen* ("Union of Dutch National Solidarities"), which called for a Greater Netherlands but, at the same time, avoided cooperation with Hitler's National Socialism. Another Flemish group, the *Vlaamich National Verbond* (VNV, "Flemish National Union") adopted an outright Fascist ideology.

French-speaking Walloons organized the even more active Rexist movement. Its leader, Léon Degrelle, was a loud demagogue who viciously attacked the Belgian parliamentary system.[3] Although Walloon-oriented, Degrelle was able to win agreement with the radical wing of the Flemish national movement. Allied with 16 deputies of the VNV in the Belgian House of Representatives, 21 Rexist members were able to weaken the functioning of the government in the late 1930s.

Walloon and Flemish extremists worked together during World War II; both collaborated with the German occupation forces. In August 1941, shortly after the Germans invaded the Soviet Union, Degrelle organized, and later commanded, units of Walloon and Flemish brigades in SS (*Schutzstaffel*) formations on the Russian front.[4] Inside Belgium, Degrelle's followers worked closely with the Germans until the end of the war.

That kind of collaboration with the Germans was not popular with the vast majority of Belgians; most of them resented German occupation, and many joined underground forces to harry the Nazis. Nor did Flemish-Walloon cooperation survive the war. By 1944 virtually the entire Belgian people turned against Degrelle. In September 1944 he fled to Spain and the following December was sentenced to death *in absentia* as a collaborationist. Even the few Fleming and Walloon extremists who had found a common cause in Belgian fascism now turned on one another and widened the rift already existing between the two peoples.

Linguistic Warfare

A linguistic wall separated Flemings and Walloons.[5] The line ran east to west, just south of Brussels. North of the wall, tucked under the wing of Holland, the people spoke Flemish, which is similar to German. Flemish was spoken in the Belgian provinces of West Flanders, East Flanders, Antwerp, Brabant, Limburg, and partly in French Flanders. Written Flemish was virtually identical to Dutch, as was the spoken language of the educated classes.[6] There were some minor differences: in contrast to Dutch, Flemish diminutives tended to end in *ke* instead of *je*. Flemings adhered strongly to linguistic traditions and resented any attempts to relegate their language to second place.

Walloons living south of Brussels in the areas of Jaimur, Namur, Liège, Luxembourg, and Brabant spoke French and preferred French cultural forms. Theirs was essentially a French dialect. They managed to retain their linguistic distinctiveness under Burgundian, Spanish, Austrian, French, and Dutch control, as well as after the establishment of the Belgian kingdom in 1830. The Walloon dialect was used in the Middle Ages in such epics as *Aucassin et Nicolette,* in chronicles, religious tracts, and folklore dramas. It gradually merged into French.

After 1830, French, the tongue of revolutionaries, became the official language of Belgium, marking a significant change in relations between Dutch-speaking Flemings and French-speaking Walloons. For 10 centuries the two peoples had lived in a common territory without relinquishing their linguistic peculiarities. Giving the French language official preference set off a feud that was to continue throughout the 19th century into the 20th. Speaking French became the key to upward mobility. It was an impelling linguistic motivation for hardening of mini-nationalistic sentiment.

The Flemish-Walloon language rivalry affected every phase of political, social, and economic life in Belgium. French became the language of administrative, managerial, and professional Belgium. Walloons made no secret of their contempt for "peasant Flemish." They considered themselves to be more progressive than the backward Flemish farmers. They saw their language as elegantly superior while Flemish was guttural and coarse.

Non-bilingual Flemings were angered by this contemptuous attitude. They resented the use of French as the language of education, courts, medicine, and everyday life. Why should French-speaking Walloons hold most of the important administrative and professional posts? And why should they be given preference in industrial employment?

The Flemish movement emerging in the late 1830s was keyed directly to the language problem.[7] From the beginning, it called for a renascence of the Dutch language and demanded that Flemish be placed on an equal footing with French. It would settle for nothing less than complete linguistic equality: (1) all state business must be conducted in both French and Flemish; (2) there must be more use of Flemish in elementary and in secondary schools; (3) Flemish must be given equal status in scientific research; (4) inscriptions on Belgian coins must be in both Flemish and French; (5) Flemish-speaking units must be permitted in the military; (6) bilinguality must be recognized for all legal cases; and (7) Flemish courses must be introduced into the universities. Flemish citizens put increasing pressure on political parties to recognize their demands, which they considered to be reasonable for a mini-nationalism.

Economic Competition

Added to the language war was an economic confrontation between Flemings and Walloons. Flemings in the north traditionally preferred farming and textiles. Walloons in the south chose commerce and industry. When the Industrial Revolution made its appearance in Belgium in the early 19th century, Walloons took full advantage of the new situation. The Walloon middle class—manufacturers, merchants, lawyers, teachers—were more successful than were Flemings in acquiring wealth.[8] Agriculture–oriented Flemings were left far behind. Their resentment stiffened as the economic gap widened throughout the 19th century. Walloons were further enriched by the discovery of new coal basins.

By the time of World War I, a dramatic change occurred in the economic status of the two regions. The port of Antwerp, which had won an important position in world trade, was in the Flemish area. Much of the Walloon region had suffered an economic depression due to exhaustion of the coal mines. The Flemish birth rate began to surpass that of the Walloons. There were now more Flemings than Walloons in Brussels, the financial center of the country, and Walloons began to fear a diminution of their favored status.

This process of economic change continued after World War II. Foreign investors turned away from Wallonia, with its declining coal mining and steel industries, and looked instead to Flanders as a preferable region for investment.[9] Although many American firms had their headquarters in Brussels, they preferred to have their plants in Flanders, to the distress of the Walloons.

Walloons were worried by this loss of economic status in commerce, industry, and finance to the "upstart Flemings." The latter, in their turn, viewed the transformation as historically justified and denounced Walloonism for its pro-Germanism in World War I and Rexist fascism in World War II. Politico-economic differences aggravated both mininationalisms.

Psychological Motivation

Psychological undertones formed a distinct element in both Belgian mini-nationalisms, as in nationalism in general.[10] Both Flemings and Walloons developed their own special national characteristics.[11]

A Flemish sense of inferiority grew out of the 18th-century Enlightenment. The wave of rationalism emanating from Paris engulfed French-speaking Wallonie and gave content to the culture of the newly prosperous society of industrialists, businessmen, and intellectuals. Parisian salon intellectuals, certain that they had discovered all secrets of the universe, science, government, and economics, displayed an overwhelming optimism which spread to the French-speaking Walloon society. Francophone Walloons in Brussels spoke knowingly of Rousseau's popular sovereignty, Voltaire's secularism, and Montesquieu's spirit of the laws. They regarded themselves as superior to ignorant Flemish farmers who knew nothing of constitutionalism, parliamentarianism, or free trade. How could one compare refined gracefulness with clumsy vulgarity?

Over the years most Flemings seemed to accept this inferior status, which developed in the presence of a French-oriented culture. This sentiment persisted to the present day. A former premier complained that his Brussels butcher always spoke to him in French, though both were Flemings. Asked why he insisted on doing this, the butcher replied: "I speak French to you because you are a gentleman."[12] A Flemish-speaking Member of Parliament criticized the government because the French word *tire* ("pull") was not accompanied by the Flemish *trekken* ("pull") in the toilets of the National Assembly.[13] Disappointed Flemings charged that Walloons held all the political offices that mattered. A common complaint was: "The boss speaks only French, the secretaries are bilingual, but only the cleaners speak Flemish."[14]

This kind of inferiority was far removed from the pride displayed by emotional Basques or self-confident Bretons. These latter dissidents would not admit for a moment that theirs was "a farmer's language" unfit for a cosmopolitan-oriented society. The Flemish sense of inferiority had dangerous implications because it could not be contained and could explode at any moment. To be mocked as social inferiors in a society theoretically composed of equals was more than the Flemings could tolerate.

Clashes in Education

Both Flemings and Walloons realized instinctively that their future was bound up closely with the educational process. Both called for recognition of "the child's mother tongue." Any attempt to deprive the child of the language of his parents was regarded as anathema. Both sides wanted their own language in primary and in secondary schools. In 1914 Flemings won the right to use Flemish exclusively in primary education. In 1932 a new Belgian law required all schools to use the language most used in their districts. The reform was angrily opposed by parents. Walloons feared that their children might be forced to study Flemish, especially in areas near the linguistic boundary line. To Walloon parents, Flemish was still "a peasant's tongue," to which they would not allow their children to be subjected.

The language issue carried over to the university level. In 1916, in the midst of World War I, German authorities occupying Belgium introduced the use of Flemish at the University of Ghent. In 1930 the university was confirmed by the Belgian Government as a Flemish institution, a step which acted as a stimulus for the Flemish movement.

In 1968, at a time when militants were active in universities throughout the world, Flemish students won a major battle against Belgian authorities in what amounted to an escalated language war. The University of Louvain, the world's largest Roman Catholic university, lay on the Flemish side of the linguistic frontier. The student body was about equally divided between 13,000 Flemish-speaking and 12,000 French-speaking students. Rivalry between the two was strong. In early 1968 Louvain's Flemish students demanded that Francophone students and faculty be removed to Wallonia.[15] Governmental authorities at first paid no attention to what they regarded as a costly, potentially damaging request. Flemish students thereupon boycotted classes, took to the streets, fought French-speaking students, sang "We shall overcome!" and hurled rocks at the police. Angry police turned fire hoses on the demonstrators.[16] The governing board of the 543-year-old university, composed of bishops, met to consider the demands, but the prelates themselves soon split along linguistic lines.

Flemish students managed to topple Premier Paul Vanden Boynants's center-right coalition government. Eight Flemish ministers belonging to the moderate Christian Socialist Party threatened to resign unless the student demands were met. With no hope for a compromise, Vanden Boynants handed King Baudouin his government's resignation.[17]

Belgian authorities then attempted to settle the Louvain problem by a parliamentary decision moving the French section of the university to Ottignies, a town near Brussels just inside the frontier of Walloon country. The shift was slated to take place over the next decade and was expected to cost about $340 million.[18] The projected compromise satisfied neither the Flemings nor the Walloons. Walloons wanted their university section moved farther from Brussels to the heart of Walloon country.

The compromise did not end the language war at the university level. With Belgium's three main political parties hopelessly split on the issue, the political pot continues to simmer in this Belgian version of the Tower of Babel.

The Continuing Controversy

University riots formed only one facet of the Flemish-Walloon confrontation. Language barriers survived in Belgian society even though Flemings and Walloons have been intermarrying for years.[19] The situation was characterized by a Walloon aristocrat: "One speaks only Flemish to one's servants."

The reaction varied from social ostracism to angry physical encounter. Belgian police were kept busy breaking up street fights between contending linguistic factions. On August 11, 1965, about a hundred Flemings ostentatiously walked out of a church service in Ostend when a priest began the mass in French for the benefit of vacationing Walloons. Gendarmes were forced to drive through the streets in armored vehicles to halt the ensuing riots.[20] In December 1965 there were clashes in the language-border region of the Fourons, an area of six predominantly French-speaking villages that had been transferred in 1962 under the new linguistic laws from Francophone Liège province to Flemish Limburg. On December 19, 1965, 200 Flemings who had motored from Antwerp bearing flags with the emblem of the Flemish lion toured Fourons villages to demonstrate in favor of their language. In the ensuing riots, several persons, including a village postmaster, were injured.[21]

Every effort to find an answer to the linguistic controversy seemed to lead to insurmountable difficulties. Belgium's major political parties agreed in 1977 on the Egmont Pact, which called for a federal system of three autonomous regions—Flanders, Wallonia, and Brussels—to succeed the centralized government at Brussels. Each region was to have an elected assembly, an executive administration, and its own economic and industrial policies under guidelines set up by the central government. Local communities were to be governed by councillors who would serve also as members of the new national Senate. These administrators were to handle all matters of language, education, culture, and "personal issues."

The projected Egmont Pact was supported by a coalition of four-fifths of the entire membership of Parliament. Public opinion on both sides of the linguistic border seemed to favor the proposal. Flemish extremists, however, voiced strenuous objections. An independent Brussels, they charged, would give the French-speaking minority of Wallonia control of two districts out of three. The ensuing controversy forced new elections for Parliament. When the ballots were counted, the result was a stalemate; nothing was resolved. The new Parliament was faced with the same troublesome constitutional issues.

In the summer of 1979, another bill similar to the Egmont Pact was introduced by the coalition government. Satiated by continuing riots, leaders of the main political parties again proposed reform, but there was violent disagreement on the specifics. Objections ranged from the trivial to the serious. What about those who spoke French and lived in the Flemish suburbs around Brussels? Would Flemings in Brussels be given status in governmental employment commensurate with their numbers? What could be done about squabbling students in the universities?

Among the complicating factors in a complex situation was ambivalence on the part of the Flemings. The vast majority held themselves to be loyal subjects of the Belgian state. Over the course of years they had won many concessions. At the same time, however, they felt themselves bound by fellowship of language and culture to their Dutch neighbors in the Low Countries. They would not go so far as to demand political union with the Dutch. Nor would they be attracted by the violent tactics of Basque or Corsican terrorists. What they wanted most of all was absolute social equality, a status giving them a greater share of governmental offices and the national wealth. Most Flemings were willing to forgo independence in favor of increased autonomy.

On October 2, 1980, after years of debate, a measure of regional autonomy took effect. Flanders and Wallonia were given their own regional assemblies and executives. The new local bodies took control of public health, the economy, urban projects, and cultural matters. The federal government retained responsibility for defense, foreign affairs, education, finance, and justice. Whether or not these concessions to mini-nationalism could ease the confrontation remains to be seen.

Frisian Separatism in The Netherlands

The half million Frisians are a Germanic people living in the Frisian Islands of Friesland, a northern province in The Netherlands, and in Ostfriesland in Germany.[22] Frisians of the prehistoric era migrated to the coastlands stretching from the mouth of the Scheldt River to the Ems River. In the process they ousted the resident Celts. From the 1st to the 5th century A.D., they were under Roman control; Tacitus mentioned them in his *Annals* as living adjacent to the Rhine.

Frisian territory was then infiltrated by Angles and by Saxons on their way to England. At that time, a close association began between the Frisian language and English, which has lasted to the present day.[23] In the 8th century the Frisians were conquered by the Franks. Charlemagne converted them to Christianity. In later centuries they were territorially divided. William of Holland restored their ancient liberties in 1248, but six years later they again revolted, suffered defeat, and were absorbed into the province of Holland. Frisians east of the Zuider Zee repeatedly opposed Dutch attempts at domination.

Frisian resistance to outside authority continued well into the 15th century. When Holland passed to the House of Burgundy, the independent-minded Frisians refused to recognize the new authority. In 1498 all Frisia came under control of Duke Albert of Saxony, but Frisians remained recalcitrant and unsatisfied. They were subjugated by Charles V, the Holy Roman Emperor, in 1523. In 1579 Friesland joined six other provinces in the Union of Utrecht against Spanish control. It remained in the union until 1795, all the time insisting on its right to appoint its own *stadthalters* ("administrators"). In 1748 William of Nassau-Siegen, *stadthalter* of Friesland, became William IV, Prince of Orange, sole and hereditary *stadthalter* of the United Provinces. In 1815 his grandson became William I, King of The Netherlands.[24]

Modern boundaries locate Friesland, one of the 11 provinces of The Netherlands, partially on the northeast side of the Zuider Zee.[25] It occupies an area of 1,325 square miles, mostly below sea level. Frisians have developed their own form of mini-nationalism inside The Netherlands. A minority in a small country, they have remained aloof for centuries from the rest of The Netherlands, partly because of their geographic remoteness and partly because of their own cultural traditions which have set them apart from both North and South Holland.

Frisians claim that they molded the first dikes by moving huge amounts of earth to form mammoth terps (mounds) rising as much as 30 feet above sea level and spanning 45 acres. Here they set up their churches and defended their lands against invaders—including Romans, French, and the ever-threatening sea. Sensitive to their past tradition of independence, they jealously insisted on their sovereign rights against the encroachments of the neighboring Dutch. They regarded their distinctive nationality as marked by their own language. At the first hint of intervention, they defended their right to be free and to maintain a culture unlike any other in The Netherlands. The spirit of a mini-nationalism was at work.

Throughout the Frisian countryside, this independent-minded people displayed their red, white, and blue flag beside Holland's official flag. They had their road signs painted in two languages.[26] Industrious, devoted to farming and stock raising,[27] they were proud of such natives as Peter Stuyvesant, prominent in the founding of New York City; Menno Simons, who started the Mennonite Church; and even Margarethe Gertrude Zelle, the notorious Mata Hari of World War I.[28]

While some extremists called loudly for independence, most Frisians were not inclined to go beyond the stage of local autonomy. Resenting what they believed to be a secondary role assigned them by the dominant Dutch, they felt that they had been left behind in a modernization process that had not taken into consideration their economic and political rights.

At the same time, Frisians were an eminently practical people. In 1933 the 21-mile-long *Afsludijki* ("Enclosing Dam") was completed, calming the Zuider Zee and opening four-lane highways from other Dutch provinces to remote Friesland, as well as providing immediate economic advantages for the Frisians. They began to see the taste of their bread improved by using Dutch butter. Like the Welsh and the Scots, they saw economic advantages in maintaining their ties with the central government.

For the moment, Frisians are inclined to settle for a liberal concession of local rights. They retain their own language, folk dances, and pride in diversity. They remain an unsatisfied mini-nationalism, but it is a muted dissatisfaction unimpressed by the terror syndrome.

The South Moluccan Dream

Of considerably more concern to the Dutch than mild Frisian separatism was an obstreperous mini-nationalism inherited from colonial days. Just as a full-blown nationalism may on occasion assume a strange and incomprehensible form, so can a mini-nationalism take on a bizarre twist. Such is the case presented by South Moluccans on Dutch soil.

After the Dutch granted independence to Indonesia on November 2,

1949, the Moluccan minority that had left the islands to settle in The Netherlands turned its wrath, not on the newly emergent Indonesian Government, but on the mother country which had relinquished its colony. Unsatisfied Moluccans insisted that the Dutch Government should have known better and should have intervened to meet their aspirations. Shocked Dutch officials regarded the Moluccan attitude as weird, illogical, and ungrateful.

In the early 19th century, the Dutch extended their rule over the 3,000-mile archipelago of the East Indies, creating an empire out of an old chain of trading posts.[29] They suppressed revolts in 1830, 1849, and 1888. By the 20th century this huge area, with its rich and varied natural resources, was exploited by the Dutch "culture system," forced labor by which local farmers were required to deliver a specified amount of such crops as sugar and coffee. Dutch entrepreneurs considered the East Indies an area of opportunity for their sons. They were careful, however, to preserve native customs as a means of shutting off Western ideas of nationalism and democracy.

Resistance gradually built up against Dutch imperialism. Islamic Indonesians resented Dutch domination. There were sporadic rebellions. In 1942, in the midst of World War II, the Dutch were forced to abandon the Indonesian archipelago under humiliating circumstances. When the Japanese left in 1945, Achmed Sukarno, the leading agitator for independence, took control. The Dutch attempted to reconquer the archipelago, but after four years of warfare, they realized that they were fighting a losing cause. They recognized the independent Republic of Indonesia, which was joined in a tenuous union with the Dutch Crown.[30] Sukarno, elected President for Life, set up a "guided democracy," in reality a personal dictatorship.[31]

During the struggle for independence, South Moluccans, a minority living in a cluster of islands at the southern tip of Indonesia, supported the Dutch. In April 1950, when Sukarno incorporated some 15 states into his new state, South Moluccans proclaimed their own republic but were quickly defeated. Some 4,000 South Moluccans and their dependents left their ancient homeland and arrived in Holland with little but their talent for soldiering. They were welcomed by the Dutch, who were grateful for their loyalty in trying times. Most South Moluccans settled in factory towns.

Although some newcomers to The Netherlands soon intermarried with the Dutch, most were inclined to resist integration. In two decades their numbers increased to 40,000, all of them settled into enclaves. Older Moluccans, inculcating a strong sense of tradition in their offspring, opposed amalgamation into Dutch society. The younger generation, tutored at home in a strict patriarchal life, clung fanatically to the dream of a future independent "Republic of the South Moluccans." A brisk mini-nationalism was in the process of formation.

There were few accommodationists among the South Moluccan exiles; virtually all supported the cause of independence. They were annoyed by what they considered to be far too close a collaboration between their Dutch hosts and oil-rich, independent Indonesia. They believed that it was necessary to carry on their traditions and seek their own way to independence. They considered it vital to pass resentment on to the younger generation.

So successful was this delegated sense of nationalism that young South Moluccans, few of whom had ever seen their native land, took up the struggle for independence. They began to blame the Dutch Government for their plight. Soon they were striking violently at their hosts in a terror campaign designed to bring attention to their cause. They demanded that the Dutch relinquish all links with Indonesia and support their demand for an independent South Moluccan state.

In December 1975 seven young Moluccans seized a train and held it for nearly two weeks. Three persons were killed in the process. At the same time, another nationalist unit occupied the Indonesian consulate in Amsterdam for 15 days. The seven hijackers were tried and sent to prison. On May 23, 1977, South Moluccans took over a Utrecht–Groningen express train with 51 passengers near De Punt, while others seized a primary school at Bovensmille, holding 105 children and 5 teachers hostage. For two weeks, all attempts at mediation failed.

Until this time Dutch officials had been indifferent to South Moluccan militancy. This new hostage situation, however, turned their attitude to raw anger. They were not appeased when the school children, endangered by unhygienic conditions, were released after four days. The Dutch public called for freedom for the 51 exhausted hostages, then in their 20th day of captivity. The train was attacked by a 2,000-man army of Dutch commando marines, a squad of sharpshooters, and armored military-police units. Overhead, six Starfighter jets of the Royal Netherlands Air Force, with afterburners roaring, dropped smoke bombs to give the troops cover and to alert the hostages. Six of the 13 Moluccan terrorists (5 men and 1 woman) and 2 of the hostages were killed; 1 terrorist, 2 marines, and 9 prisoners were wounded in the assault. The long ordeal was ended.[32]

Far from being cowed by the attack, Moluccans turned the funeral of the dead terrorists into a dramatic political protest. A crowd estimated at from 3,000 to 10,000 marched silently in a three-mile procession to a cemetery where the bodies of the slain "heroes" were buried in a common grave.[33] When the remaining hijackers were placed on trial, Moluccan extremists set fire to two schools and wounded a policeman with a burst of gunfire.[34] Dutch police and military units used armored personnel carriers and helicopters in predawn raids on Moluccan enclaves in a search for weapons.[35]

Dutch officials dismissed the demands of young Moluccan hotheads as preposterous. They pointed out that administrative control had been conceded to Indonesia nearly three decades ago and that they could do nothing to change the colonial legacy. Their attitude angered Moluccans, who, with perverse logic, continued to hold their hosts responsible for their plight.

The militancy of South Moluccans in The Netherlands indicates that mini-nationalisms may well pass beyond the boundaries of reason. South Moluccans, possessed by the ideal and dream of independence, lash out grotesquely against the hosts who gave them sanctuary in troubled times. Nationalism in all its manifestations should never be confused with rationalism.

Denmark and the Greening of Greenland

For central governments everywhere which have to contend with mini-nationalisms, one word is anathema—independence. They fear that a grant of freedom to any one region will lead to a domino effect of other unsatisfied minorities agitating for the same goal. On occasion, they will grant semi-sovereignty as the most rational solution to a perplexing problem. Such is the case of Danish Greenland.

The vast Arctic territory of Greenland, the world's largest island, lies northeast of Canada between the Arctic Ocean on the north and the Atlantic Ocean on the south. It is 5 times the size of France and 50 times that of the mother country Denmark. The coastal strip plus the nearby islands are free of ice, but the rest of Greenland is sheathed in ice 11,000 feet thick. Without interurban roads, transport is by sledge, ship, or helicopter. The population of 43,000 is predominantly Eskimo, with some Europeans living mostly on the west coast. Greenland is the world's most underpopulated country.

The Norse explorer Eric the Red landed on the beautiful but barren island in the 10th century and named it Greenland in the hope of attracting settlers from Scandinavia.[36] By the Middle Ages, most of Eric's heirs had succumbed to the harsh climate, leaving only an Eskimo population that had migrated across the Arctic from Asia. In the 18th century, Danes colonized the island and in 1953 made it a Danish province. Today, most Eskimos and a few colonial Danes in Greenland earn their living by fishing, hunting seals, shrimping, raising sheep, and herding reindeer.

During the second half of the 20th century, the Danish Government decided to modernize its backward colony. The inhabitants were removed from their igloos, installed in modern concrete-block buildings, and given the advantages of the typical Scandinavian welfare program administered by Danes. Copenhagen shops opened branch stores in Greenland. In a short time the standard of living was lifted from a low subsistance level to relative prosperity.[37]

This development, regarded by Danes as progress in civilization, soon led to an identity crisis for Greenlanders. The cost in human terms was heavy. The sudden uprooting of natives from their customary life, from their traditional fishing villages to urban centers, adversely affected them.[38] Greenlandic self-esteem and self-confidence plummeted under the modernization program. Eskimos resented control from Copenhagen and complained of lack of freedom. Worst of all were rises in the crime rate, alcoholism, and venereal diseases, adjuncts of the civilizing process.

The arrival of American forces in Greenland during World War II brought additional modernization and even more problems. The influx of Danes in the 1950s, following the proclamation of the territory as a Danish province, added to the dissatisfaction of native Greenlanders.

Greenlandic agitation for home rule began in 1975. Angered by years of poverty and what they deemed as neglect, Eskimo leaders began to call for disengagement from the mother country. On January 17, 1979, more than 70 percent of the population voted for the introduction of home rule to begin in May 1980. Faced with this situation, the Danish Government deemed it wise to grant semi-sovereignty to Greenland. It introduced provisions for self-administration.[39] Foreign policy, defense, and management of the currency were reserved for Denmark. Fundamental civil rights, similar to those noted in the Danish Constitution, were guaranteed to Greenlanders.

Greenlanders were quite willing the accept the proposal. Behind their agreement to acknowledge a status short of separation was an economic motivation—they did not want to part with their Danish subsidy. Each native received an annual grant of $250, which far exceeded the amount he usually earned from fishing or mining.[40]

This settlement of semi-sovereignty indicates that a reasonable solution to the demands of regional nationalists is possible when the central authorities recognize the justice of unsatisfied yearnings and when local dissidents are willing to eschew terrorism as an operating procedure. Both sides win in the compromise: the larger nationalism is maintained intact with guarantees against dissolution, while the smaller nationalism achieves at least a portion of its demands. Greenlanders, like Scotsmen, Welshmen, and Quebeckers, have chosen this way of moderation. Basques, Corsicans, Croats, and South Moluccans reject it as an unsatisfactory substitute for freedom. The moderates function in a peaceful society; the extremists promote bloodshed and chaos.

CHAPTER **8**

PLURINATIONAL SPAIN: BASQUE AND CATALAN SEPARATISM —————————

For nations as for individuals, character is destiny, and
moderation has been fundamentally, even extravagantly absent from Spain's political character. Fervor has seemed a
necessity of the national nervous system; perhaps Spanish
formality seems to smother the ferocity beneath the shell of the
nation's life.
                    —George F. Will, syndicated columnist

A Cult of Violence

On October 8, 1979, several weeks before the proposed Guernica Statute
calling for Basque autonomy was to be submitted to a referendum, Carlos Garaicoetxea, leader of the Basque Nationalist Party which supported the statute, stated publicly: "Between now and October 25 there
will be a dirty war of killings and assassinations."[1]

Garaicoetxea referred to the sharpened terrorist campaign of the
separatist organization *Euzkadi Ta Azkatasuna* (ETA), whose violence
brought the number of killings in Spain in 1979 to 114. Militant mini-
nationalisms differ in the intensity of their activism. To publicize their
cause, Scottish nationalists stole into Westminster Abbey and, in the dead
of night, removed the Stone of Scone. Hot-headed Basque extremists
reject such gestures as puerile and ineffective. Instead, they turn to
bullets, bombs, and grenades. They advocate the language of force—
might makes right, power to the strong.

The ETA cult of violence is but one aspect of dissent in plurinational
Spain—but it is the one that has won global attention. There is a combination of oppositions, from the relatively benign localism of Galicia in
the northwest and of Andalusia in the south to the vigorous sentiment
for autonomy in Catalonia in the northeast and the volatile extremism in
the Basque country in the north. Basque extremists prefer the way of
the Irish Republican Army; the Palestine Liberation Organization; the

101

Baader-Meinhof gang, or Red Army faction, in West Germany; and the Red Brigades in Italy. Hard-line ETA terrorists are committed to establishing an independent Basque nation through violence. They regard autonomy and moderation as the way of weaklings and fools.

Regionalism in Spanish History

Behind the separatist fires burning in Spain is a long history of regionalism.[2] Regions of Spain were once separate kingdoms, and their people have long resented the loss of their independent status. ETA terrorism is grounded as much in regional differences as in class or ideological differences. The militants' call for separatism is equated with freedom; regional rights are equated with individual rights.

On the map, the Hispanic peninsula gives the impression of a contiguous land mass, but for most of its history, Spain has been a geographical expression. In the early Middle Ages, several Spanish Christian kingdoms arose in reaction against the Muslims in a process known as the Reconquest. Christian peoples coalesced around seven regional nuclei from west to east: Galicia, Asturia, Catalonia-Castilla, western Basque country, Navarra (southwestern Basque lands), Aragon, and Catalan counties. Geographical and politico-military factors, a supposed ethnic identity in the case of the Basques, stimulated this regionalism.

In the west the Asturias took on the status of "kingdom" a little more than a generation after the Muslim conquest of most of the peninsula. By the end of the 8th century, the people of the Asturias were identified with the vanishing Visigothic kingdom. From the northwest the Asturias expanded southward and established the greater kingdom of Léon, the eastern frontier of which split off to form the kingdom of Castile-Léon. The Catalan counties of the eastern Pyrénées were originally dominions of the Frankish Crown. The county of Aragon, south of the main Pyrénées, was an early dependency of the Duchy of Toulouse, which quickly won its independence.

Not until the early 18th century did a unified Spanish state-system emerge under the control of the new Bourbon dynasty. One by one the regional constitutional systems succumbed to the centralism instituted by the Bourbons. However, there remained strong residues of regional identity. The Basque principalities in the north bordering on the Pyrénées were able, despite Bourbon pressure, to maintain their special constitutional structures. Their pattern of particularism was to have important consequences not only for themselves but also for other Spanish peoples from Aragon to Catalonia. Proud of their singular institutions, Basques were determined to maintain their own unique identity, language, and culture. They insisted that the *Generalitat*, their ancient organ of local rule, be restored. Other regionalists echoed the demands of Basque separatists.

The Evolution of the Basque Provinces

In the formation of modern states, peoples of similar roots, language, culture, and historical traditions were often split into two parts on either side of a natural or artificial boundary. That is what happened to the Basques north and south of the Pyrénées.

Seven Basque provinces share a contiguous geography: four in Spain (Vizcaya, Guipúzcoa, Alava, and Navarra) and three in France (Labourd, Basse Navarre, and Soule). Each combination forms a mini-nationalism, one in France and one in Spain. Basque nationalists wanted a reunion of all seven principalities. While French Basques were less restive than their brethren across the Pyrénées, they also proposed an independent Basque nation.[3]

Basque traditions of opposition, resistance, and conspiracy run deep in Spanish history.[4] Little is known about Basque origins, and the chances are that little or nothing will be added in the future. There is no evidence to support the contention of Basque nationalists that there is a biologically distinct Basque "race," any more than there is an American "race" or Winston Churchill's British "race." Basques are an amalgam of several peoples in the western Pyrénées, united by language, culture, and historical traditions, certainly not by an evanescent race. Although we are unable to trace the Basque language or ethnicity to any other region,[5] it does not necessarily follow that they are ethnically autochthonous or are of "pure race."

Roman historians recorded the presence of tribes of Vascones in the area today called Navarra. Attempts were made by successive waves of Visigoths (West Goths), Franks, Normans, and Moors to subdue the Vascones, who survived them all. The Vascones, later called Basques, retained a fierce sense of independence during the Middle Ages.

The Basque urge for independence continued even after the provinces were united with Castile and Aragon. Spanish Basques, as did their brethren in France, demanded and obtained a measure of local autonomy, especially in military matters, taxation, and trade. Local rights were guaranteed in legislation known as *fueros*, which defined the rights of Basque assemblies and set up rules for inheritance. French Basques were deprived of such rights during the French Revolution. Spanish Basques retained them for almost another century but lost the privileges in 1873 because of their pro-Carlist stand in the Carlist Wars.[6]

Angered when they lost their old privileges, Basques thereafter lent their support to any movement that opposed the centralism of Madrid.

There was, however, a split among Spanish Basques when the Spanish Republic was proclaimed in 1931. Three of the four provinces—Vizcaya, Guipúzcoa, and Alava—were content with semi-autonomy inside the Republic despite its anti-clerical stand. The Basques of Navarra hewed to the line of independence. Basque separatism was strong in Navarra, but Bilbao, the capital of Vizcaya, became an additional center of Basque separatism.

During the Spanish Civil War (1936–1939), Basque provinces became an isolated Republican conclave. Republicans gave them autonomy at the beginning of the conflict. In return, Basques supplied the Republicans with some of their most effective troops during the civil conflict. The Basque republic lasted just eight months before it was overthrown by the insurgents in 1937. Guernica, in Vizcaya, became a symbol of lost Basque liberties.[7]

The Role of the Basque Language

Language played a major role in the formation and development of Basque nationalism.[8] *Euskera,*[9] one of the most distinctive of non-Castilian languages, is also one of the most complex of all tongues.[10] It is akin to no other European or any other language. The origin of this guttural, highly inflected language is unknown. Linguists have been unable to find its roots in any other family of languages. Some connect it to Hebrew because of its similar pronouns, or to Aztec or Dakota Indian tongues because of similar verbs. Scholars link elements of its roots to many other languages, usually with meager results.[11] Others find a slight relationship between Basque and Mongolian dialects.

Basque is probably the only remnant of a language spoken in southwestern Europe before the area was brought under Roman control. Currently, it is the language of about half a million people in the Pyréneés region of Spain and France. It is spoken in the Spanish provinces of Guipúzcoa, parts of Navarra and Vizcaya, and a small portion of Alava. In contemporary France it is spoken in the western region of the *département* of Pyrénées Atlântiques.

This unique and complex language was a powerful vehicle for Basque separatism. It remained a symbol of dissent even though its use has diminished recently; it is spoken mostly in countryside and fishing villages, rarely in Bilbao, the capital of Vizcaya, or in San Sebastian, the capital of Guipúzcoa. The language retained its special phonology, grammar, and vocabulary. It contributed little to neighboring Spanish, French, or Occitan and bypassed the sort of cultural diffusion by which languages influence one another.

Basques regarded their language as the binding cement of their society. They rejected any orders from Madrid that Spanish be used for local signs. For them, *Euskera* meant pride in a mystical relationship between people and territory, between themselves and Basque hills, plains, and shore. It was the heart of their mini-nationalism.

Basque Cultural Affinity

As in other mini-nationalisms, added to pride in language was Basque respect for cultural traditions. Over the centuries, Basques developed their own dress, customs, and folkways, which they guarded diligently against outsiders. The ancient Romans never succeeded in absorbing Basque culture, nor did the Visigoths, Muslims, or Carolingians.

Special Basque customs differed from those of the rest of Spain. Living in a rugged countryside quite unlike the arid fields of the middle or southern Iberian peninsula, Basques were active as fishermen, sailors, and shepherds. They were immensely fond of choral singing. A local saying explained: "One or two Basques are nothing much, but three Basques are a choir." The favorite Basque game was *jai alai,* in which players used scoops attached to their hands to throw balls at great speed. Youngsters played the game either with bare hands or with primitive wooden bats. Basques enjoyed hotly contested community games, including such trials of strength as boulder lifting, log splitting, wood chopping, hay cutting, and towing heavy boats through rough seas. These activities continue today.

Basque community-mindedness revealed an urge to be free from outside interference. The people were happiest under local administration and resented any meddling from Madrid. Their strict adherence to their special culture was closely related to their political aspirations. They saw not only their customs but also their ancient privileges as inviolable. They reacted strongly against either cultural or political amalgamation. Theirs was a proud, highly sensitive nationalism.

Basques Under the Franco Dictatorship

With the collapse of the Spanish Republic in 1939 and the beginning of the Franco dictatorship came a long period of Basque martyrdom. The dictator's goal was simple: plurinational Spain must be united into one centralized state. Franco would throttle regionalism and any movements for separatism: he discouraged regional languages; he executed those extremists whom he regarded as traitors.

The Basque provinces proved to be a special problem for Franco, who favored the carrot-and-stick technique used by the Kremlin in dealing with its recalcitrant nationalities. He would grant a small measure of autonomy, but the moment dissent turned to terror, he would fight fire with fire. The carrot first; the stick second. If Basque officials could hold the extremists in line, they would be given limited concessions. If not, they would be subjected to an iron hand from Madrid.

Basque resistance to Franco's centralism increased in the decade from 1940 to 1950. The dictator retaliated with a series of harsh emergency measures. Proclaiming a "State of Exception" as legal justification, he ordered the Civil Guard to suppress Basque dissidents. The Civil Guard, drawn from non-Basque regions, hunted down activists, subjected them to torture, and turned them over to harsh judges. Basques were executed for "military rebellion." The dictator wanted no opposition in his monolithic state.

ETA Militancy

Stubborn Basque militants reacted strongly against Franco's policy of repression. Some gave up in disgust and, to avoid the dictator's police, went into exile, especially to Argentina, Mexico, and Cuba.[12] Exiled Basques organized an emigré government in Paris to await the day of liberation.

Basques who remained in their homeland were split by a generation gap. Older nationalists, who hoped for more autonomy, were placed in a dilemma. If they condemned activism, they would be discredited in the eyes of their compatriots. If, on the other hand, they remained silent, they would be regarded by Madrid as accomplices of the extremists and would have to pay a penalty for it.

Young militants, however, were in a hurry. Unwilling to wait much longer, they turned to a revolutionary solution. They denounced the moderate Basque Nationalist Party (PNV) as ineffective and called for all-out war on Madrid's centralism. In 1959 they organized the *Euzkadi Ta Azkatasuna* (ETA), or "Basque Homeland and Liberty." They announced their goal as full independence for the four predominantly Basque provinces in Spain and eventual union of the Spanish Basque provinces with the three in France.[13]

Mostly from middle-class families, ETA activists adopted their own version of Marxist-Leninist ideology. As the first generation of Basques to be free from the traumatic memories of Civil War days, they turned to direct action to win Basque freedom. They kept their ranks small in numbers but allotted every member a specific task. The military branch comprised 300 members trained for direct action, while another 300 were designated for intelligence, cover, and shelter. The military section was divided into self-contained command units of three or four men, occasionally including romantic teenagers. Both military and civilian branches were expected to hold normal jobs and to fuse into the general population. Militants went into action only on orders from above, usually from a shadowy leadership often residing in southern France.

To gather funds, ETA leaders organized "revolutionary" bank robberies and "revolutionary taxes" extorted from frightened Basque industrialists. Youngsters in the underground organization plastered walls with ETA slogans, placed booby traps in the cars of governmental officials, and dynamited deserted Civil Guard posts. This kind of activity was followed by a more dangerous terror campaign.

ETA militancy was violent and deadly. In August 1968 bearded ETA gunmen assassinated Meliton Manzanas Gonzales, police chief of the Basque region, after naming him "the butcher of our people." An ETA militant justified the killing: "We set up our own tribunal, condemned him to death, and executed him. Our Central Committee has decided on additional executions."

The Franco Government countered with mass arrests. Six ETA members were found guilty and condemned to death before a firing squad. Basque workers called protest strikes. Public opinion elsewhere urged leniency: the governments of West Germany, Britain, Sweden, and Italy urged Franco to grant clemency. Pope Paul VI was prepared to call for mercy, and even the Kremlin, itself under attack for death verdicts against Jewish hijackers, joined in the call for mercy. Franco commuted the death sentences to 30 years' imprisonment.

Among those who lost their lives in 1968 in actions attributed to the ETA were policemen, governmental officials, and others, 63 in all.[14] Militants bombed Civil Guard headquarters and blew up homes of those they suspected of opposition to their tactics. They claimed that they were responding in the only possible way to Franco's police, who, they charged, were under orders not to take prisoners but to kill. In December 1970, 16 ETA militants were tried by tribunal, of whom six were found guilty of armed rebellion and sentenced to death.[15] On January 19, 1972, four armed ETA men kidnapped an industrialist near one of his factories on the outskirts of Bilbao and drove off with him in a stolen car. The ETA announced that it would execute Lorenza Zabala as a "Fascist bourgeois" unless he reinstated 183 Basque workers he had dismissed the preceding month because they had started a strike for higher wages.[16] On September 24, 1972, four persons, including a policeman, died after an ETA attack.

Post-Franco Violence

It might be supposed that ETA militancy would subside after the death of Franco in 1975 and the subsequent movement of Spain along the road to democracy. If anything, ETA activism increased.

Prime Minister Adolfo Suarez and King Juan Carlos proposed a new plan of devolution to meet the demands of separatists. They would balance regional desires with Madrid's centralism and prevent dangerous polarization in the transition to democracy. In late September 1977, they recognized the Catalonian *Generalitat,* the ancient governing body, and moved to grant limited home rule to Galicia, Aragon, and the Canary and Balearic Islands.[17] In mid-1977, by royal decree, the Basque *Generalitat* was recognized officially as a "pre-autonomy" body with powers to take complete control of industry, agriculture, commerce, and urban development in the Basque provinces.[18]

The government's offer of pre-autonomy seemed to be a reasonable one. Basque citizens, including Socialists and Communists, were attracted by the promise that additional powers would be granted in due time. Many Basques were pleased by the concession enabling them to display their once-forbidden red-white-and-green flag.

Unfortunately for the moderates, this governmental appeasement came at a time when the economy of the Basque regime was in a state of decline. Active Basque capitalists already had begun to move out, investments lagged, and unemployment increased. Along with the deteriorating economy went political unrest and stepped-up ETA activity. Extremists denounced Madrid's concessions for home rule as too little and too late. "Orders from Madrid," said one militant, "sound as if they came from another planet." ETA terrorist attacks were intensified. The polarization feared by the government took place when army officers loyal to Franco, angered at losing their old positions of power, denounced governmental "softness" and came close to mutiny. The police, angered by ETA excesses, resumed their warfare against dissidents.

It was an explosive mixture of ETA violence and police counteraction. On December 5, 1977, 20 people were injured in Pamplona, the capital of Navarra province, in clashes between right-wingers armed with pistols, chains, and clubs and Basque nationalists similarly equipped and waving nationalist flags.[19] On February 23, 1978, ETA terrorists fatally shot a federal policeman as he stopped his car at a crossroad in Guipúzcoa.[20] On July 10, 1978, Basque demonstrators and riot police turned Pamplona into a bloody battleground, with 1 man killed and 135 injured. A fiesta in honor of a local saint was broken up when Basques threw bottles at police and the officers countered with smoke bombs and rubber bullets.[21] Five days later, a public meeting protesting police overreaction set off a violent confrontation in San Sebastian.[22]

Bitterness increased on both sides. On September 1, 1978, ETA proclaimed a death list of governmental officials.[23] On November 16, 1978, a man on a motorbike rode up to a judge outside his home and shot him dead in revenge for his judicial action of imprisoning dissidents during the Franco regime.[24] On December 6, 1976, on the eve of the referendum on the new Spanish Constitution, three young men burst into a crowded bar in San Sebastian and killed three policemen. They left shouting: "Long live a free Basque land!"[25]

This kind of political violence extended from Madrid to the Basque provinces.[26] At the same time, Basque activists made certain to gather funds for their cause: in 1968 alone, ETA militants stole an estimated $2.5 million from banks and payrolls, in addition to enormous sums extracted from Basque industrialists and businessmen.[27]

ETA terrorism was condoned by a large proportion of the Basque people, whose attitude was: "We do not like ETA methods but we do admire their idealism."[28] Privately, many Basques believed that violence was necessary to give priority and urgency to their special claims. On March 26, 1978, more than half a million Basques marched through the flag-draped streets of Bilbao in the first celebration of their national day since the Spanish Civil War of 1936–1939. Nationalists, left-wing political parties, and trade unions simultaneously held similar marches in San Sebastian, Vitoria, and Pamplona. Through festooned streets the marchers chanted such slogans as "Long live an autonomous Basque country!" and "Independence and autonomy now!"

In the summer of 1979, the ETA struck at the prosperous tourist industry in the Costa del Sol in the south. Thousands of Europeans, including wealthy Germans who had come to Spain on holiday, suddenly were endangered by bomb explosions set off by ETA terrorists. The goal of the dissidents was to free a hundred comrades from prison or have them transferred from central Spain to the Basque provinces. They also attacked French trains moving into Spain from Paris, in order to force Paris to recognize captured guerrillas in French jails as political fugitives.[29] The violent separatist campaign took 120 lives during 1980. There was little sense of moderation in this mini-nationalism.

Bandit Priests of Basqueland

A unique feature of Basque separatism was its attraction for the lower ranks of the Roman Catholic clergy. Basques were most loyal Catholics in a strongly Catholic nation. They were proud of Ignatius Loyola and Francis Xavier, both of whom were Basques, and both of whom had the spirit of independence long associated with their provinces. For the community-minded Basques, the village church was always regarded as a traditional stronghold of regional culture and values.

The Basque clergy was split by differing opinions. The upper hierarchy, the largely conservative bishops, objected to ETA violence and ETA championing of the class struggle. The Archbishop of Madrid worked hand in hand with government officials. Bishops urged a moderate stand and supported cooperation with the centralist state apparatus. Clergymen who held seats in the legislature and were paid by the government opposed ETA militancy.

Younger Basques of the regular clergy (monks) and secular clergy (priests) had an altogether different attitude. They felt themselves closer to the people of their parishes than to the ecclesiastical authorities in Madrid. In an organization known for discipline and obedience, Basque priests and monks opposed their own hierarchy. Some even called for a purely evangelical church that would guarantee the rights of all men—including Basque separatists.

The ecclesiastical situation took a sensational turn when lower-ranking members of the clergy moved from moderation to extremism. "One can be a Christian," said a young Basque priest, "and still work with the ETA." Another declared: "Violence is imposed upon us. We have no other recourse because the [Franco] regime has made dialogue and negotiation impossible."[30] ETA membership rolls in all probability included several young Catholic priests. Others made no secret of their opposition to their own national, state-supported hierarchy and even flew the illegal Basque flag.[31] Militants in trouble found sympathy and support among young priests. In mid-May 1969 a taxi driver was murdered outside Bilbao shortly after police raided an ETA meeting there. The next morning two priests bound up the bullet wounds of a man they found unconscious in a nearby village. Police rounded up eight priests whom they suspected of ETA sympathies. The accused were sent to prison at Zamora, where there was a special wing for the confinement of priests and monks.[32]

Spain's "bandit priests" turned to the ETA because they opposed the Franco regime as dictatorial, anti-democratic, and anti-Basque.[33] Franco in turn, regarded them as dangerous traitors. He ordered the arrest of those who preached human rights or said mass for ETA guerrillas killed by the police. His Civil Guards raided monasteries in the Basque country, confiscated banned books from cells, searched for banned Basque flags, and subjected clerical prisoners to psychological and physical torture. Those prelates who dared complain were charged with insulting the armed forces, a serious matter in Franco's Spain.[34]

In Rome, the Vatican, while concerned by the confrontation between high ecclesiastics in Madrid and lower-level Basque clergy, made only feeble efforts at mediation. The papacy regarded Franco as its loyal protector and was reluctant to interfere in what it saw as local Spanish affairs. With or without intervention from Rome, Franco's authorities continued to arrest, mistreat, or exile rebellious Basque priests. The practice was halted after the death of Franco.

Homage to Catalonia

Catalonia, the second major area of regional discontent, encompasses the provinces of Barcelona, Tarragona, Lérida, and Gerona. Occupying about 12,000 square miles, it stretches from the southeastern Pyrénées down to the Costa Brava, past Barcelona, and westward to the Ebro River. Catalonia also formed part of the geographical, economic, political, and cultural continuum extending northward into France and greater Occitania.

The origins of the Catalan people are lost in the mist of time. Their language, a separate tongue and not a Spanish dialect, was derived from a Latin dialect spoken by colonizing Romans. Today, it is the mother tongue of some 8 million people in Catalonia, Valencia, part of western Aragon, and several French provinces.

The history of the Catalans, like that of the Basques, comprises a series of conquests by Romans, Goths, Moors, and West Franks.[35] The most important influence on them was Roman. Belonging culturally to the Meditarranean world, Catalans retained Roman customs during the feudal-manorial era.

With the decline of the Carolingians in the 10th century, Catalan counties were divided into separate centralized jurisdictions. These localities gradually coalesced into a small principality in the northeastern part of the Iberian peninsula. In 1137 the area was combined with the independent kingdom of Aragon. In the later Middle Ages, Catalonia expanded throughout the central Mediterranean and formed a powerful thalassic empire extending, at one time, as far eastward as Greece.

Catalonia became a major mercantile and industrial power in the western Mediterranean. Behind its success was a wealthy and powerful middle class. Administratively, the counties had a well-developed representative system of their own. The Catalan Cortes retained for itself an almost complete power of the purse. It supported a constitutionally delimited royal authority in the belief that Catalan prosperity was due to independence of action. Most of all, Catalans revealed their independent spirit in the *Generalitat*, a permanent executive board of the Parliament. They retained this body for some six centuries, although it was ended for a time by the French-Castilian occupation of 1744. Since then, Catalans have worked energetically to revive the *Generalitat*, which has become the focal point of Catalan nationalism.

The Catalan urge for independence persisted throughout the 19th century despite fluctuations of political power. Like the Basques, Catalans had a profound distaste for Madrid's centralism. In five centuries as a part of Spain, they never relinquished their dream of an independent Catalonia with its own special red-yellow banner.

Catalans came close to realizing their dream during the short-lived days of the Spanish Republic in the 1930s. Franco's forces required three months to conquer the four provinces of Catalonia. The dictator attempted to hold Catalonia in line by the same repressive measures he used in the Basque provinces: centralized administrative and economic control, discouragement of local dialects, arrest, trial, and execution of dangerous separatist leaders. Catalans resented Franco's iron hand, but their reaction was considerably less violent than that of the Basques. Proud and industrious, they reasserted their nascent nationalism in biting satire, in pinpricks instead of bullets and bombs.

Post-Franco officials took steps to appease the Catalans. In an effort to defuse the situation, they granted the newly restored regional government the power to legislate, levy taxes, administer schools, and organize the police force. They hoped that such liberal measures would lessen dissent. While grateful for a status of semi-autonomy, Catalans did not lose their desire for independence. Their mood was revealed in a haunting song, "*Els Segadors*": "Catalonia triumphant, will again be rich and full!"[36] In Barcelona, teenage girls wore T-shirts showing the map of Catalonia. Young men proudly displayed their red-and-yellow jacket patches proclaiming: "*Soc cintada dela paisos Catalans*" ("I'm a citizen of the Catalan nation").[37] School children, who learned their language at home and flaunted it in public, called Spanish "the language of the oppressor."[38]

In July 1977 thousands of Catalans jammed a Barcelona park in a ceremony to restore to its old pedestal a statue of Pau Claris, a 17th-century Catalan hero.[39] The following October, Josep Tarradallas, a Catalan nationalist who had been in exile for 39 years, returned to Barcelona to a tumultuous welcome. Several hundred thousand Catalans jammed the streets to greet the former president of the *Generalitat* which had been abolished by Franco. Appearing on the balcony of the *Palau de la Generalitat,* where the Spanish Second Republic had been proclaimed in 1931, Tarradallas spoke: "Citizens of Catalonia! We are here—to share your sufferings, your struggles, your sacrifices. I am here to work with you for a prosperous Catalonia in freedom."[40] Although the *Generalitat* had been restored the previous month, Tarradallas still spoke of Catalan freedom.

Catalans have never relinquished their dream of independence. Theirs is another case of a mini-nationalism with an unfulfilled mission.

Devolution or Civil War?

After a two-year constitutional process culminating in the home-rule referendum of 1979, Catalonia and the Basque country formally became autonomous regions inside Spain. Decrees of autonomy, overwhelmingly approved in the referendums, gave the two regions power to elect their own parliaments, to control taxation, education, and police, and to supervise broadcasting. On the surface, it seemed that, at long last, democratic devolution had solved Spain's most pressing and depressing problem.

Nevertheless, residues of regionalism remained strong and dangerous for the stability of the state. Separatist violence continued in the Basque country. Moderates called for even more autonomy in Catalonia. In addition, there were home-rule demonstrations in Galicia, Andalusia, and Aragon. Proud Spaniards retained their sense of passionate fractiousness. Solutions were difficult in an atmosphere of contempt for Madrid.

The issue was complicated by economic realities. For the central government, the loss of the Basque provinces and Catalonia, the country's most valuable industrialized regions, would mean mortal danger. If Basques and Catalans were to win all they wanted, Madrid would starve. If they seceded, they would take the country's wealth in steel, textiles, and natural gas with them.[41]

For Madrid, which saw national centralized unity in quasi-religious terms, regional independence was plainly and simply impossible. It had a choice—it had to appease or resist, and it had already gone as far as it could on the road of accommodation. The best it could hope for was continued division between moderates and extremists in the provinces. The latter had caused some alienation among their fellow citizens. The Guernica Statute for Basque autonomy, submitted to a referendum on October 25, 1979, was negotiated almost singlehandedly by the mainstream Basque National Party, composed of moderates strongly opposed to ETA terrorism. Predominantly middle class and inspired by European Christian Democracy, the Basque Nationalist Party at one time had been united with the ETA in hostility to Madrid, but now it took a stand against ETA efforts to block the home-rule statute.

In the first election for a parliament in the troubled Basque country on March 10, 1980, the Basque National Party emerged as the victor. The outcome of the vote presaged further confrontations between Basque legislators and Madrid. The Basque Nationalist Party had already withdrawn its representatives from the Cortes in Madrid. Now it was faced with the difficult task of taming the ETA guerrillas on its own territory. A moderate party also won victory in the elections for the home-rule legislature in Catalonia.

Within three months it became clear that the whiff of autonomy had failed to stem violence. Moderates and extremists, once united against Madrid in the demand for home rule, now slid into a conflict rapidly approaching the status of a civil war. Unemployed steelworkers burst into the regional parliament. Basque Nationalist Party leaders, outraged by profanation of the new institution, mobilized 30,000 followers for a street demonstration. In July 1980 violent skirmishes took place between moderates and ETA partisans.

It was again the clash between autonomy and independence, moderates versus extremists. Positions hardened on both sides; each called the other "Fascist." Moderates denounced the ETA's idea of a military solution as insane and excoriated its type of nationalism as "below the level of maturity that is necessary for a people who live in Europe." Basque Nationalist Party leaders criticized the "insensitivity" of the Madrid Government and concluded that a limited civil war might be the only solution. They saw no other way to meet the ETA's unrelenting campaign of assassination.

Basques now had their carefully circumscribed autonomy, but they had additional problems on top of ETA terrorism. They claimed Navarra as part of their "colonized" provinces, but Navarrans had their own ideas on the subject. Once connected with a separate kingdom, they supported Franco in the Civil War when most Basques sided with the Republicans. In December 1977, at the funeral of a Navarran police chief who had been killed by terrorists, Navarrans chanted "ETA assassins!" and disavowed the separatist cause.[42] The entire issue of Basque autonomy was clouded by this Basque-Navarran rivalry.

The central government at Madrid saw behind the shadow of regionalism the specter of republicanism. Leaders of the democratic monarchy felt that accommodation was necessary as a matter of prestige for the royal house. They sensed that regional autonomy must be granted if the monarchy was to endure.

Added to the domestic problem was the uncomfortable fact that the Basque issue was hurting French-Spanish ties. The matter periodically strained relations between the two countries and flared up with special vehemence in late 1980. It was the ease in passing from Spain to France and back again that allowed ETA terrorists to survive under both Franco and the succeeding democratic regime. France became a refuge, a kind of rest camp, and an important means of supply for the guerrillas. The two countries had an extradition treaty, but the French declined to consider tightening it, a refusal that annoyed Spanish authorities. In late November 1980, the tension was increased when three men machine-gunned a cafe in Hendaye, on the French side of the border, killing two and injuring one. Escaping in a car, the assailants crashed through the French border-police post and sped to the Spanish side. Despite urgent calls from the French police, they were released.[43] French Interior Minister Christian Bonnet said that the French Government "cannot tolerate such behavior, which smacks of complicity."[44] French officials were worried not so much about the minor Basque separatist movement on its side of the Pyrénées, but about ETA penetrations from across the border.

The political frustrations that nourish the rise of Spanish separatism still exist. The issue of autonomy versus independence remains a central problem. Madrid continues to seek strengthening of its authority in the violence-torn provinces and to forge closer ties with the fledgling home-rule authority. Moderate Basques and Catalans say that they are dissatisfied with what they regard as foot-dragging by Madrid. ETA terrorists continue to express their arguments by bullets and bombs.

Central to the problem in Spain is the hard-line intransigence of the ETA. Nothing appears to calm the revolutionary ardor of the terrorists. Attempts at negotiation have failed, and counter-violence does not seem to have worked. Despite the efforts of moderates, the average Basque citizen at heart supports the way of ETA guerrillas. The judgment of Robert P. Clark would seem to be correct: "It is probable that ETA and its violent strategy will continue to play a key role in Basque politics for months and perhaps years to come."[45] Extremists continue to raise clenched fists and chant "*Eusko Gudariak*," the hymn of Basque defiance to central authority.

Authorities in Spain's young democracy, as elsewhere in Europe, seek cautiously to appease their mini-nationalisms. Despite persisting terror, they made concessions by granting the Basque Nationalist Party additional powers over education, industry, transportation, and health. It was much less than Basque Nationalists demanded—such paternalism never really buried the dreams of Basque independence.

The ETA, with its Marxist-Leninist orientation, sought an independent *socialist* nation, a critical factor closely observed by the Kremlin. Some Spanish politicians and intelligence officials were convinced that the Soviet Union was abetting Basque terrorism by training ETA guerrillas in Cuba and South Yemen, both Soviet clients.[46] By Moscow's peculiar code, Ukrainian and Georgian mini-nationalisms were equated with treason, but ETA Basque terrorism was merely the way of liberation.

The current status of terror in Basqueland was described succinctly by a Basque journalist in an interview with the American journalist Claire Sterling:[47]

The terrorists are trading on our sentiments today, reminding us of how stupendous they used to be when Franco was on our backs. They *say* they're killing for the sake of Basque nationhood, but their sole purpose has changed. They're really doing it to destabilize the Spanish state—to hit the police, the army, judges, institutions, for the same reasons the Baader-Meinhof Gang does, or the Italian Red Brigades.

CHAPTER 9

SEPARATISM IN THE BALKANS

Croat chauvinism, if left unchecked, would lead to the renewal
of fratricidal civil war between the national groups and eventually to the breakup of the Yugoslav state.

—Marshal Tito

Tito, the "champion of human freedom," is one of the greatest
mass murderers of all time.

—Croatian National Congress

Heterogeneous Nationalities

Karl Marx, regarded by his followers as a champion of human rights,
dismissed the Balkans as "ethnic trash."[1] The variegated peoples of the
embattled peninsula would not agree. Each points to its own special
background, and each would like the blessings of freedom. Granted,
there is political confusion in the entire area, with its many minorities
clamoring for the limited space available. Each mini-nationalism has its
own characteristics and its own demands. The case of Yugoslavia presents an excellent example of how one mini-nationalism emerged
victoriously out of the quagmire with full nationalism, only to be subjected in turn to assault by its own unsatisfied nationalisms.

The pattern for dissolution originated as early as the consolidation of
the Austro-Hungarian Empire in the 19th century.[2] The Dual Monarchy
was formed of varied eastern European peoples, each with its own con-
geries of special, linguistic, cultural, and psychological peculiarities. Diverse peoples from the area of the Sava and Danube Rivers southward
had already known conquest, assimilation, and disruption while seeking
to retain their own special institutions. Serbs, Croats, and Slovenes were
thrown into an incongruous and illegitimate union.

The Dual Monarchy under Hapsburg rule was created in 1867 in a
constitutional compromise between Austria and Hungary known as the
Ausgleich ("settlement" or "agreement"). There was nothing like this
multi-national empire in European history. A land of dissimilar peoples
ruled by a German-Magyar minority, it was an anachronism in the Age
of Nationalism. Both the Austrian Empire and the Kingdom of Hungary

117

were to be equal partners, each with its own constitution and parliament. The administrative language of Austria was to be German, that of Hungary, Magyar. Hapsburg ruler Francis Joseph was named emperor in Austria and king in Hungary. There was no common parliament, but there were combined ministries for foreign affairs, finances, and war.

On paper, this seemed to be a workable compromise for a large area in central and southeastern Europe with peoples of common economic interests. From a political point of view, however, there was a dangerous defect in the Dual Monarchy. Just as the statesmen at the Congress of Vienna had paid far too little attention to the rising nationalism, so, too, did the Viennese manipulators of 1867 show too little regard for regional sensibilities. The *Ausgleich* favored two peoples—Germans and Hungarians. The Germans formed less than half the population of Austria; the Magyars, less than half the peoples of Hungary. What about the rest of the peoples in this conglomerate empire?

In effect, the agreement of 1867 solidified separatist sentiment by paying insufficient attention to it. In Austria there were unsatisfied Czechs, Slovenes, Poles, Italians, and Ruthenians. In Hungary there were equally dissatisfied Croats, Serbs, Slovaks, and Transylvanians. Most aggrieved of all were the fiercely independence-minded Croats and Serbs.

It was a hopeless hodgepodge of angered nationalities. Francis Joseph attempted to keep the squabbling minorities under control by a divide-and-rule policy. His treatment was unequal, favoring some and ignoring others. He knew that the kind of Russification process favored by his giant neighbor to the east was impractical in his jumbled mixture of a nation-state.

There was disaffection everywhere. Italians living in the Dual Monarchy were attracted by the national cause of Italy (irredentism). Rumanians in Transylvania resented their Hungarian masters. German-speaking Austrians called for union (*Anschluss*) with Germany, with the argument that linguistic brothers belonged to the same political family. Even though they had been granted dominant status, unsatisfied Hungarian extremists demanded a separate state of their own. Vienna gave Croats a special grant of semi-autonomy, a decision which infuriated other nationalities.

Equally dissatisfied were the Slavs—Serbs and Czechs who felt bound to each other by linguistic affinity and who were angered by being forced into union with Germans and Magyars. They had hoped for a Triple Monarchy, an Austro-Hungarian-Slavic Empire, in which they would have equal rights and responsibilities. Instead, they were given inferior status in a state dominated by rival peoples. Emboldened by the rising Pan-Slavic movement, Slavs began calling loudly for autonomy. In the expected confrontation between Pan-Slavism and Pan-Germanism, the Slavs hoped to emerge with an independent state of their own.

It was just too much for the Hapsburgs. Francis Joseph and his associates never were able to find a solution for the vexing problem. A viable centralism seemed impossible in this maelstrom of bickering nationalities, each with its own territorial imperative. There were some regional leaders who saw economic sense in a union of this kind, but most others were attracted by the heady wines of either autonomy or independence. With the exception of courtiers in Vienna, few Europeans were surprised by the dissolution of the Dual Monarchy in 1919.

The Emergence of Yugoslavia

Inside the old Austro-Hungarian Empire, four peoples—Croats, Serbs, Slovenes, and Bosnians—spoke basically the same language.[3] With the growth of nationalism in the 19th century, all four peoples came to feel that they were one nation. By 1900 their sentiment was transformed into a political movement. It was obvious that the Hapsburg monarchy had no intention of granting them the equal status they wanted. Looking forward to eventual dissolution of the empire, they saw common interests with Slavs in "occupied" Bosnia and in independent Serbia across the border.

This Pan-Slavic agitation was one of the contributory causes of World War I. Irredentist Slavs finally saw partial fulfillment of their dreams. Out of the crucible of war came a new independent state, the Kingdom of the Serbs, Croats, and Slovenes (not until 1929 was the name officially changed to Yugoslavia). The new state was enlarged by the victor powers at the expense of defeated Austria and Hungary. The subsequent history of the new succession state of Yugoslavia reveals how a mini-nationalism won its way to success, only to be split eventually into warring factions.[4]

The confrontation began as early as 1920, when Serbs set up a centralized government and Croats immediately demanded autonomous rights. Croats and Slovenes, who had had limited rights under the old regime, saw no reason why that status should not be maintained. From that moment on, contending factions faced one another in hostility.

On August 16, 1921, Alexander, second son of Prince Peter Karageorgevich of Serbia, became the first monarch of the new country. His reign was unsteady. There were increasing demands from Croats under the leadership of Dr. Stephen Radić.[5] When the Croats set up a separate parliament in 1928, Alexander replied by turning to dictatorship. He dissolved the parliament and changed the name of the country to Yugoslavia. He was assassinated in 1934 by a Croatian nationalist.

Meanwhile, Croatian separatism was encouraged by Hungary and

Italy, both of which hoped to benefit by the factionalism. At this time, a Croatian nationalist organization called the *Ustachi* turned to terrorism to enforce its demands. In 1939, under the regency of Prince Paul,[6] Croats were granted limited autonomous rights. In March 1941, in the midst of World War II, Paul signed a pro-Axis pact, which led to his overthrow within two days. When the Germans invaded Yugoslavia the next month, the *Ustachi* seized power, issued a declaration of independence, and set up a dictatorship under Ante Pavelich, chief of the *Ustachi*. At that time Croatia came under Italian military control.[7]

Restive under Axis domination, many Yugoslavs joined the underground. At first the more important guerrilla force was composed of *chetniks,* led by the Serb Draja Mikhailovich. In 1942 another army of underground fighters was organized by a Croat, Josip Broz, supported by both the Soviet Union and Britain. Serbs and Croats fought not only against the Germans but also against each other. Josip Broz, called Tito, took part in this fierce infighting. In late November 1945 he established the Federal People's Republic of Yugoslavia. The Tito dictatorship immediately began to eliminate all opposition, including Mikhailovich, who was executed in 1946.[8] Tito managed to survive the wrath of Stalin and to maintain Yugoslavia's independence.[9]

Yugoslavia's Inner Tensions

Once in power, Tito gave highest priority to the maintenance of a viable federal system within a Socialist framework. It was not easy for him to solve his inherited problem of nationalities. Any attempt to accommodate one nationality was sure to be followed by outraged protests from others. One of Tito's greatest accomplishments was his success in forcing quarrelling nationalities into a single unit. With the Constitution of 1963, Yugoslavia became a federal republic comprising Serbia, Croatia, Slovenia, Bosnia-Herzegovina, Montenegro, and Macedonia. Administrative control was exercised by a Federal Executive Council, but power lay in the hands of Tito.

Tito's will to national unity was dominant, but there were strains in the multi-national structure. It was impossible to eliminate Slavic, Eastern, and Western imprints. In this regional melange, Croat nationalism remained the most militant dissenting force.

Croats form the second largest nationality in contemporary Yugoslavia.[10] Serbs make up approximately 42 percent of the population; Croats, 23 percent; Slovenes, just under 9 percent; and the rest is spread among various small groups. This intermixture resulted from the historical development of the Balkans. When the great Slavic influx into the area began in the 6th century, Serbs and Macedonians settled in the eastern region, Croats and Slovenes settled in the western part. Both considered themselves to be Slavs, but there rose between them a mutual antagonism which lasts to the present day.

There was no significant linguistic base for Serbo-Croatian differences. Both peoples spoke similar dialects; the only important variation was the Serbian use of the Eastern Cyrillic alphabet and the Croatian use of Western Roman letters. Rivalry between the two, however, was accompanied by strong religious differences. Serbs and Macedonians in the east came under the influence of the Byzantine Orthodox Church, while Croats and Slovenes turned to Roman Catholicism. These religious preferences, passionately felt, helped divide the two peoples.

Of considerable importance in Croatian nationalism was a driving sense of territorial imperative.[11] Hardy mountaineers of western Croatia, they were motivated by an ardent sense of independence and had never in their history willingly accepted a subservient status. Violence was always their answer to repression.

In consolidating his dictatorship, Tito had to take into account the diverse nationalities in his state.[12] "We have nurtured our sovereignty with the blood of our people, and no one is going to take it away from us."[13] He suppressed "bourgeois nationalism" by force. He never wavered from the task. His greatest achievement, he said, was "the unity we have attained." Tito managed to win public support at critical moments: on two occasions, just 20 years apart, when threatened by Stalin in 1948 and again by Brezhnev in 1968, the Yugoslav people rallied to support Tito against outside interference.

A Croat himself, Tito believed that his Croatian brothers, as well as all other nationalities, should subjugate their own aspirations in the interests of a higher nationalism. He was willing to grant a certain amount of decentralization in administration, industry, and agriculture, and allowed considerable local autonomy. But it was not enough.

High on the list of Tito's problems was the deep-rooted hostility between the Serbs and the Croats. When the Germans overran Yugoslavia in 1941, Croats, at that time ruled by a puppet regime, became Hitler's ally. Serbs and Croats began to kill one another in a deadly confrontation, and the bitter rivalry extended into the Tito era.

Relations between Serbs and Croats were exacerbated by economic differences. Croats were convinced that dominant Serbs treated them unfairly. They accused the government of using the economic bonanza from tourism (Croatia was a favorite vacation spot for western Europeans) to assist non-Croatian regions. They demanded a greater share of tourist revenues for themselves. At the same time, they objected to the governmental policy of expropriating hard German marks being sent home by thousands of Croats working in the Federal Republic of West

Germany. Moreover, they charged that while they provided a third to a half of Yugoslavia's exports, they were never rewarded for their industry.[14]

There are differing assessments about the separatists' claim that Croatia had been exploited systematically by the Tito Government.[15] Croatians insisted that they were victimized by economic exploitation. Many were convinced that an independent Croatia could achieve a Swedish standard of living within four years after independence. Here again, we see, as in many other mini-nationalisms, the close affinity between nationality and economic drives.

The Tenor of Croatian Separatism

Croatian dissenters included moderate intellectuals, emotional students, and hard-line extremists. Each had its own version of opposition, resistance, or conspiracy.

Croatian intellectuals organized the *Matica Hrvatka,* a cultural association centered in Zagreb. Its leaders worked to prepare an ideological base for the secessionist movement by accenting every aspect of Croatian culture. Like similar societies elsewhere, it supported research into the distant past, published books and pamphlets, and encouraged regional folkways, customs, and songs.

There was also a mounting tide of student alienation. Unresponsive to old revolutionary slogans, Croatian students denounced Tito's guerrilla comrades as fat and lazy parvenus attracted by a consumer society. They also criticized what they called the "sandwich generation"—those between 39 and 50—as flabby and hypocritical.[16]

The third group of dissenters went beyond cultural autonomy and called for outright independence. They would break away from the federal union and set up their own separate nation with its own foreign policy, membership in the United Nations, and even a Croatian national air line. They would fight the established regime with terror.

The extremist position, held by resistance forces inside Croatia and by Croats living in exile and scattered throughout the world, was highly critical of Tito's leadership.[17] It accused Tito of spending the first half of his life as a Comintern agent. It held him responsible for denouncing and betraying his colleagues of the Yugoslav Communist Party leadership, causing them to be liquidated. He was not chosen by Yugoslav Communists as their leader but was imposed by Stalin. He came to power, it was charged, to some extent through the Teheran agreement between the Great Powers and the entry in 1944 of the Red Army into Belgrade. Critics accused Tito of unleashing an unprecedented reign of terror in Yugoslavia in the postwar era. In 1948, fearing for his own position of power, they said, he turned against Stalin. The West welcomed Tito's opposition to the USSR as a means of undermining Soviet leadership of the Communist world. Opponents said that Tito managed to play the superpowers against one another and took as much as he could from both sides in order to bolster his economically bankrupt state.

Croat extremists denounced Tito as a mass murderer and listed "only a few" of his crimes against the Croat people:[18]

- In 1945 Tito ordered the massacre of 300,000 Croat soldiers together with many women and children.
- Tito's agents brutally murdered scores of Croat political exiles in Western countries—often unhindered by Western police forces.
- Tito persecuted religions, killing or imprisoning thousands of clergymen, including Cardinal Stepinac, who was kept in confinement until his death in 1960.
- Tito imprisoned and tortured thousands of Croat political prisoners in such terrible prisons as Stara Gradiska, Lepoglava, and Goli Otok.
- Tito's economic policies impoverished and exploited Croatia causing more than a million Croats to leave the country in search of a livelihood.
- In the 1960s Tito encouraged young Croatian idealists to set forth their demands for freedom, but in 1971 reversed himself and imprisoned thousands of intellectuals, students, and workers.

This denunciation of Tito and the litany of grievances was in the classic mold of propaganda for a cause, but it did explain the motivations behind the determination of Croatian separatists for independence. For militant Croats, Yugoslavia was an imperialist state set up by force, violence, and terror, and the only way to meet its repression was to strike back with equal violence and terror. They claimed they were waging a national liberation struggle for "a free, democratic, independent, and neutral Croatia." It was the familiar call of extreme dissidents everywhere.

Croatian Extremism Abroad

The intensity of dissent inside a centralized state usually varies with the nature of the society. In democratic countries, with their concern for free speech, dissenters, especially those moderates who want autonomy and not independence, are tolerated. In dictatorships, both moderate autonomists and extreme separatists are treated as traitors. Those who rebel against authority have a choice of prison, exile, or execution.

So it was with Yugoslav dissenters.[19] Endangered in their homeland, Croatian and Serbian nationalists stepped up their opposition abroad. Many left Yugoslavia and settled in sizable communities abroad, especially in the Federal Republic of West Germany, South America, and the United States. Some 100,000 Croatians were scattered in pockets in Chicago and Indiana. An equal number of Serbian exiles kept alive their own national aspirations.

The Croatian National Council, with its headquarters in Chicago, and the Croatian National Congress, with its offices in New York, carried on the "national liberation struggle against imperialist Yugoslavia." Similarly, the Serbian National Defense Council represented Serbs in exile. Both Croats and Serbs retained the political, cultural, and religious animosities that long had divided them, and both were united only in their contempt for Tito and the government ruling their homeland.[20] Both also denied any relations with their military wings and terror tactics. At times this hostility broke into violence. When the editor of a Serbian weekly newspaper and his 9-year-old daughter were murdered in Chicago in 1977, Serbs blamed local Croats, while the latter called it the macabre work of agents of the Yugoslav Government.[21]

Throughout the 1970s, militant Croats operated from Canada and Australia.[22] One group known as *Otpor* ("Resistance," in Croatian) was founded in Spain after World War II and operated throughout the world. It had an extraordinary record of violence ranging from bombing to hijacking to assassination. In 1971 Croatian activists assassinated the Yugoslav ambassador to Sweden. The killers were captured but were freed later when other Croatians hijacked an airliner and threatened to destroy it. The unpunished conspirators moved to Paraguay.[23] Emboldened by this success, a Croatian attempted to kill the Yugoslav ambassador to Paraguay, but mistakenly took the life of the Uruguayan ambassador. That same year Croatian terrorists were suspected of blowing up the main terminal at La Guardia Airport in New York City.[24]

In September 1976 Croatians of the *Otpor* group hijacked a Trans World Airline jet that had taken off from La Guardia Airport and ordered the pilot to fly successively to Canada, Iceland, England, and, finally, France before surrendering to authorities in Paris. While the hijacking was in progress, an unknown telephone caller directed the New York police to a locker in Grand Central Station, where they found a long statement accusing the Yugoslav Government of terrorism and genocide.[25]

In mid-June 1977 Croatian nationalists invaded the building housing the Yugoslav United Nations Mission in New York City, shot one person, and then threw leaflets out of the window.[26] Later that year the U.S. Federal Bureau of Investigation looked into the matter of several dozen extortion letters written in Croatian dialects and sent to people in Chicago, Cleveland, and San Francisco. Signed by "Coordinator of the Operation," the letters aimed to raise funds for Croatian separatist activities.[27]

The campaign was accelerated in 1978, when Stephan Bilandzic, founder and leader of Croatian People's Resistance, was arrested by West German police. Croatian militants reacted violently when a court in Cologne ordered that Bilandzic be extradited to Yugoslavia. To discourage the process of extradition, they took hostages in Chicago.[28] The following December, two Croatian separatists were convicted of taking over the German consulate in Chicago.[29]

Here, again, as in Ireland and Spain, moderate autonomists deplored the violence of the extremists, but at the same time, they tended to look upon guerrilla fighters as heroic liberators who were fighting for a sacred cause. Many among them admired and excused the hotheads who were regarded as fighting fire with fire.

The Muslim "Nation"

The nationality problem in Yugoslavia was not limited to the demands of Croats and Serbs. Far from being the union Tito wanted, the plurinational state was rather a conglomeration of six peoples, each with its own national sentiment, plus two autonomous regions (Voyvodina and Kosovo) and several other minorities, including Hungarians and Albanians. Even the small Albanian minority was preoccupied with its own "national identity."[30]

Added to this already complicated tangle was the proposal to establish a new Muslim "nation" in Yugoslavia. The republic of Bosnia-Herzegovina, in addition to its Serbs and Croats, was inhabited by a Muslim community which came into existence under Turkish rule. These Muslims created a mini-nationalism of their own.

For Belgrade authorities, Muslim nationalism was an unwanted phenomenon, dangerous and divisive. As Marxists, they wanted no coexistence with organized religions. They refused to recognize any legal distinction between Muslim nationality and the Islamic faith and insisted that this could not be allowed in a Communist society.

Behind the Muslim "nation" was a long religious tradition. For centuries, Bosnia-Herzegovina, with its capital at Sarajevo, had been the European outpost of the Ottoman Empire. In 1878 the Congress of Berlin placed Bosnia and Herzegovina under Austro-Hungarian administration and occupation, but the process of Germanization could not eliminate Turkish customs or the Islamic faith. Bosnian Muslims retained their regard for mosques, muezzin, and the Koran. Of the three major nationalities in the province, they formed the largest element of the population.[31]

The Bosnian Muslims provide a striking example of how a people can make a nationality out of a religion instead of out of ethnicity, political goals, or language. Situated in the very center of the multi-national Yugoslav state, they presented the Yugoslav authorities with a troublesome form of separatism—based, as it was, on strong religious sentiment.

Communist officials, already concerned about the Orthodox Church and Roman Catholicism, were reluctant to take too oppressive measures against Bosnian Muslims. They sensed that religious oppression was counterproductive. There were enough problems with Croatian and Serbian separatists without adding more strains. For the moment, they were satisfied that Muslim nationalism remained mute and dormant.

Yugoslavia's Dilemma

During the latter years of his rule, Tito, in order to reduce tensions, granted his disparate nationalities a measure of autonomy, including decentralized economic planning. For a time the concession worked. Energetic Yugoslavians had one of the best standards of living in western Europe. Busy Belgrade, with its new glass-and-aluminum office buildings and packed restaurants, contended daily with a heavy traffic jam. Shops teemed with consumer goods of Western quality—in contrast to those of the Soviet Union and its satellites. Money flowed into the country from tourists and from Yugoslavs working in prosperous western Europe.

In the late 1970s, however, the Yugoslav economy began to slump badly. After years of growth came widespread unemployment and declining productivity. Inflation hit the country with a rising rate each year. Each nationality considered itself to be hit especially hard by the economic slump. Governmental steps to alleviate the situation had little success.

For three and a half decades Tito had managed to force his varied peoples to live together, not always happily, in national unity. In his declining years, the aging dictator found it increasingly difficult to grant more concessions. Croatians continued to demand privileges far in excess of what he was willing to grant. Like leaders in the Kremlin faced with the same problem, Tito feared a domino effect leading to dissolution of his state. "Destructive separatism," he warned, "is a weapon for fascism that could tear us apart." He ordered his secret police to reply to terrorism with its own version of "instructive violence."[32]

In his last days, Tito pointed to a choice between recentralization or civil war. Opponents claimed that, on his death, the country of disparate nationalities would become ungovernable. The only solution for an impossible situation, they said, was a division of the country into its varied parts.

With his death, the iron hand of Tito disappeared. Yet, the problem of Yugoslav nationalities remained very much alive. As in conglomerate states throughout the world, mini-nationalisms refused to wither away in favor of a unity they condemned as artificial.

Diaspora Nationalism in Czechoslovakia

Yugoslavia was by no means the only Balkan state suffering the strains of separatism. Czechoslovakia, too, had its troubles with Magyars, who formed a dissenting unit in the hodgepodge of the Balkans.

A nomadic people, speaking a Finno-Ugric tongue, the Magyars migrated ca. 460 A.D. from the Ural Mountains to the region of the Northern Caucasus Mountains. Ferocious warriors mounted on swift horses, they penetrated deep into the Balkan peninsula, absorbing other peoples within Hungary proper. Eventually, the words "Magyar" and "Hungarian" came to be used interchangeably.

By the Treaty of Neuilly after World War I, three million Magyars were transferred from Hungary into three successor states— Czechoslovakia, Rumania, and Yugoslavia.[33] Some 700,000 became citizens of Slovakia, the eastern province of Czechoslovakia. Here, the Magyars, in a typical example of diaspora nationalism, created a zealous mini-nationalism of their own. They reacted like other unsatisfied minorities in a hostile environment by resisting assimilation into the ruling Slovak majority. Distributed in settlements in three countries adjacent to Hungary, they retained their language, customs, and traditions. They took on the status of a mini-nationalism in a multi-national society.

Opposed to absorption, the Magyars of Czechoslovakia were careful to retain their cultural autonomy. They created societies to preserve their language and prevent the intrusion of Slavic or Germanic tongues. They resisted the imposition of Slovak as a compulsory subject in Magyar schools. They demanded more books, newspapers, and literary gazettes in their own language and opposed restrictions placed on the Magyar press. Because there was no Magyar university, they established several cultural and scholarly organizations as substitutes.

Magyars in Czechoslovakia, like mini-nationalists elsewhere, complained of political and economic exploitation. Politically, they saw themselves as second-class citizens. They claimed that, in the process of industrialization, they had been relegated to agriculture. They charged that the central government had worsened the economic status of Magyars by settling Slovak peasants on former Magyar-owned estates. They received some accommodation in later years, but it was not enough to satisfy their demands.

The status of Magyars in Czechoslovakia reveals a persistent problem troubling Communist as well as capitalist states—how to satisfy the demands of minorities against the central government. The dominant Slovaks quoted Lenin as justification for their opposition to cultural self-determination for minorities. They insisted that, in a Marxist society, all antagonisms must be thrust aside, that nationalities must work on a class basis, and that minorities should eventually adapt to the cultural standards of the majority. This view, also held by the Kremlin, denounced as unacceptable bourgeois nationalism any attempt by a minority to hold on to its special character, preserve its own culture, or seek a separate status at the expense of national unity. Communist leaders boasted of their adherence to internationalism but, at the same time, held national centralism to be sacred and separatism to be a traitorous and insane dream.

Germans in Rumania

Problems of regionalism versus centralism existed throughout the Balkans, in the traditions of shifting boundaries and citizenship. Mini-nationalisms do not respect boundary lines; they may exist in countries with natural borders or in areas with historically flexible boundaries. The British are identified with an island, the Italians with a peninsula, the French and Spanish with relatively natural boundaries. In the Balkans, on the other hand, boundaries expanded alternately like bellows in reaction to war, colonization, purchase, exchange, and royal marriages. Where there were no natural frontiers, regionalism thrived in a chaos of geographical fragmentation.

From the heart of central Europe, Germans spilled over into France, Switzerland, Poland, Denmark, and the Balkans. From time to time, they settled in Rumania.[34] As early as the 13th century, Teutonic Crusaders settled in Transylvania; others later settled in the Banat region. Subsequently, these Germans developed their own separate cultural institutions and refused assimilation with Rumanians or Magyars.

Germans were distributed in six Rumanian regions—Transylvania, Banat, Sathmar, Bukovina, Bessarabia, and Dobrudja. In 1868 they lost their political privileges by the union between Rumania and Hungary.[35] Toward the end of the 19th century, the Germans in Rumania began to oppose the Hungarian policy of Magyarization in education and religion. In 1919, at the end of World War I, some 750,000 Germans in Rumania were incorporated into Greater Rumania, created after the ruin of the Austro-Hungarian and Russian Empires. At first they were granted the rights of self-government, education and courts in their own language, and representation in national legislative bodies in proportion to their numbers.

The Germans in Rumania, although forming a foreign conclave, remained loyal subjects for some time to whatever regime was in power. Both German-speaking Rumanians and other Rumanians had a common interest in opposing the policy of Magyarization. Each preferred the Hohenzollern dynasty to Hungarian rulers. Rumanian Germans, although separated from Germany, maintained close and cordial relations with the German Fatherland. At the same time, they were careful not to offend the central government by calling for separatism.

This situation changed with the advent of National Socialism. Dr. Paul Joseph Goebbels and his propaganda machine hammered away at the theme of *Volksdeutschtum*—Germans everywhere belonged to the Third Reich. Nazi ideology found adherents among young Rumanians. In the 1930s, a group organized by Fritz Fabrius and called the Movement for National Mutual Assistance of Germans in Rumania became an important political force in the German community.

For the Germans in Rumania, World War II was an ongoing tragedy. Their numbers were reduced from 750,000 to 500,000. After the invasion of Soviet troops in 1944, Marshal Ion Antonescu and the Iron Guard were overthrown, and Rumania switched to the Allied side. In 1945 a Communist government was set up, which, for the next two decades, was not especially favorable to the Kremlin. Politically, the German minority maintained its tradition of cooperation with the existing regime. In 1969 the Communist head of state, Nicolae Ceausescu, declared in a speech: "We have achieved complete equality of rights for all citizens of our country regardless of nationality, an excellent result of the Marxist-Leninist national policy of our people."[36] Exiled Rumanians living in West Germany ridiculed the assertion as ridiculous.

Yet, it is fair to say that the cause of German separatism in Rumania did not approach the intensity of that shown by Croats in Yugoslavia or Ukrainians in the Soviet Union. Though the older generation looked with nostalgia at the ties with the German Fatherland, younger Germans in Rumania seemed reluctant to opt for either autonomy or independence. While not altogether satisfied with their minority status, most Rumanians rejected violence or terror to win liberation, a freedom that might not turn out to be in their own interest. They preferred to remain advocates of a quiescent nationalism, sensitive to their own culture but unattracted by the heady wine of independence.

CHAPTER **10**

MINORITY NATIONALISMS IN
THE SOVIET UNION _____

We regard the Ukraine and other regions not inhabited by
Great Russians as territories annexed by the Czar and Great
Russians.
                              —Vladimir Ilyich Ulyanov Lenin

Nationalism and Communist Ideology

The multi-national Union of Soviet Socialist Republics is bound together
by bonds of steel. The Kremlin is not impressed by calls for human
rights or for demands by its minorities for independence. It sees any
attempt at separation, be it Ukrainian, Georgian, or Armenian, as
treason. It will not grant independence to any part of the union because
it fears that any concessions would result in an unwanted domino effect
leading to dissolution of the national state.

In Marxist eyes, nationalism is a disease of capitalism, an evil fostered,
nurtured, and promoted by bourgeois ideals. It is charged that
nationalism, by its very nature, makes for suppression of the proletariat
and that it ultimately leads to war. In the type of society envisioned by
Lenin, national differences and national loyalties were to give way to
Socialist unity, and there would be no need for the excesses of
nationalism. Satiated with the compounding inconsistencies of
capitalism, working men of the world would unite and overthrow their
class oppressors. Nationalism would then disappear in the solvent of
internationalism as surely as the feudal order vanished in the era of
rising nation-states.

Marxist theory thus sounded the death knell for bourgeois
nationalism. There is, however, a fatal flaw in that conception of society.
At the core of Marxist teaching is the "fact" that all human motivation
can be reduced to materialist causation. Unfortunately for Marxist intellectuals, the view of man as an economic animal has been disproved
regularly by eruptions of nationalisms, macro-nationalisms, and mini-

131

nationalisms, none of which is necessarily grounded in materialism and all of which have important psychological as well as economic motivations.

The trend of Russian history itself reveals the weakness of the Marxist analysis of nationalism. As early as 1918, British pacifist-mathematician-philosopher Bertrand Russell visited the fledgling Soviet state in search of his own proposed "roads to freedom." He came away convinced that "there is too much government there." Far from taking the lead in setting up the structure of a global international society, the Soviet state, Russell found, had turned to the road of nationalism.[1]

Subsequent developments confirmed Russell's judgment. In the confrontation between Trotsky (world-wide revolution) and Stalin (Russian nationalism), the latter was the victor. Trotsky paid with his life for his beliefs. Stalin made it plain that Russian proletarians must be loyal to the national state. Karl Marx, prophet of internationalism, would have regarded Stalin's decision for a neotribalistic community as grotesquely heretical and atavistic.

Stalin's successors hewed to the same basic line—that national interests transcended any vision of fraternity with Communist brethren throughout the world. Soviet ideology still retained the Marxist-Leninist vocabulary praising the glories of internationalism, but the reality was nationalism triumphant. It diluted its orthodox eschatology to justify the existence of Russian nationalism. For the Kremlin, global revolution took second place to necessary centralism.[2]

Nationalism, indeed, affected everything concerned with Russian social life. It was less a cohesive dogma than a set of attitudes, beliefs, and emotions ranging themselves in different patterns. Just as western Europe, after the French Revolution, applied nationalism to every phase of political, economic, social, and cultural life, so, too, did Soviet ideologists place nationalism at the core of the "New Society," while loudly proclaiming the supremacy of internationalism.

Nationalism in the Soviet Union appeared at two levels. The larger nationalism reflected the existence of a highly centralized state. The new nationalists, who called themselves the *Russity,* controlled all layers of Russian society, especially the military and the secret police. They regarded Jews, among others, with contempt[3] and opposed any efforts by any minorities to weaken the centralized structure.

Added to this larger nationalism were many mini-nationalisms, dissenting movements fired by visions of freedom. They resented the Russification policy inaugurated under the Czars and continued after the formation of the Soviet state. The unsatisfied mini-nationalisms represented a grave danger to the larger nationalism. The Kremlin was convinced that, once released, these latent nationalisms might have a devastating effect on the Soviet state and on society.

Russification in the Czarist Empire

The problem of national minorities was of much concern to Czarist authorities in the mid-19th century.[4] In early 1863 they suppressed armed rebellion in Polish areas by taking severe measures against dissidents. They also faced open resistance in the Ukrainian and Lithuanian borderlands. Despite suppression, the Poles managed to retain their language and sense of national consciousness.[5] Taking steps to counteract rising Ukrainian nationalism, the central government banned publications in the Ukrainian language. Across the border, several million Ukrainians who had settled in eastern Galicia made certain to maintain their literary traditions and continue their political activities.

In the last decade of the 19th century, the Czarist response to dissenting nationalities was to promote a policy of systematic Russification. Centralized authorities, supported by the Orthodox Church, a strongly nationalistic press, and a growing bureaucracy, hit hard at nationalities throughout the Empire. They banned the German language in favor of Russian in the Baltic provinces. They Russified secondary schools and universities throughout the country. They forced Lutherans to abandon their faith and accept Russian Orthodoxy.

This policy of Russification was extended even to the Muslim Tatars of the Volga Valley region. Here, the religious conflict was especially severe as authorities sought to convert Muslims to Christianity. For the Jews, Russification was a long era of martyrdom. Russian officialdom regarded them as radical Socialists, while the lower classes looked on them as oppressive capitalists. The government officially promoted pogroms as a means of diverting popular discontent.

There was some passive resistance to Russification: on occasion, it took what the government saw as a dangerous turn. Christians, Muslims, and Jews all resented interference in their affairs.[6] Armenians in the Caucasus, who had been friendly in the past, reacted angrily when Russian authorities closed schools that had been maintained by church funds. Efforts to Russify Finland led to the murder of the Russian governor-general in 1904. The Russification process was not popular.

Resistance by the nationalities and nationalist discontent were among the important factors leading to the fatal weakening of the old Russian Empire. The greater the efforts at centralism through Russification, the more resistant was the reaction. The problem of the nationalities was never resolved in the Czarist Empire. It carried over into the even more centralized Soviet Union.

Nationalities and Federalism

Immediately after the October Revolution of 1917, leaders of Bolshevik Russia had to contend with the continuing complex problem of the nationalities. Regionalists throughout the vast expanse of the country saw the revolution as an opportunity for freedom. In the north, Lithuanians, Latvians, and Estonians began to think in terms of liberation and the formation of their own national states. In the south, Ukrainians, Georgians, Armenians, and Azerbaijanis hoped for recognition of their national aspirations.

During the chaos of the post-revolutionary civil war, some nationalities were able to enjoy a short period of independence. This happy state of affairs for them ended abruptly with the triumph of the Red army over the White armies, the failure of the Allies to throttle the new regime, and the subsequent solidification of Communist control. At one time Lenin favored self-determination, but he dropped the idea when faced with the reality of forging a new society. The state he fashioned was a highly centralized republic. The first four members of the Union of Soviet Socialist Republics were the Russian Soviet Federated Socialist Republic, the Ukrainian Soviet Socialist Republic, the White Russian Soviet Socialist Republic, and the Transcaucasian Soviet Socialist Republic.[7] The name "Russia" was not used officially.

Lenin was well aware of nationalism and its concomitant problems for his new state. He was faced with the dilemma of how to offer a small measure of autonomy to the nationalities while at the same time holding them together in a higher union. The Constitution of 1924 provided for an expansible union with the provision that any member might secede.[8] None took advantage of that provision.

The special type of federalism was designed as a response to the problem of the nationalities. Lenin and his successors were acquainted with the history of the Austro-Hungarian Empire and its clamoring nationalities and of the dissolution of that conglomerate state in 1919. There were 117 different peoples and more than a hundred languages in the Soviet Union. The government granted 50 nationalities the privilege of using their own language, running their own schools, wearing their traditional dress, and pursuing their own cultural folkways. They could perform their own dances, sing their own songs, and collect their own folklore.[9]

To cultural concessions, Soviet authorities added certain political rights. They placed the nationalities into administrative categories based on size and importance: federated socialist republics; autonomous republics; autonomous regions; and national districts.[10] They made an effort to satisfy the nationalities by giving them a measure of self-respect and pride in their way of life. But in the matter of ultimate political power, they were adamant: it was reserved for Moscow, for the Communist Party apparatus, and for the dominant Slavic population.[11] They were not inclined to recognize the "political sovereignty" of each republic.[12] Not for them were the dangerous ideals of Jean-Jacques Rousseau or John Locke. They would grant strictly limited concessions, perhaps even semi-autonomy, but never the goal of independence.

Lenin sought diligently to heal the wounds through a moderate nationality policy, but he was never successful. Stalin replaced Lenin's efforts with a revived type of Russian nationalism, presented as Soviet universalism.

Ukrainian Nationalism

The separatist movement most feared by the Kremlin was in the Ukraine. One of the 15 constituent republics and one of the four founding republics, the Ukraine held a dominant place in the Soviet economy. It was the country's life-giving soil belt and chief wheat-producing area.[13] For Moscow, this was the vital heartland. Hence, its severe reaction against Ukrainian separatism and the continuing campaign to stamp it out.

Lying in the southwest of European Russia, the Ukraine, the third largest region in Europe, spreads over 233,100 square miles. Despite its size, it was still dwarfed by the total Soviet territory.

The history of the Ukraine is the story of a long, unending search for independence.[14] In ancient times, a major part of what is today the Ukraine was in contact economically and culturally with the Greek and Roman worlds. Early in the Christian era, one invader after another, including Goths, Huns, and Avars, moved into the Ukrainian steppes. It is not known when Slavs settled in the area, but by the 12th century, they had established a powerful state centered in Kiev. By the 13th century, the Kievan state was conquered by the Tatars (Golden Horde), after which the center of gravity of Russian history shifted westward. In the late 14th century, most of the Ukraine was conquered by Lithuanians, under whose rule the Ukrainians flourished. The territory became Polish in 1569. Persecution of the Ukrainian Orthodox Church led to violent opposition by Zaporogian Cossacks, who rose in rebellion in the 17th century and won their independence from the Poles.

Russians from the north then penetrated into the Ukraine and, by the 18th century, captured the Black Sea area from the Ottoman Turks. In the early 19th century, the Ukrainians became as much dissatisfied with Moscovite control as they had been with Polish domination. At this time, Ukrainians, including compatriots in the Austro-Hungarian Empire (Galicia, Bukovina, and Ruthenia), renewed agitation for national revival.

The Brotherhood of Cyril and Methodius, a secret political organization founded in Kiev, was the spearhead of the new Ukrainian nationalism. The Brotherhood called for a federation of Slavic states, including Ukrainians, which would be free of Moscow's domination. The most revered apostle of emergent Ukrainian nationalism was Taras Grigoryevich Shevchenko (1814–1861), poet, artist, and thinker, who won the accolade of "the Ukrainian Pushkin." Shevchenko's poems, using the rhythm of Ukrainian folk songs, called incessantly for Ukrainian liberation.[15] His poetry was filled with nationalistic fervor and compassion for Ukrainian victims of Czarist injustice. His *Free Cossacks* (1841) told the story of a Ukrainian uprising against Polish rule.

Shevchenko's nationalist poetry aroused the anger of Czarist authorities, who made certain to suppress both the popular poet and his subversive Brotherhood. In 1847 they sentenced him to compulsory military service and ordered him to the Urals as a private soldier. Czar Nicholas I was believed to have given orders banning the poet's activities. Though he was released by amnesty in 1857, Shevchenko never fully recovered his health and died in 1861 at the age of 47.

Ukrainian national consciousness, though still confined mostly to an educated elite, gathered momentum. From both inside the Ukraine and from exiles living in foreign countries there were increasing calls for independence.[16] By the end of the 19th century, the movement was drawing support from workers in the newly industrialized Ukraine. Intellectuals and laborers alike now saw their best prospects in a revolutionary situation.

The Provisional Government set up after the February 1917 Revolution granted Ukrainian autonomy and recognized the authority of the Ukrainian *Rada* ("council") over the central Ukraine. After the Bolshevik Revolution of October 1917, the *Rada* proclaimed independence of the Ukraine on January 22, 1918. As we have seen, Lenin, earlier in his career, had preached the desirability of recognizing the rights of national minorities and, at the same time, had denounced "Russian chauvinism."[17] Now, faced with the realities of political power, he changed his mind. There would be no separate identity for the Ukraine. After a complicated struggle,[18] Ukrainian independence was vetoed, and the territory was absorbed as one of the original constituent republics of the Soviet Union.

Ukrainian national consciousness survived. It was not smothered even by Stalinist terror. The dictator was determined to throttle any movement that might endanger national unity. His purge of the nationalities from 1936 to 1938 was even more harsh than that of the Czarist regime. He denounced Ukrainian separatists as traitors, as "bourgeois nationalist deviationists." He sent Nikita Khrushchev to the Ukraine with the special mission of purging its nationalist leadership.[19]

Neither Czarist *knout* nor the Stalinist bullet was sufficient to stamp out Ukrainian separatism. Ukrainians saw an opportunity for their cause during World War II, when on June 22, 1941, Hitler's mechanized forces moved into the Ukraine. At first the invading Germans were greeted as liberators. It was a golden opportunity for the *Fuehrer* to win support for his invasion, but unfortunately for him, he did not take advantage of it. In a key blunder, he treated the Ukrainians as if they were Slavic beasts. Faced with a choice between two dictators and certain that Hitler intended to enslave them, Ukainians returned reluctantly to the Russian union. Stalin welcomed Ukrainians back for the defense of Mother Russia in the Great Patriotic War.

After three years of German occupation (1941–1944), with its accompanying devastation, the Ukrainians were again brought under Soviet rule. With reborn centralism came a revived movement for national independence.[20] For several years, a Ukrainian Insurgent Army (UPA) operated from the Carpathian Mountains in a large-scale guerrilla campaign against Moscow. The movement for independence gathered strength both inside and outside the Ukraine.[21]

After the death of the dictator in 1953 and the subsequent era of de-Stalinization, Ukrainian separatism was promoted even more vigorously. Intellectuals felt free to devote more attention to their historic and national identity. In the 1960s the *shestydesyatnyky*, the new generation of Ukrainian intellectuals, began to express the national theme with increasing vigor. They revived the poetry of Shevchenko and spoke passionately of freedom. They denounced Moscow's polycentrism as infringing on the rights of Ukrainians. There were accented themes:

1. The Ukraine was deprived illegally of its sovereignty and its people were denied the right of entering into political and economic relations with other states.
2. Ukrainian political and economic rights were harshly limited.
3. The Ukrainian language was banned in government agencies, scholarly institutions, lower schools, industry, and in the social and cultural life of the nation.
4. The Ukraine was being stifled economically by the removal of two-thirds of its natural resources to beyond its frontiers.
5. "Great Power Russian chauvinism" weighs heavily over the entire Ukrainian people.

Soviet authorities reacted severely to these serious charges. The secret police began a manhunt to find those "dedicated to the overthrow of the Soviet national state." They organized two major waves of arrest in 1961 and in 1965. In 1961 their target was the Ukrainian Union of Workers and Peasants, many of whose members were arrested and sent to camps in the Moldavian Republic. In 1965-1966 they took into custody a hundred Ukrainian separatists, of whom 20 were tried in secret for "disseminating anti-Soviet propaganda and agitation" and sent to labor camps under sentences of up to seven years.

Vyacheslav Chornovik, a young Ukrainian journalist, revealed details of these arrests and trials in *The Chornovik Papers.* His account of inhuman practices by Soviet secret police and of illegal activities by the judicial authorities aroused the anger of Ukrainian intellectuals in the West.[22] Emigré circles throughout the world protested bitterly against violations of "Socialist legality" inside the Ukraine.

Ukrainian separatists were emboldened in 1967 by a letter sent to the Fourth Congress of Soviet Writers by Aleksandr Solzhenitsyn, in which the exiled poet and novelist condemned the oppression of Ukrainians and added that censorship of their literature was no longer tolerable.[23] In his major work, *Gulag Archipelago,* published in 1976, Solzhenitsyn also denounced "the principles concerning our relations with the Ukraine."[24]

The Kremlin's suppression of what it called "this ugly strain of nationalism" continued throughout the 1970s. In 1972 it dismissed Pyotr Y. Shelet as Ukrainian Party chief because he had been too permissive in countering the growing spirit of nationalism in the republic. Shelet's successor, Vladimir V. Scherbitsky, more amenable to Moscow, excoriated the Ukrainian press for its "low ideological level, its priority of local interests, and its national narrow-mindedness and conceit." It was impermissible to oppose Moscow's centralism.

The subsequent experiences of Valentin Moros, a central figure in *The Chornovik Papers,* showed the seriousness with which the Soviet authorities took Ukrainian separatism. After his arrest and trial in 1965, Moros was sent to a camp with other Ukrainian dissidents. Released at the end of 1969, he was taken into custody again in 1970 and sentenced to six years' imprisonment to be followed by an additional three years of "strict regime" and, after that, five years of internal exile. He refused medical treatment although he was suffering from a liver complaint as well as from wounds inflicted by fellow prisoners. At his trial he delivered a fiery statement in which he refused to compromise his views.[25]

The confrontation continued with ill will on both sides. Ukrainian nationalists insisted that secession was their right guaranteed by the 1936 Soviet Constitution as well as by the 1975 Declaration of Human Rights signed by the Soviet Union in Helsinki. "If you forget what is yours," said a Ukrainian nationalist, "God will not forgive." To such views the Kremlin replied with harsh suppression of "unacceptable deviationism." There seems to be little ground for conciliation[26] between rigid Soviet centralism and fervent Ukrainian separatism.

Fires of Independence in Soviet Georgia

Soviet dictator Joseph Stalin was born in the provincial Georgian town of Gori, but once in power, he had little patience for Georgian separatism. Once he had consolidated his dictatorship, he opted for socialism in one country, a strongly centralized union, and pitiless extermination of deviationists.[27] Although he spoke Russian with a Georgian accent, he dismissed the idea of Georgian independence as grotesque nonsense. The words "autonomy" and "independence" were not in his vocabulary.

Situated on the southern slopes of the Greater Caucasus and the Lesser Caucasus around the mountainous tip of the Black Sea, Georgia had its own language, historical traditions, and long-standing Christian community. The Georgian language was developed in pre-Christian antiquity. Among its many dialects were West Georgian and East Georgian. Scholars have attempted, without much success, to relate Georgian to either Semitic, Indo-European, or Basque tongues. Georgian literature began with the conversion of Georgians to Christianity in the 4th century and the subsequent translation of the Scriptures into the vernacular. Georgia's distinctive culture was a combination of Byzantine, Greek, and Persian elements, as well as Caucasian folklore. Many monuments and buildings, including monasteries and churches, gave evidence of a long traditional culture.

The history of Georgia, like that of the Ukraine, is a story of recurrent invasions, leading eventually to Czarist colonialism and Soviet centralism.[28] Here, we can detect the same pattern existing in the background of other mini-nationalisms—a long tradition of opposition to successive overlords. Persians who ruled the country in the 3rd century A.D. left their imprint on Georgian culture, but they were expelled in the early 4th century. After a period of Armenian control, Georgians succeeded in re-establishing their independence. There was a flowering of Georgian culture in the 12th and 13th centuries. Out of this era came Shota Rustaveli's great epic poem, *The Knight in the Tiger Skin*, which, to this day, Georgians regard as an expression of their special national genius.

In the 13th century, Georgia was ravaged by Mongols. There was a period of decline from the 16th to the 18th century, during which the area became an object of contention between Turks and Persians. In 1783, caught between these two warring factions, Georgians accepted vassalage to Russia. After the Russian Revolutions of 1917, the Georgian Menshevik Party proclaimed Georgia's independence in May 1918, which was recognized by Moscow in May 1920. That status did not last long: in 1921 Red troops invaded and occupied the province; in 1936 it was made a separate republic in the Soviet Union.

Despite this history of successive invasions, Georgians, like other peoples with a sense of national consciousness, retained their preference for cohesion. Georgian intellectuals probed deeply into their past to find the roots of their heritage, a typical activity of mini-nationalists everywhere. Angered by Stalin's policy of strict Russification, they sought ways of expressing their discontent. Aware of the dangers of opposing the Soviet dictatorship, they used subtle means of indicating their national sentiment. They saw to it that busts at the University of Tbilisi were mostly of Georgian poets and painters, rarely of Lenin. It was an oblique way of giving notice that they had no intention of relinquishing their own culture in an era of Russian dominance.

The Kremlin was concerned especially by the survival of Menshevist sentiment in Georgia.[29] It considered Menshevism to be as dangerous as Trotskyism or deviationism of any kind. Vestiges of Menshevism in Georgia provided a clear and present danger for Soviet authorities. It was not to be tolerated. In mid-May 1972 Moscow struck at the Menshevik heresy in Georgia. Opportunity came with the publication of what was regarded as a seditious book written by Ushangi I. Sidamonidze and sponsored by the Georgia Institute of History, Archaeology, and Ethnography. It was titled *Historiography of the Bourgeois-Democratic Movement and the Victory of the Socialist Revolution in Georgia, 1877–1921.* Despite the imposing title, the Kremlin was not pleased. From its point of view, the author had made far too much use of Menshevik rather than Bolshevik sources. This kind of scholarship was not to be tolerated.

Soviet authorities condemned the author, the house editor who had allowed the manuscript to go through to publication, and the academicians who had endorsed it. They accused the author of "objectivism," a dirty word in the Soviet vocabulary. He had presented heretical Menshevik views without the kind of examination expected of orthodox Communist historians. (Parenthetically, professional historians at international meetings are much amused by what Soviet historians regard as "objective history.") Soviet authorities ordered Sidamonidze to recant his political errors. When he submitted, he was allowed to retain his Party membership, a concession of sensational importance.

In November 1976 the Central Committee of the Georgian Communist Party, on orders from Moscow, issued a decree designed "to intensify the struggle against harmful tradition and customs." The measure banned Georgian religious festivals, the celebration of name days for various saints, animal sacrifices during religious ceremonies, blood feuds and vendettas, arranged marriages, and extravagant wedding and funeral feasts. It denounced especially the excessive drinking for which Georgians were known throughout the Soviet Union.[30]

The issue remained unsolved. Georgians, like other Soviet nationalities, resented the power of the Kremlin's centralism but could do little about it. In recent years, their dissent has been muted, and few militants dared risk the wrath of Moscow. On its part, the Politburo saw Georgian separatists as dangerous non-persons with twisted minds. Guardians of the larger Soviet nationalism did not intend to ease the way for dissolution of the USSR. They would grant neither autonomy nor independence to "traitors."

Armenians against Russification

The spirit of Armenian independence survived centuries of conquest by Assyrians, Macedonians, Persians, Arabs, Mongols, Turks, and Russians. None of these powerful peoples succeeded in stifling the Armenian sense of independence. Like Georgians, Armenians had their own language, literary and cultural traditions, a deep-rooted attachment to Christianity, and a feeling of national identity. Like other nationalities in the Soviet Union, they resented the process of Russification and the effort to hold them under centralized control.

Historically, the land of the Armenians stretched from the Black Sea to the Caspian Sea, from the Mediterranean Sea to what is today Iran. For more than 5,000 years, this area was a strategic crossroad as well as the scene of war, conquest, dismemberment, and political fragmentation.[31] Mini-nationalisms eventually thrive in such areas. What remained of this large territory shrank to 11,000 square miles in South Transcaucasia as a constitutent republic of the USSR. Armenians survived decimation, despoliation, and transplantation.

In 519 B.C. Armenians were conquered by Persians, who regarded them as a backward people. In 334 B.C. they were absorbed by Alexander the Great in his burgeoning empire. By the 2nd century B.C., they had emerged as one of the most powerful people in the Middle East. Armenian merchants controlled a rich trade between the Mediterranean region and India and China. They fell, however, to Roman domination.

The conversion of Armenians to Christianity in 301 A.D. was the supreme event of their history. In the mid-7th century, their ties to Byzantium were broken by a *jihad*, a holy war, but they managed to regain their independence in 886 A.D. In the 11th century, their country was occupied successively by Seljuk Turks and Mongols, and in the 12th century by Persians and Turks. Armenians resisted Mongol-Tatar onslaughts in the 13th and 14th centuries. They were divided again among Persians and Turks in the 16th century.

Armenians came under Ottoman rule in the 19th century. They could not be shielded altogether from the century's currents of nationalism, liberalism, and democracy. The new Armenian bourgeoisie took advantage of the Industrial Revolution to better their position under Turkish domination. They adhered rigidly to their old Christian traditions. Because they were dependent upon Turkish authorities for economic prosperity, they moved only slowly in the direction of separatism.

A people with this history could not be satisfied with Ottoman domination. Armenian philosophers, poets, artists, teachers, and musicians called attention to the glories of their ancient past.[32] Despite long Muslim control, they continued to accent their Christian ethics. Armenian peasants, with their own folk songs and dances, joined city intellectuals, petty bourgeoisie, and wealthy businessmen in calling for autonomy.

The intensification of Armenian nationalism coincided with efforts of various Balkan peoples to break away from Ottoman control. Sultan Abdul Hamid II saw such efforts as treasonable. In the first half of his reign, he allowed his soldiers to burn and loot the Armenian quarter of Constantinople. Starting in 1894 and continuing for two years, a series of Armenian massacres aroused global attention. More than 200,000 were slaughtered in this tragic blood bath. Armenian militants desperately turned to violence in a vain hope to stem the killings. For a time they expected help from the Young Turk reformers, but they were disappointed. Eventually, the Great Powers, including the United States, intervened to stop the slaughter.

During World War I and the immediate postwar years, there was another period of Armenian martyrdom under Turkish rule. Those who spoke up for the Allied cause were suppressed mercilessly; others deserted to the invading Russians. Outraged Turkish authorities eliminated tens of thousands of Armenians by starvation or massacre. Many were deported to the deserts of Syria, where they perished. Others fled to Russia or emigrated elsewhere.[33]

After 1919 the Allies proposed to establish an independent Armenia, along with the new Polish and Czechoslovakian states. Their promises, however, were never implemented. In November 1920 President Woodrow Wilson ordered his aides to draw up definitive borders for Armenia. By this time, the Turks, who had recovered their strength, were able successfully to resist the formation of an independent Armenia on what they regarded as their own sacred soil.

Meanwhile, Armenians drifted into the Soviet sphere of influence. In October 1917 the victorious Bolsheviks declared Armenia to be a part of the Transcaucasian Federation. On December 20, 1920, Armenian Communists proclaimed a new Soviet republic. The Kremlin smothered a subsequent revolt in February 1920. In 1936 Armenia became one of the 15 constituent republics of the USSR.

It seemed at first that Armenians were more reconciled to Soviet than to Turkish rule. The process of Russification, however, was not successful in eliminating the old traditions of dissent. Armenians preferred their own language to Russian. Families discouraged intermarriage with Russians. Armenians used subtle ways to express their sense of national identity. On May 9, 1977, the holiday celebrating the victory of the Soviet Union over the Germans 32 years earlier, Armenians in the capital city of Yerevan displayed their own flag—a gold hammer and sickle split by a blue stripe—in preference to the national Soviet flag—a red background with hammer, sickle, and star.[34] The famous Armenian Dance Ensemble performed its own national dramas in Victory Park, Yerevan, before a 170-foot statue of Mother Armenia. Dancers faced the 17,000-foot snow-capped peak of Mount Ararat, an Armenian symbol lost to Turkey but never forgotten.[35] Retaining their Christian belief in a state now devoted to atheism, Armenians held to their Christian beliefs, crowding 35 churches and baptizing their infants.

Although Armenian nationalism is dedicated to the task of re-establishing an independent Armenia in a homeland spreading across the borders of both the Soviet Union and Turkey, the current war is directed more against Ottoman Turks than against the Kremlin. Armenian nationalists have never forgotten the slaughter of a million Christian Armenians in 1915 by the Ottoman Turks. They see it as a new "Hundred Years' War." In recent years Armenian terrorists took world-wide revenge against Turks for the late 19-century genocidal slaughter. They gunned down the Turkish vice consul in Los Angeles in 1973; killed the Turkish Ambassador in Austria in 1975; assassinated the Turkish envoy to France two days later; and in 1979, shot and killed the son of the Turkish Ambassador to The Netherlands. Armenian terrorists were desperate enough to make the Turks suffer for the sins of their ancestors. The Armenian Secret Army claimed some 136 terrorist attacks against Turks from 1975 to 1981.

In contrast, dissenting Armenians inside the Soviet Union remained quiescent. For the moment, they were inclined to accept their overlapping identity. The Kremlin, always worried by its dangerous mini-nationalisms, kept a close watch on Armenian separatists.

Grass-Roots Nationalism in the Baltic States

Estonians, linguistically related to the Finns, settled in their land before the Christian era. Northern Estonia was conquered by Danes in the 13th century; the southern part, by Livonian Knights. The north passed successively to Sweden in 1629, to Poland in 1629, and to Russia in 1710, under Peter the Great. Moscow's suzerainty was broken only between 1918 and 1940, when Estonia was incorporated into the USSR as a constituent republic.[36]

The history of Latvia followed similar lines. Livonian Knights conquered and Christianized the country in the 13th century. Portions passed to Polish suzerainty in 1561, to Sweden in 1629, and to Russia in 1721. In the 18th century, Latvia was dominated by German merchants who were settled there by the Hanseatic League and by German landlords. German Baltic barons maintained their control over Latvia until 1885, when the German language was replaced by Russian. In the closing years of World War I, Latvian patriots expelled both German volunteer bands and Red troops. Peace with the Soviet Union was concluded in 1920. Latvian independence, however, was ended in 1940, when the country was incorporated into the Soviet Union.

Lithuanians also fell under control of Livonian Knights and Teutonic Knights in the 13th century. Establishing a strong national state, they added to their territory by raiding their neighbors. Lithuania was one of the largest medieval states, incorporating in its borders sections of Byelorussia, the Ukraine, and Great Russia. Christianity was introduced in the late 14th century, and Lithuania became strongly Catholic. It was merged with Poland in 1569. In the three successive partitions of Poland (1772, 1791, and 1799), Lithuania passed to Russian control. In February 1918 it became an independent kingdom under German protection. Occupied by the Russians in 1940, it was absorbed into the USSR as a constituent republic.

All three Baltic states, which had returned only reluctantly to Russian domination, reacted adversely to Moscow's efforts at Russification. The Kremlin sought to allay discontent by offering minor economic privileges not granted to other minorities, but it was not able to divert the Baltic peoples from their ancient demands. They remained stubbornly separatist, thorns in the side of the Russian bear.

The pattern in the Baltic states was much the same as that in other Soviet mini-nationalisms: intellectuals called for regeneration of their own language and literature; historians dwelled on the traditions of a common past; Baltic Christians denounced Marxist atheism; and peasants held to their customs and folklore. Resistance often passed the boundary line of moderate dissent. In Lithuania, where the spirit of separatism was strongest, even a minor event such as a soccer game could set off a riotous reaction.[37] There were more underground newspapers (samzidat) in Lithuania than in any other Soviet republic.[38] There remained a residue of sullen discontent throughout the Baltic states.

The Kremlin's Predicament

These and other mini-nationalisms[39] were viewed with much alarm in Moscow. The Kremlin had failed to eliminate anti-Russian sentiment in its nationalities, a situation affecting its ambition to draw all nationalities into a single mold. From its early days, the Soviet Union faced the over-whelming task of preserving its centralism. It had hoped to eliminate regional particularism and create a united people in a highly centralized state. It had assigned a large proportion of its national budget for military power to guard against internal dissent.

To meet the challenge of its mini-nationalisms, the Kremlin was will-ing to grant a minimum of autonomy. Its moderation, however, van-ished immediately at that point where local mini-nationalisms appeared to challenge the cause of national unity. It would not tolerate what it called "political deviationism." It equated dissent with mental deficiency—what individual in his right mind would challenge the glori-ous unity of the Soviet Union? In late October 1980, police in Kiev ar-rested an elderly Ukrainian nationalist and sent her to a mental hospital. For the Kremlin, a psychiatric hospital was the only place for such dis-senters.[40]

Despite its superpower status, the Soviet Union faced serious prob-lems. Added to the entanglement in Afghanistan, which began in 1980, were endangered relations with her satellites, including the critical im-position of martial law in Poland in late December 1981. Her economic growth declined steadily as defense costs rose dramatically. Soviet agri-culture was unable to meet the needs of the people, who were troubled by the lack of food and consumer goods.

Above all, the Communist system was being challenged by a crisis in ideology. Original Marxist egalitarianism disappeared when Lenin turned to one-party totalitarianism. According to the London *Economist*, Marxism-Leninism has lost its gleam as a revolutionary force. It might still be a useful rationalization for seizing power in the name of the future, but even in those terms it now looks less attractive than did the old appeal of nationalism.[41]

The Kremlin is faced with the same troubles of capitalist states—the familiar clash between a unifying nationalism and disruptive mini-nationalisms, between centralism and regionalism. At the present time, the urge for separation may be relatively quiescent, but underneath, there is a deep well of unsatisfied ambitions that may well erupt as internal and external problems multiply. The Kremlin may be threatened by increasing centrifugal pressures inside its own borders. Zbigniew Brzezinski observed that the nationality problem in the Soviet Union has become politically more important than has the racial issue in the United States.[42] There could be a similar conclusion inside the walls of the Kremlin.

CHAPTER 11

IRAN AND IRAQ _____

You know how the Jews of Russia feel now. That is how I
feel—like a slave.
               —Mustafa Barzani, Kurdish rebel leader

Nationalities in Revolt

For unsatisfied mini-nationalisms, a revolutionary situation or a war
means opportunity. When the centralized state—the enemy—is faced
with revolution or war, liberators see a possibility for fulfillment of their
dreams. Instead of begging for autonomy, they point to a newly opened
road to independence.

Iran, formerly Persia, furnishes a prime example of a centralized state
in political chaos. With an area in the Middle East of 686,363 square
miles and a population of 37,430,000 (Government estimate 1979), Iran
lies between the Caspian Sea on the north and the Persian Gulf on the
south. It shares frontiers with the Soviet Union, Turkey, Iraq, Pakistan,
and Afghanistan.

Iran houses a hodgepodge of disparate elements, virtually every one
of which wants independence. Though its base is Persian, its population
is not homogeneous. At its core are 14 to 16 million Persians, inheritors
of an ancient civilization. Living in the central and eastern parts of the
country, they are surrounded by a conglomeration of variegated tribal
minorities. Moving clockwise from the north, these are:

Turkomans. Descendents of Mongols, some 10 million Turkomans live
in the northeast near the Caspian Sea. They adhere to the Sunni branch
of Islam rather than to the majority Shi'ite sect.
Baluchis. The major tribal group in the southeast corner of the country, 2 million Baluchis spread over into Pakistan and Afghanistan. Originally from the area near the Caspian Sea, they are tough warriors related to the Kurds.
Quasqais. An indigenous tribal group numbering about half a million,
they live on the eastern shore of the Persian Gulf. Speaking a dialect
related to Turkish, they have long been a threat to Iran's central government.

147

Arabs. Just to the north of the Quasqais are the culturally distinct Arabs, who control the oil-field city of Ahwaz and the port of Khorram-shahr on the north side of the Persian Gulf.

Bakthiaris. A tribal group of sheep-herding nomads living in the Sag-ros Mountains, many Bakthiaris work in the oil fields.

Lurs. Although related to the Bakthiaris, the Lurs speak a different dialect but agree on the necessity for autonomy.

Kurds. Several million Kurds, the most active large group, are settled in the Zagros Mountains in the west and are deeply committed to the cause of separatism.

Azerbaijanis. Originating in Turkey and settled on the northwest frontier with their central city at Tabriz, 5 million Azerbaijanis speak a language related to Turkish. Many of their compatriots live across the Soviet border.

All these nationalities had their own heritages, and all were affected by an upsurge in national feeling. Added to powerful tribal loyalties were religious differences. The dominant religion was Islam, but there were minorities of Zoroastrians, Christians, and Jews. The central authority found it almost impossible to control these varied nationalities and religions.

The problem was complicated by Iranian nationalities spilling over into neighboring countries. The Baluchis of Iran and neighboring Pakistan and Afghanistan, like the Spanish and the French Basques, had a sense of common destiny. Similarly, the Azerbaijanis felt attached to their comrades across the Iranian-Soviet border. These interlocking relationships stimulated the cause of separatism.

The Historical Continuum

Iran has a long and rich history,[1] replete with invasion, conquest, and assimilation—the familiar pattern behind the mini-nationalisms. Its central location in the Middle East made it a crossroads of migration. Village life began in the Caspian littoral and central Iranian plateau as early as 4000 B.C. This was the home of such religions as Zoroastrianism, Mithraism, and Manicheanism, with a later swing to Islam.[2]

Aryans, an Indo-European people related to the people of India, arrived in the Middle East about 2000 B.C. and divided into Medes and Persians. After periods of Assyrian, Median, and Achaemenian rule, Medes and Persians were united by Cyrus, who, in 550 B.C., set up a huge empire reaching from the Indus to the Nile. To Persians, Cyrus was always the father of his people; Xenophon made him the hero of a special treatise. Darius I conquered Thrace and subdued Macedonia but failed in two expeditions against the Athenians ending in the Battle of Marathon in 490 B.C.

Persia was subsequently ruled by Seleucids, Parthians, and Sassanians and then fell to Arab conquest in the 7th century. After several invasions by Mongols, order was restored by the Safavid dynasty from 1502 to 1736. There were frequent wars with the Turks over religious differences. Iran then began steadily losing territory to neighboring countries and to Europeans, especially to the Russians. In the early 19th century, she was forced to relinquish much of the Caucasus to the Russians.

The discovery of oil in 1901 intensified rivalry between the British and the Russians, both of whom were attracted by valuable oil deposits. In 1907 the country was divided into two spheres of influence between the British and the Russians. In World War I, Iran was neutral but was occupied by both the British and the Russians. In 1918 the agreement of 1907 was annulled, and Iran was admitted to the United Nations as a sovereign state. The USSR renounced its claims on Iran in 1921 and withdrew its forces from the country. That same year Reza Khan, an army officer, led a military coup and set up a military dictatorship and a new Pahlavi dynasty.

Iran again drew the attention of major powers in World War II. On August 25, 1941, two months after the German invasion of the Soviet Union, British and Soviet forces occupied Iran. On September 16, 1941, the pro-German Shah abdicated in favor of his son Mohammed Reza Pahlavi. At the Teheran Conference in 1943, the Soviet Union guaranteed the territorial integrity of Iran. The Kremlin, however, was dissatisfied with the extent of its oil concessions there. Fomenting a revolt, it helped establish the People's Republic of Azerbaijan and the Kurdish People's Republic. After Iranian protests to the United Nations, the Russians withdrew from Iran.

Mohammed Reza Pahlavi operated under Allied occupation, which lasted until 1945. During the next eight years, Iranian society witnessed various forms of nationalist movements calling for linguistic autonomy and self-determination. There were demonstrations and strikes throughout the country against the exploitation of Iran's raw materials. Early in the 1950s, Mohammed Mossadegh, the Iranian Prime Minister, nationalized oil ownership. Western European countries and the United States countered by boycotting the sale of Iranian oil. The Shah and his Queen, fearing for their lives, escaped from their country.

In August 1953, Mossadegh's government was overthrown, and the Shah and his family returned to the throne.[3] With the monarch's return, the SAVAK, the secret police, was organized to deal with opposition.[4] The Shah claimed that he was working for the Westernization of his country and that he had to be protected against those who would hinder

the process.[5] In 1979 he was overthrown. The Ayatollah Ruhollah Khomeini, a revered religious leader, returned from his exile in Paris to set
up an Islamic regime. The country soon fell into political chaos. Khomeini demanded that the cancer-stricken Shah be returned to Iran to
face charges of terrorism and embezzlement of national funds. The
religious leader blamed the "satanic United States" for Iran's compounding troubles.

In the ensuing confusion, Iran's nationalities saw a perfect opportunity. They would take advantage of the chaotic situation to win their
long-awaited independence.

The Kurdish Experience

One characteristic of nationalism is that it has many faces.[6] People without a territorial base may well have a sense of national consciousness.
That sentiment can flare up among peoples who inhabit either large or
small regions in a unified state. In some cases, it can be expressed by
those who have progressively lost parts of their territory and have been
forced to settle on a fraction of their former land.

Such is the case of the Kurds, a fiercely independent-minded people
whose ancient homeland, which they call Kurdistan, is now divided
among Iran, Iraq, Turkey, and Syria. Again and again they have rebelled against dominating masters, but they have never been able to win
complete freedom. It is the familiar story recapitulated at trouble spots
throughout the world.

Kurdish aspirations, similar to those of mini-nationalisms elsewhere,
were based on both territorial and human factors. Kurds claimed exclusive right to ownership and control of their special share of the world's
surface because they believed themselves to be a distinct people with
common characteristics—the essence of nationalism. Unfortunately for
them, the wheel of history left them in a status of subjugation, a situation
they refused to accept as final.

Contemporary Kurdistan (Persian, *Kordestan*—Land of the Kurds), occupied more or less continuously by Kurds and claimed as their own, is
an extensive plateau and mountainous region with 10,000-foot summits
in the heart of the Middle East.[7] Covering an area of about 74,000
square miles, it stretches north and south about 450 miles from Mount
Ararat to a tributary of the Tigris River and approximately 375 miles
east and west. The area straddles the frontier between the old Persian
and Ottoman Empires. The exact boundaries cannot be defined and do
not coincide with any internationally recognized frontiers.

This large area, plagued by bitter winters, was inhabited by 7 million
Kurds[8] distributed over eastern Turkey (where they were called
"mountain Turks"),[9] Iran, and Iraq, with small enclaves in the eastern

extremity of Syria and in Soviet Transcaucasus (Armenian SSR). Their economy was dominantly pastoral and agricultural. During the summer, they traditionally migrated from the lowlands with their herds of cattle, sheep, and goats to the mountain pastures of the highlands. Others lived on farms and in villages as settled agriculturalists. They were organized along tribal lines and owed allegiance to either chiefs (*agas*), landlords, or dervish sheiks.

Kurds were generally tall, with aquiline features, fair skin, and blue eyes, which they attributed to their Aryan ancestry. A stiff-necked, freedom-loving people, they often rebelled against any authority they did not recognize. Like Croats, Basques, and Corsicans, they had a reputation for violent behavior in their drive for self-determination.

Kurdish was an Indo-European tongue belonging to and resembling the northwestern division of Aryan languages but distinct from southern Persian. There were several mutually unintelligible Kurdish dialects, divided into southeastern and western groups, attributable in part to the mountainous nature of the land and to the difficulties of communication. Most Kurdish dialects probably were derived from a basic language such as Median. Kurds also spoke the language of the country in which they lived.

The majority of Kurds were devoted Sunnite Muslims, unlike most Iranians, who were Shi'ites.[10] Over the centuries they fashioned their own special culture. They liked to quote from their national epic, *Mem u Zim*, a kind of Kurdish *Romeo and Juliet*, composed by Ahmad-e Khan Botan (1650–1706). They were devoted to the patriotic poetry of Haii Qadir of Koi (1815–1892), who urged independent-minded local chiefs to cease their divisive feuds and unite in Kurdish grandeur.[11] Kurdish culture was accented in newspapers, journals, literary groups, and patriotic societies, all of which claimed that Kurdistan had been partitioned unjustly and kept in subjugation by usurpers.

Kurdish resistance had its roots in Kurdish history.[12] Much of it dissolved into legend, but Sumerian records tell of a people called Gūtū, or Kūti, who held the middle Tigris region between 2400 and 2300 B.C. Unwilling to submit to a dominating empire for long, they outlived conquests by Sumerians, Hittites, Assyrians,[13] and Persians. They were Aryanized under both Cyrus and Darius. Later, from their mountain strongholds, they fought indiscriminately against Greeks,[14] Romans, Arabs, and Turks.

Although conquered by Arabs from the 7th to the 9th century A.D., Kurds were never completely subdued. In the 11th century, they fell under the domination of Seljuk Turks. Kurdish power reached its height under Saladin (1138–1193), who was himself of Kurdish origin and who eventually became sultan of Egypt and Syria. The most formidable opponent of Christian Crusaders, Saladin put the rulers of the steadily weakening Latin Kingdom of Jerusalem on the defensive. He won an important victory over the Christians in 1187.[15]

Kurds fought steadily against assimilation by the Turks. Dissatisfied with proposed Turkish reforms, they rose in rebellion in 1832. Their Turkish masters replied by replacing Kurdish tribal chieftains, called "Derebeys" ("Lords of Valley"), with their own administrative officials. Kurdish resentment increased.

The sense of Kurdish nationalism was strengthened during the late 19th century at a time when other subjugated peoples were restive in the Ottoman Empire. In 1890 Abdul Hamid II[16] attempted to appease the Kurds by allowing them to organize their own cavalry units. Operating for Turkish benefit, they became a scourge in the area. For a time, they retarded the growth of Kurdish national consciousness, but not for long.[17]

Kurdish national sentiment increased at the turn of the century. The first Kurdish newspaper, *Kurdistan,* founded in 1897, appeared in Cairo, Geneva, and London at intervals until 1902. The first political club and the first literary society emphasizing Kurdish aims were organized in 1908. Books of Kurdish verse and anthologies were printed in Constantinople to further the cause of Kurdish nationalism.[18] Kurdish deputies in the Turkish Chamber and Senate began to push for national regeneration.

Kurdish separatists saw an opportunity with the fall of the Ottoman Empire in 1918. They were encouraged by Point 12 of President Wilson's Fourteen Points, announced in January 1918, which referred to "an absolutely unmolested opportunity of autonomous development" for nationalities in the Ottoman Empire.[19] They reaffirmed their demands at the Versailles Peace Conference in 1919. By the Treaty of Sèvres, they won recognition of a new Kurdistan, including the vilayets of Turkey south of Armenia and the Mosul vilayet then under British occupation.[20] There was, however, unexpected Turkish resistance. Fired by the leadership of Mustafa Kemal Ataturk, the Turks rose against the victorious Allies and managed to replace the Treaty of Sèvres, which was never ratified, with the Treaty of Lausanne in 1923. No mention of a new Kurdistan was made in the new treaty.

The Kurds were appalled by the sudden loss of independence, but they were determined to continue their campaign for freedom during the Long Armistice between world wars. They began armed uprisings in Turkey, Iran, and Iraq. In 1937 the latter three governments concluded the Treaty of Saababad, which was designed to insure cooperation in containing the menace of Kurdish unrest.[21] There were major rebellions in Turkey in 1925, 1930–1931, and 1937, all of which were savagely suppressed by Turkish armed forces. The February 1925 uprising had some initial successes, but it was broken when Kurdish nationalists were captured and executed. Turkish authorities transferred thousands of Kurds from their historic homeland to the unhealthy coast of Anatolia. Talk of separatism and secession was made illegal and punishable. At the same time, an attempt was made to appease Kurdish national sentiment by giving a modicum of recognition to Kurdish cultural interests.

The Kurds of Iraq

The status of Iranian Kurds was closely bound with that of their Iraqi compatriots. They rebelled indiscriminately against Turkish, Iraqi, and Iranian masters, all of whom used savage methods of reprisal. Only in Iraq did they finally manage to obtain legal recognition as a special minority, but here, too, they remained unsatisfied. The Kurds in Turkey were unable to win this kind of accommodation.[22] There was no real Kurdish national movement in Turkey as there was in neighboring Iraq and Iran, although attempts were made to awaken Kurdish nationalism behind a screen of cultural activities. The sizeable minority of Kurds in Turkey was assimilated partially into Turkish society.

The first and only attempt to set up a separate Kurdish province in Iraq was made in the immediate post-World War I years. With British support, a semi-autonomous regime was proposed for Kurds in Iraq, in accordance with the concept of self-determination held by President Woodrow Wilson. To combine religious prestige with tribal authority, Sheik Mahmoud, head of a local Sayyid family in the region of Sulaymani, was nominated to head the new government. Mahmoud, who resented British intrusion, led a rebellion and proclaimed himself King of Kurdistan. The proclamation was nullified when Mahmoud and his followers were ousted in a military operation and deported from Iraq.

Kurdish national consciousness increased despite the political defeat. Iraqi Kurds insisted on using their own language and holding tightly to their traditional customs. They supported a steadily rising output of newspapers, anthologies, poetry, historical treatises, fiction, and Kurdish grammars.[23] They also made a conscious effort to resist the encroachment of Arabic words into their own language.[24]

Concerned by Kurdish intransigence, the Iraqi Government, in the early 1930s, began to install new civil administrators in the remote northern district, which, until then, had been largely under Kurdish control. This move stimulated a new opposition centering around the flamboyant Mustafa Barzani, son of a Kurdish rebel hanged by the Turks before World War I.[25] An able mountain warrior, Barzani led his men against governmental troops in 1932 but was driven over the border into Turkey. During his exile, he joined forces with Kurdish intellectuals in the south.

In 1943 Barzani gathered a guerrilla force of 1,000 men in the mountains and resumed his campaign of harassing the Iraqi administration. His rebels soon numbered 6,000. Attacked by superior forces, Barzani led his followers on a long march across the mountains into Iran, where they were welcomed by Kurdish nationalists. The Soviet Union, then occupying that area of Iran, set up a Kurdish republic and commissioned Barzani a major general. When the Russians left in 1947, Iranian authorities began the task of eliminating the Kurdish movement inside its borders. They captured Kurds and condemned them to death. Barzani fled to the Soviet Union, where he remained until the overthrow of the Iraqi regime in 1959 in one of several coups by Army juntas.

During the 1960s, Barzani's guerrilla army, the *Persh Merga* ("Forward to Death") fought Iraqi forces to a standstill. A cease-fire was arranged in 1966 when the Iraqi Government indicated that it was willing to grant a measure of autonomy to the Kurds. Complaining that the government had not lived up to its promises, Kurds began raiding valuable oil installations. A governmental military operation was accompanied by a new gesture of political appeasement. In March 1970 the government ordered a truce: it recognized the Kurds as a national minority, with special rights in local administration, education, and law courts. It set a four-year deadline for these autonomy proposals, but just before the expiration date, the Kurds, still dissatisfied with limited self-rule, again resumed fighting.

The Kurdish struggle in both Iraq and Iran was complicated by the oil issue. Kurds insisted that they were not given their due proportionate share of the rich oil income. The United States was involved: when in 1975 the Shah of Iran reached an agreement to cut off supplies to the Kurds, Washington, at the insistence of Secretary of State Henry Kissinger, withdrew its support for Barzani. Soviet-supplied Iraqi tanks quickly defeated the guerrillas. Again, the Kurdish chief went into exile.[26]

The Baath Government of Iraq tempered its efforts at conciliation with renewed operations against the Kurds. It forcibly removed inhabitants from Kurdish villages situated a dozen miles from Iraq's borders with Iran and Turkey, burned their homes, destroyed orchards and crops, and sent Kurds to detention centers in the south. Its goal was to create a free zone between Iraq and Turkey as well as Iran. The result, as was to be expected, was even more Kurdish resistance.

The Kurds of Iran

Kurdish separatism was the most active of the minority nationalisms in Iran. Here, the confrontation was strong in the religious sphere between the majority Shi'ites, the official state religion, and the minority Kurdish Sunni Muslims. Each side held adamantly to its own doctrines, and neither one was inclined to compromise.[27]

Behind Kurdish aspirations in Iran were centuries of accumulated resentment. In the immediate post-World War I years from 1919 to 1922, Kurdish tribal chieftains, religious leaders, and middle-class townsmen combined in a drive to separate their northwestern area from the central government. They were unsuccessful. In August 1941, in the midst of World War II, Kurdish separatists again rose in rebellion, this time to take advantage of the no-man's-land between the Soviet forces in the north and the British forces in the south. As we have seen, the Russians set up an independent Kurdish republic, with its capital at Tabriz, while the British held on to the oil fields in the south. The Kurds then proclaimed a "Free Kurdish State" in the mountains of northwest Iran in December 1945. It lasted only 12 months.

Kurdish separatists were not discouraged. They organized a political party called the Society for the Revival of Kurdistan (JK), with headquarters at Mahabad. There were rebellions in 1946, 1950, and 1956. Teheran authorities considered these acts treasonous. They hunted down Kurdish leaders and condemned them to prison or execution. This kind of treatment only intensified opposition, which continued into the 1960s and 1970s.

The Kurdish cause was weakened by internal rivalries among rightists, moderates, and leftists. On the right were the conservative farmers and shepherds who made up a majority of the Kurdish population. One rightist resistance group was led by Mustafa Barzani, the Iraqi Kurdish chieftain, whose activities extending along the border were discussed in the preceding section.[28] The most popular resistance movement was headed by Sheik Ezzedine Hosseini, a moderate religious leader.[29] On the left were several guerrilla units, each of which hoped to take the lead in the struggle for Kurdish independence.[30] Each group was reluctant to unite with the others.

During his regime, which began in 1941, Shah Mohammed Reza Pahlavi used force to throttle Kurdish separatism.[31] Kurds, believing that at long last the day of *sarbasti* ("freedom") had arrived, supported the revolution which overthrew the Shah. They assisted in the roundup of SAVAK, the governmental terror agency, and joined the revolutionaries in what they believed was the formation of a new government friendly to their regionalist demands.

The Kurds soon found that they had made an error in judgment. Ayatollah Ruhollah Khomeini, the 79-year-old Imam[32] and driving force behind the revolution, intended to set up an Islamic state under his own control. Consumed by hatred for the fallen Shah, the United States, and Westernization, he had no intention of allowing the Kurds or any other separatists to break his control of the state. His Revolutionary Council made it clear that there would be no regional autonomy or independence for any Iranian minority.

Kurdish reaction was predictably violent. The Islamic Republic was only 11 days old when a skirmish took place between revolutionary troops and Kurdish separatists near the Iraqi border. More than 100 men were killed in this first large-scale clash in what seemed to be turning into a veritable civil war.[33] Even the moderate Ayatollah Hosseini was angered: "We fought in the revolution not out of religious conviction but for political goals. We want autonomy—our own Parliament, our own language, our own culture." It was the familiar cry of mini-nationalists everywhere. And again: "The revolution has destroyed despotism, but it has not ended discrimination against minorities. The revolution must go on until all the major minority groups—the Kurds here, the Turks in Azerbaijan, the Baluchis in the East—win a measure of autonomy."[34]

On May 10, 1979, Kurdish rebellion erupted again in the mountain-ringed city of Santanda in Iranian Kurdistan about 250 miles northwest of Teheran. When a local revolutionary council attempted to send some of the town's wheat to Teheran, angry Kurds armed themselves at the provincial local headquarters and asked Khomeini's local representative for permission to draw ammunition from the army garrison on the outskirts of the city to defend their wheat silos. Their request was refused. One of the revolutionary deputies pulled a gun and started shooting, killing a high-school student and wounding two passersby. That was all the Kurds needed. They moved through the city, captured governmental buildings, and placed the local garrison under siege.[35]

The full-scale insurrection left several hundred dead in the next few days. Holding alleyways and roof-top positions, paying little attention to their losses, rampaging Kurds poured gunfire into the barracks. They tore down posters of Ayatollah Khomeini and ripped them to shreds. Others attacked with machine guns and mortars. The government responded with buzzing P-4 Phantom fighting planes and 20-mm. cannon fire from helicopter gunships.[36] "Given our history and culture," said a doctor attending the wounded, "only a fool would not have seen this as inevitable."[37] A tenuous peace was finally restored when governmental ministers from Teheran beseeched the Kurds to remember that "the soldiers are our brothers." They promised a grant of semi-autonomy.

The truce was short-lived; fighting started again April 21, 1979. When thousands of Kurds met at a sports stadium in western Azerbaijan Province to inaugurate a branch of the Kurdish National Party, a shot was heard. In the ensuing panic and clash between government troops and Kurdish and Turkish minorities, about 70 or 80 people were killed.[38] On

July 18, 1979, Kurdish tribesmen fought a skirmish with national police in the frontier region near the western town of Serow.[39] On August 16, 1979, Kurdish rebels overran the town of Paveh near the Iraqi border and, for two days, attacked Islamic Revolutionary Guards and the state police force. Thirteen were killed and 50 wounded.[40]

Iranian authorities, responding to Khomeini's directive for increased revolutionary action, resisted fiercely. During the continued fighting, they executed 29 Kurds within a few days. The Ayatollah denounced the Kurdish Democratic Party and accused it of being a party of Satan (his favorite designation for his enemies) and its members as being "American agents."[41] "We see that you are not good people, that you are not Islamic, and that you have connections with foreigners."[42] The pious judgment failed to influence angry Kurds. From the northwestern city of Mahabad, Kurdish spiritual leader Hosseini issued a statement: "We say again to the masses of Iran that the Kurdish people will fight for the basic rights in a united Iran and will not stop the fighting for a moment."[43] An estimated 50,000 armed Kurdish insurgents moved to the mountains near the Iraqi border.[44]

Kurdish resentment was deep and bitter.[45] In late November 1979, there was a period of relaxation as Khomeini transferred his polemics from the Kurds to the Americans.[46] Where before he had singled out Kurds for special hostile treatment, he now invoked the needs of Iranian nationalism and urged them to join him. He pleaded for understanding. He was, he said, "a servant of the nation who is passing the last days of his life."[47]

Unlike the Welsh or the Scots, Kurdish tribesmen saw little advantage in limited autonomy—in accommodation or appeasement. They wanted their own nation and were willing to fight for it. They were not attracted either by Khomeini's dictatorship or by any Marxist state that might succeed it. If anything, their sense of national consciousness grew even stronger. Modern means of communication enabled even the older villagers and nomads to be swayed by separatist propaganda. In the process, old feudal ties and new intellectual patriotism were fused into a national movement uniting all classes.[48] Kurdish students living outside Iran also supported the separatist movement.[49]

The issue was highly charged with emotion. Well-armed Kurds, eager for combat, became walking arsenals with guns and cartridge belts at their hips and hand grenades in leather pouches at their sides. Kurdish women in homespun garments worked at their chores with a child on one hip and a rifle on the other. Guerrillas gathered heavy equipment, including artillery, machine guns, and anti-tank weapons, in the mountains and valleys. The outbreak of the Iraqi-Iranian War in September 1980 gave Kurds the opportunity for which they were waiting.

With weapons, with an undiminished will to win, Kurdish tribesmen were fixed in their determination to transform their separatist sentiment into a full-fledged nationalism.

Iran Against Itself

Kurdish separatism was not alone in its opposition to Khomeini's centralism. Azerbaijanis, rugged mountain people settled in the northwestern tip of Iran, went from protest to demonstration to open revolt.[50] There was continuing tension in Tabriz. Azerbaijanis complained that they had been given an inferior status in the new government. Their spiritual leader, Ayatollah Kazen Shariat-Madari, once Khomeini's mentor, proposed moderation and accommodation, but he was unable to restrain his zealous followers. Activists of the Muslim People's Republican Party (MPRP) drove governmental officials from Tabriz and held nine of Khomeini's men hostage for a week.[51]

Khomeini, castigating Azerbaijani separatists as a threat to the very survival of his regime, denounced them as "mere heathens, foreign-led agents whose dossiers are in our hands." He urged Azerbaijanis to join his anti-American campaign against the "Great Satan."[52] "Any gesture," he said, "or utterance weakening the government is apostasy."

The apostasy, however, proliferated. There was unrest in the southeastern province of Baluchistan-Seistan, where, in late December 1979, clashes between Baluchi tribesmen and Persians in the town of Zahidan left 3 persons dead and 48 wounded.[53] In early January 1980, two revolutionary guardsmen were killed when their 12-man unit was attacked on a road.[54] Tribal warfare spilled across the frontiers into neighboring Pakistan and Afghanistan.

Nomadic Baluchi tribesmen overwhelmingly refrained from voting in the December 1979 national referendum on the new Iranian constitution. The issue was complicated by gun battles between rival Baluchis and Seistanis, as well as between Baluchis on the one side and Seistanis and revolutionary militiamen on the other.[55] Unsatisfied Sikhs, a minority living among the minority Baluchis, also called for autonomy.

This kind of factional infighting threatened the very existence of Iran. Rebellious minorities complained about the way Khomeini was running the country. Each one saw in the chaotic political situation an opportunity to win its independence. In late 1980, the activities of a militant Arab minority led straight to war.

The Iranian-Iraqi War

Arabs living in Khuzistan in the oil-rich southwestern corner of Iran made up only 4 percent of the population of the country. Iranians, though Muslims, were not of Arab stock but were Indo-European in origin. There is a long history of rivalry between Arabs and Persians, dating back to the Muslim Arab conquest of the Persian homeland.

There were strong religious differences between Iranians and Arabs. The ruling clergy of Iran held to the Shi'ite brand of Islam, while the Arabs espoused the cause of Sunni Islam. Arab dissidents, who called themselves citizens of "Arabistan," regarded themselves as an unsatisfied minority in Iran and called for autonomy and eventual independence. Faced with stern opposition from the new revolutionary regime in Teheran, Khuzistan Arabs began a campaign of sabotage in Iranian oil fields, blowing up pipe lines and rail tracks and reducing the flow of oil to domestic refineries.

Neighboring Iraq was soon involved in the confrontation. Arab Iranian guerrillas were undoubtedly trained in Iraq. President Saddam Hussein of Iraq was annoyed by Khomeini's repeated calls to the Shi'ite Muslims of Iraq to rise in revolt against Iraq's Baath Party Government. This was, Hussein claimed, an outright call to war. The Iraqi strong man saw his own system of secular-oriented Arab socialism being challenged by Khomeini's militant Islamic regime. Roots of difference were deep: for over a century, a battle had been raging over the correct dividing line to be drawn down the Shatt-al-Arab waterway. The problem was intensified on the issue of oil.

The tempo of sabotage increased as armed guerrillas infiltrated from Iraq into Iran to face the fanatical forces of Khomeini's Revolutionary Guards. Teheran replied with harsh measures: between March and July 1979, the Teheran regime put to death dozens of young Arabs on charges of sabotage.[56] On April 30, 1980, armed Arab dissidents, calling themselves "Group of the Martyr," seized the Iranian Embassy in London and held some 20 hostages inside it in a demand for more rights for the Arab minority in Iran.[57]

By the fall of 1980, Hussein was convinced that Iran was militarily weakened and on the verge of chaos. On September 22, 1980, he sent his troops on a surprise invasion of Iran along a 500-mile front. Iraqis headed for four cities inside Khuzistan Province. Hussein's Soviet-equipped forces met head-on with Iranian Revolutionary Guards, army troops, and border guards. Iraqi MIGs, supplied by Soviet Russia, hit Iranian oil fields, while Iranian Phantoms, made in the United States, struck at Baghdad. Each side reacted with nationalistic fervor.

The Iraqi thrust into Iran came to a halt within a month as both sides dug in, exchanging artillery barrages and bombing strikes. There was a brutal battle for control of the Iranian port of Khorramshahr on the Shatt-al-Arab waterway. Claims on both sides were equally inflated, but thousands were killed or wounded, and property damage ran into billions of dollars.

The war brought Kurdish separatism into focus. The Kurdish problem was one of the causes of the war. Under the late Shah, the Iranians had supported a rebellion against Baghdad by Iraqi Kurds in the early 1970s. The Iraqi Government was forced into signing a 1975 agreement with Iran, which Iran unilaterally abrogated immediately before the war began. Under the accord, Iran abandoned support for the Iraqi Kurds in return for a new border agreement between the two countries.

As the war progressed, well-armed *Pesh Merga* Kurdish guerrillas, operating from mountain bases behind the Iraqi front line, began to strike at Iranian troops. Although they did not trust their new-found Iranian comrades, Iraqis backed Kurdish demands for greater autonomy from the Teheran Government. The most active mini-nationalists in the Middle East, the Kurds had already won recognition from Baghdad after their rebellion in Iraq in 1975, which had ended with 60,000 dead and injured. Iraqi Kurds now had their own autonomous region and their own national assembly.

The Iranian-Iraqi War had international repercussions. There was fear throughout the world that the conflict might spread to the Persian Gulf states. Washington and Moscow were supposedly neutral, but there was increasing danger that they might be drawn into the war. People everywhere were concerned that the conflict might cause massive disruption of the world's oil supplies. If tanker traffic were interrupted through the Strait of Hormuz at the southern end of the Persian Gulf, some 40 percent of the non-Communist world's supply of oil would be cut off.[58]

There were fears that Iran's position was being weakened. On October 23, 1980, Donald F. McHenry, chief American delegate to the United Nations, warned the Security Council that the Iraqi invasion threatened to break up Iran. "All of us must be opposed to the dismemberment of Iran. The United States believes that the cohesion and stability and prosperity of Iran are in the interests of stability and prosperity of the region as a whole. The national integrity of Iran is threatened by the Iraqi invasion."[59] He urged Iraq to withdraw from the occupied territories in Iran.

Others saw an immediate danger in a possible collapse of the Khomeini regime. In that case, one observer noted, Iranian Communists would seize control of the government and then invoke a 1921 treaty with Russia to preserve the integrity of Iran against all those groups seeking to dismember the country. Soviet troops would then march in to implement the treaty.[60] The implication was clear: mini-nationalisms could work not only to dissolve a chaotic country but also to attract the attention of aggressive superpowers.

CHAPTER **12**

PLO, ISRAEL, AND LEBANON —

We have the intention of utterly destroying the state of Israel.
                    —Ahmed Shukairy, first head of the PLO

We shall attack these murderers at every opportunity. We shall
give them no rest.
                    —Israeli Prime Minister Menachem Begin

Palestinian Self-Rule

For more than three decades, the Palestinian quest for a homeland has
kept the Middle East in turmoil. Nearly 4 million Palestinian Arabs, most
of them living in exile, claim as their birthright the land of Israel and the
occupied territories on the West Bank and Gaza Strip. There is a deep,
seemingly irreconcilable conflict of competing nationalisms in the Holy
Land, a situation fraught with danger for the peace of the world.

Both Israelis and Palestinians claim historic and religious rights to the
land. When Israel became an independent state in 1948, hundreds of
thousands of Palestinians were sent to refugee camps. Israel refused to
take them, and Arab countries declined to absorb them for fear that this
act might mean recognition of Israel. Thereafter, Palestinians were
transformed from a dispirited band of exiles into a dispossessed people
united by anger and a sense of injustice. Their cause emerged as one of
the most aggrieved mini-nationalisms in a global conglomeration of unsatisfied peoples.

Like the Poles before 1919, Palestinian Arabs claimed that they were
left without a country, without a land base. Israelis replied that the Arabs
had found a home in Transjordan. Unwilling to accept this solution,
Palestinians expressed their bitterness by turning to the extremist Palestine Liberation Organization, which announced its goal of fostering
unity "among a displaced people" and of forming an independent Palestinian state. Leaders of the extremist wing of this organization, despairing of defeating Israel in war, turned to terrorism as a means of calling
attention to their cause.

In October 1967, Islamic leaders in 34 countries declared a holy war (*jihad*) on Israel. Arabs who fell in the struggle were promised a passport into paradise and the respect due to prophets. They were glorified as *fedayeen* ("men of sacrifice"), fighters for freedom. In scores of incidents they used bullets, grenades, and bombs to carry their message: "This land is ours!"

In this classic conflict of nationalisms, Israelis reacted in kind under the principle of an eye for an eye. They saw their very existence at stake. They denounced what they called the "Palestine Murder Organization" as a gang of terrorists. They fought back with raids on guerrilla headquarters and training camps. They would not allow the formation of a new Palestinian state on the West Bank and argued that they would not be neighbor to a people dedicated to their destruction. They, too, made it plain: "This land is ours!"

Palestine in History

Palestine, the historic region on the eastern shore of the Mediterranean Sea between Syria and Egypt, has seldom had firm borders.[1] Usually, it included territory between the Mediterranean and the Jordan River, an area about 140 miles long and from 30 to 70 miles wide. This was the Holy Land of three religions—Jews, Christians, and Muslims—all of whom shared shrines in Jerusalem, Bethlehem, Nazareth, and Hebron.

Roots of dissension were traditional in the Holy Land. The Hebrews established a state after the decline of the New Kingdom in Egypt.[2] By 1000 B.C., they had established a state with Jerusalem as its center. King David reduced the sea-faring Philistines to subjection. After the reign of Solomon, the kingdom was split into two parts: Israel, with its capital at Samaria, and Judah, with its capital at Jerusalem. Israel was destroyed by the Assyrians (ca. 722 B.C.) and Judah by the Babylonians (586 B.C.). An autonomous community was set up under Persian sponsorship.

In the 4th century B.C., Alexander the Great conquered Palestine. Efforts to impose Hellenism resulted in the Maccabean revolt. A Jewish state was organized in 141 B.C., which finally yielded to Rome. At the time of Christ, Palestine was controlled by puppet rulers who never were successful in reconciling Jews and Romans. To suppress a revolt, Romans destroyed the Temple and expelled the Jews from Judea in 70 A.D.

At the time of Constantine in the 4th century A.D., Palestine became a center for Christian pilgrimages. There was a period of prosperity under Justinian. Like the entire Mediterranean area, however, Palestine fell to Muslim invaders, starting in 640 A.D. with Omar. The Islamic invasion was accompanied by a period of decline as the highlands were deforested and the cultivated valleys turned into swamps.

In the 9th century, Palestine came under Egyptian control. The Fatimate rulers, who molested pilgrims and destroyed the Church of the Holy Sepulcher, provoked the Crusades undertaken by European Christians between the 11th and 14th centuries to recover the Holy Land from Islam. However, the Latin Kingdom of Jerusalem, set up in 1099, lasted less than a century.

The next rulers were the Mamelukes, also of Muslim background. In 1517 they were conquered by Ottoman Turks, whose rule of Palestine was regarded generally as a period of decay. It remained under the rule of the Ottoman sultan at Constantinople, except for a few months of Napoleon's invasion and several years of Mohammed Ali's occupation, until the time of World War I.

Toward the end of the 19th century, large numbers of European Jews, fearing that assimilation might lead to a loss of identity and even to the disappearance of Judaism itself, emigrated to the United States.[3] Others found solace in the new Zionist movement which called for the establishment of a Jewish state in Palestine.[4] The First Zionist Congress, held at Basel in 1897, urged that Jews from all the world find refuge in a Palestinian homeland.

At the beginning of the 20th century, the British failed to work out a satisfactory relationship with Arab Palestine. During World War I, on November 2, 1917, A. J. Balfour, the British Foreign Secretary, in a letter to Lord Rothschild, a Zionist leader, declared British support for the establishment of a Jewish national home in Palestine, provided that safeguards could be reached for the rights of the "existing non-Jewish communities" in Palestine.[5] The Balfour Declaration was soon confirmed by the Allied governments and formed a basis for the League of Nations mandate for Palestine in 1920.

By making contradictory promises to Jewish Zionists and to Arab nationalists, the British created a situation which was to plague them until their departure in 1948 with the Middle East in turmoil. They underestimated the dynamism of both Zionist and Arab nationalisms. They had hoped that the two peoples would live in peace. They were aware of Arab-Jewish hostility but misjudged its depth.

As early as 1921, riots broke out between the Arab population and Jewish immigrants.[6] On August 23, 1929, the conflict took on menacing proportions when grave disorders erupted in Jerusalem over access to the Wailing Wall.[7] Similar disorders spread to other parts of the country. After Hitler's accession to power in 1933, the persecution of Jews in Germany stimulated their emigration to Palestine.[8] Muslim-Jewish hostility turned into serious bloodshed. Caught between two irreconcilable nationalisms, the British vacillated. In traditional reaction to such differences, London sent royal commissions to investigate conditions and propose solutions, it called round-table conferences, and it published white papers. At times, London seemed to favor the Jews; at others, it discouraged them in favor of the Arabs.

The British found a solution impossible because neither Jewish Zionists nor Arab nationalists were inclined to compromise. Each side, driven by religious and nationalist fanaticism, looked upon its cause as sacred and judged compromise as unacceptable. At one time, the British had enjoyed the good will of Jews and Arabs; in the end, they incurred the hostility and wrath of both.

Further discussions were shelved throughout World War II. During the war, Palestine became an important center of British power in the Middle East, especially as the base for an attack on the Vichy French in Syria and Lebanon in 1941. Jews, who looked upon Hitler as their main enemy, suspended their struggle for a Jewish Palestine for the duration of the war and rallied to the Allied cause. Arabs, on the other hand, distrusted the Allies and welcomed the war as an opportunity to throw off the British and French yokes.

The Emergence of Israel

After the end of World War II, homeless survivors of nazism sought out Palestine as a place of refuge. Jews hoped that the new British Labour Government would open Palestine to them, but the white paper published in 1939 severely restricted Jewish immigration and land purchase and also envisaged the creation of an "independent Palestinian state." Jewish hopes were soon disappointed when it became clear that British policy in Palestine was not to be changed. Arabs were heartened by the growing importance of Arab states in the Middle East and by the formation of the Arab League.

A new wave of terrorism culminated on July 22, 1946, when Zionist extremists blew up British headquarters in the King David Hotel at Jerusalem, resulting in the loss of 91 lives. British authorities arrested Jewish leaders, deported illegal immigrants, and proposed the Morrison Plan for dividing the country into provinces or cantons. The plan was rejected unanimously by both Arabs and Jews. Despairing of a solution, London announced on February 15, 1947, that it would submit the Palestine problem to the United Nations.

In May 1947 the United Nations proposed a territorial division of Palestine into an Arab state and a Jewish state, with Jerusalem and its environs remaining a *corpus separatum* under United Nations trusteeship. The plan was adopted by the Assembly in November 1947 with a required two-thirds majority. The British agreed to terminate the mandate on May 15, 1948, and to evacuate their 100,000 troops by August 1.[9]

Palestinian Arabs regarded the creation of Israel as an unmitigated disaster. Reacting violently, they were joined by irregular forces from neighboring states. The confrontation turned into veritable civil war between Jews and Arabs, with the British caught in the middle. During the chaotic conflict, the Jews transformed the Haganah, their main military force, into a national army. At midnight on May 14, 1948, the British High Commissioner left Palestine. At the same time, the new Jewish state of Israel was proclaimed at Tel Aviv. It was recognized immediately by the United States (*de facto*) and by the Soviet Union (*de jure*).

Wars for Survival

Israel was able to establish its right to survival only in the crucible of war.[10] Armies of surrounding Arab states, united in the Arab League, quickly crossed the frontiers at several points. Israel had to surrender the old city of Jerusalem but held on to the new city. After a four-week truce supervised by the United Nations, fighting resumed on July 8, 1948. Israeli troops gained footholds in all areas except Jerusalem. By the time of the armistice in January 1949, Israel had increased its territory by more than 50 percent of the original land grant.

There was no general peace settlement. There was little likelihood of a new Palestinian state, for Jordan annexed nearby territory and Egypt held on to the southwest coastal strip. Though defeated in their goal of exterminating Israel, the Arab states continued their policies of economic boycott, blockade, and incitement of local guerrilla activities. Israelis responded in kind to terrorist activities.

On October 29, 1956, Israel, helped briefly by British and French forces, invaded Egypt's Sinai Peninsula. Within a few days, fast-moving Israeli troops conquered the Gaza Strip and the Sinai, while Britain and France simultaneously invaded the area of the Suez Canal. Eventually, Israel yielded to pressure from the United States, the Soviet Union, and the United Nations and removed its troops from Gaza and Sinai.

By 1965, the population of Israel had grown to 2.5 million, of which 90 percent were Jewish. About 900,000 Arab refugees, living in misery in neighboring states, were given minimum care by the United Nations Relief and Works Agency. An uneasy truce was supervised by a United Nations Emergency Force.

There was another dramatic outburst in the full-scale Six-Day War of 1967. On May 19, 1967, the UN force withdrew at the insistence of Egypt's President Gamal Abdel Nasser. Arabian troops occupied the Gaza Strip and the Sinai Peninsula and captured Old Jerusalem, Syria's Golan Heights, and Jordan's West Bank. Israeli reaction was quick and effective. On June 5 planes attacked 10 enemy air bases and put an end to Egyptian air power. Three Israeli armored columns invaded the Sinai Peninsula and smashed the Egyptian forces there. Israeli troops took both Jerusalem and the Golan Heights. The fighting was halted on June 10 with a UN-arranged cease-fire.

Terrorist attacks continued for the next several years. On October 6, 1973, on Yom Kippur, the most solemn day on the Jewish calendar, Egypt and Syria launched a surprise attack on Israel. The Soviet Union sent supplies to the invaders by massive airlifts, while the United States began its own airlift to Israel. Israeli troops drove the Syrians back and crossed the Suez Canal, surrounded Suez City, and trapped Egyptians in their own Sinai salient. A UN cease-fire went into effect on October 24, 1973. Later, Israel withdrew from the Canal's west bank, and by a second withdrawal in 1976, she yielded additional Sinai territory, including an oil field.

Israel had won its right to exist by the ultimate test of the battlefield. Palestinian Arabs, however, were in no mood to accept the situation. They staged one terrorist attack after another, killing scores of civilians in the process. Israelis conducted massive retaliatory raids on Palestinian guerrilla camps across the border into Lebanon. The pattern was repeated in an escalation of assaults. Terrorist attacks were almost invariably followed by Israeli reprisal raids.

Yasir Arafat and the PLO

Meanwhile, in the cascading confrontation between Israeli Jews and Palestinian Arabs, dispossessed Arabs found their latter-day Saladin in a short, stocky man with a prominent nose, receding chin, and a bald head concealed by Arab headdress. Yasir Arafat, leader of the Al Fatah, the most active Palestinian guerrilla unit, and head of the Palestine Liberation Organization, the coordinating body of 10 commando groups, gave the movement the leadership it needed. He was born in Jerusalem in 1929 and claimed descent from Palestinian nobility.[11] By 1949 he and members of his family were members of the Holy Struggle Army fighting against the emergence of Israel.

When the 1948–1949 war ended, Arafat and his parents were refugees in Gaza. He moved to Cairo, where he enrolled as an engineering student in the university there. Among the founding members of the Palestinian Student Confederation, he became its chairman. He helped lead Palestinian and Egyptian commandos who harassed the British in the Suez Canal area. He also served in the Egyptian army as a demolition expert and fought against the British and French in 1956 at Port Said and nearby areas.

In the next decade, the Arab world began to hear the name of Arafat's Al Fatah.[12] At the time, it was only one of several guerrilla groups then working against Israel. In 1964 the leaders of the Arab states sanctioned the formation of the Palestine Liberation Organization (PLO) as an umbrella organization. The 1967 war against Israel had left Arab armies shattered and discredited. Disgruntled Arabs began to look to Arafat's guerrillas as offering some hope in a humiliating situation. They were impressed by his confident words: "I have no time to spare arguing over left foot and right. What is important is action and its results. We believe that the only way to return to our home and land is the armed struggle. We believe in this theory without any complications, and this is our aim and hope."[13]

By 1969 Al Fatah had become the largest and most important of the guerrilla units. Arafat gained control of the PLO and was named chairman of its executive committee. Earlier, he and his followers were regarded as outlaws and were subjected to punishment in Arab countries, but now, he appeared as a liberator and the creator of a new legend. He and his *fedayeen* would bring down the hated Israelis and avenge Arab humiliation. The paunchy little man, who had "married a woman called Palestine," scarcely cut the figure of a dashing guerrilla leader, but to Palestinian Arabs, he became an immensely heroic figure.

Arafat's followers began their guerrilla campaign with small acts of destruction. They ambushed Israeli citizens, assaulted *kibbutzim* (Israeli settlements), and mined roads and bridges. In addition to military targets, they attacked civilians in market places, movie houses, and school buses. Their chief base of operations was originally Jordan, from which they ventured across the border into Israel. They encountered swift retaliation.

When fighting broke out in Jordan in early 1970, King Hussein at first took a conciliatory attitude toward the guerrillas. When he agreed to back Egypt in a truce and negotiated with Israel, Hussein was opposed by the guerrillas. *Fedayeen* sought to take control in several Jordanian cities. Forced to a showdown, Hussein ordered his troops to strike at the guerrillas. He and Arafat signed a truce on September 27, 1970.

Arafat was more successful in maintaining a base in Lebanon, where the PLO was able to operate more openly. By 1970 there were some 4,000 commandos stationed in Lebanon, of whom one-third were members of Al Fatah.

After the PLO defeat in Jordan, Palestinian guerrillas turned increasingly to international terrorism. In 1970 a splinter group of *fedayeen* held 60 foreigners hostage in Jordanian hotels for three days and also dynamited a TWA Boeing 707 on an airstrip outside Amman. The renewed policy of terrorism culminated in an event that aroused horror throughout the world—the murder by Palestinian guerrillas of Israeli athletes at the 1972 Olympic Games in Munich.

The PLO suffered a setback in the Yom Kippur War of October 1973, although it played almost no part in that conflict. Israel's decisive defeat of Egypt and Syria resulted in a split in PLO leadership. Moderates inside the organization indicated that they would be inclined to accept a Palestinian state limited to the Gaza Strip and the West Bank of the Jordan River, both of which had been occupied by Israel after the 1967 war. The extremist wing of the PLO, however, rejected this compromise and continued to insist on the elimination of Israel as a sovereign state.

Meanwhile, Palestinian Arabs began to win more and more international recognition. On October 14, 1974, the United Nations General Assembly invited representatives of the PLO to participate in a debate on the Palestine issue. Arab heads of state agreed that the PLO was to be "the sole legitimate representative of the Palestinian people" in their campaign for independence. On November 13, 1974, Arafat addressed the UN General Assembly, which passed a resolution stating that Palestinians had a right to self-determination and national sovereignty. Israeli leaders replied that they would never, under any circumstances, deal with the terrorist PLO.

For more than a decade and a half after its formation in 1964, the PLO waged a war of terrorism against Israel. In March 1975 a bus was attacked and 38 Israelis were killed. The PLO campaign in Europe diminished as its leaders mounted a diplomatic offensive. It called itself a government-in-exile and established more than 80 offices throughout the world. The PLO was governed by a 100-member council and an executive committee. Its aim was twofold: to put an end to inside rivalries that had plagued the movement for years, and to win international recognition. Nevertheless, moderates and extremists inside the movement continued their quarrels. The pattern of PLO terrorism and Israeli reprisals persisted.

The Palestinian Case

The Palestinians' claim was simple and clear: they saw themselves as a people who once owned land from which they had been driven by terror or reduced to second-class citizenship.[14] They regarded themselves as survivors in a dispossessed community with no sovereignty of their own and kept in subjugation by an alien state. They were a people, they said, who had "an indissoluble bond with the land." They saw their self-assertion as violated. They claimed self-determination as a fundamental right and absolutely essential need. "History has taught us," said one

Palestinian, "that ultimately one cannot circumvent the rage of a people trying to regain its freedom and independence."

To charges of inhuman terrorism, Palestinians replied that Zionists had treated them with equal violence. Were they not driven from their own land by physical and psychological terror?[15] They insisted that their own militancy did not begin to match Zionist assaults on Arab, British, and United Nations forces. They saw their PLO not as a terrorist organization but as a legitimate response to Zionist terror. They were fighters for liberation, they said, patriots in a war to the death against Israel.

Palestinians claimed that they had suffered for six decades—30 years of British occupation and 30 years of fragmentation, exile, and Israeli occupation. They pointed out that those of their compatriots still living in Israel were subject to mass arrests, deportation, torture, expropriation of land, harassment at check points, and harsh military rule. Why were they lepers in their own land?

All this, said the Palestinians, was abysmally unfair. More than half a century ago, they claimed, the League of Nations had determined that the Palestinian people were entitled to self-government and national independence. Now they were offered "autonomy" for one-third of their people in one-fifth of their legitimate territory. That involved, they charged, a severe diminution of their national rights. They would have no settlement divorced from their aspirations for nationhood. "We are alarmed and angered by the present mutation of our hope for a comprehensive regional peace into a partial bilateral settlement."[16]

Palestinians resented the idea of autonomy and considered it less desirable than independence. An autonomous region, in their view, was, in the final analysis, still a part of a larger and dominant state. They would not accept any solution that ruled out the possibility of independence. They saw no reason why they should negotiate a settlement that would prohibit the option of independence. They believed that they would legitimize Israeli occupation of their land by agreeing to a thinly camouflaged version of autonomy.

Arafat himself denounced talk of autonomy as "a tragedy for my people, a new slavery. It is not self-rule. It is self-administration, and I call it garbage. The Israelis have control of everything, even the source of water.... I say of autonomy ... that we reject [it]. And we will continue to resist until we are able to live freely in our own homeland."[17] So much for the choice between autonomy and independence.

According to Arafat, Palestinians had been transformed from refugees to freedom fighters, able to resist for a just cause. On his feelings about Palestine: "There are birds that fly around the world but come back to their original nest. There are fish that swim from the rivers to the sea, but somehow their sons go back to their original sources. Home is something in the heart of every human being. In appearance, perhaps, I look happy, but in my heart something has cracked. I live the tragedy of my people. But I am optimistic because sooner or later our people will achieve their goal."[18]

The Palestinian case was much the same as that of separatist mini-nationalisms everywhere: Palestinians would accept only a comprehensive settlement that would include realization of their own right to self-determination, including the right of political independence in a national state on their own native soil.

The Israeli Case

Israelis rejected each and every claim made by the Palestinians. They denounced as one of the great falsehoods of contemporary history the Arab contention that Jews were strangers in Palestine, foreigners who had no right to the land, outsiders who did not belong in the Middle East. On the contrary, Israelis asserted their fervent attachment to their historic homeland. They saw themselves as linked to a land from which they had been expelled forcibly. They were determined to maintain their right to live in their own land.

The Israeli argument was also simple and direct: Jews had lived in the land of Israel without interruption for 3,000 years. Even at the time of the destruction of the Temple, when Jews were scattered and forbidden to set foot in Jerusalem, many of them managed to remain in Palestine as guardians of the homeland to await the day of return to power.

The Israeli case stressed the continuity of Jewish aspirations. Palestine, it was said, had remained the Promised Land for Jews throughout the world. Celebrations of the Jewish Passover everywhere had always ended with the words: "Next year in Jerusalem." It was pointed out that, in their prayers, Jews turned their faces toward Zion; Arabs faced Mecca. A pertinent Jewish psalm was: "If I forget thee, O Jerusalem, let my right hand wither."

To Israelis, Jewish presence in the Holy Land began with the Old Testament and was affirmed by generations of Jews who prayed each morning for the eventual return to the Holy Land. Those who came from the ghettos of Europe, those who were in flight from persecution, had transformed a despoiled country of desert, swamp, and stones into a land flowing with milk and honey. History, said the Israelis, was on their side—it had decreed that Palestine was theirs.

In Israeli eyes, Palestinian Arabs had no just claim to the Holy Land. That area of Palestine once occupied by Arabs was not, said the Israelis, a country proper but a sparsely settled province of the Ottoman Empire. Most Palestinians who left in 1948 departed on orders from their lead-

ers. Israelis rejected the argument that Palestinians had a unique grievance, which was that no other people in modern times had been evicted
from their homeland to accommodate newcomers who claimed better
title to the land. Israelis pointed out that other refugees had been reset-
tled by their countrymen: in 1923 nearly one and a half million Greeks
had been thrown out of Asia Minor; after World War II, 12 million
Germans were expelled from Poland and Czechoslovakia; Finns and
Poles had been driven out of the Soviet Union. All these refugees had
settled elsewhere. What then, asked the Israelis, was unique about dis-
placement of Palestinians? They were living in the midst of populations
that easily could have absorbed them.

To Israelis, the PLO was a terrorist organization dedicated to the
destruction of their country. They saw no alternative other than to strike
back at those who refused to recognize Israel's right to exist. Had not the
United Nations Security Council voted in Resolution 242 for "acknow-
ledgment of the sovereignty, territorial integrity, and political independence of every state in that area"? Surely that resolution applied to Israel
as well as to Palestinian Arabs. Yet, the PLO was continuing its campaign
calling for destruction of the sovereign Jewish state. Israel would meet
the challenge. Prime Minister Menachem Begin expressed the will of his
people: "We shall attack these murderers at every opportunity. We shall
give them no rest."[19]

The Israeli case held that to give Palestinian Arabs self-determination
in occupied territory would be like inviting a time bomb in one's own
home. It called a Palestinian state a military threat, even if Israel remained the strongest military power in the Middle East. It saw no end to
PLO terrorism. Any new Palestinian state, from Israel's viewpoint, could
not support all the returning exiles and would almost certainly degener-
ate into poverty. Worst of all, said the Israelis, an artificial state on the
West Bank and Gaza would come under the influence of the Soviet
Union and eventually cause an even more dangerous situation in the
Middle East. In Israeli eyes, Palestinian nationalism was a historical
anachronism.

Repercussions

This clash of diametrically opposing views revealed the depth of emotion
behind an angry, unsatisfied nationalism. Participants moved dangerously in a mine field.

The issue was not settled by clash of arms. Palestinians refused to
accept the verdict of Israeli victories in 1949, 1956, 1967, and 1973 as
final. They pointed to several million of their homeless compatriots scattered as refugees throughout the Middle East and to their comrades still

living in Israel as second-class citizens. In theory, they would replace Israel with a democratic, secular state of Palestine in which Muslims, Jews, and Christians lived in equality. On a more practical level, they would settle for an independent Palestinian state on the West Bank and Gaza. They demanded an immediate end to "Israeli occupation" and a voice in determining their own future. Pending achievement of this goal, they would support the PLO in its recruitment and training of guerrillas as justified in a holy war against Israel. "Palestine," they cried, "will be liberated by terror, blood, and fire."

Israelis replied with scorn. Their status, they said, was won in the crucible of war. Their sons and daughters had died to preserve their land. They had no intention of retreating. Their backs, they claimed, were to the wall, and they had no choice—fight or perish. They would never give in to PLO violence and its reprehensible sneak attacks. They would not renounce their ancient right to the West Bank and Gaza, nor would they allow the formation of a state on the West Bank that would place every spot of their small country within the range of Arab guns.

Despite its intensified campaign, the PLO never became strong enough to prevail in a head-on encounter with Israel's small but powerful forces. It was weakened by constant quarrels among its members, traditional behavior among Arabs.[20] At the same time, the PLO won much support. It was recognized by many governments and had representatives in more than 50 countries.[21] It won the sympathy of circles in Italy, France, Belgium, Portugal, and Greece.[22]

Mention has been made here of increasing United Nations support for Palestinian Arabs. The program drawn up by the Committee on the Exercise of the Inalienable Rights of the Palestinian People was designed to enable the Palestinian people to exercise these rights and was endorsed repeatedly by the General Assembly. The 1974 General Assembly pro-Palestinian resolution reaffirmed:

(a) the right to self-determination without external interference,
(b) the right to national independence and sovereignty, and
(c) the inalienable right of the Palestinians to return to their homes and property from which they have been displaced and uprooted.

On January 30, 1981, in accordance with a General Assembly resolution, the United Nations Postal Administration issued a set of three stamps including the slogan: "Inalienable Rights of the Palestinian People." Outraged Jewish-American groups protested what they claimed was an endorsement of the PLO. Some stamp collectors denounced the politicizing of their hobby, the first time United Nations stamps had been used for a political cause. United Nations postal officials pointed out that the stamps honored Palestinians, not the PLO, and that, in any case, they were following orders of the General Assembly.

For the United States, the Israeli-Palestinian clash posed a serious dilemma. American policy supported democratic Israel, but that attitude was complicated by U.S. dependence on Arab oil. Washington tried to find some solution guaranteeing Israel's existence as well as Palestinian autonomy. The Camp David accord, reached by Egypt and Israel with the help of U.S. President Jimmy Carter, called for a five-year period of Palestinian self-rule; withdrawal of Israeli troops to special locations; and negotiations among Egypt, Israel, Jordan, and elected Palestinians to determine the final status of the West Bank and Gaza. Israel insisted that the accord did not ban new Jewish settlements in the area, a stand opposed by both the United States and Egypt. It was a somewhat shaky solution.

The confrontation between Israelis and Palestinians was but one facet of an increasingly precarious international situation. The Middle East, more heavily armed than most regions in the world, was a danger spot. There were critical imponderables, including geopolitical interests, oil, U.S.-Soviet rivalry, and, worst of all, nuclear options. There was the possibility that an unsatisfied minority might ignite a spark leading to a global explosion of incalculable consequences. There was a vast difference between a benign mini-nationalism asking only for cultural autonomy and a fanatical mini-nationalism demanding not only independence but also the destruction of what it deemed to be a usurper state. In this respect, PLO nationalism went far beyond the goal of other regional nationalisms which are content merely with the winning of autonomy.

Chaos in Lebanon

How fanatical nationalisms can threaten the dissolution of a country is indicated by the case of Lebanon. In theory, the Republic of Lebanon, bordered in the west by the Mediterranean, on the north and east by Syria, and on the south by Israel, was a united sovereign state. Its national anthem, "*Kulluna lil Watan*" ("All for the Fatherland"), proclaimed unity. In practice, however, the country was beset by religious separatism, splintered ideologies, and squabbling clans.

In ancient times, what is now Lebanon was occupied by Hittite and Aramaic kingdoms and later by the great sea-trading empire of the Phoenicians.[23] It was invaded successively by Assyrians, Persians, Greeks, Romans, and Byzantines. Maronite Christians established themselves and survived the influx of Islam in the 7th century.[24] In the 16th century,

Lebanon was absorbed into the Ottoman Empire while retaining considerable autonomy. From 1861 to 1864, massacres of Maronite Christians by Islamic Druses led European governments to force Ottoman sultans to agree to a pro-Christian government for Lebanon. Since then, the population of Lebanon has been split almost evenly between Christians (Maronites, Roman Catholics, Armenians, and Greek Orthodox) and Muslims. Religious confrontation was frozen into the fabric of Lebanese society.

With the collapse of the Ottoman Empire at the end of World War I, Lebanon became an independent state under French mandate. In 1941, under Free French occupation, it was declared independent, a status not generally recognized until early 1945. Opposition to pro-Western policies eventually grew into full-scale rebellion. In 1958, American troops, ordered into Lebanon by President Dwight D. Eisenhower, were withdrawn after the formation of a new Lebanese government.

The situation in Lebanon was complicated by increasingly hostile relations with Israel. Lebanon joined the Arab side in the Arab-Israeli War of 1948. Thereafter, relations were strained. Although Lebanon disclaimed responsibility for PLO commandos operating against Israel from Lebanese territory, Israeli troops made retaliatory raids on Lebanese soil. On December 28, 1968, an Israeli helicopter raid on Beirut Airport resulted in the destruction of 13 Lebanese airliners. Israeli raids persisted through the 1970s.

Inside Lebanon the pluralistic communal structure was shaken by bitter struggles during which an estimated 35,000 people were killed. Opposing groups dominating the political life of the country were constantly in conflict. Leftist Muslims and PLO units fought against a combination of Christian Maronite militia, the rightist Phalange, and other Christian units. Lebanon, too, was subjected to the political and religious vicissitudes of the Middle East. In 1976 some 15,000 Syrian troops entered the country to "restore order."

Israel gave active support to Lebanese Christians in the south. In the summer of 1968, a 6,000-man United Nations peace-keeping force moved into southern Lebanon to hold the factions apart. Thirty men of the UN force were killed in the process.[25] The situation was aggravated by rivalry among the Christian factions: each side rounded up enemies and held them as hostages.[26]

The recurrent internal regional crises have made the continued existence of Lebanon questionable. The separate identity of the country has been undermined by seemingly insurmountable religious differences.[27] Once considered to be one of the most prosperous and stable countries in the Middle East, Lebanon fell victim to irreconcilable mini-nationalisms. It provides the classic case of vertical religious hierarchies dominating the political structure of the state. Horizontal relationships extending beyond sectarian beliefs had little interest in a unified system of government. For centuries, the mountainous country had been an asylum for diverse quarreling religious groups. Now, in the closing years of the 20th century, the Lebanese system was in danger of collapse. Separatist movements thrive in this kind of atmosphere. Autonomy loses its appeal in favor of outright independence.

CHAPTER 13

CANADIAN QUANDARY: FRANCOPHONES VERSUS ANGLOPHONES ————————

Most Canadians understand that the rupture of their country
would be a crime against the history of mankind.
—Prime Minister Pierre Trudeau

The Unity Crisis in Canada

The Canadian experience fits no category of nationalism. From its beginnings, Canada developed as a state, not as a nation. It was composed
of two disparate elements which never became assimilated in the New
World but, instead, degenerated into a tradition of rivalry which lasts to
the present day. The confrontation between French-speaking Canadians
(Francophones) and English-speaking Canadians (Anglophones), based
largely on linguistic and cultural differences, affected the economic,
political, and psychological life of the two peoples. Francophones, who
had settled largely in Quebec Province, asserted an increasingly vocal
mini-nationalism which threatened the unity of the Canadian state.

The clash, in essence, was between two differing concepts of the nation.[1] Anglophones supported the idea of a single federal state comprising one nation, but with two languages, two cultures, and a single future.
Unsatisfied Francophones called for the separation of Quebec from the
century-old federation and the creation of what would amount to two
sovereign nations—one French-speaking, with its capital at Quebec City,
and the other English-speaking, with its capital at Ottawa.

Canada was created by two different peoples in what was then called "a
supreme act of faith." For more than a century and a half, these two
peoples, of French and British origin, fought for control of the rich
North American territory. Eventually, they were combined in a federal
union that was unstable from its start. Canadians were divided by geography, language, and economics in a way that made their country less a
nation than a combination of regional population pockets scattered over

177

vast areas. The proclaimed unity was never consummated. The possibility for a fragmented Canada was always there.

The conflict became the central issue of Canadian politics. The two levels of opinion represented what was actually a complicated issue. Canadians did not possess the power to amend their own constitution. In the British North America Act (BNA) of 1867, the country's founding document, important powers were reserved for the British Parliament. A key passage refers to the division of powers between the centralized federal government and the provinces. The latter had never been able to agree on a formula that would remove all colonial ties with Britain. In this respect, the country was not yet master of its own affairs.

The constitutional situation has led to much dissatisfaction throughout Canada. Quebec is not alone in its discontent. The peoples of western Canadian provinces, especially Alberta, Saskatchewan, and British Columbia, also have a sense of alienation from the federal system.[2] They are dissatisfied with their economic progress and especially by outside control of their rich natural resources. British Columbia, far removed from Quebec and facing the Pacific Ocean, has no language problem: only 2 percent of its people speak French. A province rich in forest and mineral products, it feels economically deprived—a sentiment it shares with Quebec. Both British Columbians and Quebeckers resent the power of Ontario, the largest and strongest province. They contend that federal politics favor Ontario's industrial, commercial, and financial growth. They denounce the protectionist tariff policies of the federal union, which, they charge, favor industrial provinces at the expense of the rest of the country.

The objections of British Columbians to federal power do not extend, however, into a separatist ideology. They deplore Quebec's nationalism, though they would use it as a convenient springboard for their own goals. The national union, they say, must be kept inviolate. At the same time, they complain about federal intrusion in their own affairs and demand that they be consulted in political matters that concern them.

In Quebec Province, on the other hand, the movement for separation has gathered momentum. Here, Francophones were unimpressed by the British contention that the country was built in freedom and equality with two languages and two cultures. They opposed what they called "foreign control" and resisted any policy of appeasement or accommodation. They insisted upon the creation of a French state in Canada.

The Roots of Confrontation

The history of Canada is a story of conflict and tension between rival partners.[3] Unlike the United States, Canada did not become a social melting pot; rather, it became a home for a combination of peoples, among whom the English and the French formed the two largest groups.[4] English-speaking immigrants and their descendants eventually outnumbered French Canadians. The population remained divided into two major streams: both English and French languages were given legal equality. Added to linguistic problems were political, economic, cultural, social, and psychological differences. There was also a religious barrier: French Canadians preserved their Catholic faith, while the majority of Anglophones hewed to Protestantism. All these differences, frozen in tradition, kept the two peoples apart. Canada became one country but two nations.[5] The impulse for separatism came early in Canadian history.

In global clashes between centralized governments and unsatisfied nationalisms for more autonomy or independence, one of the principal arguments presented by mini-nationalists is the claim: "We got there first!" In the case of Canada, both Anglophones and Francophones plead priority.[6] John Cabot and Sebastian Cabot, Italian explorers working for England, reached Cape Race and Labrador in 1497 and 1498. French explorer Jacques Cartier landed on the Gaspé Peninsula in 1534, sailed into the Gulf of St. Lawrence, reached Quebec in 1535, and began fur-trading in the area.[7] Cartier is regarded by Francophones as the founder of Canada. Samuel de Champlain established the first French settlement in 1604 and moved it to Port Royal in Acadia. A French company called the One Hundred Associates became active in the lucrative fur trade. Frenchmen settling at Quebec and in Montreal were attracted by riches in the interior of the vast territory.

French rule in Canada lasted from 1664 to 1760. The way of life in New France emphasized feudalism and a settled ecclesiastical organization. The feudal order transplanted from France took on, in rural districts, a modified form of the seignorial system, in which peasants, or habitants, rendered customary feudal services. The Roman Catholic Church, under centralized control of the bishop at Quebec, assumed a powerful position in the colony. Both the government and the system of law were under centralized control. French mercantilists expected New France to function on behalf of the mother country.

The English had no intention of remaining idle while the French appropriated Canada's riches. Pointing to the discoveries of the Cabots as evidence of priority, they encouraged settlements in the new territory. Where the French penetrated into the interior, English settlers preferred the Atlantic coastal regions. From the beginning, each side regarded the other as an interloper without a just claim to the territory. In the seesaw conflict, the English won Port Royal in 1614 and Quebec in 1620; the French took Quebec in 1629.

Competition between the French and the English in Canada was reflected in a long-standing rivalry between the two peoples on the Continent, which included King William's War (1688–1687) and the War of the Spanish Succession (1702–1713). By the Treaty of Utrecht in 1713, the English were given Nova Scotia and had confirmed their occupancy of Newfoundland and the forts on Hudson Bay. The French attempted to confine the English to the eastern part of the continent by setting up a series of forts anchored at Quebec and extending through the Great Lakes region to the Mississippi Valley and Louisiana.

The European Seven Years' War (1756–1763) was also fought in North America, where it was known as the French and Indian Wars. Most Indian tribes, with the exception of the Iroquois, sided with the French, while American colonists fought for the British. In the early stage of the war, the French maintained the advantage, due primarily to the brilliant leadership of General Louis Joseph de Montcalm, as well as to the inefficiency of British commanders. In 1758, however, the British were able to capture key French ports. The next year, British General James Wolfe defeated Montcalm on the Plains of Abraham, bringing about the fall of Quebec. Montreal fell in 1760. The Treaty of Paris in 1763 brought an end to New France and established British rule in Canada.

The issue was thus settled by force of arms. Several factors contributed to British supremacy in Canada. British colonists there were careful to develop resources of their own without too much reliance on the mother country, while the settlers in New France remained dependent on France. In Europe, the French were so weakened by their campaigns against Frederick the Great that they could not maintain their widely separated forts in Canada. British sea power was effective in cutting supplies from France to Canadian strongholds. British persistence eventually won the struggle in Canada.

From 1760 to 1867 Canada was a part of British North America. London was faced with a new problem in Canada: how to deal with the French Canadians, a proud people of European background with a culture as old as that of the English. It was important to work out a system to ease the antagonism felt by people who believed that they had been robbed of their territory. Early efforts at appeasement failed. The Quebec Act of 1774, the great charter of French Canadian liberties, was designed to stabilize British rule by recognizing French rights in language, religion, and civil law. French civil law and English criminal law were to exist side by side.[8]

French Canadians, encouraged by concessions granted by the Quebec Act, did not join the American colonists in their War of Independence. American revolutionists hoped to annex Canada, but the attempt was a dismal failure. During the Revolution, American loyalists (United Empire loyalists) fled northward to Canada in large numbers and settled there.

Anglo-French rivalry continued into the opening decades of the 19th century and culminated in the rebellions of 1837. London showed its alarm by sending Lord Durham (1792–1840), known as a colonial reformer, on a mission to win back disaffected Canadian opinion by recommending political reforms. His *Report*[9] (1839), despite its low opinion of French Canadians, became the Magna Carta of the British colonial system.[10] Its main proposal was to provide responsible government for Canada in a dominion status within the framework of British colonial unity. Durham also recommended the union of Upper and Lower Canada into one colony.

A great landmark in Canadian history came on July 1, 1867, with the British North America Act (BNA) proclaiming the union of Ontario, Quebec, Nova Scotia, and New Brunswick. The union originally included only four provinces, but it became the nucleus to which other provinces were later added. A federal system of government was modeled after the British Parliament as well as a Cabinet structure under the Crown. By Section 33 of the BNA, the French language was given equal status with English in the Parliament at Ottawa, in the Quebec Legislature, and in the federal law courts. Each province retained control of its local affairs, but an appointed Senate and a House of Commons elected by the people held authority over national matters. The British sovereign was represented by a governor-general who acted as the constitutional head of state. As in Great Britain, a Cabinet of ministers responsible to Parliament exercised essential executive functions.[11]

From 1867 to 1914, the Dominion of Canada made progress in nation-building by extending and developing its economic life. It played an important role in the Allied campaign against Germany in World War I. In 1930 it was proclaimed a self-governing dominion in the British Empire. When the Empire gave way to the Commonwealth, Canada became an independent member.

This maturation of Canada as a nation took place in an atmosphere of increasing French dissatisfaction. The *Québécois* and the French minorities outside the province complained of discrimination at the federal level and lack of responsibility for governing the country. They rejected English efforts at accommodation. They especially resented a foreign policy which they considered to be too submissive to British imperial designs. Quebec, they said, was not a province like Ontario and Manitoba but the homeland of a distinct people with separate language, culture, institutions, traditions, and economic resources. They were not a minority under English rule, they said, but a distinct people. This kind of dissatisfaction crystallized into a strong mini-nationalism calling for separation and independence.

The Bilingual Gap

In Scottish nationalism, language played a comparatively insignificant role, but in Quebec, it was of major importance. Linguistic rivalry between French and English became the focus of differences between the two communities. Conflict over language policy led to a series of confrontations.[12]

French-speaking Canadians make up about 20 percent of the 22,998,000 Canadians.[13] In Quebec the French-speaking majority runs to 80 percent. It claimed to be a French island in an English-speaking sea. Quebeckers argued that a common language such as theirs provided the main ingredient of a nation-state. Their linguistic pride was expressed in the slogan: "*De plus en plus en Québec c'est en français qui ça se passe*" ("More and more in Quebec it's in French that things are happening"). They saw the language issue as appropriate to self-government. Any national group of substance, they said, deserves to govern itself.

To Anglophones, this attitude was a threat to national union. Quebec's English-speaking minority, about 20 percent in a population of 6,224,000,[14] rejected the idea of separatism. Anglophone grievances came from little things. An Anglophone housewife stormed out of a store because the salesclerk, who knew English well, insisted on speaking French. An English-speaking journalist in Quebec City was denied permission to transfer his daughter from a French to an English school. English-speaking bosses ordered their employees to "speak white," an insulting term to Francophones. The Anglophone Freedom of Choice movement agitated on the ground that their linguistic rights had been abrogated.[15]

This long-standing bilingual clash was intensified in August 1978, when the Quebec Government made an attempt to preserve French by restricting the use of English. The Legislative Assembly approved a Draconian law, known as Bill 101, which made French the only "official" language in Quebec. The bill gave official standing only to the French version of laws, though English translations would be provided. French was to be spoken in the courts, except where the contending parties agreed beforehand on English. Only the French version of a legal judgment was to be regarded as legitimate. All business with the provincial government was to be conducted in French. Doctors and lawyers were expected to display "appropriate fluency" in French in order to practice. French was to be "the official language of work." The bill also limited the right of new Quebec residents, including Canadians from English-speaking provinces, to send their children to English-speaking schools.[16]

According to Camille Layrin, then Quebec's Minister of Cultural Affairs, Bill 101 was designed to make Quebec "as French as Ontario is English." Anglophones reacted angrily to the new law. The Positive Action Committee, which claimed the support of 32,000 English-speaking Quebeckers, announced that Bill 101 "conveyed a message to all non-French speakers in the province that is clear and unequivocal. The present government in Quebec does not respect their rights to continue as healthy, viable and creative minorities."[17] The Association of English-speaking School Boards of Quebec proclaimed its strong opposition to Bill 101. The Quebec administration, warning that public funds and diplomas would be withheld from children registered illegally, appealed to Anglophones "to uphold the British tradition of respect for the law."[18]

Some businesses, which, under the new language law, had to operate in French, moved from Canada. The Quebec Government was adamant: it would not settle "for a few words of French." It directed *L'Office de la Langue Française* to supervise conversion of all business enterprises to French. It also ordered police to arrest any strikers whose picket signs were in English. It decreed that all posters and signboards were to be in French.[19]

The explosive language issue revealed that a wide gulf separated Francophones from Anglophones in Quebec. The gap was destined to widen soon into political confrontation.

Dual Culturalism

The accommodation of Scottish and English cultures served to lessen the impact of Scottish separatism, but in Canada, there was little amalgamation of differing cultures. Cultural differences were, in effect, an extension of the language issue. There was little cross-fertilization, no fusing or melting of diverse strains.[20]

English Canadian culture, largely derivative, was imported from Britain and the United States. In theme and attitude, the "native" Canadian strain had its origin primarily in England. Britain was the model in the colonial era as well as in the 19th and 20th centuries. Canadian novelists, historians, poets, dramatists, and musicians looked to London for inspiration. They glorified the Canadian landscape and life on farms, in towns, and fishing villages, but the impulse came from across the Atlantic. There was a nationalistic emphasis, but it was diffuse and subtle, a dominantly English culture making its way in a perturbed federation. It paid little or no attention to French strains.

Francophones, on their part, deemed it expedient and, indeed, a matter of survival to maintain their own special cultural heritage. There was an efflorescence of French Canadian literary activity in the middle of the 19th century conterminous with the rise of Quebec nationalism.[21]

Writers in French hoped to inculcate in Quebeckers a sense of pride in their past and a determination to protect their heritage. They emphasized the theme of nationalism in one form or another.[22] Richard Jones described it: "The French Canadian of our day considers himself, consciously or unconsciously, to be part of a colonized minority. It is this particular image that is the source of his nationalism."[23]

While French Canadian writers agreed on the desirability of maintaining their own special cultural traditions, they took differing positions: (1) advocacy of a French-language culture in Canada as a whole (la survivance); (2) call for a special status for Quebec inside the federation; and (3) demand for outright independence.[24]

Abbé Lionel-Adolph Broulx (1878–1967), clergyman-historian, supported the idea of two nations in a federal union rather than separation. This view was held also by novelist Félix-Antoine Savard, whose Menaud Maître-Draveur (1937) was strongly nationalistic in tone.[25] Both Broulx and Savard deplored French "economic servitude" and denounced the sale of their "nation" to foreign countries as the main danger for French national survival.

Other French Canadian writers also stressed the original French idyl but called more emphatically for separation instead of autonomy. Hubert Aquin, political activist and leader of the Rassemblement pour l'Indépendance Nationale, demanded outright independence. In his novel, Prochain Épisode, a spy story, Aquin pointed to the "next episode" as a revolution to be accomplished. He denounced English conquest and colonization and gave historical examples for the impending revolution (Roman Empire, France, Italy, and Cuba). The novel took a clear-cut political position.[26]

Other poets and playwrights also emphasized the uniqueness of French Canadian culture. Gaston Miron, who became known as the voice of Quebec nationalism, urged his compatriots to unite in the cause of separatism: "The majority of our creators—the novelists, playwrights, artists, poets, and singers—are in favor of independence as well as a strong proportion of the intelligentsia, the scholars, the university people."[27] Miron's poems asserted his pride in French Quebec and his bitterness against the more numerous English Canadians.[28] The trend to independence, he insisted, was "irreversible."

Playwrights, too, joined the chorus for independence. One of the most popular recent plays staged in Quebec City, La Complainte des Hivers Rouges (The Red Winters' Lament) by Roland LePage, paid tribute to an abortive 1837 rebellion against the British.[29]

Despite efforts to build a bridge between the two cultures, the conflict extended to education from primary schools to universities. At the lower levels, parents adamantly supported their own language and culture and resented efforts to impose "foreignisms" on their children. McGill University in Montreal, regarded as a symbol of Canada's Anglophone elite, had to face an increasingly assertive French-speaking student body. Among Francophones, McGill University had a local reputation as an arrogant bastion of QWASP (Quebec White Anglo-Saxon Protestant) culture in a dominantly French-speaking province. On one occasion thousands of French-speaking students marched on the campus shouting *"McGill Française!"* In retaliation, the provincial government, responsible for a major portion of the university's budget, began a fiscal squeeze.[30]

The accelerating cultural conflict indicated a lack of success for the hoped-for diversity in unity. The accent on separate cultures was a barrier to political accommodation.

Economic Grievances

As in the case of mini-nationalisms elsewhere, added to alienating bilingualism and biculturalism were economic grievances which helped polarize federal and provincial relations. Many Quebeckers felt that they were allowed only a secondary role in Canadian economic life. Their traditional fear of insecurity was intensified. Like the Catholics of Northern Ireland, Quebeckers claimed that they were unjustly shut out of the country's economic life.

Despite its considerable distances and harsh climate, Canada had been converted into an urban, industrialized state. Its rich natural resources had provided raw materials for industry since the early days of exploration and colonization. Agriculture was a major pursuit, although its share of the total economy tended to diminish as industry drew the bulk of people from the countryside into urban centers. An important part of the economy was the exportation of wheat, especially grain. The manufacturing establishment, too, compared favorably with those of other highly developed countries.

The Canadian economy has undergone significant change.[31] There was a period of rapid growth in the first decade after World War I. A slowdown followed by a severe recession came in 1957, due partly to world economic conditions and partly to overexploitation of rich but nonrenewable resources.

French Canadian resentment increased in direct proportion to this unfavorable economic development. Quebeckers already considered themselves second-rate citizens in the economic structure of the country. Throughout most of Quebec's history, French families had shunned business and commerce—activities which they were inclined to leave to Anglophones. They preferred to stay on farms, although those who could afford to sent their sons to urban centers to be educated. The result was that English-speaking Canadians took over a virtual monopoly in business and industry.

Only after World War II did Quebeckers make a serious effort to take a more active share in the country's economic life. With new opportunities, they began to demand a greater share in business and industry. No longer would they be regarded as "hewers of wood and drawers of water." They were not satisfied with their subsidiary role in a federal union in which they were supposed to have equal rights. They claimed a greater share of Canada's riches and more economic security.

Unfortunately for them, Quebeckers made their economic demands at a time when the country was sliding into a severe recession. The situation worsened in the late 1970s. Within a year after the separatists had won political power in Quebec in 1976, the economy plummeted to a new low. Unemployment rose to a record 11.4 percent, 23 percent above the national average and 43 percent larger than that of Ontario. Joblessness in Montreal rose to 49 percent above the 1976 level. In the first five months of 1977, 186 more federally chartered companies left Quebec than had moved in. Private investment lagged. More than 40,000 Quebeckers left the province to seek a living elsewhere.[32] Quebec was threatened by a flight of people, capital, and business.

Canadians, both federalists and separatists, were deeply concerned by these proliferating economic difficulties. Federalists judged the economic decline to be a nationwide phenomenon running through all sectors of the national economy. The proposed secession of Quebec, they insisted, was no solution: it would bring disaster for everyone. If Quebec left the union, it would immediately lose financial support from Ottawa. Unemployment, already severe, would double overnight because at least a third of Quebec's manufacturing jobs depended on sales to the rest of Canada.

Quebec's nationalists were unimpressed by these arguments. Quebec, they said, had resources, business, and industry of its own, including global markets for its pulp, iron ore, and asbestos. If it separated from the rest of Canada, it could still retain its business and industrial relations with the United States, Europe, and the developing nations. If some businesses left Quebec, that was due to scare speeches, to "a poisonous climate maintained in great part by the English-speaking media and by federal propaganda."[33]

The clash between federalists and separatists on economic viability revealed how mini-nationalisms, like the larger nationalisms, were impelled by a complex combination of motivations. The economic factor was an important one in the solidification of separatist sentiment, but it was by no means the only one. It should be added to linguistic, cultural, social, political, and psychological elements to ascertain the real nature of a mini-nationalism.

Quebec's Political Road to Separation

Canadian bilingualism and biculturalism led inevitably to political differences. Quebec nationalism was crystallized from 1885 to 1911 at a time when French Canadians were seeking equal political status at the federal level. Wilfred Laurier, Prime Minister from 1896 to 1911, was of French Canadian origin, but he favored cooperation between the French and the English.[34] In 1885 Honoré Mercier formed the Nationalist Party out of former Liberals and Conservatives. His viewpoint on nationalism was quite different from that of Laurier. He emphasized an embattled French defending their culture against the Anglo-Saxon majority and intimated that separation was the eventual goal.[35] His defense of French institutions was reinforced at the end of the century by still another nationalist theme—an unwillingness of French Canadians to take part in foreign wars for the benefit of British imperialism.[36] Quebec's nationalists opposed conscription and denounced Canadian participation in the Boer War (1899–1902).

The pace of Quebec national sentiment increased dramatically in the 20th century. Québecois novelists, poets, and historians, calling the confederation a failure, supported a French Canadian renascence. The breach was widened during World War I, when conscription again led to a crisis.[37] The issue was complicated by the new status of Canada inside the British Empire: because of her contribution to Allied victory, Whitehall gave her recognition as an autonomous country. The idea of Canadian autonomy was strengthened further by Canadian participation in World War II. From Quebec, however, came even louder cries for independence.

In the 1950s, Quebec's nationalists intensified their opposition to "federal authoritarianism" and what they claimed to be federal anti-labor policies. A group of young French Canadians took over the Quebec Liberal Party. With a platform dedicated to reform, they came to political power in 1961. Reelected in 1962, they began what they called "the Quiet Revolution," which was designed to modernize the province and give preference to its French culture.

Worried about this reformist trend, the central government in Ottawa offered special status to Quebec: it would not be required to participate in the federal welfare program. English-speaking Canadians immediately denounced the concession as unwarranted appeasement. Quebec extremists reacted by a series of bombings in the English-speaking districts of Montreal. Faced with this crisis, Prime Minister

Lester Bowles Pearson appointed a royal commission of investigation in July 1963. He ordered the Bilingual and Bicultural Commission, consisting of five Anglophones and five Francophones, to recommend what steps should be taken "to develop the Canadian Confederation on the basis of equal partnership between the two founding races."

The Commission's task was even more difficult than at first believed. It examined historical and legal backgrounds and held hearings and regional conferences to assess public attitudes. A preliminary report in 1965 documented the existence of two societies inside Canada, a fact already well known to the Canadian public, and stated that "Canada, without being fully conscious of the fact, was passing through the greatest crisis in its history." The final, multi-volumed report, which appeared in 1967, proposed to establish nationwide equality in languages at both federal and provincial levels.

Quebec's extremists, especially the *Front Libération de Québec*, were unsatisfied by the Commission's report. In October 1970 came the so-called Quebec crisis, triggered by the kidnapping of James Cross, British Trade Commissioner in Montreal, and the abduction and murder of Pierre Laporte, Quebec's Labor Minister. At this time Prime Minister Pierre Trudeau invoked Canada's 1914 War Measures Act and placed the entire country under martial law.[38] Moderate Quebeckers, shocked by extremist actions, approved Trudeau's harsh anti-terrorist measure.

The situation gradually eased, but it stirred again in the mid-1970s. In November 1976 the electorate of Quebec, in a stunning decision, rejected the liberal government of Robert Bourassa and returned René Lévesque and his separatist *Parti Québecois* (PQ) to power.[39] The PQ had no specific program of separatism, but it clearly hoped for eventual independence. Lévesque and its leaders damned "this sick Confederation" and presented the slogan: "Quebec for *Québécois!*" There was no satisfactory coexistence, they complained, "only a continuous aggression of the language of the majority."

The *Parti Québecois* had its own solution for the language problem. It introduced in Quebec's Legislative Assembly the measure known as Bill 101 (mentioned earlier), which made French the only official language in Quebec. The proposed law sent a shock wave through the English community, which saw it as a clear affront and which dreaded its effect on business and education. Anglophones began to speak of the bankruptcy of appeasement and denounced the situation in which French Canadians were given a disproportionately large share in federal affairs.[40]

PQ leaders stated that they would support a referendum on the separatist issue. Suspicious Anglophones replied that, even before any vote was scheduled, separatists would make doubly sure of victory by proposing referendum rules in their favor.

FLQ: Hard-Line Terrorists

Most Quebeckers were moderates who hoped to see the issue solved through legal and non-violent means. During the decade from 1960 to 1970, however, the *Front Libération de Québec* (FLQ), a small extremist element, began to agitate for separatism. Rejecting reform as inconsequential, these hard-liners would settle for nothing less than independence.

Beginning in 1963, the FLQ launched an activist program of bombing, burning, and looting. Its members planted bombs in the mailboxes of Anglophones in Montreal's suburbs. At first they used small devices, but in 1969, they set off a powerful detonation at the Montreal Stock Exchange which caused 27 injuries. Bombings increased from 35 (1963–1967) to 50 (1968–1970). Holdups by FLQ members multiplied from 8 (1963–1967) to 20 (1968–1970). By the fall of 1970, FLQ terrorists had claimed 6 lives.[41]

Most Quebeckers, alienated by FLQ tactics, approved harsh anti-terrorist measures taken by the central government. FLQ extremism, especially the murder of Laporte, was discredited. The Quebec public, aware of political assassinations throughout the world, which they had regarded as distant thunder, now saw unwelcome incidents on their own soil.

Trudeau Versus Lévesque

The issue of federalism or separatism became the focal point of both Canadian and Quebeckian politics. Political leaders and the public alike were divided; Canadian Prime Minister Pierre Trudeau and Quebec's Premier René Lévesque took diametrically opposed positions on the future of Canada.

Trudeau and Lévesque had much in common: both advocated the democratic process and both believed the issue could be solved without violence; both sought to preserve the French language in a country in which three-fourths of the people spoke English. Trudeau, a one-man bridge, would safeguard the French heritage inside a bilingual Canada. Lévesque saw the solution in the eventual formation of an independent state controlled only by Quebeckers.

Pierre Trudeau was born in Montreal on October 18, 1919, the son of a millionaire oil and land investor.[42] After taking a law degree at the

University of Montreal, he spent several years studying politics at Harvard University and in Paris and London. Returning to Montreal in 1949, he worked as a labor lawyer and economist. He entered politics as an opponent of the provincial government of Premier Maurice Duplessis. Erudite, debonair, fluently bilingual, he became known as a philosopher-statesman. He advanced rapidly in his political career and, in 1968, became Canadian Prime Minister.[43]

Trudeau sought to persuade his fellow French Canadians that their best hope for political, economic, and cultural survival lay inside the federal system.[44] He had two goals: "One was to make sure that Quebec would not leave Canada through separation, and the other was to make sure that Canada would not shove Quebec out through narrow-mindedness."[45] Quebeckers, he said, must be masters in their own house, but it was essential that the house must be the whole of Canada. Above all, they must be assured equality inside the Canadian Confederation.

Trudeau saw the consequences of an independent Quebec as disastrous for the rest of Canada. "It is a hypothesis I cannot contemplate because we would be renouncing our heritage. So for me it is unthinkable. It would be a major setback in the course of history. And the burden would lie with those who would like to break up one of history's greatest achievements—the Canadian Confederation."[46] For Trudeau, any political theory which called for sovereignty for diverse Canadian groups could only be regressive and destructive. He urged that the Canadian Confederation be maintained as a real confederation, not as a union of quasi-independent states in economic association. As a model, he pointed to the Swiss cantonal system, with its French-, German-, and Italian-speaking autonomous cantons and its use of three official languages at the confederation level.

As Prime Minister, Trudeau regarded himself as the federal standard-bearer, but at the same time, he made sure to expand the role of Quebeckers and their language in the Canadian system. As a French Canadian, he could speak to the people of Quebec in terms that would be closed to Anglophones. He could tell them about the dangers of independence and the advantages of federation. He could use terms of brutal frankness that would be perceived as patronizing if they came from an outsider.[47] He favored a degree of centralization, but not to a point where national government became impossible. Canada, he said, was already one of the most decentralized countries in the world. His views had a sobering effect on a people who seemed favorably inclined to the views of separatists.

Despite Trudeau's efforts to maintain national unity, the nagging question of Quebec's place in the confederation remained. Opposition crystallized in the person of René Lévesque. In contrast to Trudeau's affluent background, Lévesque came from one of Quebec's farming regions. The son of a lawyer, he earned his college degree at Laval University in Quebec City but was suspended from its law school for smoking in a lecture hall. After a stint as a popular television newsman, he turned to politics. Described as "a chain-smoking, disorganized, hot-tempered bundle of emotional energy,"[48] he was actually shy and self-deprecating. His platform speeches were extemporaneous, his meandering style contrasted with Trudeau's formal but subtle delivery. Lévesque, like Trudeau, advanced rapidly in politics, serving as a Liberal member of Parliament and as the country's Justice Minister and Attorney General. A fervid Quebec nationalist ("I am first a *Québécois* and second, with a rather growing doubt, a Canadian"), he urged his fellow Quebeckers to throw off the English yoke. In 1967 he formed the *Mouvement Souveraineté Association,* the forerunner of his *Parti Québécois.* His PQ moved steadily forward until, in the election of 1976, it toppled the Liberal Government of Robert Bourgassa in Quebec and won 69 of 110 seats in the provincial assembly. Lévesque became Quebec's Premier.

Lévesque ran on a platform of good government. He was careful to play down the separatism issue but made it clear, nevertheless, that he favored political separation "in a positive way." He expressed distaste for the word "secession." In an interview he declared that separation should be accomplished peacefully and in a democratic manner. The people of Quebec, he said, form a national entity with a different language, culture, and outlook existing over several centuries. The language issue was critically important: "There are two nations here, and the *Québécois* will make it clear what they want through a referendum which should be as democratic and well-prepared as possible—not improvised. The Confederation has been a negative force and only force of habit has held Quebec to it. We are like two trains getting farther and farther away from each other. For 30 years Quebec has been moving towards self-affirmation, self-determination, and self-government, which does not mesh with the federal system."[49]

Lévesque was certain that Quebec would be viable as an independent state, even more so than most members of the United Nations. "In terms of gross national product, Quebec would rank 23rd in the world. In per-capita income, No. 11. In terms of potential material resources, we would be recognized as one of the most advanced and enlightened societies in the world."[50] Such arguments were convincing, in the opinion of Francophones who dreamed of their own French state on Canadian soil.

The French Connection

Since the British victory on the Plains of Abraham in 1759, France regarded her one-time colony as irretrievably lost. Paris kept strictly out of
Canadian domestic affairs. Then, in July 1967, came a sensational incident which gave global publicity to Quebec nationalism. After a trium-
phal motorcade through the heart of French Canada, French President
Charles de Gaulle arrived on an official visit to Montreal. In his sepul-
chral tone recognized by audiences everywhere, de Gaulle, in a speech
delivered from the balcony at City Hall, shouted the catch phrase "*Vive le
Québec Libre!*"—Long live Free Quebec!"

De Gaulle's words were wholly unexpected—and astonishing. They
were, however, quite in line with his character and personality. Patriot
par excellence, one of the great egotists of the 20th century, the French
President looked upon himself as the embodiment of France. He believed that he not only spoke for France—he was France.[51] His mind was
filled with battle pictures in which his beloved compatriots were always
winning. France, he was certain, was assured of an exalted destiny.
France could not be France without greatness. Allied leaders in World
War II had to contend with that kind of Gallic arrogance. Churchill regarded de Gaulle as one of his most annoying problems, and Roosevelt
dismissed him as a latter-day Joan of Arc.

It is possible that de Gaulle's words were designed not only as an
expression of French grandeur but also as a reminder for his fellow
Frenchmen that they had a special cultural association with their distant
cousins. Some patriotic Frenchmen saw, indeed, the glimmer of a prospect that there might be a reversal of Britain's conquest of French
Canada, but most of them, knowing their bombastic President, dismissed
the incident as merely an exaggerated but friendly salute to the second
largest French-speaking community in the industrialized world.

English Canadians were not amused. Anglophone authorities informed the visiting President that his statement was unacceptable and
intimated that he was no longer welcome in Canada. For English Canadians, the Confederation was not a British or a French idea but a union
of separate ethnic Canadians. The accomplishments and progress of
their country were due, they believed, to joint efforts of both peoples,
and any attempt by de Gaulle to divide them was an unwarranted interference in Canadian affairs. They urged the French President to concern
himself with his own separatists in Brittany, Corsica, and the Basque
country. In pointed words, they invited him to keep his prominent Gallic
nose out of Canadian affairs.

Quebec's nationalists, as was to be expected, were delighted. For them,
de Gaulle's clarion call was an endorsement of their views. They did not

forget the gesture. On November 1, 1977, Lévesque, who was in France to solicit support for his movement, paid a visit to de Gaulle's tomb in the tiny village of Columby-les-Deux-Églises. After a moment of silence, Lévesque described de Gaulle as "a clear-minded friend of Quebec." Most French Canadians, he said, would have liked to have said the same thing. The French President had been prophetic—success of the *Parti Québécois* had been part of an inevitable evolution toward independence. French villagers watched approvingly.[52]

When asked in an interview whether he felt that President Valéry Giscard d'Estaing and other French leaders wanted Quebec to become independent, Lévesque replied: "The general trend of our discussions with our various interlocutors—both government and opposition—was that they would like to see us opt for independence. They were all sympathetic to the changes we are proposing because they dovetail with their own confederal perceptions for Europe's future."[53]

It was an optimism not shared by federalists in Canada. The French connection between Quebec and Paris was ephemeral at best. Realistic Frenchmen, busy with problems of their own, did not want renewal.

Quebec Votes "Non"

Appearances concerning the vitality of a mini-nationalism may be deceiving. The apparently cascading strength of a national movement does not necessarily mean that it has won the support of the majority of the people. When the issue is finally put to the test in a referendum, especially in democratic countries, those who in the past have warmly supported separatism often have second thoughts in the polling booth. Deciding that their security lies in union, they are reluctant to enter an uncharted realm. More autonomy—yes; independence—no. This tendency was revealed clearly in Scottish and in Welsh referendums. Such was also the case in Canada.

The Canadian debate grew ever sharper, public rhetoric on both sides more threatening. The principal arguments used by each side on a proposed sovereignty referendum were:

YES—The major crisis in Canada between the French majority in Quebec and the English majority in Canada can be resolved only by establishing equality between them. Like mini-nationalists everywhere, French Quebeckers believed that the federal system inhibited their development. In 1831 Alexis de Tocqueville called them "the conquered race." The situation, they asserted, had not changed. Equality could be achieved only by giving Quebec the sovereign right to protect its culture and insure its development. Quebec's citizens had achieved a maturity that enabled them to assume control of their own destiny. They would settle for a temporary nation with two languages.

NO—The federalists stayed with their vision of a large Canadian nation with two languages. They pointed to the genius of their founding fathers who gave them a constitution which had worked for 110 years and which provided for necessary adjustments. Liquidation of the Canadian Confederation would be a disaster. It was untenable. Federalists admitted that, in economic terms, French Canadians had not been treated generously. They also acknowledged a certain amount of intolerance, but they promised fair accommodation with French Canadian views.

Canada, said the federalists, was one of the freest and most prosperous nations in the world. Quebeckers, they insisted, have actually benefitted from these advantages. The proposed association between two sovereign entities was not desirable because the rest of Canada would not accept it. A solution of the crisis, they believed, lay not in dissolution of the Canadian state but in the perfection of democratic federalism. Canada, they warned, must not be allowed to slide back into Balkanized provincialism. An independent Quebec, they said, would eventually turn out to be a French-speaking ghetto in a land of Anglophones.

For several months before the referendum, the balance between the "Yes" and the "No" sides seesawed in newspaper polls. In the weeks before the vote, the "No's" maintained a slight lead, making the federalists increasingly confident of victory. On May 18, 1980, however, the "Yes" side took a surprising lead in a poll published by the Montreal newspaper *Dimanche-Matin.* The poll showed 40 percent in favor of the proposal and 37 percent opposed, a reversal of the survey by the same polling organization a week earlier. The remaining 23 percent were undecided or declined to answer.[54]

The question given voters in the referendum read as follows:[55]

The Government of Quebec has made public its proposal to negotiate a new agreement with the rest of Canada, based on the equality of nations.

This agreement would enable Quebec to acquire the exclusive power to make its laws, levy its taxes and establish relations abroad—in other words, sovereignty—and, at the same time, to maintain with Canada an economic association, including a common currency.

No change in political status resulting from these negotiations will be effected without approval by the people through another referendum.

On these terms do you give the Government of Quebec the mandate to negotiate the proposed agreement between Quebec and the rest of Canada?

The issue came to a head in the historic referendum held on May 20, 1980. In one of the heaviest turnouts in Quebec's electoral history, voters rejected the move to sovereignty.[56] The "No" vote was 2,140,814, or 59.4

percent; the "Yes" vote was 1,475,509, or 40.6 percent. The separatists did not win even a majority of the Francophones, who made up 80 percent of the province. About 54 percent of the French joined with more than 80 percent of the Anglophone minority to produce a decisive federalist victory.

Jubilant federalists who had assembled in a Montreal sports arena cheered their victory. Thousands of nationalists, gathered in another sports arena, had hoped to celebrate a triumph, but they turned into a sullen, weeping crowd which booed the results displayed on a huge bulletin board. Young militants from East Montreal marched toward the English-speaking western part of the city, shouting, "We want a country." Blinking back tears, Premier Lévesque conceded defeat, but in a final gesture of defiance, urged his followers to "fight on until the next time."[57]

The Inflamed Controversy

The people of Quebec had voted for Canada. In decisively rejecting independence, they had checked, for the moment, the dissolution of the country. Through democratic means, they had decided that Canada would not become, like pre-Bismarckian Germany or pre-Cavour Italy, a geographical expression. They had been attracted by the idea of sovereignty, but they also sensed great economic dangers. If separated from the rest of Canada, they would become economically vulnerable, with new problems of currency, capital, movement of goods, new relations with the European Economic Community and the International Economic Fund, and the imposition of external tariffs. They understood that such economic dislocations might be crippling.

Added to this fear was an uncomfortable feeling that a small, independent Quebec might not long endure and might become subservient to the giant neighbor to the south. Graham Spry, a Canadian journalist, expressed this sentiment: "In the course of time and of increased economic and communications pressure, the several parts [of Canada] would almost certainly fall, whatever the political terminology, into subordination to the United States."[58]

Quebec had given its vote, but not its deep sentiment, to the cause of federation. There was a sense of relief not only in Quebec but throughout the country as well. At the same time, few Canadians believed that the issue was dead; in fact, it was not.

Prime Minister Trudeau, champion of federation, was faced with a herculean task. He called for peace "with my fellow Quebeckians who have been wounded in defeat." "We have all lost a little in this referendum. If you take account of the broken friendships, the strained family relationships, the hurt pride, there is no one among us who has not suffered some wound which we must try to heal in the days and weeks to come."[59] He acknowledged that the Canadian federation would have to be reshaped to take Francophone grievances into account. He would make what he called "a most solemn commitment" in return for Quebec's "*Non*" vote to separatism.

Trudeau believed that Canada was already one of the most decentralized countries in the world. He would resist further decentralization by proposing a new constitution and a new charter suitable for Canada's regional diversity and bilingual culture. In his mind, this was the key issue. It was necessary, he said, to remodel an archaic constitutional system to succeed the British North America Act of 1867 that ceded substantial powers to the provincial governments. He called for "patriation" from London. He felt that it was necessary to halt the trend to autonomy—cultural, as in Francophone Quebec, and economic, as in oil-rich Alberta. He summoned representatives of the rebellious provinces to discuss a new federal parliamentary structure, a new system of elections, and the adoption of a Canadian Bill of Rights.

In Trudeau's view, the national charter would take precedence over any bill of rights enacted by individual provinces. Among other freedoms, the charter would guarantee minority-language education. Until that time, Canadian education was almost entirely a provincial responsibility. The proposed "Charter of Rights" would give the federal government additional powers.

Representatives of the federal and provincial governments met in Ottawa throughout the summer of 1980 to reach an accord on constitutional change. Provincial premiers bitterly criticized the proposed changes because they would lose many of their powers. Lévesque demanded that no restrictions be placed on Quebec's legislative powers over education. He charged Trudeau with "erecting a monument to himself on the tombs of our aspirations and rights."[60] He was joined by most of the provincial premiers who opposed a bill of rights with the argument that Parliament, not the courts, should guard civil liberties. Western leaders also warned Ottawa to keep its hands off their vital oil and gas deposits.

The conference collapsed in acrimonious failure. Trudeau threatened to bring the issue to a national referendum. "Let us put reason before passion. Let's talk a little bit more with our intelligence. Then our gut feeling will be more for Canada than for any particular province or division of the country."[61]

In calling for "reason before passion," Trudeau pointed to the heart of the problem: both separatists and federalists feel deep emotions. Jane Jacobs, who favors peaceful separation, reveals the depth of conflicting passions: "Trying to argue about these feelings is as fruitless as trying to argue that people in love ought not to be in love, or that if they must be, then they should be cold and hard-headed about choosing their attachment. It doesn't work that way; our feelings are their own arguments."[62] Yet Jacobs sees a historical model in how Norway, in the last century, gradually and persistently broke its ties with Sweden and became a separate nation in a classic case of peaceful separation. That shows, she says, how a mother country and its formerly dependent province can combine their respective energies as autonomous states to the greater benefit of both.

Anglophones reject the parallel and call for sacred union. They profess to be disappointed by the obstinate refusal of the Francophones to give up their language and customs. They condemn the French as tradition-bound, clannish, backward, and indifferent to national honor. They match the French in accenting old resentments and nourishing new grievances.

That mini-nationalist sentiment has a way of persisting despite temporary defeat was indicated once more, when, in the elections of April 13, 1981, Premier Lévesque and his *Parti Québecois* were elected to a new term. Some 4 million voters who had rejected Quebec's separation from Canada in 1980 turned around and gave Lévesque a sweeping vote of confidence in his ability to lead Quebec as a Canadian province. The stunning victory resulted in a new spontaneous outpouring of French Canadian nationalism, despite the fact that Lévesque had based his campaign on a promise that he would seek no new separatist initiative during his second term. Lévesque's new mandate encouraged bitter separatist demonstrations in the oil-and-gas-rich western provinces of Alberta, Saskatchewan, and British Columbia.

Lévesque bitterly opposed the proposal before the federal Parliament to establish a new Canadian Constitution. Prime Minister Trudeau proposed to ask Britain to abolish the British North America Act of 1867 and to transfer to Canada exclusive power to amend its constitution in the future. In mid-November 1981, all but one of the eight provincial premiers who had opposed Trudeau's plan dropped their opposition. Only Lévesque continued to protest.

The unhappy result of this latest attempt to solve the crisis was political and legal confusion. Canada remained a tormented country with national unity at stake in the continuing power struggle. An all-out Canadian consensus remains difficult in the face of emotional differences. Not even the democratic process of referendum has been able to heal the deep wounds. Here again an unsatisfied mini-nationalism threatens the structure of what was supposed to be a coherent state. The prognosis is not good—either here or in all those other pluralistic countries.

CHAPTER 14

THE AMERICAN MOSAIC ———

You cannot spill a drop of American blood without spilling the
blood of the whole world. . . . We are not a nation as much as a
world. . . . We are the heirs of all time and with all nations we
divide our inheritance.

—Herman Melville

The American Experience

That the United States has been able to avoid a multiplicity of mini-
nationalisms such as those burdening nations elsewhere is due to its
special historical development.[1] It has many regional divisions, varied
groups, religions, and economic interests, but it has been successful in
moderating these internal conflicts that have burdened other countries.
A persistent problem in Europe has been to find a way to unite various
sectional interests and traditions within a national whole that would
allow liberty of development to all its parts without imposing the
hegemony of one of them.[2] Whereas in Europe this tendency to federation found a rough road, it persisted and survived in the United States.

From its beginnings, the peopling of the United States presented a
unique tableau. The American nation was born during the 18th-century
Enlightenment with its accent on liberty, constitutionalism, and parliamentarianism. A fabulously rich and virtually empty continent was
occupied and taken over by Europeans of differing backgrounds. This
new society had little use for relics of medieval feudalism and man-
orialism. It placed great emphasis upon the right of every individual to
life, liberty, and the pursuit of happiness. The poor, the weak, the oppressed of Europe, who had been subjected to political and religious
disabilities, flocked to the New World. They enthusiastically accepted the
rough frontier life, abolished monarchy and aristocracy, separated
church and state, and forged a new society—a nation of many nations.

The fledgling American society was blessed with a number of in-
telligent and far-sighted Founding Fathers, among them Thomas Jefferson, John Adams, and Benjamin Franklin. Like other European
rationalists of the Enlightenment, they were exuberantly optimistic.
"Our sure, virtuous, public-spirited federative republic will last forever,"

199

said John Adams, "govern the globe, and introduce the perfection of man." While this utopian goal was not to be achieved, the Founding Fathers were successful in avoiding the kind of internal and external quarrels that complicated the European scene. They set up a careful balance between centralism and sectionalism, between centralization and decentralization, a balance that survived and gave the nation a generally effective political union. The tradition left little room for the emergence of a host of clamoring mini-nationalisms. The Founding Fathers held a diffuse society together by carefully balancing conflicting interests.

There were heavy and tragic costs. Europeans who created the American nation subjugated the native Indian population and made slaves of Africans. There was a terrible loss of life when ideological and economic differences could not be bridged: the disastrous Civil War of 1861–1865 nearly ended the promising American experiment. The nation managed to emerge intact from that tragedy, with new common denominators of society, politics, and economy—certainly enough to hold the national union together.

Immigrants came to the United States from all corners of Europe.[3] Most of the early national minorities settling in the New World retained much of their culture, but succeeding generations moved deliberately into the American mold. American society took on a national bias instead of local prejudices. Common attributes were solidified inside a larger nationalism. Different sections, varied groups, classes, and religions merged into a common centralism. The American constitutional system extended that balance between federal and states' rights recommended by the Founding Fathers. There were recurrent strains, but the system seemed to work. Minorities felt themselves to be part of the larger American dream. Each immigrant group saw its salvation in loyalty to the Union. Each rejected the psychology of separatism. Mini-nationalisms could not blossom in this balanced society.

Americans of varying backgrounds shared the fruits of prosperity and the onus of hard times. There was effective national unity in both world wars.[4] Polish-Americans, Italo-Americans, German-Americans, Norwegian-Americans, Swedish-Americans, Hispanic-Americans, American Indians, American Blacks, American Jews—all took pride in their overall Americanism. There was no language confrontation such as that dividing Francophones and Anglophones in Canada.[5] There was no fear of national dissolution such as that which worried the masters of the Kremlin.[6]

American minorities saw their security in the larger nationalism, not in their own special character, culture, and economy. Any urge for separation remained miniscule and ineffective. That there were advantages in the American Union was demonstrated by Alaskans (January 3, 1959) and Hawaiians (August 21, 1959) when they voted for statehood.

Two ethnic groups—Indians and blacks—played a special role in the amalgamation process: both were left behind in the progression of American life. Neither group, however, turned to a full-blown separatism to confront the national state. Instead, both sought to obtain a share of the national wealth inside the federal Union.

The predicted polarization between minorities and the centralized authorities did not take place, despite the views of pessimistic observers. Americans in general internalized their target of aspirations. This was due in part to economic and technological achievements and in part to the successful discrediting of foreign ideas promising high degrees of freedom, such as socialism, communism, internationalism, and world government.[7] American minorities were well aware of the nature of promised "freedoms" in either Bolshevik or Fascist ideologies. They had witnessed confrontations between Irish and English, between Muslims and Christians, between the Russians and Jews, and they wanted as little as possible of such clashes. Each minority was aware of its role in building America, and each hoped to share in the fruits of its technological achievements rather than press for autonomy, independence, or racial war. American blacks did not form ghetto states, nor were they moved by ideas of territorial imperative or Return-to-Africa. They had problems, but no alien ideology—they were Americans.

This kind of thinking by no means implied that perfect society envisioned by John Adams. Yet by and large, there has been no severe fragmentation into many squabbling antagonists on a large scale. Admittedly, there were relics of exploitation, but these had no legal justification, and efforts were made through legislation to correct injustices. There was a goal—to recognize the rights and aspirations of all minorities. This was not a perfect society, but it had elements of great strength. It was most difficult for mini-nationalisms, with their disintegrative characteristics, to flourish in an atmosphere of accommodation.

Aboriginals in the United States

It is believed that aboriginal peoples existed in North America more than 25,000 years ago. Of Mongoloid stock, at one time they presumably crossed the Bering Strait and spread eastward and southward from Alaska. Physically similar in appearance, they generally had straight black hair, copper-colored skin, aquiline noses, and prominent jaws. Most Indians today have intermingled with other stocks, especially with whites.

Indians settled in distinct tribes throughout North America. Hundreds of tribes lived in 59 recognized "families" north of Mexico. Aboriginal areas were marked by differences in language, culture, economy, and social organization. Among the varied languages were: Algonquian in the Atlantic coastal area; Iroquoian in regions bordering Lakes Ontario and Erie; Muskogean in the Gulf region; Siouan in the South Plains; and Salishan on the northwestern coast. Culture areas included: the eastern woodlands, based on maize and squash; the plains of the Midwest, geared to bison hunting; California, where the acorn was the staple food; and the Pacific Coast, based on salmon and seafood.

The history of the American Indian is a complex one.[8] Friction with early settlers began with the first colonies. Armed only with bow and arrow, tomahawk, and war club, aboriginals were no match for hungry, well-armed settlers. In New England the confrontation ended in 1637 with the virtual destruction of the Pequot tribe. The struggle between Virginia settlers and the Powhatan Confederacy ended in utter Indian defeat. King Philip of the Wampanoag Indians was defeated in New England; Tuscorars and Yamasses, in South Carolina.

In the French and Indian War, the North American phase of the Seven Years' War in Europe (1756–1763), some northern tribes were allied with the French but, in the end, were defeated decisively. With the formation of the Union, some attention was given to the plight of displaced Indians. Thomas Jefferson promoted the purchase of their lands and helped them move westward. In the War of 1812, British agents in Canada supported the able Chief Tecumseh. There were tragic consequences as the American frontier was pushed westward. Settlers appropriated Indian lands in defiance of treaty rights and destroyed the game on which aboriginals depended for food and clothing. There were bloody encounters in the South, where Andrew Jackson was victorious over the Creeks in Alabama and the Seminoles in Florida. Indian men, women, and children were slaughtered by American militiamen in the brutal Black Hawk War.

Congress then sought to remove eastern Indians to the Great Plains beyond the Mississippi. From 1832 to 1837, Indians were removed to the trans-Mississippi area in what was supposed to be new "Indian Country." By 1840 most of the Five Civilized Tribes—Creeks, Chocktaws, Chickasaws, Cherokees, and Seminoles—were settled there. In the continued territorial expansion to the West, hostile Comanche, Arapaho, and Cheyenne Indians opposed the formation of a new American road. By 1890 the old frontier was gone, and between 5 and 6 million white settlers were farming on what had been Indian land.

The march of the white man westward was destructive for the Indian. Shameful atrocities were committed in the process. Herds of buffalo were wiped out. In the "civilizing process," whole tribes were exterminated. Countless Indians succumbed to diseases which they could not withstand and to alcohol which was introduced by their white conquerors.

Toward the latter part of the 19th century, there was a dramatic change in the attitude of white Americans toward native Indians. At one time, most Americans regarded them as savages who had to be eliminated. Now that Indians were conquered and "civilized," it was not forgotten that they were the original owners of the soil and that their rights should be recognized more fully. It was an extended exercise in guilt: attempts were made to reward Indians for past brutal treatment and for excesses against their forebears.

The U.S. Government began to help Indians in farming, education, industry, and health. Public-spirited individuals and societies promoted the education of young Indians. As early as 1873, boarding and day schools were established on Indian reservations. In 1887 Congress passed the Dawes Severalty Act, which established the modern policy of absorbing American Indians into the body politic of the nation.[9]

From then on, a long series of steps followed to improve the status of the Indian and to compensate him for his lost land. The development culminated in a striking decision by the United States Supreme Court in the summer of 1980. Behind the decision were decades of dissension. In 1868 the United States and the Sioux Nation signed the Treaty of Fort Laramie, granting to the Sioux title to 7 million acres of their sacred Black Hills in South Dakota. Washington promised that the reservation would be "set apart for the absolute and undisturbed use and occupation of the Indian."

Sioux resistance led to the Battle of the Little Big Horn, where American army officer Col. George Custer and his men were killed on June 25, 1876.[10] When gold was discovered in the area, Congress cancelled the treaty and took over the land, granting the Sioux $6 million in subsistence provisions. Dissatisfied with the land-taking, the Sioux began to fight in court. On June 30, 1980, the U.S. Supreme Court ordered the Federal Government to pay not only $17.5 million for the land but also an extra $87.5 million in interest compounded at 5 percent since 1877. The Court's 8-to-1 majority affirmed an earlier ruling by the U.S. Court of Claims that the Fifth Amendment required the U.S. Government to provide compensation for all property it had seized.

This award, the largest ever made by the U.S. Court of Claims, was designed to be distributed eventually to 60,000 members of the Missouri Sioux tribe living on eight reservations.[11] There were some problems: Sioux tribes involved as plaintiffs in the case (six in South Dakota and one each in Nebraska and Montana) were more or less independently governed tribes. Many simply wanted their land back. There was some sentiment against accepting the cash settlement because it would in all probability extinguish future claims to the land itself.[12] Some Indians claimed that they had been bribed, threatened, and starved into signing away their land and, in its place, had been given desolate, eroded land, known today as the Badlands National Monument.[13] Others recognized that the action on accommodation was fair and that it served to discourage zealous separatism among American Indians.

Indian Nationalism

In 1924 Congress granted full citizenship to Indians. This act explicitly rejected the principle of the Dawes Severalty Act, which had implied that citizenship for Indians should be contingent on individual ownership of land. This reversed policy led to the Indian Reorganization Act of 1934, affirming the right of Indians to local self-government based on Indian customary law. Indians were to have a tribal council of representatives, and tribes would be organized as business corporations to manage their own resources.

Critics denounced the new relationship as "re-Indianizing the Indians." To the Indians themselves, however, the new situation offered the possibility of operating at the national level rather than as members of special tribes. In their past confrontation with the centralized government, they had chosen to form confederacies. Now they began to think in terms of a strengthened political, economic, and cultural union at the national level.

The result was the emergence of an American Indian nationalism.[14] In 1944, under the influence of John Collier, then Commissioner of Indian Affairs, the National Congress of American Indians (NCAI) was formed. Its original sponsors were Indians from various parts of the United States, mainly from Oklahoma and the Plains. Membership was exclusively Indian. The following is the preamble to the constitution of the organization:[15]

We, the members of the Indian tribes of the United States of America invoking the Divine guidance of Almighty God in order to secure for ourselves—the Indians of the United States and the Natives of Alaska—and our descendants the rights and benefits to which we are entitled under the laws of the United States, thereof, and the Territory of Alaska; to enlighten the public toward a better understanding of the Indian people; to preserve Indian cultural values; to seek an equitable adjustment of tribal affairs and tribal claims; to secure and preserve rights under Indian treaties or agreement with the United States; to promote the common welfare of the American Indian and to foster the continued loyalty and allegiance of American Indians to the flag of the United States; establish this organization and adopt the following Constitution and By-Laws.

From its very beginning, this new concept of national consciousness among American Indians was by no means a budding recalcitrant mini-nationalism but a movement tinged with loyalty and a sense of accommodation. Although a small minority chose the way of separation, by far the large majority opted for self-determination within the framework of the United States.

The new national organization, the first non-religious grouping of Indians, was, in part, a reaction against various individuals and societies assuming for themselves the right to act as spokesmen for Indians. Its first president was N. B. Johnson, a mixed-blood Cherokee from eastern Oklahoma, who served for eight terms. Later executives and officers included representatives of the Plains tribes, the Pueblos, and others. These leaders made it a point to watch Congressional legislation on Indians. They also disseminated information about Indian affairs. They organized a lobbying unit in Washington, D.C., and published a periodical as a means of increasing Indian solidarity.

The NCAI began to exercise an important influence on national Indian affairs, but there was some dissatisfaction, especially among the younger generation. Young Indians accused the organization of being dominated by "mixed bloods." In 1961 they formed the National Indian Youth Council in the hope of exercising influence at the national level. They sponsored "fish-ins" to remind Americans that Indians had prior rights in important fishing streams. They also called for more educational opportunities.

Both organizations were content with a moderate line. Both preferred to work inside the American society to improve their status in national life, to overcome tribal differences, and to express the solidarity of all American Indians. They resisted the idea of conformity to Anglo-American cultural values, which they rated as inferior to their own.[16] They still had grievances, which they expressed in the Chicago Declaration of June 1961 summarizing detailed demands on matters of law and jurisprudence, taxation, and treaty rights.[17]

Despite the violence done to them in the past, Indians were reluctant to take an extremist position. They asked for technical and financial assistance to regain some measure of the status they had enjoyed as original possessors of the land. When they spoke of the continent they had yielded, they referred not only to the loss of millions of acres of productive land but also to things they had known, valued, and loved. They meant to hold "the scraps and parcels as earnestly as any small nation or ethnic group was ever determined to hold an identity and survival."[18] What they asked for was not charity or paternalism, even when benevolent, but that their situation be recognized and made the basis of policy and action.

It was, indeed, a moderate position, indicating that American Indians, in general, had accepted the realities of modern life. They knew that the American Union could not and would not be dissolved in order to return to them the continent they had yielded. They were dissatisfied with efforts made by the Federal Indian Administration, which, they said, tended to place their social adjustment on a money-time-interval scale. This resulted in unwanted pressures and frustrations. They believed that they no longer had any word in determining where and under what conditions they could live. They complained that their method of existence had been destroyed or materially modified, their ranks decimated by disease, and their internal tribal and family life subjected to unfair shifts.

Governmental authorities, impelled by decades of guilt, did much to alleviate the situation. On October 10, 1980, President Jimmy Carter signed an $81.5 million settlement resolving Indian claims to two-thirds of Maine (the Penobscot and Passamaquoddy Indian tribes had asked for return of the northern two-thirds of the state). The deal, the largest ever made by the Federal Government, included a $27 million trust fund and money to buy 300,000 acres of land.[19]

While Indian nationalism remained unsatisfied, it was muted and temperate. Despite accommodation, Indians still believed they were subject to a dominant power. "This is said, not in a spirit of complaint: we understand that in the lives of all nations of people, there are times of plenty and times of famine. But we do speak out in a plea for understanding." Indians felt themselves to be part of the American nation: "For the problem we raise affects our understanding which our nation sustains before world opinion."[20] They spoke confidently of "our nation"—the nation of many minorities.

It remained an unsatisfied nationalism, but one based on restraint and understanding. As such, it set a standard for a mini-nationalism far removed from the violence-prone techniques of the Basques, Croats, and Corsicans.

Black Americans

Like the American Indian, the American black[21] was concerned with an identity crisis and with conflicting strategies for integration or self-determination. Both these minorities called for basic rights accorded to all Americans. Although small groups among them called for separation, most saw themselves as distinctly American and asked for a just share in the fruits of their society. They gave little support to movements for separate states or, in the case of the blacks, for expatriation to Africa. Most blacks, as well as Indians, advocated recourse to judicial decision, executive orders, and legislation. Instead of violence, they supported direct action in strikes, boycotts, freedom rides, demonstrations, and sit-ins.

The status of blacks in the United States hinged on two pertinent questions: were they a nationality or a race? were they a nation in the making or a racial minority on the way to integration?

Politically motivated Soviet scholars, anxious to show any weakness in the rival American society, portray American blacks as an oppressed people who cannot be absorbed into American life and who are progressing to a point of becoming a nationality.[22] Both Lenin and Stalin, aware of Soviet nationality problems, were uncertain of how to classify black Americans. In the mid-1920s, the official propaganda line from Moscow addressed to American blacks turned from the designation "racial inequality" to "oppressed nation."[23] The implication was that the United States had a problem of separatism which might lead to national dissolution. To the Kremlin, obsessed with its own problem of nationalities, such a problem was enticing.

Black leaders, unimpressed by Soviet propaganda, did not accept the designation of "proto-nation" or the idea that they were developing a separate nation out of a common ethno-national identity. They understood well the process of nation-building elsewhere. They had witnessed the collapse of colonialism in the mid-20th century and the formation of new countries in the Third World. They saw these not as nations in the Western sense, but rather as peoples moving toward nationhood. True, tribal units in Africa had been set up as successor states to the old colonial states, but this "nationalitarianism" was far removed from the black experience in the United States.[24]

There were, indeed, calls for black separatism, for the formation of a new black American nation.[25] Most American black leaders, despite disappointments and setbacks, rejected the radical solution and the Soviet wish. They preferred to work as Americans inside the boundaries of a united nation. This land, too, was theirs. They won important legal decisions in the 1950s[26] and patiently awaited action by legislative and executive branches to buttress Supreme Court rulings. They rejected the language of the bomb to call attention to their grievances. They were unsatisfied Americans, not unsatisfied nationalists. There was an important difference.

From Slavery to Citizenship

Only the high points of a familiar story need be presented here.[27] There had been slaves in America since 1517, the year marking the formal opening of the lucrative slave trade.[28] In 1619 the first 20 slaves in English America were brought to Jamestown, Virginia. Slavery in Virginia received statutory recognition in 1661. Native Indians were regarded as unsatisfactory workers, and indentured servants, committed to work for seven years, did not satisfy the growing demand for labor. English settlers turned to the large supply of slaves available in the West Indies who had been imported from Africa.

Colonists set up special codes for handling slaves. Regulations were mild in New England but severe in the South.[29] Whites in southern states were alarmed by the growth of the slave population due to a combination of natural increase and forced immigration. The inhuman trade in slaves was bound to have repercussions. As early as 1663 there was a slave rebellion in Virginia. Not until after the French and Indian War in the mid-18th century was there any significant sentiment against the excesses of slavery. Those colonists who felt themselves trampled by the British began to realize that they, too, were oppressors of slaves. The death of Crispus Attucks, a runaway slave and the first to fall in the Boston Massacre of March 5, 1770, aroused the conscience of those who already had guilt feelings about slavery. In Massachusetts, it became common practice to denounce domineering England and amoral slavery in the same breath.

Thomas Jefferson wrote a denunciation of slavery, but his words were deleted from the Declaration of Independence. Despite harsh treatment, at least 5,000 blacks fought for the patriot cause in the American Revolution in the belief that their loyalty would give them a step toward freedom. They fought alongside their white comrades, not in segregated units.

The ordinance of 1787 barred slavery and involuntary servitude in the Northwest Territory. Reaction set in as constitutional guarantees were made for the slave system.[30] The institution of slavery declined temporarily during the early 18th century, but the situation changed drastically with the invention of the cotton gin in 1793. There was an augmented demand for slaves to work in the fields as new territory opened up west of the Mississippi. By 1832 there were more than 2 million slaves working on plantations from sunrise to sunset.

The brutalization of slavery was depicted in Harriet Beecher Stowe's controversial novel, *Uncle Tom's Cabin* (1852). Slaves were mistreated on the large plantations. They were given less food than were northern workers and were whipped or beaten for infractions. The breakup of families was not uncommon. Those who defended slavery spoke piously of the beloved "Mammy" helping raise the planter's children and run his household.

Many slaves grudgingly accepted their bondage, but there were uprisings against the system. An insurrection led by Nat Turner in Virginia in 1831 resulted in the death of 50 whites and more than 100 slaves. The plight of slaves led to an abolitionist movement which denounced the institution as morally wrong. In the opening issue of his magazine

Liberator, William Lloyd Garrison favored unqualified emancipation, a stand that infuriated many southerners.

In 1818, when Illinois was admitted to the Union, there were 10 slave and 11 free states. In 1819 Alabama and Missouri applied for admission. Alabama, by the terms of Georgia's original land cession, had to be a slave state; its admission would restore the balance between slave and free states. Northerners rallied to oppose the entry of Missouri except as a free state. A compromise was arranged: Missouri was admitted as a slave state; Maine came in as a free state; and slavery was excluded forever from the territory acquired by the Louisiana Purchase north of the southern boundary of Missouri. In 1857 a majority of the Supreme Court declared, in the Dred Scott decision, that Congress had no power to exclude slavery from the territories.

The country was drifting into war. Interpretations of the Civil War differ: one side cites slavery as its main cause; the other insists that it was of minor significance—slavery was either focal or peripheral. Despite the controversy, the fact remains that the northern victory eventually brought an end to slavery following the proclamation issued by President Lincoln on January 1, 1863.

During the era of Reconstruction from 1865 to 1877, white supremacy was eventually restored. Toward the end of the century, sectionalism and racialism erupted once again and the position of blacks worsened. In 1895 Booker T. Washington appealed for help for 8 million of his people "who had without strikes and labor wars tilled your fields, cleared your forests, builded your railroads and cities, brought forth treasures from the bowels of the earth."[31]

On May 18, 1896, the Supreme Court, in *Plessy* v. *Ferguson,* gave impetus to the growing cause for segregation in the South by giving sanction to the doctrine of "separate but equal" accommodation in interstate travel.[32] Black intellectuals denounced this decision as reflecting "exploitation, segregation, disfranchisement, discrimination, and contempt." Their status was, indeed, at a low point at the turn of the century. Disfranchisement and segregation had been solidified in the South. Laws segregated blacks on trains and street cars, at station windows, in waiting rooms, theaters, restaurants, and other public places.

The Flowering of Black Nationalism

Black intellectuals, concerned by the deterioration of their status in the late 19th century, turned to a broad spectrum of nationalist ideologies, ranging from advocacy of race solidarity to territorial separatism and emigration. The institutional organization of the black community, rooted in church and fraternal orders, went back to the late 18th century. Nationalist manifestations were expressed in the convention movement, beginning in 1830 and lasting throughout the century. The goal was the recognition of blacks in the American social order. In the ante-bellum period, there was a distinctly elitist movement among disillusioned black intellectuals which called for emigration to or colonization in Africa or Latin America.

During the half century after the end of Reconstruction, a number of black nationalist movements arose which variously advocated integration, territorial separatism, or emigration. In the late 1870s, the augmented racism which accompanied the end of Reconstruction, combined with economic distress, led many working-class blacks to migrate to a more favorable location. Disillusioned with the South, many black families moved to Kansas. Toward the end of the century, there were attempts to create all-black towns in the United States. The most important of these was Mound Bayou, Mississippi, founded in 1887, in which Booker T. Washington was deeply interested. Even more significant was an attempt to turn the Oklahoma Territory into an all-black state in the 1890s. In all, some 25 black towns, such as Boley and Langton, were set up in Oklahoma. These communities endured great difficulties and often failure but were regarded by their sponsors as based on race pride and solidarity.

There was also a revival of sentiment for a return to Africa. Bishop Henry M. Turner, a gifted orator, called for an indemnity so that blacks could "go home to Africa." He even questioned the intelligence of his people:[33]

We remained in slavery two hundred and fifty years, and have been free the best end of fifty more years. In other words we have been dominated over by the buckra, or white race, for about three hundred years. We have worked, enriched the country and helped give it a standing among the powers of the earth, and when we are denied our civil and political rights, the fool Negro who has no more sense than a jackass, yet he wants to be a leader, ridicules the idea of asking for a hundred million of dollars to go home, for Africa is our home, and is the one place that offers us manhood and freedom. . . .

Every man that has the sense of an animal must see that there is no future in this country for the Negro. In the north we have some kind of civil rights, we grant, and the same in the east and west, but in the south, where the great bulk of our people are, we haven't the rights of a dog. . . .

Can't the fool Negro see that there is no future in this country for him? If he cannot, then he should return to slavery. We would be better off as slaves than as freemen. . . .

Before God I believe that we are inferiors, and were born to be slaves. We are certainly a set of fools.

Bishop Turner's oratory gave dramatic evidence of one form of black nationalism, but he represented the viewpoint of only a small minority. Most black intellectuals aimed to lift their people from their "low rugged plateau" but preferred to call for reform inside the American system. Many placed their faith in President Theodore Roosevelt, who seemed to understand their plight, but they were disappointed when he yielded to a hands-off policy.[34]

In June 1905, black intellectuals led by Dr. William Edward Burghardt Du Bois, meeting on the Canadian side of Niagara Falls,[35] demanded freedom of speech and criticism, manhood suffrage, abolition of all distinctions based on race, recognition of the basic principles of brotherhood, and respect for the working man. The next August, adherents of what was then called the Niagara Movement met at Harper's Ferry, West Virginia,[36] and called again for equal rights. Du Bois expressed the goal: "We shall not be satisfied to take one jot or tittle less than our full manhood rights. We claim for ourselves every single right that belongs to a freeborn American, political, civil, and social, and until we get these rights we will never cease to protest and assail the ears of America."[37]

Starting with its formation in 1910, the National Association for the Advancement of Colored People (NAACP) made a remarkable record in a series of successful suits before the U.S. Supreme Court. This organization worked inside the American social system, but there were smaller fringe movements calling for separation. Among them was the plan of Arthur Anderson to set up a black nation within the confines of the United States. Calling himself the "Prophetic Liberator of the Colored Race," he demanded that the United States Government pay an indemnity of $600,000,000 "for slavery, for the trail of blood sacrificed in human lives, the loss of country." He asked for even more:[38]

In addition, we the colored people of the U.S.A. and our representatives, demand of the U.S.A. Government a suitable territory, a part of the United States of America, not some distant land over the sea, but the U.S.A. The land, every inch of which is hallowed by the blood of the Negro, shed in the upbuilding of the Empire. A suitable territory of ample spacious dimensions—in which to propagate, to develop their resourcefulness, necessary to its maintenance as a modern nation, a race apart, the people to be free from further oppression. . . .

The whole to be under the protection of the U.S.A. . . . But the protectorate is in no way to interfere with the civil affairs of the colored people's territory. . . . And I would like to state here that a Monarchy would be preferable to a Republic. . . .

American blacks were intrigued by Anderson's assertion that they were the original race of mankind from which the whites, an inferior and diseased race, had evolved. However, they displayed little interest in his plan for a "Colored Liberty League" and for a separate black territory. In World War I, as in the Spanish-American War, black troops had had a share in victory.[39] Service in both wars gave blacks faith and pride in themselves as part of the American society. There was a setback after 1919, caused by increasing race riots in which several hundred blacks and whites were killed or wounded. An attempt by Congress to adopt an anti-lynching law was frustrated by a filibuster led by southern Senators.

Expatriation, Separatism, and Integration

Black nationalism took on three conflicting strategies—a Back-to-Africa Movement, a separate black state within the United States, and the fullest possible participation in American life.

From the early 18th century to the present day, there have been proposals by organizations and individuals for forced or voluntary emigration of blacks to Africa. In the early 19th century, a scheme was proposed by the American Colonization Society, with such sponsors as Henry Clay and Thomas Jefferson. Awarded a grant of $100,000 by Congress, the society established the colony of Liberia in Africa in 1821.[40]

A second plan was advanced by President Lincoln before he signed the Emancipation Proclamation. At his suggestion, Congress passed a bill authorizing the colonization of blacks in the West Indies, at an initial cost of $12 million. A contract was signed with Bernard Kock, a promoter of questionable reputation who had obtained a lease on the Island of Vache, off the coast of Haiti. The first contingent of 500 men, women, and children was sent to the island. The venture was a miserable failure and led to the death of 200 colonists. Lincoln sent an army transport ship to bring survivors back to the United States.

Despite the enthusiasm of the promoters behind these two schemes, most black Americans were unimpressed by the arguments for expatriation. Black leader Frederick Douglass wrote in February 1859: "No one idea has given rise to more oppression and persecution of the colored people of the country than that which makes Africa, not America, their home."[41] Douglass's call for assimilation rather than colonization was an important reason for the failure of expatriation schemes in the 19th century.

The Garvey Movement

The most grandiose scheme for the expatriation of American blacks abroad came in the early 1920s with the emergence of a flamboyant demagogue who revived the Back-to-Africa Movement. Marcus Garvey was born in Jamaica, British West Indies, in 1887, the grandson of African slaves.⁴² He grew up under a color caste system—white, mulatto, and black. His resentment against whites and mulattos was later adopted as a cardinal tenet of his movement.

Garvey moved to London, where he worked for several years as a printer. Encouraged by native Africans whom he met there, he began to dream of an empire ruled by black men. In 1916 he came to Harlem, in New York City, and began to promote the idea of a black nation in the African homeland. At first he was ignored or ridiculed as an immigrant carpetbagger, but he soon began to attract attention to his views.

Garvey was convinced that whites would always be racists and that the black man should develop a distinct racial type of civilization of his own and work out his salvation in the motherland. He founded the Universal Negro Improvement Association (UNIA) and gave it a set of slogans: "One God, One Aim, One Destiny"; "Ethiopians Awake!"; "Back to Africa"; and "Africa for Africans!" He presented a specific program.⁴³

The Program of the Universal Negro Improvement Association is that of drawing together, into one universal whole, all the Negro peoples of the world, with prejudice toward none. We desire to have every shade of color, even with those of one drop of Negro blood, in our fold; because we believe that none of us, as we are, is responsible for our birth; in a word we have no prejudice against ourselves in race. We believe that every Negro is just alike, and, therefore, we have no distinctions to make, hence wherever you see the Universal Negro Improvement Association, you will find us giving every member of the race an equal opportunity to make good.

Garvey believed that it was only a question of a few more years before Africa would be completely colonized by blacks, as Europe had been by the white race. "No one knows when the hour of Africa's redemption cometh. It is in the wind. It is coming. One day, like a storm, it will be here."⁴⁴ In his Back-to-Africa Movement, Garvey was, in effect, reviving colonization schemes that had already been advanced on other occasions in the American past.

Garvey expressed his ideology in his newspaper, the *Negro Weekly*. In ringing editorials, he paid tribute to the "glorious history" of his people. He recounted the story of slavery and called attention to Africa's regal past. He wrote admiringly about Nat Turner and the slave revolts, about the exploits of Zulu and Hottentot warriors against British imperialism in the African homeland, and about Toussaint L'Ouverture's Haitian rebellion. He proposed a "black economy" inside the white world and urged his fellow blacks to become independent of the grasping white businessman.

Garvey's black nationalism took on bizarre tones with his use of eccentric methods of organization, promotion, publicity, and propaganda. He assumed for himself the title of "Provisional General of Africa." He set up a "Court of Ethiopia," and elevated trusted aides and financial contributors to dukes, duchesses, and ladies-in-waiting. He adopted an official flag: black (for skin color); green (for hope); and red (for blood), as well as a special anthem titled "Ethiopia: Land of Our Fathers." In his African Orthodox Church, God, Christ, and the Madonna were all black. He made every effort to support black culture—even promoting the manufacture of black baby dolls for children. He set up auxiliary organizations such as the Universal Black Legion, outfitted in blue and red uniforms; the Universal Black Cross, with its own special corps of nurses; and the ill-fated Black Star Line.[45]

Money began to roll into the coffers of the UNIA. American blacks, including British West Indians and those of French and Spanish backgrounds, disillusioned by continued humiliation despite their war records, were more than ready for a leader who could offer them some hope. Alienated by the resurgence of the Ku Klux Klan in the South, they saw the stocky, little black nationalist leader as a new Moses. They flocked to his headquarters at Liberty Hall, a great zinc-roofed shed in Harlem. UNIA membership rolls enjoyed phenomenal growth in response to Garvey's eloquence during a whirlwind tour of 38 states.[46]

Garvey's extraordinary oratorical talent and his showmanship created a sense of pride and chauvinism that no black intellectual could match.[47] Black intellectuals like Dr. Du Bois were shocked and dismayed by Garvey's type of black nationalism. Du Bois called the movement "a poorly conceived but earnest determination to unite the Negroes of the world."[48] A. Philip Randolph, later to become the revered President of the Brotherhood of Sleeping Car Porters, denounced Garvey as an ally of anti-black forces and as "the only black who could hold rallies in the South and not be driven out [by whites]." Randolph declared that black exploiters and tyrants were as bad as white ones.[49] Black intellectuals pointed out that Garvey had won the enthusiastic approval of white demagogues, including leaders of the Ku Klux Klan.[50]

Despite its mass appeal, Garvey's movement encountered difficulties. In early 1923, after repeated complaints, the Federal Government investigated the Black Star Line. Garvey was indicted and put on trial for using the mails to defraud. He blamed crafty associates for the poor economics of his program and for illegally appropriating his funds.[51] After a trial which lasted for a month, during which Garvey dismissed his black attorney, hired a white one, and then brushed his lawyer aside and handled his defense himself, he was convicted. He was fined $1,000 and sentenced to five years in prison. His appeal was denied.

Without its dynamic leader, the UNIA dissolved into quarreling factions. Garvey tried to revive the movement, but he was unsuccessful. He finally gave up and moved to London, where, deserted by his followers, he died in obscurity in 1940.

Although Garvey's version of black nationalism gave a new sense of dignity to American blacks, it foundered because the vast majority had no intention of leaving the United States for Africa. His views were seductive but not altogether convincing. He was unable to maintain a mass following, nor could he win the assistance of black intellectuals. To most black leaders, the idea of a black empire in a raging sea of imperialism was ludicrous. They preferred to seek redress as Americans in an American society. Historian Rayford W. Logan pronounced the Garvey movement "almost a complete failure." In Logan's view, the most disastrous result of Garvey's meteoric rise and fall was the widening of the gulf between West Indians and American blacks, between those of dark and light skins.[52]

The Black Muslim Nation

Proposals for expatriation did not cease with the collapse of the Garvey movement. In the 1930s, Mississippi Senator Theodore Bilbo, with some support from a few blacks, introduced a new scheme for colonization in Africa. His bill calling for support of black colonization there failed to win passage. In the mid-20th century, when one African nation after another was winning its independence, the movement in the United States for expatriation gained additional support.

Meanwhile, there was a revival of the case for a separate black nation inside the United States. The proposal, as expected, attracted the interest of black American Communists. The Sixth World Congress of the Communist International passed a resolution calling attention to the economic, social, and class conditions of black Americans: "There are increasing forces which serve as a basis for the development of a Negro nation within the United States."[53] A small minority of black Americans dutifully responded to the call, but the vast majority rejected the Communist proposal. Equally unsuccessful was the National Movement for the 49th State, organized by middle-class blacks in the 1930s. In 1967, at the Newark Conference on Black Power, held in Newark, New Jersey, 700 delegates resolved "to initiate a national dialogue on the desirability of partitioning the United States into two separate and independent nations, one to be a homeland for whites and the other to be a homeland for black Americans."[54]

In the early 1930s, black nationalism took a new turn with the emergence of the Nation of Islam, whose leadership called for "a complete separation in a state or territory of our own either on this continent or elsewhere." Founded in 1930 during the Depression by W. Fard Muhammad as a breakaway faction of the Moorish Science Temple, the sect organized a paramilitary corps known as the Fruit of Islam. From a small beginning, its membership grew to 8,000. The founder disappeared mysteriously in early 1934, after which the Lost-Found Nation of Islam was taken over by Robert Poole. Born in Sanderville, Georgia, in 1897, Poole took the name of Elijah Muhammad.

The Black Muslin Nation was both a religious and a national movement. The faith was fundamentally Islamic: belief in Allah as One God, the prophets, and the Holy Koran. "We believe in the truth of the Bible, but we believe that it has been tampered with and must be reinterpreted so that mankind will not be snared by the falsehoods that have been added to it."[55] Black Muslims asserted that they were the people of God's choice because it had been written that God would select the rejected and despised: "We can find no other persons fitting this description in these last days more than the so-called Negroes in America." They believed that Allah appeared in the person of Master W. Fard Muhammad in July 1930 as the long-awaited Messiah of the Christians and the Mahdi of the Muslims.[56]

Added to these religious beliefs was a demand for social reform. Black Muslims rejected integration as hypocritical nonsense and held that the time in history had arrived for separation from the whites of the United States: "If the white people are truthful about their professed friendship toward the so-called Negro, they can prove it by dividing up America with their slaves." Elijah Muhammad presented a decalogue of demands, condensed as follows:[57]

1. We want full and complete freedom.
2. We want equal justice under the law.
3. We want equality of opportunity.
4. We want our people in America to establish a separate state or territory of their own—either on this continent or elsewhere.
5. We want freedom for all believers of Islam now held in federal prisons.
6. We want an immediate end to police brutality and mob attacks.
7. We demand equal employment opportunities—NOW!
8. We want the government of the United States to exempt our people from ALL taxation as long as we are deprived of equal justice under the laws of the land.
9. We want equal education and all black children educated, taught, and trained by their own teachers.
10. We believe that intermarriage or race mixing should be prohibited.

At first, Elijah Muhammad built up his strength among lower-class blacks and prison inmates. He won attention to his cause in an era of black protest and rebirth of African nations. The numbers and influence of his Muslim nation increased dramatically. He set up Muslim schools and Muslim-run businesses such as dry cleaning shops, grocery stores, and restaurants. Like Marcus Garvey, he supported the idea of a prosperous, black capitalist class.

The movement underwent a critical challenge to its leadership in the person of Malcom X.[58] Born Malcom Little in Omaha, Nebraska, in 1925, he was, by his own confession, a dope addict and pedlar, a pimp, a numbers runner, and a draft dodger in his youth.[59] After a stretch in prison for armed robbery, he became a spokesman for Elijah Muhammad. In 1964, following a trip to Mecca, he renounced the doctrines of hate and racial supremacy. He supported the doctrines of black nationalism—self-determination, self-defense, and separatism, but he preferred to work inside the American system. He emphasized land as an essential prerequisite to black nationhood, but for the time being, he placed a low priority on the Muslim demand for complete separation. To him, the political philosophy of black nationalism meant only that the black man should control the politics and politicians of his own community. He opposed an immediate breakaway. "As Americans, we will not give up a single right guaranteed under the Constitution."[60]

For Elijah Muhammad, this was heresy. He had insisted repeatedly that all blacks in America whose parents or grandparents were slaves should establish a separate state or territory either on the North American continent or elsewhere. A power struggle broke out between the two. Malcom X left the Nation of Islam and, in March 1964, issued a declaration of independence. He formed the rival organization of Afro-American Unity, which took on a more secular and international orientation. On October 21, 1965, he was assassinated by three blacks while addressing his followers in New York City.

Since the assassination, the status of the charismatic Malcolm X grew to that of a martyr in the cause of black nationalism. He became an important symbol in the cultural revolt of young blacks against white domination, as an advocate for black self-discipline and unity, and as a revolutionary nationalist.

Victorious in the conflict, the orthodox Nation of Islam, claiming a membership of 200,000, continued to be the leading organization promoting black separatism and a separate black nation. Like mini-nationalisms elsewhere, it had no mass basis and little prospect for implementation of its demands.

Black Power: Extremism and Moderation

Black nationalism took on a menacing tone in the mid-1960s. In August 1965, riots in Watts, the black section of Los Angeles, led to 34 deaths, injuries to hundreds, and the arrest of 4,000 persons, as well as property damage estimated at $35 million. These riots, plus disturbances in Chicago and Cleveland the next year, led to a widening rift between younger militants and older moderates. Stokely Carmichael introduced the term "black power," which became the protest cry of young militants.[61] There was growing disillusionment with the progress of the civil rights movement in the South. Young blacks in urban ghettos and on college campuses called not only for racial solidarity but also for black revolution. "We have got to get rid of some of the people who have white power," said Carmichael in a typical speech. "We have got to get us some Black Power. . . . We have to organize ourselves to speak for each other. That is Black Power."[62] Young militants insisted on control of political power when they were in a majority and proper representations when they were in a minority. Economically, they called for the liberation from exploitation of "black colonies" at home and abroad.

The spirit of militant extremism spread to Oakland, California, where the Black Panthers[63] emerged under the leadership of Bobby Seale and Eldridge Cleaver.[64] United at first with the SNCC (Student Nonviolent Coordinating Committee), the Black Panthers used a distinctive dress— black leather coats and black berets—and carried side arms. By 1970 there were Black Panther units in 30 cities.

Black power organizations, advocates of violence, began to proliferate. Among them were the Revolutionary Action Movement (RAM), the Black Liberators, the Black Liberation Army, and the Republic of New Africa. Some leaders urged "guerrilla warfare on the honkie white man." Some began to demand "reparations" from white churches and synagogues because of centuries of exploitation. Others called for partition of the United States into separate white and black nations.

At the root of this revolutionary nationalism was the feeling that a violent confrontation had to take place before blacks could really win their freedom. The essentially religious nationalism of Elijah Muhammad and Malcolm X was changed into a secular political nationalism. This viewpoint separated white and black nationalisms. White nationalism, it held, was capitalist, reactionary, and dedicated to keeping the emerging, oppressed Third World in bondage; revolutionary black nationalism, on the other hand, was described as an extension of black patriotism, "the identification and consciousness of our own kind and self." The black nation, it was said, must break from its captivity. The black man must learn to think not only of armed defense but he must also act aggressively.

This philosophy of violence was opposed by older leaders who were resolved to obtain redress of grievances through legal means. For years the NAACP had advocated a moderate biracial policy in the search for equality of opportunity. The National Urban League, founded in 1911, also supported biracialism and negotiation. The Congress of Racial Equality (CORE), founded in 1942, proposed nonviolent direct action such as sit-ins and freedom rides. The Southern Christian Leadership Conference (SCLC), led by Dr. Martin Luther King, Jr., until his assassination on April 4, 1968, was dedicated to "full citizenship rights and total integration of Blacks into American life."

Although much media attention was given to incidents concerned with militant black extremism, only a miniscule minority of the 20 million American blacks gave their active support to revolutionary nationalism. Most American blacks, sensitive to the nature of the American mosaic society, asked only that their rights be recognized in that society. They took pride not only in their own culture but also in their status as American citizens. They looked with interest and even with some approval on the activities of extremists, but it was a matter of limited attention.

It is reasonable to conclude that the vast majority of American blacks see themselves as advocates of the larger American nationalism. True, they are an unsatisfied minority, but they are not willing to extend that sense of dissatisfaction into a full-blown effective mini-nationalism. Racial pride and cultural awareness—yes; separation—no. Improvement in matters of jobs, housing, and business—yes; dissolution of the union—no. Reliance on the Supreme Court, the executive, and regulatory agencies—yes; support of violent nationalism—no.

Puerto Rican Nationalism

The strength of a mini-nationalism should not be confused with the loudness of its extremists. Revolutionary nationalists have little use for the ways of democracy. They contemptuously reject the idea of majority rule. They see themselves as fighters for freedom, as liberators who one day will receive the homage of their enslaved compatriots. They resort to terror as a preferred *modus operandi*. As prospective martyrs, they are quite willing to die for the cause in the belief that others of like mind will move in to continue the struggle.

Such is the case on the Caribbean island of Puerto Rico, with its 3.4 million people, which currently holds the status as a United States commonwealth. Most were satisfied with their ties to Washington, but a small group of fanatics carried on a campaign of sabotage and terror to win independence. Their demands were punctuated with acts of violence. Again, a miniscule minority won attention far beyond its actual strength.

Puerto Rico was discovered by Columbus in 1493 and later explored by Ponce de León.[65] Originally a Spanish dependency, it was ceded to the United States by the Treaty of Paris in 1898. It was under military rule until 1900, when Congress set up an administration with a U.S. governor, an executive council appointed by the U.S. President, and an elected house of delegates. In 1917 the Jones Act granted U.S. citizenship to Puerto Ricans.

From the beginning of United States control, there were evidences of unsatisfied Puerto Rican nationalism. Many Puerto Ricans criticized their new status on the ground that it threatened the Hispanic roots of their culture. They pointed to their pre-Columbian Indian background and their Hispanic roots, the Spanish language, and their own art and literature as bastions of their culture. They saw their own indigenous culture expressed in the work of the colonial artist José Campeche, the educator Eugenie María de Hostes, the composer Juan Morel Campos, the poet Luis Palés Matos, and the historian Salvador Brau. They were proud of their folklore.

Puerto Rican nationalists were concerned by what they called the "interference" of American culture and values, which they feared might some day altogether supplant their Hispanic values. In fact, the process of Anglo-Saxon acculturation did become accelerated and intensified, especially since the 1940s, when the United States adopted a liberal policy in Puerto Rico.[66] Washington no longer used crude denationalization tactics that had previously aroused much resistance.

The U.S. influence brought improvements in education, health and sanitary services, and communications. In addition, the growth of American industrial plants resulted in an improvement in the standard of living. These favorable developments attracted the support of both the Puerto Rican bourgeoisie and proletariat and eased the Anglo-Saxon assimilative process.

There were, however, serious economic difficulties. Absentee ownership and the one-crop sugar economy added to the ills of overpopulation. During the Depression of the early 1930s, when the sugar market dropped precipitously, Puerto Rican workers, who had always lived on the verge of starvation, became even more desperate. Under the Franklin D. Roosevelt New Deal and the governorship of Rexford G. Tugwell (1941–1945), there were distinct improvements. The first popularly elected (1948) governor, Luis Muñoz Marín, began a program of agricultural reform and industrial expansion while maintaining cordial relations with Washington.[67] In 1950, Puerto Rico was allowed to draft its own constitution.[68]

Meanwhile, a small band of unreconciled nationalists, angered by the Anglo-Saxon acculturation process, political ties to Washington, and economic control by "foreigners," began to express their dissatisfaction. At first they called attention to their cause by nuisance raids but later turned to violence. On November 1, 1950, while President Harry Truman was across the street at the Blair House during remodeling of the White House, Oscar Collazo, holding a German P-38 automatic pistol, opened fire on a guard stationed in front of the house. Simultaneously, another nationalist, Griselio Torresola, killed a guard and injured a plainclothsman; Torresola was killed in an exchange of fire.

The Blair House incident was followed on March 1, 1954, with a shooting attack at the U.S. House of Representatives. Lolita Lebrun walked down the aisle of the visitors' gallery, pointed an automatic pistol at Speaker Joe Martin, and shouted: "Puerto Rico is not free!" Behind her, two other nationalists, Rafael Cancel Mirando and Andreas Figuerea Cordero, holding similar guns, sprayed the House floor with bullets. Speaker Martin managed to escape behind a column, but five Congressmen were wounded. The three nationalists were quickly seized.[69]

Most Puerto Ricans did not share the objective of extremists. Gradually, sentiment turned in three directions—assimilation, statehood, or independence. Assimilationists, headed by Marín and the Popular Democratic Party, believed that it was essential for Puerto Ricans to cast their lot with the United States. Conservative republicans favored statehood. Independents, led by Gilberto Conceptión, and the nationalists, headed by Pedro Albizu Campos, favored independence.

In 1952, 67 percent of the island's electorate supported the commonwealth status that went into effect that year. Only 13 percent favored statehood, while 19 percent wanted independence.[70] The issue was finally brought to a referendum on July 23, 1967. The vote was: commonwealth, 425,481; statehood, 273,315; and independence, 4,205.[71]

Despite this democratic decision, small bands of unreconciled terrorists insisted on maintaining the schism. Among them were: the *Fuerzas Armadas de Liberación Nacional* (FALN), or Armed Forces of National Liberation, and the *Ejercito Popular Boricua*, or Boricuan Popular Army, also called *Macheteros*, or machete wielders. The FALN claimed responsibility for more than a hundred bombings since 1974 in Chicago, New York City, Miami, Washington, D.C., and Puerto Rico, killing 5 people and injuring at least 70 others.[72] The *Macheteros* took credit for an attack on the U.S. Navy's SECA communications center in Puerto Rico on December 3, 1979, when 2 seamen were killed and 10 others wounded.[73] On January 12, 1981, the terrorist group claimed responsibility for bombing 11 Air National fighter jets in a midnight raid, causing an estimated $45 million in damages.[74]

Gov. Carlos Romero Barceló called the attacks the work of "fanatics or madmen." In contemporary Puerto Rico, the entire independence movement drew only 6 percent of the vote in recent elections, although pro-independence sentiment appeared to be stronger than these returns indicated.[75] Sentiment for statehood soared to about 55 percent. Governor Barceló, an aggressive supporter of statehood, scheduled a plebiscite later on the island's status. Some observers predict that Puerto Rico will become the 51st state of the Union.

The situation in Puerto Rico provides a classic case of fanatical nationalists refusing to accept a democratic decision. The relatively few supporters of Puerto Rican independence condemned the violent tactics of the fanatics among them and agreed that the future of the country should be determined democratically. This argument had little effect on the fervent militants who saw themselves as heroic guerrilla fighters, as saintly liberators who refused to compromise with Yankee tyranny. They believe that one day they will be regarded by their compatriots as genuine heroes who won freedom for their country.

CHAPTER 15

FRAGMENTATION IN AFRICA —

The dawn is here, my brother, dawn! Look in our faces, a new
morning breaks out in our old Africa.
                                        —Patrice Lumumba

The Road to Nationalism

Only recently has Africa begun to take an active role in world affairs.
With the exception of Egypt, which is, along with the Tigris-Euphrates
crescent, a cradleland of Western civilization, most of Africa remained
silent and passive over the centuries. In the 16th century, European
adventurers and discoverers began to explore its coastal regions but
were careful not to venture into the interior of the great continent. Only
in the late 19th century did European imperialists turn their attention to
regions south of the Sahara Desert.

Attracted by rich natural resources, Europeans carved the large land
mass into colonies and protectorates. They imposed their own
regulations—territorial, political, social, cultural—on African life, with
scant regard for the natives. Pressures either for unification or disruption were exerted from the outside. European imperialists disregarded
tribal sensitiveness as they herded together peoples of differing linguistic and cultural backgrounds in territorial units satisfactory only to themselves. They imposed new and artificial boundaries on what had been a
complicated pattern of tribal and sub-tribal groupings. It was truly the
despoliation of a continent.

European conquerors paid considerably more attention to the riches
of the continent. They built roads and power plants, cultivated plantations, and dug mines, all to ease the task of extracting the wealth of
Africa for themselves. To salve their European conscience, they gave a
modicum of attention to education and to the reduction of disease. After
all, they were bringing civilization to backward peoples, were they not?
Considerably more attractive was the possibility of economic exploitation
and acquisition of naval bases.[1]

In the early years of World War II, the Japanese inflicted a series of
humiliating defeats on the white man. Africans who were serving over-

seas during the war began to see their own relations to Europeans in a different light. They asked questions about foreign exploitation of their homeland. Why should colonial masters who were being taught a lesson by the Japanese continue to exploit Africa and its riches? African leaders began to talk in terms of independence. The movement gathered momentum—after the war all Africa exploded in a drive for emancipation that has been called "a revolution of rising expectations." Throughout the continent there were calls for *Uhuru* ("freedom"). Then came an extraordinary development—one after another, European colonial powers began to leave the continent, on occasion with haste.[2]

There were varied patterns in the European process of abandonment. The British, who sensed the coming revolution, took limited steps to train their Africans in the responsibilities of self-government. As a result they were able to withdraw from their African possessions without the ignominy of being pushed out. The French, on the other hand, who had attempted a policy of assimilation, had to face severe difficulties in the process of liquidation. They nevertheless saw to it that close ties were retained with their old colonies. The Italians lost all their colonies on the continent. In June 1960 the Belgians suddenly granted independence to the Congo, which, altogether unprepared for this major concession, descended at once into chaos. Only Portugal and Spain managed to hold on to their small African possessions—with concomitant problems.

Literally overnight the vast continent entered the age of nationalism. Primitive tribal societies in sub-Saharan Africa were plunged into a battle for equality and human dignity.[3] They faced dangers because of their lack of experience and training in self-government, unlike such colonial dependencies as India and the Philippines.[4] They were to endure a transition period filled with perplexities and critical tensions similar to those that existed in Europe and the Americas before nationhood.

Nation-building in Africa recapitulated the European experience. Africans had won liberation from their colonial masters but not necessarily from European ideology. Everywhere, they turned joyously to nationalist symbols—flags, anthems, stamps, and coins. Africans, too, could weep with fervor in the presence of the national flag. Some African parliaments were careful to retain the British traditional form as an expression of a newly found veneer of civilization—the right way to do things. Judges wore wigs in the British fashion, and soldiers marched in the impressive British style. However, the masses of people, untrained in the ways of democracy, were called upon almost overnight to form political parties and vote in approved democratic style.

The new African nationalism operated at two levels. On one level, negatively and externally, it was a response to European imperialism— the right of black Africans to win freedom from white rule. In this sense it was a reaction against alien control and racial supremacy. On the other level, postively and internally, it represented the aspirations of Africans to win the benefits of modernization. They would propel themselves into the 20th century with all its promises. Both the educated African elite and the illiterate masses were convinced of the desirability of European customs and technology. At the same time, they wanted reform on their own terms, without subservience or patronizing orders. They saw their new nationalism as the combination of the best of their past and the advanced technology of their former European masters.

African Tribalism

The term "tribalism" is used on occasion in a deprecatory sense to describe the fragmentation of African society. Actually, whether it be called "regionalism," "communalism," "ethnicity," or by some other nomenclature, tribalism is merely a part of an international trend that is denoted here as mini-nationalism. Whether it be the Islamic Hausa-Fulani in northern Nigeria, the Bengalis in Pakistan, the Croats in Yugoslavia, or the *Québécois* in Canada, all these peoples are infused with elements of tribalism and all have an urge to separation.

European imperialists, despite zealous efforts, were not successful in overcoming the strength of tribalism. In the spoliation of Africa and the subsequent Balkanization of the continent, they took little account of the wants of tribal communities. They divided some tribes and kept the land for themselves; they combined others, even rival tribes, inside the same borders. They set up artificial units without any relation to the history, language, or culture of the peoples herded together.

Colonial masters showed little understanding of the nature of African social life. Most Africans found their security in special groups of comparatively small size. They lived in a series of concentric circles, of which the largest was the tribal unit. Parts of this larger group included kinship clans and villagers. The larger unit generally had a common history, language, traditions, and customs. Thus, in separate groupings, Africans found their spiritual and temporal needs from birth to death. Their neighbors recognized them as distinct entities.[5]

This larger unit—the tribe—was far closer to the older clan than to the newer nation. For the average African, the closely knit and exclusive tribe, the supremacy of the family in the social order, was his preferred form of society. It was, in essence, a part of the overall African personality, which placed manners above principle, family above self, race above humanity.[6]

This does not necessarily mean that the older tribes remained static as a social institution. They were always in the process of change over the centuries, moving from one area to another in search of territory, food, and security or in waging warfare. Colonial administrators gave little attention to the altered status of tribes but, instead, treated them as fixed, immovable units. Yet, despite their changing status, the tribes remained remarkably resilient as a form of society throughout the vicissitudes of centuries.[7]

This engrained sense of tribalism, which was to have a strong effect on the new mini-nationalisms, persisted after the wave of independence arose in the mid-20th century. Tribalism as a way of life was to be a serious obstacle not only to national unity but also to the continued existence of new nation-states. True, some tribes were eroded by urbanization, new mobility, inter-tribal contact, and education. Nevertheless, the centrifugal force of tribal separatism remained strong. Many Africans found it difficult, if not impossible, to join in the kind of collective action required in the larger nation-state. Dissatisfied with their new artificial boundaries, they became enmeshed in tribal convulsions. Their leaders continued to speak of national unity while at the same time pandering to tribal sensitiveness. Hundreds of African tribes, each with its own traditions, taboos, and prejudices, looked upon their newly centralized governments as foreign and unwelcome. Few had expressed any such desires for unification in the past.

Africa's new nation-builders had one thing in common: they worked together in racial solidarity to loosen the bonds imposed by the white man. Once they had won independence, they were faced with a different and unwelcome set of circumstances. Inexperienced in the complex process of nation-building, they made the same mistake as had 19th-century imperialists: they paid little attention to tribal patterns. Once again, heterogeneous tribes of differing wants and aspirations were herded together in newly formed artificial structures. This kind of forced welding of differing units was bound to have negative repercussions. African nationalists, in a burst of enthusiasm, sought to create new, alternative societies which could supersede the traditional forms.[8] Paying too little attention to tribal loyalty, they merely exacerbated what was already a divisive element in African life. It was a cardinal mistake.

European experience revealed that efforts to win supremacy of national centralism over regional loyalty was beset with extraordinary difficulties. In some cases, such confrontations had lasted for centuries. It was too much to expect that Africans, in the short era after the wave of independence, could solve similar problems in short order. European minorities were only half convinced of the desirability of national over regional loyalty. Africans, too, held the same sentiment. Many among them favored a return to the traditional local sense of security. The phenomenon, as we have seen, was global, not especially African. In Africa, its effect on a tribalistic society was especially fractionalizing.

Nigeria and Biafran Secession

Nigeria presents a classic case of the clash between the new nationalism and the older tribalism in Africa. Located on the west coast in an area of 356,669 square miles, it is the continent's most populous country, with a population of 74,595,000 (1979 World Almanac estimate). Its earliest known culture flourished around 700–200 B.C.[9] At one time the region was sparsely inhabited. Some tribes lived there for centuries, while others moved in from other parts of Africa, bringing with them differing languages, customs, and religious patterns. Later developments were marked by the rise of rival tribes and regional differences.

More than 250 different linguistic groups settled in Nigeria. The four dominant tribes were the Hausa and the Fulani in the north, the Yoruba in the west, and the Ibos in the east. Others included the Edo in the west, the Ijaw in the east, and the Kanuri, Nupe, and Tiv in the north. Each tribal group had its own distinct language, and each struggled for power and control of natural resources.

Between the 15th and 17th centuries, British and Portuguese explorers engaged in slave trading on the coast. In 1861 the British annexed Lagos and gradually set up administrative control over the area. British supremacy over all of southern Nigeria was recognized by the Conference of Berlin in 1885. In 1914 northern and southern Nigeria were combined into the British colony and protectorate of Nigeria.

In this amalgamation process, typical of similar moves elsewhere in Africa, little attention was paid to tribal hostilities which had torn the region throughout the 19th century. Scores of distinct tribes, each with its own traditions, taboos, and prejudices, were herded together without regard to their wants. To facilitate their rule, the British set up three, and later four, internal regions. Each region was given a federal parliament and an electoral system with proportional representation.[10]

From 1952 to 1954, at a time when colonialism was ebbing on the African scene, the British took successive steps to prepare the Nigerians for self-government. In 1960 Nigeria became an independent federal state within the British Commonwealth and, in 1963, a federal republic inside the Commonwealth. The damage, however, was already done. The custom of welding antagonistic tribes into a centralized state was to have dangerous consequences.

After independence, a critical issue arose on the matter of who was to control the new government. There were long-standing rivalries between the Muslim Fulani in the north and the Ibos and Yoruba elsewhere. The differences soon resulted in disorder and violence. The federal elections of 1964 were marred by voter-intimidation, ballot-box stuffing, and political assassination. For a people whose training in democracy had been severely limited, victory in elections was viewed, not as a mandate for exerting political influence, but as a license for political domination.[11] This behavior pattern was set by past experience under colonial rule as well as by a simple lack of assurance.[12]

Regional leaders set up a compromise after the unsuccessful elections, but little was settled. Northern Muslims, led by Sir Abubakar Tafawa, dominated the government. There was no national unity: Nigeria was still divided into mutually suspicious regions separated by tribe and religion.

The chaotic situation came to a head in 1966 with military coups. Army officers, more and more disillusioned by bitter political conflicts, ousted the civilian government and established a military regime under Major General Johnson Aguiyi-Ironsi, an Ibo from the east, who aimed to do away with the country's federal constitutional structure and make Nigeria a unified, centralized state. Sensing a loss of power, the northern Hausa-Fulani rebelled. Aguiyi-Ironsi was murdered when anti-Ibo elements in the army staged another coup of their own. In the ensuing clashes, 50,000 Ibos were massacred, and more than a million of them were driven from the north. A new military government was formed under Major General Yakubu Gowan.

In 1967 the federal government announced the creation of 12 regionally based states to replace the four previous regions. The move immediately aroused intense opposition. The eastern region, led by Lieutenant Colonel Odumegwu Ojukwu, seceded and proclaimed itself the independent Republic of Biafra. Federal troops at once invaded the area. The country was plunged into civil war.

The fratricidal conflict was accompanied by mass starvation. Hundreds of thousands fled from the north to the east, where the federal government set up a blockade.[13] The secessionists lost ground steadily. Ojukwu fled to the Ivory Coast. Gowan announced a general amnesty, only to be ousted himself in another military coup.

Although the Biafran secession failed, it indicated the intensity of strong regionalism in Nigeria. The new military government attempted to ease tribal diversity by adding several states. It was an impossible dilemma.

The British had created the situation in which neither a common Nigerian nationalism nor the many diverse nationalisms could grow.[14] Nigerian leaders, each impelled by tribal considerations, added to the difficulties. Instead of solving their problems, they merely added to ethnic suspicions. The Nigerian experience revealed the strength of tribal communities in African life. It was repeated across the entire continent, with variations. The centrifugal instinct, the consuming urge to fragmentation, had a weakening influence on the process of nation-building in Africa as well as in Europe.

The Ivory Coast

The most successful leaders in the new Africa were those skilled in "ethnic arithmetic." Felix Houphouët-Boigny in the Ivory Coast, Léopold Senghor in Senegal, Julius Nyerere in Tanzania, Jomo Kenyatta in Kenya, and Kenneth Kaunda in Zambia were able to retain power in the seventies in part because they could balance tribal ambitions.[15] All were faced with tribal demands against central authority, and all considered it to be of the highest priority to give their attention to tribal wants.

One part of Africa made much progress in the task of overcoming tribal rivalries. Economically the brightest area in western Africa, the Ivory Coast, under the experienced leadership of President Houphouët-Boigny, maintained close ties with France and consistently supported the policies of French governments while at the same time giving priority to the sentiment of its many tribes. The combination of foreign capital, expert local administration, and attention to tribal housing and health enabled the young nation to maintain an unusually successful growth.

The Ivory Coast had its first contacts with Portuguese and French explorers in the 16th century. The Baoulés and Agnis, tribes related to the Ashantis of Ghana, came to the area in the 18th century.[16] Other tribal groups had their centers in neighboring countries. The French took control in the 19th century despite fierce tribal resistance.

The Ivory Coast won its independence in 1960 but retained close ties with France; both countries saw advantages in association. French personnel stayed to assist coffee production,[17] diversification of crops, foreign investment, hydroelectric power, manufacturing—from textiles to automotive assembly—and the packing of tuna caught by a large fishing fleet. Such relations and their resulting economic benefits impressed other similarly Francophile African states, including Volta, Dahomey, and Togo.

Favorable economic benefits did much to break down the kind of tribal nationalism apparent elsewhere on the continent. Successful urbanization,[18] education, and careful attention to the wants of some 60 tribes, eased the way for the new centralized state.[19] Recognition of the problem by the administration helped avoid open conflict or hidden dissatisfactions. President Houphouët-Boigny, himself a member of the

Baoulé tribe, took a realistic position: "The Ivorian nation does not yet exist. France left the Ivory Coast with a mass of tribes unaware of each other's existence. We are only gradually breaking down tribal barriers." Many Ivorians turned to Islam or to Roman Catholicism, but most still placed their faith in animism. Houphouët-Boigny continued to consult witch doctors. "Africa is animist," he said. "We have no right to be ashamed of our animism. It is the basis of our lives."[20] This recognition of tribal culture did much to lessen the intensification of ethnic conflict.

Tribal Conflict in Burundi and Rwanda

The favorable development of the Ivory Coast was not duplicated in equatorial Africa, especially in Burundi and neighboring Rwanda. The earliest inhabitants were the pygmy Twa people, who were later supplanted by the Bantu Hutu from the Congo Basin. In the 15th and 16th centuries, the Bantus were, in turn, supplanted by the Watusis, or Tutsis, a tall, warrior tribe specializing in cattle-keeping and probably originating in Ethiopia. The Watusis gradually established a feudal overlordship over the more numerous Bantus. European explorers came to the area in the 19th century, and in 1885, it was taken over by the Germans. It was ceded to Belgium as the Trust Territory of Ruanda-Urundi after World War I.

After World War II, the Belgians disengaged themselves from their mandate, and Ruanda-Urundi was made a United Nations trusteeship, which was terminated in 1962, when the independent states of Burundi and Rwanda were set up.

Independence did not solve the traditional tribal rivalries between the pygmy Twas, the average-sized Bantus, and the seven-foot-plus Watusis. Even before national freedom, the more numerous Bantus, wielding machetes, chopped down the towering Watusis and burned their villages. Thousands of the tall people fled to become refugees in Tanzania and Zaire.

In Burundi, two premiers were slain by extremists and a third was wounded. Hutu activists opposed a government controlled in part by the minority Watusis. In 1965 some 76 Hutu leaders were executed after an abortive coup. Another Hutu revolt in late April 1972 was suppressed, with 10,000 Watusis slain by the rebels and 100,000 Hutus killed by governmental troops.

Rwanda suffered similar chaos. In 1963 a Watusi invasion from Burundi resulted in the massacre of 12,000 Watusis in Rwanda, followed by a renewed Watusi exodus. The Hutus, with 90 percent of the population, continued to dominate the Watusis (9 percent) and the Twas (1 percent). There was little prospect of tribal accommodation in this chaotic situation.

South Africa and Apartheid

That nationalism appears in a cloak of many colors is revealed by the case of the Republic of South Africa. In a unique transferral of roles, centralized nationalism here represented a minority, while the mini-nationalism was the sentiment of the large majority. The Europeans who came to North America overwhelmed the native Indians in number and decimated their ranks, but those European colonizers attracted by South African gold and diamonds eventually set up a state in which they remained a minority. The Boers (Afrikaners), oriented by the Bible, felt that they were chosen, like the Israelites in Egypt, to enter a Promised Land where they were predestined to be masters over "hewers of wood and drawers of water."[21]

Bartholomeu Dias, Portuguese explorer, discovered the Cape of Good Hope in 1488.[22] The area of South Africa was peopled in the north with Bushmen, primitive nomadic hunters; in the south and east by pastoral Hottentots; and by Bantus in the north and east. In 1652 Dutch settlers established Cape Colony, which was seized by the British in 1814. In 1835 disgruntled Boer descendants of the original Dutch settlers trekked north and founded the republics of the Transvaal and the Orange Free State. The discovery of diamonds in 1867 and gold in 1886 stimulated British and Dutch rivalry, which led to the Anglo-Boer War (1899–1902). As a result of the war, the Boers acknowledged British control of the two republics in the north. In 1910 the Union of South Africa incorporated the Cape Colony and Natal, the Transvaal, and the Orange Free State. Following a referendum, the Union became the Republic of South Africa and withdrew from the Commonwealth.

During these developments, little attention was paid to the feelings of the native population. There was no sharp division between whites and blacks for a long time.[23] The blacks accepted their subordinate position in society and did not especially regard whites as obstacles to their aspirations. The idea of black racial identity is of relatively recent origin and stems from the general African independence movement in the 1960s.

Beginning in 1926, ruling whites inaugurated the official governmental policy of *apartheid*, the strict separation of whites and non-whites. Supported by the large majority of whites, *apartheid* was aimed at the segregation of blacks, coloreds, and Asians. In the past century, progressive industrialization of South Africa had led to a need for skilled and semi-skilled labor, which ran counter to a policy of segregation. But emotional social obsessions overcame economic interests. Hard-line Afrikaners saw their dominant position as a right won by the sacrifices of their ancestors. They had built the richest and most developed of Africa's countries, and they had no intention of releasing their control over what they felt to be their own country. To them, *apartheid* was an absolute necessity.[24]

Behind *apartheid* was a gnawing fear in the Afrikaner community that their birthright was under siege. Over the centuries, Afrikaners had developed a sense of inferiority in their struggle against the Anglophone whites.[25] Once they had won their political campaign against the English, they were faced with a rising tide of black conciousness. They felt themselves to be beleaguered: as white Africans, they had no other place to seek refuge.

With the decolonization process in Africa fully under way after mid-century, South Africa's black population became more and more aware of a sense of racial identity. Like tribes elsewhere on the continent, the Bantus, Zulus, Xhosa, Transkei, and others began to call for self-determination.

To meet the danger, the government adopted a policy of setting up a series of "homelands" for the varied tribes. On the surface, this seemed to be a liberal concession to tribal sentiment, but actually it was a divide-and-rule policy by which the various tribes were separated so that they could be ruled indefinitely.[26]

An unusual aspect of black nationalism in South Africa was the support it gained throughout the world. The opposition to *apartheid* reflected political ideologies: Americans saw the situation in South Africa as undemocratic in that there was a black majority without a franchise; Russians supported an exploited black proletariat; and other Africans sympathized with colonized blacks.[27] The United Nations, most of whose members took an anti-colonial position, also opposed the policy of *apartheid*.[28]

The situation in South Africa remains explosive. Bantu riots culminated in June 1976 with the killing of 140 Bantus who protested *apartheid*. Here, as elsewhere in Africa, the struggle between centralism and divisive tribalism goes on.

UNITA in Angola

A basic tenet of Communist ideology is the denunciation of capitalist, bourgeois, imperialistic exploitation. Ironically, following the retreat of western Europeans from the African scene, the Kremlin saw an attractive vacuum—a vast, rich continent with many strategically important areas. It began to support "liberation" movements in Africa and sent in troops from its satellite nations to implement its professedly altruistic motives.

Typical was the case of Angola in Southwestern Africa. Stretching for a thousand miles along the Atlantic, twice the size of Texas, Angola was rich in iron, copper, manganese, diamonds, and oil deposits. It flanked the tanker route from the Middle East oil fields to the United States. Portuguese settlers, who arrived originally in 1575, founded the port of Luanda and increased its colonizing efforts in the 19th and 20th centuries. Angola became independent on November 11, 1975.

The Angolan independence movement split into three groups: Holden Roberto's National Front for the Liberation of Angola (FLNA), pro-Western and supported by the United States; Jonas Savimbi's National Union for the Total Independence of Angola (UNITA), representing a strong mini-nationalism; and Agostinho Neto's Popular Movement for the Liberation of Angola (MPLA), a Marxist group receiving massive support from the Soviet Union, Cuba, and East Germany.

By late 1975, the Marxist Popular Front, backed by 15,000 Cuban troops, several thousand East Germans, and Russian "advisers," succeeded in winning control of the country. In the ensuing clashes, more than 100,000 Portuguese fled the country.

The nationalist UNITA movement had no intention of capitulating to the Russians. For fifteen years the charismatic Savimbi had led his guerrilla warriors, first, against the Portuguese and, then, against the Marxist regime supported by Moscow. With 16,000 well-trained men and another 5,000 partially trained militiamen, Savimbi claimed support of the country's 7 million people and asserted that his forces controlled at least a third of the countryside. In the summer of 1975, he joined FLNA and South African troops to fight the Marxists. When the two latter allies withdrew, Savimbi and his guerrillas were left alone to face the Moscow-supported regime.

In February 1976 Savimbi pulled his forces back into the bush and continued his struggle against the Communists. His tactics were effective. Not an ounce of copper from Zambia in the interior moved across Angola's 836-mile Benguela railway to the Atlantic coast since independence. Savimbi's guerrilla bands moved freely over much of central Angola and struck at the government in the cities.

Meanwhile, the Marxist regime was faced with the virtual collapse of the economy. Coffee production and the exploitation of the diamond mines plummeted. Once self-sufficient in food, Angola now had to import more than half of its requirements. Savimbi's guerrilla warfare was costing the Kremlin $1.5 million a day, as well as many Cuban lives.

Moscow was learning the hard way that a strongly motivated mini-nationalism does not bow easily to either ideology or guns. Savimbi's well-disciplined guerrillas, with financial support from African and Arab states, were giving their own response to the Kremlin's efforts to "liberate" them.

A Continent Divided

Seemingly incurable factionalism and fractionalizing are repeated in varying degrees across the continent. Only a few more of these confrontations need be mentioned here. In Uganda the dominant Baganda were faced with recalcitrant Kabaka.[29] In January 1971, when Gen. Idi Amin seized control of the country, he began to persecute the Langi and Acholi tribes.[30] The South-West Africa People's Organization (SWAPO), a black guerrilla organization, called for "Namibian" independence and an end to South African domination. Namibian guerrillas waged a low-level but unremitting campaign against South Africans. In Ciskei, a small tribal territory on the southeast coast of South Africa, natives singing "*Enkululele kweni*" ("Go forward to independence") voted by a huge majority to break away from South Africa and establish their own Republic of Ciskei. Black critics called it a part of South Africa's grand strategy to segregate 30 million blacks in 10 autonomous homelands scattered across the country.

At the opposite end of the continent, in Chad and the Sudan, there was continuing warfare between Muslims and Christians. In Algeria, Arabs and Berbers worked together to drive out the French, only to resume their traditional rivalry once independence was won. In Tanzania, located in eastern Africa, there were bitter quarrels between numerically superior African and Arab Muslims (31 percent) and Christians (23 percent).

It is the familiar global pattern—a mosaic of cultural imperatives, tribal identity, linguistic pride, economic interests, and psychological drives. Whether it be called "tribalism" or "mini-nationalism," it was the same story of a larger centralism pitted against small unsatisfied regionalisms. The African experience was not an imitation of European experience, but it arose out of similar aspirations. At its roots was a deep psychological need for the dignity of freedom, for the right of a people of similar likes and dislikes to function as extended-family units. As long as this sentiment exists, so long will mini-nationalisms seek to break the unwanted bonds of union.

CHAPTER 16

CENTRIFUGAL FACTIONALISM IN ASIA _____

Nearly all our major problems have grown up under British rule and as a direct result of British policy [including] the minority problem.

—Jawaharlal Nehru, former Prime Minister of India

Nationalisms and Mini-Nationalisms

The impact of nationalism and mini-nationalism on the vast land mass of Asia, homeland of nearly one-third of the human race, was fully as significant as it was in the Western world. For Asians, too, nationalism was all-important.[1]

Anti-imperialism, opposition to colonialism in all its forms, was a compulsive force in Asia since the late 19th century. Accessible areas had become either dependent colonies of European powers or were forced to submit to the system of unequal treaties. Angered by European extraterritorial rights and leaseholds, which implied inferiority, Asians began to call for the withdrawal of foreigners. Their resentment against unwanted intrusion stimulated a sense of national consciousness, a sentiment which came into full bloom after the two world wars.

Nationalist rebellions in Asia at first took the form of boycotts against Western products; later, there were political demands, propaganda campaigns, and guerrilla warfare. There were outbursts in the immense area all the way from the western areas of Asia to the East China Sea. Yearning for national identity and freedom from foreign control became more urgent than any other sentiment. Jawaharlal Nehru described it as "a strong force today in every part of Asia. Any other force that may seek to function must define itself in terms of that nationalism."[2]

The new Asian nationalism was basically similar to its European counterpart, but there were some special characteristics. It was distinguished by a mercurial, psychologically exciting quality. It was "a huge emotional reservoir which [could] be tapped for good or ill depending on the kind

235

of leadership which captures it."[3] In country after country, Asian nationalism started as a progressive, liberating force, only to descend into an unhealthy reaction after liberation. Dynamic energies devoted to freedom soon became tarnished when private interests intruded upon a sense of public service. With few exceptions, Asian nationalism turned out to be undemocratic. Those who had access to power apparently regarded dictatorship or paternalism as preferable to democracy.[4]

Along with the creation of larger nationalisms came the expected plethora of unsatisfied mini-nationalisms. The pattern of centralization versus decentralization was the same as on other continents. Post-independence governments quickly found themselves enmeshed in the usual problem of how to deal with minorities in a plural society. Such conflicts extended to all corners of Asia: Kachins and Karens in Burma; Nagas in India; Sabahs, Sarawaks, and Singapores in Malaysia; Muslims in the Philippines. Everywhere in Asia it was the same story—the centralized state versus rebel regionalists.

The volatile peoples of Asia had their own ethnic, religious, and linguistic differences. Their communal rivalries were so bitter that nation-building became a process of the utmost complexity. Cultural differences were accentuated by ethnic concerns. African black-white antagonisms were mild when compared with Asian ethnic conflicts.

Religious differences were also harsh and disagreeable. Throughout the vast continent, there were feuds between Hindus, Buddhists, and Muslims.[5] Both India and Pakistan were torn by quarrels between Hindus and Muslims. Buddhism, despite its professed tolerance, was equally divisive.

Added to racial and religious differences were linguistic rivalries which broke the continent into a hodgepodge of opposing regionalist factions. More than 3,000 languages and dialects were distributed throughout Asia. Minorities held to their special linguistic affinity, a practice which encouraged clashes with the central authority. When attempts were made to designate as official one language spoken by fewer than half the people in one nation, other linguistic groups rioted on behalf of their own language. The same kind of linguistic drive governing the Basques in Spain, the Walloons in Belgium, and the *Québécois* in Canada impelled varied Asian peoples to demand autonomy or independence.

Any viable melting-pot process was improbable under such conditions. There were far too many hostilities spread over the continent. To resentment against Westerners was added hatred of Asians against Asians. It was a bewildering kaleidoscope of antagonisms—Tamils in Sri Lanka, Indonesians against overseas Chinese, Assamese against Bengalis, Kashmir Muslims against the Indian union, Muslim Sikhs against Hindu Indians. Europe had no monopoly on mini-nationalisms.

The Asiatic pattern, indeed, was much the same as elsewhere. Dominant power groups forged nation-states as an agglomeration of contending factions. The larger nationalism was always an artificial sentiment which supposedly united diverse peoples into a centralized state. Invariably, however, there were unsatisfied ethnic, religious, linguistic, and cultural sentiments resisting control from the center. Unified centralism was threatened with becoming a dissolving factionalism, the familiar theme of an unsettled social order throughout the world.

Regional Revolts in India

The vast subcontinent of India, 1,261,483 square miles in south central Asia, has long been a battlefield for contending factions. The spirit of separatism cut through the structure of the society everywhere. Karl Marx once referred to "the idyllic villages of India, each of which forms a little world in itself."[6] Jawaharlal Nehru saw provincialism in India as disruptive of national unity and as linked with caste and communalism.[7] Nehru warned that "fissiparous tendencies" some day might shatter the Indian union.[8] There was no firm fusion among the half billion people on the subcontinent. Instead, there was a real possibility of dissolution because of regional insurgencies, especially in the northeast, as well as cascading demands for autonomy.

India was divided by parochial, ethnic, linguistic, religious, and caste differences. There were four major ethnic stocks—Caucasoid, Mongoloid, Negroid, and Australoid. Caucasoids included dark-skinned Dravidians in the south and lighter-skinned peoples in the north. The other three stocks were dispersed in the south. There were more than 1,000 languages and dialects broken into 14 linguistic groups, 12 of them originating from Sanskrit. Hindi was spoken by 30 percent of the population; Urdu was the main Muslim tongue. The religious distribution was approximately 83 percent Hindu, 10 percent Muslim, 2 percent Christian, and 2 percent Sikh.

An important factor in Indian factionalism was the caste system, the rigid hereditary Hindu class differences based on birth and wealth. Although such distinctions existed elsewhere, it was in India that they were most developed.[9] The system began in the 3rd century A.D., when Brahmanic priests, as a means of validating their claim to highest status, divided the people into four major divisions (varnas): Brahmans, said to have sprung from the head of Brahma; Khsatriyas, or warriors, from his arms; Vaisyas, farmers and merchants, from his belly; and Sudras, or workers, from his feet. Under this classification, Untouchables, or pariahs, formed the lowest level of the Sudras. As they developed, the castes reflected differences in locale, occupation, language, religion, or tribal affiliations, sometimes exclusively or in part. The process of fission was constant, with the emergence of new offshoot castes. There was some consolidating influence in theistic communities, but by and large, the main tendency was toward isolation of the caste unit. The whole concept of caste leaned in the direction of division instead of union.

India was the homeland of one of the world's oldest civilizations.[10] About 1400 B.C., the subcontinent was conquered by invading Aryans. From 327–325 B.C., Alexander the Great moved into northwest India only to be driven out. In the next century, most of the vast land mass was united under Asoka the Great, who established Buddhism as the state religion. Buddhism was soon eclipsed by the rise of Hinduism. In the 8th century, Islam was introduced by Arab invaders. European contact began in the 16th century with successive infiltrations of Portuguese, Dutch, and British explorers and adventurers, all of whom were interested in carving out colonial domains. From 1743 to 1763, India was a battleground between the French and the British, a conflict that ended with the Treaty of Paris in 1763 which assured British supremacy.

In 1600 the British chartered their East India Company as a means of controlling important positions in administration as well as in trade. In 1784 Pitt's East India Bill set up a board of control over political, financial, and military matters. During 1857–1858, the Sepoy Rebellion by native soldiers in the employ of the British East India Company was suppressed brutally.[11] The company was dissolved and the administration was taken over by the Crown. In 1876, at the behest of Prime Minister Benjamin Disraeli, Queen Victoria assumed the title of Empress of India.

From then on, this "brightest jewel in the British crown" became a continuous source of trouble for Westminster. The British found it a major task to introduce some kind of viable rule in the subcontinent with its disruptive parochial elements. They were able to achieve a certain amount of peace and order, but they never succeeded in welding disparate parts into a unified whole. They exerted some administrative control over three-fourths of the great subcontinent, but there remained 562 states administered by major or petty princes, with varying degrees of autonomy under British protection.

The British faced truly staggering problems of modernization. They made efforts to improve agriculture and industry, but the processes remained painfully slow.[12] They introduced measures to combat epidemics, food shortages, local famine, and the ravages of poverty. Despite herculean efforts, they made little headway in a country overpopulated relative to its food supply. Added to this major problem was the burden of regional differences and rigid parochial factionalism, all of which contributed to the complexities of Indian life. The British were anxious to produce a showcase, a prosperous country in the Orient under their paternal supervision. It was plainly an impossible dream. Nehru's "fissiparous tendencies" were far too strong to permit a simple solution to India's problems.

Indian nationalists began to challenge the British exploitation and manipulated division of the country. They were aware that much of their weakness was due to hostile and disparate elements, disunited principalities, and conflicting religions and castes. In 1885 the Indian National Congress met in Bombay in the first Asian conference dedicated to setting up a public platform for political aspirations.[13] Its goal was to unify the squabbling regionalists of the country.

Consciousness of Indian nationalism grew rapidly after World War I. In 1919 Mohandas K. Gandhi organized the first of many passive-resistance campaigns against British rule. In that same year, Parliament passed the Government of India Act, partly in recognition of India's loyalty during the war[14] and partly as a concession to growing nationalist sentiment. In 1927 the Simon Commission, aiming to satisfy those nationalists who were calling for autonomy at both national and provincial levels, submitted a report recommending greater Indian responsibility in administration, an extension of suffrage, and a decentralized government. Nationalists dismissed the Simon Report as "a cup of milk for the hungry lion."

Gandhi's campaign of civil disobedience gathered increasing momentum. The frail, little Hindu lawyer, preaching *satyagraha* ("soul force"), captured the imagination of his people. Impressed by his saintly life and ideals, they revered him as a Mahatma, or great-soul. His word spread through thousands of factories and slum districts, stimulating what turned out to be a true mass movement. He called for *swaraj* ("home rule"), and the people responded with civil disobedience and boycott.[15]

In 1947 the subcontinent was partitioned into the independent nations of India and Pakistan. After the assassination of Gandhi by a Hindu fanatic who blamed him for the partition, his work was carried on by Jawaharlal Nehru, who had spent 13 years in prison for illegal and subversive activities.[16]

India had won its independence, but its new government was plagued by the same decentralizing tendencies that had disturbed the British during their days of authority. The triumph of the larger Indian nationalism did not solve the problems of a pluralistic society. There were the same religious and tribal antagonisms, the familiar unwillingness to accept control from outside. Immediately after independence, bloody riots broke out between Hindus and Muslims. Millions fled in crisscross migrations of peoples desperately seeking security among their coreligionists.[17] There was little common ground between the two religions. Muslims charged that Hindus were caste-ridden; Hindus countered that Muslims were unclean. Muslims ate the meat of cows; Hindus worshipped them. Both religions were now freed of British domination, only to settle into a bitter campaign of mutual slaughter.

British control was succeeded by a new Hindu centralism. This larger nationalism was, in turn, burdened by a host of revolts throughout the subcontinent. The Indian National Congress, which had long advocated a policy of accommodation for regionalism, gradually began to advocate the larger nationalism. It could scarcely conceal its anti-Muslim bias.

Only several of these clashes need be mentioned here. A regional demand for identity was especially strong in Kashmir, a predominantly Muslim section in the north. There was a long history of violence in this Himalayan state which bordered Pakistan.[18] When British rule ended in 1947, Indian and Pakistani troops entered the area. A cease-fire, negotiated by the United Nations in 1949, gave India control of two-thirds of the region; Pakistan was awarded one-third. Riots and outbreaks in 1955 led to an agreement to keep the opposing forces six miles apart. Tribal insurgencies and proliferating demands for autonomy or independence continued. The issue was complicated by Chinese demands for some of the territory. Kashmir separatists agitated for independence from either India, Pakistan, or China. In late July 1980, angry mobs in Srinagar, the Kashmir capital, set fire to army trucks and protested what they claimed to be harassment by the military.[19] In mid-August 1980, the death toll reached 142 from upheavals involving Muslims and Hindus, from confrontation between students demanding independence, and from federal troops.[20]

The drive for disintegration was also strong in the Punjab, a historic region in the northwest. Here, the Sikhs, who constituted about 35 percent of the population, called for the creation of a Punjabi-speaking separate state. Worried about possible contagious separatism, the Indian Government granted liberal concessions to the Punjab. Nevertheless, here, as well as throughout the subcontinent, the clamor for regional identity persisted. There was real fear that Indian mini-nationalisms would thrust the country into dissolution.

Turbulence in Pakistan: Emergence of Bangladesh

Like Nigeria in Africa, Pakistan presents the case of a mini-nationalism gaining its independence only to be faced with the aspirations of other unsatisfied nationalisms within its new borders. Here, too, there were clamoring separatist minorities in a supposedly centralized nation-state.

The history of Pakistan is a story of continuous conflict.[21] For thousands of years, the northwest corner of the Indian subcontinent, West Pakistan, was a historic invasion route for invaders through the

Kyber Pass and other passes from central Asia to the Indian heartland. Of major importance was the arrival of Islamic Arabs in the area. Muslim warriors swept through the Kyber Pass and converted millions to Islam. In the 12th century, Islam was also brought to what became East Pakistan. Here, until the mid-18th century, the people were ruled either by Afghan or Mogul dynasties or by Muslim kings.

The northwest saw successive waves of Persians, Afghans, Sikhs, Baluchis, and Pathans from the mountainous hinterlands. Each of these peoples was motivated by a fierce sense of independence and opposition to centralized rule, an attitude which persisted throughout Pakistani history, including the era of British rule.

Hewing to their monotheistic belief, Muslims refused to be assimilated into Hindu society. They had a sense of political as well as religious homogeneity. Hindus who enjoyed British patronage managed to acquire dominant positions in industry, education, civil service, and the professions, a situation that infuriated Muslims. Conflicts between the two peoples became acute in the early 20th century, with the formation of the Muslim League, which was dedicated to the winning of political rights.

In 1947 Pakistan was set up as a separate British dominion. At this time there were some four major groups in West Pakistan: the Sindhi, the Baluchis, the Islamic Rajputa and Jats, and the nomadic Pathans. The Bengalis were in East Pakistan. Most inhabitants of West Pakistan spoke Urdu, those in East Pakistan Bengali. Islam was the state religion, but there were many Hindus and Buddhists.

Conflicts between Muslims and Hindus cost more than a million lives and uprooted millions of others. The religious issue carried over into political confrontations. From 1948 to 1949, Pakistan and India were involved in an undeclared war over Jammu and Kashmir, whose Muslim population was ruled by a Hindu prince favorable to India. In 1956 Pakistan became a republic within the British Commonwealth.

The new country faced powerful regionalist sentiment. Along the northwest frontier, Pathan tribesmen, encouraged by Afghanistan and with Soviet support, agitated for independence. More important, however, was the separatist sentiment in East Pakistan, the smaller but more populous of the two parts of Pakistan. Here, a mini-nationalism impelled the birth of a new nation.

The two sections of Pakistan were 1,000 miles apart, on opposite sides of the subcontinent. The Hindu community of East Pakistan resisted control by Muslim West Pakistan and tended to gravitate toward Hindu India. As the result of a rebellion in 1971 and the Pakistani-India War (December 3–17, 1971), East Pakistan became the separate, independent state of Bangladesh ("Bengal Nation").

Behind the emergence of Bangladesh was a proliferating series of confrontations.[22] Bengalis in East Pakistan, with 55 percent of the total population of 109,520,000, were dissatisfied with both their political and economic status. For a time, the widely separated parts of Pakistan worked together in their hatred for Hindus and in their common claims to Kashmir. Religious interests were strong but not as powerful as regional separatism. The Muslims of East Pakistan felt that they were being treated as second-class citizens and began to call for secession.[23]

Bengali nationalists were led by Sheikh Mujibur Rahman, the charismatic *Bangabandhu* ("Friend of Bengal"), who urged his compatriots to rebel against the autocrats of West Pakistan. In the December 1970 elections, the Awami League, which demanded greater autonomy for East Pakistan, won a majority in the National Assembly. When the convening of the legislature was postponed, East Pakistan was swept by riots and a general strike. As West Pakistani troops launched attacks to quell the rebellion, Awami League leaders declared independence.

It is estimated that, in the succeeding months, millions died in a nightmare of violence. It is probable that as many as a million Bengalis were slaughtered and approximately 10 million refugees crossed the borders into India for safety.

There were excited calls for war from both Islamabad and New Delhi. On December 3, 1971, India and Pakistan, each accusing the other of responsibility, went to war.[24] Twelve days later, Pakistani troops surrendered and the Pakistani Government accepted India's offer of a cease-fire. India recognized Bangladesh as a sovereign state.[25]

The attempt of the centralized government to stifle Bengali nationalism failed. The greening of Bangladesh was another victory for nationalism over religious ties. Strong regionalism had won the cherished goal of independence. Sheikh Mujibur Rahman, who had served nine months in a West Pakistani prison, was released and flown back to Dacca on a Royal Air Force plane to be received tumultuously as a national hero. He became Bangladesh's first Prime Minister. "I never wept during all those months in solitary confinement," he told the rapturous crowd. "But when I arrived back here and saw my wonderful *sonar Banga* ["golden Bengal"], I wept." From hundreds of villages, the green-red-and-gold banner of Bengal was brought out from secret hiding places.

Bengali mini-nationalism disappeared in the solvent of a new larger, recognized nationalism. Immediately, the new centralized state, with its capital city at Dacca, had to face tribal insurgencies of its own. A new divisive pattern replaced the old.

The strongest move for separatism was in the area east of Chittagong in southeast Bangladesh. During British rule, a hill tract in this area had been maintained as an exclusive reserve for the mountain people of

Tibet-Burma who were organized into 16 tribes. Population pressures in the Bangladesh delta induced hundreds of thousands of Bengali-speaking Muslims to seek a new homeland in the relatively desolate hill regions. Chittagong natives protested angrily to the central government about the "invasion."[26] They reacted with acts of sabotage and ambushes of government troops sent to restore order. A guerrilla band known as *Shanti Bahini* ("Army of Peace") at first called for more autonomy but soon escalated its demand to full independence. It turned on both the government forces and the unwanted migrants from the plains.

The government at Dacca, concerned about national unity, sought to forestall secession by granting funds for schools and by offering jobs to tribal youths. However, faced with continued rioting, it resorted to force. Bengalis in Dacca, who at one time had opposed the West Pakistan Government in the same way, now angrily denounced separatists inside their new borders. They had to contend with other secessionist movements in addition to that in Chittagong. Tribal groups living in areas that cut across the borders of Bangladesh, India, and Burma intensified their calls for independence. Karen tribesmen in Bangladesh, in neighboring Mizoram and Trioura, and in Burma waged terror campaigns in support of their "natural rights." In small enclaves, tribes which considered themselves to be culturally homogeneous insisted on independence. It was the familiar pattern of regional dissatisfaction typical of artificially structured societies throughout the world.

Sri Lanka and the Tamils

Antagonism between the Singhalese majority and the Tamil minority in Sri Lanka had its roots in the island's history. Formerly known as Ceylon, whose ancient name was Taprobane, Sri Lanka is an island of 25,322 square miles in the Indian Ocean south of India. Most of its inhabitants, of aboriginal origin, now live in remote mountain areas.[27] Conquered in the 6th century by Singhalese, they adopted the Buddhist religion. Muslim Tamils who invaded the island from India became a significant minority in the country. Buddhist-Muslim rivalry became traditional in the lives of both peoples.

As in other parts of Asia, Ceylon attracted the attention of Europeans interested in gold, glory, and God. Portuguese explorers conquered the coastal areas in the early 16th century, but they were supplanted by the Dutch in the mid-17th century and later by the British, who made Ceylon a colony in 1798. In 1948 the island became independent, with dominion status in the British Commonwealth.

Long-standing rivalry between Buddhist Singhalese and Muslim Tamils continued during successive Portuguese, Dutch, and British occupations.[28] Of the approximately 12 million inhabitants in the mid-20th century, 70 percent were Singhalese; 11 percent, Ceylon Tamils; 10 percent, Indian and Pakistani Tamils; and 5 percent, Moors.

The small island developed its own version of union versus disruption, of larger nationalism versus a mini-nationalism. In 1958 there were serious riots between Tamils and Singhalese when the latter demanded official recognition of their language. In September 1959 Prime Minister S. W. R. D. Bandaranaike was assassinated. New elections brought the wife of the slain leader to power as the world's first woman Prime Minister. Following new disorders, the government outlawed the Tamil Federal Party in 1961. Ultra-leftist revolutionary Tamils embarked on a terror campaign. Those Tamils who were captured were executed.

On May 22, 1972, Ceylon became the Republic of Sri Lanka, with a president, a prime minister, and a national assembly. Tamils, still unsatisfied, opposed the new regime and demanded equal federal status.

The minority issue was complicated by the differing status of Ceylon Tamils compared to the Indian and Pakistani Tamils. Ceylon Tamils had been established for centuries on the island, and their claim to citizenship was granted. Immigrants from India, on the other hand, most of whom had arrived in the country in the 19th and 20th centuries for plantation work, were much less integrated and often retained connections with their kin in southern India. Most found it difficult to choose citizenship either in Ceylon or in India. The problem exacerbated relations between India and the new Sri Lanka.

Both groups of Tamils, indigenous and newcomers, had grievances on linguistic and cultural grounds. Like mini-nationalists elsewhere, they were undecided whether to call for more autonomy in a federal state or for outright independence.

Burma and the Mons

The same situation of intensified centralism versus rebellious tribal groups exists in Burma, bordering China in southeast Asia. Mongoloids from Tibet invaded the area before the 9th century and settled along the Irrawaddy River. After a series of Burmese dynasties, Burma was annexed piecemeal by the British in the 19th century and was ruled from London as a part of the Indian Empire. A dominion-like status in 1937 was followed by independence in 1948 as the Union of Burma.

There followed the usual pattern of struggle between central government and unsatisfied tribal groups. The most important regionalism was in the Mon state of Kawthoolei, with its capital at Moulmein in southern Burma. Numbering only 100,000, the Mons were once creators of the first great civilization in the Burma-Siam area. They were subjugated by the Burmese in the 18th century and, since then, were forced to accept a minority status.

In recent years, the Mons tightened their sense of regionalism without rising in rebellion. Large numbers, angered by Rangoon's centralism and by shrinking economic opportunities, crossed the border into Thailand. "Our people came here with empty hands," said U Ba Oo, one of their leaders. "Now they have motorcycles, cassette players, and even motorcars."[29]

Other Mon leaders, both inside Burma and in exile in Thailand, had more radical goals. As an unsatisfied minority, they contended that their ancestors had built the temples and pagodas of Burma's age of gold and that they had been rewarded by inferior status in their own land. It was the usual clarion call of a dissident mini-nationalism.

Separatism in Malaysia

Equally difficult was the problem of minority rights in Malaysia, which had been aggravated by conflicting tribal, linguistic, and religious differences. Located in southeast Asia, Malaysia is composed of 11 states of the former Federation of Malaysia and the states of Sabah and Sarawak in northern Borneo. Here, too, efforts at union were met with bitter factionalism.

In the Middle Ages, the coastline was dotted with trading posts where the natives, mostly of Malay stock, fished and gathered spices. The lucrative spice trade attracted Portuguese, Dutch, and British merchant adventurers. In 1867 the British established the Straits Settlement as a Crown colony and, in 1888, declared Sabah, Sarawak, and Brunei as British protectorates.

In this process, there was the usual blending of varied peoples and differing languages and religions. Of the nearly 12 million Malaysians today, Malays constitute about 45 percent; Chinese, 35 percent; Sabah and Sarawak tribesmen, 11 percent; and Indians and Pakistanis, 9 percent. Malay is the official language, but English, Chinese, Borneo, and Indian dialects are spoken in addition. The state religion is Islam, though religious freedom is constitutionally guaranteed.

Behind this tribal melange is a long history of tensions between the dominating Malays and the Chinese, who formed a clamoring minority. In 1948 Malaysian Chinese, stimulated by events on the mainland, started a series of insurrections and were finally defeated in 1960.

The problem of Singapore was especially acute, with increasing rivalry between Malays and Chinese. In 1963 Singapore was included in the independent Federation of Malaysia, but the union was a precarious one. Malays were opposed to Chinese dominance. In 1965 Singapore seceded from the Federation. Far from subsiding, tensions increased between the Chinese and the Malaysians, especially in the capital city of Kuala Lumpur, where, in May 1969, 180 people died in riots. The constitution was suspended, and an emergency ruling council was set up.

In Malaysia, as well as in large and small states throughout Asia and the world, the term "federation" was supposed to be the magic solvent that would eliminate tribal, linguistic, and religious factionalism. Only rarely, as in the case of Switzerland, has a centralized federation won the support of culturally diverse regions.

Papua New Guinea Versus Bougainville

Mini-nationalisms emerged in Asia when minorities felt themselves to be victims of an imposed unity. They sought redress against old colonial wrongs. Such was the case of the people of Bougainville in New Guinea, or Papua, which is the second largest island in the world. Situated off North Australia, the island has an area of 312,000 square miles and a population of 2,630,000. Politically, New Guinea is divided into two parts—Indonesian-administered West Irian (formerly Netherlands New Guinea) and the Australian territory of Papua New Guinea (PNG) in the east. After World War I, the territory of Papua and New Guinea was administered as a mandate by the League of Nations. After World War II, it became a United Nations Trust Territory under Australian control. In 1963, following turmoil in Netherlands New Guinea, that part of the island was transferred to Indonesian administration.

Included in the Territory of New Guinea was Bougainville, the largest of the Solomon Islands. During World War II, it was the last Japanese stronghold in the Solomons. For the 80,000 people of Bougainville, there was little compulsion to ratify PNG's independence as an integrated country.[30]

The tiny mini-nationalism which arose was the result of a long tradition of dissatisfaction. Bougainvillians complained that, in past imperialist territorial exchanges, they had been shuttled about "like human chattel" with little regard for their own feelings. In 1889, by a mere exchange of notes between Britain and Germany, they were designated as residents in a German sphere of influence. After 1919 they were subjected to Australian control. With PNG independence, they were shifted arbitrarily to unwanted masters.

It was the classic cry of mini-nationalisms everywhere: "We do not want to be a fixed, unchangeable, hopeless minority in the midst of an overwhelming majority." Bougainvillians wanted no part of revived colonialism from an imposed centralism. They began to talk of secession.[31] In September 1968 their leaders demanded a referendum to decide whether Bougainville should be independent, unite with the Solomon Islands as a separate unit, or remain with New Guinea.[32]

The issue was complicated by racial differences. Most Bougainvillians were black, identifiable from other Papua New Guineans, who abusively call them "black bastards" or, in Pidgin English, *bilong suspen* ("black as the soil at the bottom of a saucepan"). Bougainvillians retaliated by ridiculing their tormenters as *skin i red* ("red skins").[33] There were also cultural distinctions. Bougainvillians had their special type of dancing (kuma, panpipe, or mamboo). They regarded human life as sacred and pointed with disgust to those clans and tribes in the Highlands who indulged in almost daily killings.

Bougainville's factionalism was accentuated also by a strong economic motive. One of the largest and most lucrative copper mines in the world was on the island, and it was controlled by an Australian multi-national corporation. Migrants from all over New Guinea came to seek work in the mines. Bougainvillians denounced the newcomers as rowdy and uncivilized, as unwelcome foreigners. More importantly, they accused the central government of extracting taxes from the mines for its own benefit.[34]

The government refused Bougainville's request for a referendum. In September 1975 Bougainville declared its independence, an act promptly disavowed by the authorities. Moves were then made to grant a certain amount of autonomy. In January 1975 the government renamed the island the North Solomon Province and granted it provincial autonomy with an interim assembly.

As elsewhere, the attitude of Bougainville's secessionists wavered between autonomy and independence. The issue is still unresolved. It provides yet another microcosmic case of the familiar global pattern of conflict between territorial integrity and divisive regionalism.

New Zealand and the Maoris

The two principal islands of New Zealand have an area of 103,736 square miles in the South Pacific, about 1,200 miles southeast of Australia. Discovered in 1642 by Dutch navigator Abel Janszoon Tasman, the coasts of New Zealand were explored in 1769 by British Captain James Cook. Settlers, mainly from Scotland, began arriving in 1840. Retaining sentimental ties to their homeland, they fashioned a largely Anglo-Saxon country with representative institutions. The colony became a dominion in 1907. Today, it is an independent member of the British Commonwealth.

The 3,148,000 New Zealanders, mostly Anglo-Saxon, enjoy a high standard of living.[35] They are proud of what they describe as a successful multi-cultural society. Not quite. There is an increasingly dark spot in this bland social order, a growing sense of identity among the Polynesian population. Early in the 19th century, native Maoris numbered about 200,000. From 1845 to 1848, angered by London's failure to honor past land guarantees, they rebelled against English rule and were suppressed by military force. During the decade from 1860 to 1870, they renewed their war against the British but were defeated again. By the end of the century, the Maori population was cut to 40,000.

Today, the Maoris number about 240,000. They complain that they have not shared in New Zealand's agricultural and industrial prosperity. Unemployment in the diversified economy stands at only 60,000, or 5 percent of the work force, but almost all the jobless are Polynesians.[36] The situation has been aggravated by a recent economic downturn. Maori leaders admit that their people have won grudging acceptance by the white majority, that tribal intermixture is frequent, and that they have been given protection in equal-rights legislation. They ask, however, for something more: recognition of their culture and a greater share in the country's economic life as well as in the decision-making process. They accept the reality of their status. Unlike their ancestors who fought against British control, they do not use the term "independence," and they indicate that they will settle for more autonomy in an Anglo-Saxon-controlled society.

Self-Rule for the Marshall Islands

The issue of autonomy versus independence may hinge upon strategic value. Such is the case of the Marshall Islands, which, in 1980, was offered limited independence by the United States.

The Marshall Islands, an archipelago of 2,141 islands covering 70 square miles in the central Pacific north of New Zealand, comprise 34 atolls and extend 700 miles. Discovered by Spanish explorers in the 16th century, they were visited by British Captains James Cook and John Marshall in 1788. In 1885 they were made a German protectorate, which fell to Japan in 1914. Following its mandate over the islands in 1922, Japan claimed sovereignty in 1935. In World War II, the Marshalls, especially Kwajalein, became a major target in the American island-hopping campaign from the Solomons to the doorstep of Japan. In 1947 the Marshalls were included in the U.S. Trust Territory of the Pacific Islands under UN trusteeship.

The earliest natives were Micronesians, who are believed to have migrated from southeast Asia. For four centuries, they withstood Spanish, German, Japanese, and American conquest. Recent American rule in the islands was troubled by nuclear tests at Bikini and Eniwetok, during which there was a wholesale evacuation of natives to neighboring islands. Micronesian leaders also complained about the use of the huge Kwajalein Atoll as a missile range. Their relations with Washington became increasingly contentious.

On January 14, 1980, after 11 years of heated discussion, the United States proposed a pact giving limited freedom to the 115,000 islanders but retaining military rights for at least 15 years.[37] The natives would be autonomous in domestic and foreign affairs, except in matters relating to defense and security.[38] In return for military rights, Washington agreed to supply economic assistance of $50 million a year for the combined Trust Territories.

The projected agreement, formally called a "Compact of Free Association," represented gains for both sides. The United States retained military control of an area regarded as critical for defense. At the same time, the proposal was designed to appease a budding mini-nationalism.

Restive Micronesians were guaranteed increased political autonomy and desperately needed economic aid, but not full independence. President Amata Kabua of the Marshall Islands Government hailed the proposal as "a wonderful thing restoring more than anything a kind of dignity and respect, mutually speaking."[39]

It was, indeed, a rare political event in the history of relations between a government with central power and a people under control.[40] Micronesians would have virtually all attributes of sovereignty outside the defense and security spheres. They could even make treaties with foreign countries and use their own resources as they saw fit.

It was not likely that this kind of free association would appeal to all-or-nothing-at-all separatists elsewhere and appease the cause of mini-nationalisms. To IRA or PLO zealots, to Basques and Corsicans, "limited independence" was a contradiction in terms; it was simply a means of retaining sovereignty while denying real freedom. Independence, they claimed, was not negotiable—people were either free or in bondage. For Micronesians of the Marshall Islands, however, half a loaf was preferable to none at all.

POSTSCRIPT IN DECALOGUE —

> It is the national institutions which form the genius, the
> character, the tastes, and morals of a people, which make
> themselves and not another people.
>
> Jean-Jacques Rousseau

Common Denominators

What conclusions can be drawn from this survey of global mini-
nationalisms? Among the more significant are these, expressed in the
form of ten characteristics.

1. Nationalism may be a force for unity or for disruption. One of the most
powerful historical phenomena of the contemporary age, nationalism is
a two-edged sword with both inward and outward impulses. The accent
here has been on those disruptive mini-nationalisms which reject the
larger nationalism of the centralized state and call for decentralization.
Regionalist minorities demand either autonomy or independence. Their
incurable factionalism acts as a disintegrative force in current society.

*2. Omnipresent mini-nationalisms present additional evidence of the impor-
tance of change in human affairs.* The process of continuing flux in human
affairs was recognized as early as the 5th century B.C. by the pre-Socratic
cosmologist Heraclitus, who maintained that, while the world was eter-
nal, it was always in a state of change. "Everything flows, nothing abides."
The principle holds for both the larger and the smaller nationalisms.
Mini-nationalisms exist because centralized states everywhere do not
adequately take into account the history, or psychological wants of regions forced into the national union. The larger nationalisms see unity as
paramount and force heterogeneous peoples into the national fold without regard for their special rights.

The result is a persistent call for change. Throughout the world,
mini-nationalisms break through the surface of "national" societies and
present their own claims for autonomy or independence.

Hegelian dialectics explain the struggle as a clash between thesis and
antithesis in the march of history. From this point of view, the confrontation reflects a normal historical process in which change comes from the
struggle between antagonistic historical impulses.

251

3. The conflict between centralization and decentralization has existed since the formation of the national state in early modern times. The concept of the modern nation-state called for national unity, the will to fight for common interests, a uniform political and ideological indoctrination, an able and homogeneous leadership, the confidence of the masses, and a willingness to fight for national existence. This kind of unity, however, was won at some cost. The birth of modern nation-states was almost always a painful process in which a dominant majority subjected reluctant minorities to amalgamation and assimilation. The artificial structure was composed of either a few or many special groups with either related or distinct languages, cultures, and historical traditions. From the beginning, there were difficulties between the central authority and the component parts.

The process may be observed most clearly in the formation of France as a nation-state. From small beginnings on the Île de France, the nation gradually expanded to its present natural boundaries. Diverse elements of differing traditions, languages, and cultures were absorbed into what became a strong centralized state. Bretons, Basques, Alsatians, and Corsicans, each with their own sense of national consciousness, were absorbed into the national union. There were similar developments elsewhere recapitulating the same course of digestion.

The process resulted in the problem of regional imbalance. People who were only half convinced of the supremacy of national loyalty above local ties were herded together in an unwanted union. Minorities were not convinced that the central authority was acting in their interest. Excluded from the center of power, they demanded political equality, economic opportunity, and social justice. Cumulated dissatisfactions led to proliferating unrest in the social order.

4. The phenomenon is universal. There are mini-nationalisms on all the continents. There are currently approximately 163 nations in the world, of which 153 are members of the United Nations, and 50 other political units, chiefly colonies, territories, and the like. In most of these territorial units, there are minorities dissatisfied with their current status. They project the regional "we" against the larger national "they." They see their own sense of national consciousness throttled.

The confrontation exists in both old and new national states—in Britain, France, Spain, and Italy—as well as in the newly emergent nation-states of Africa and Asia following the dissolution of British, French, Spanish, and Dutch colonialism. On the surface, the mini-nationalisms of the underdeveloped states of Africa and Asia may appear to be imitations of European experience, but actually, they are a product, not of diffusion, but of political parallelism.

5. Mini-nationalisms, like the larger nationalisms, are suffused with ir-

rationalism and emotion. The development of nationalism and its peripheries ran counter to reason or common sense. In a world in which transportation and communication have brought peoples everywhere closer together, the nation-state has become an anomaly fit for discarding in the ash can of history. However, instead of disappearing in favor of a viable world order, nation-states became even more powerful as the preferred units of society. At the same time, suppressed minorities clamored for recognition of their rights.

There is little that is logical or rational in the pattern. The same Charles de Gaulle who called for a free Quebec reacted in horror when Bretons proposed a free Brittany. Those Englishmen who supported Greek independence in the 19th century saw nothing unreasonable in opposing Irish freedom. Canadians who argue the cause of Armenian, Kurdish, or Palestinian separatists denounce Quebec separatism as an unnecessary step to dissolution of the state.

These irrational inconsistencies are intensified by deep emotions on both sides. Dogmatism replaces tolerance; bizarre hatreds of the past are kept alive. Such dangerous emotions lead to acts of terrorism, tyranny, even war.

6. *Separatists, too, are rationally inconsistent.* Once they are successful in their demands, separatists promptly forget the heady cause of self-determination and throw barriers in the way of any additional separation in their own society. The new centralized state turns to a full-blown nationalism of its own: the Zionist movement led to the establishment of the State of Israel and the partitioning of Pakistan led to the independent State of Bangladesh. There is no logic in the reasoning of the mini-nationalisms: they call for self-determination as a means of winning independence, but they deny it to others once freedom is won. Successful separatists call themselves liberators; they label new dissenters and new mini-nationalists as traitors. This is the way of all nations—old or young, powerful or weak, developed or undeveloped.

7. *Goals vary between autonomy and independence.* Regionalist sentiment may take either a moderate or an extreme stance. In some cases (Britain, Belgium, Canada), most of the concerned peoples are willing to settle for protection of their special rights as a minority in a centralized state. Such moderates are influenced by powerful economic ties that make total separation inadvisable. Dissidents accept the larger nationalism because it is in their economic interest, but at the same time, they demand political, linguistic, and cultural rights of their own, preferably in a federated state.

In other cases, secessionists call for full independence (Basques, Croats, Corsicans). Where moderates limit themselves to argument and persuasion, extremists prefer bullets or bombs. Such hard-line separatists may form only a tiny minority of the population (PLO, IRA, FALN), but they have the support of many fellow citizens. They reject democratic decision as a sham. They see themselves as liberators who are willing to accept martyrdom on the road to independence. They regard tension as a creative factor in their work and guerrilla tactics as a desirable *modus operandi* to extend the power of their revolutionary nationalism.

8. Like the larger nationalisms, mini-nationalisms may be either a blessing or a curse. Not all mini-nationalisms are reprehensible or dangerous. The Hayes formula for blessing-or-curse, which he applied to nationalism, holds true for the smaller form as well. Regionalist sentiment may mean merely that the people are attached to the community of which they feel themselves to be a part. They care that they have a community of interests. The Welsh take joy in preserving their own language, folklore, songs, and traditions. At the same time, they are willing to remain inside the United Kingdom as long as their cultural interests are recognized.

Basques and Corsicans, on the other hand, contemptuously reject this kind of moderation and accommodation as useless. In turning to the bomb, they abandon civilized behavior. If innocent children are blown to bits in the public square, that is too bad—the only matter of importance is ultimate independence.

9. The predictability factor is of little value in estimating the future of the mini-nationalisms. The social behavior behind nationalism and its corollaries does not lend itself easily to quantitative analysis. This has not deterred the new generation of computer-minded young scholars who believe thay are on the right track in solving the mysteries of nationalism. One can only wish them well, while at the same time expressing a sense of pessimism about the possibility of elevating history to the status of a pure science.

10. The struggle continues. There is little to support the view that the confrontation between centralization and decentralization is in decline. If anything, it seems to be strengthening as the end of the 20th century approaches.

Retrospect and Prospect

Modern nationalism was born—an ironic anachronism—in the optimistic 18th-century Age of Reason. Reasonable men, however, now describe it as an irrational curse, as moral insanity, as an atavistic phenomenon revealing human aggressiveness. Nationalists show little regard for such denunciations.

From its inception, the building of nations tended to increase the sense of separation it was designed to reduce. Political integration was the goal, but it did not overcome varied linguistic and cultural rivalries. In fact, it exacerbated them. Confrontation between centralization and decentralization increased everywhere. Dangerous tensions progressed from riots, rebellions, and small wars to the two world wars of the 20th century. Realignment of borders, far from solving the problem, led only to the formation of new mini-nationalisms.

The sore spots exist wherever there are nations. Britain, faced with rebellion in its Celtic fringe, turns to devolution to avoid dissolution. France, seemingly the most centralized of European states, uncomfortably faces the ogres of Breton and Corsican separatism. Authorities in Spain contend with bomb-throwing Basques. The Kremlin casts a suspicious eye on Ukrainian regionalists and worries about a domino effect that would mean the disintegration of the huge conglomerate Russian state. Sicilian and Sardinian separatists call for independence from Italy. Centralists and separatists clash in the successor states of Africa as well as in Asia, from Sri Lanka to New Zealand and Malaysia. Small as well as large states are affected: in northwestern Jerusalem, leaders of a religious anti-Zionist sect have started their own brand of "local autonomy" as a protest against policies of the current Israeli Government. The Neturei Karta refuses to accept laws passed by the Israeli Knesset, the parliament, and declines to recognize a Jewish state until the arrival of the Messiah.

Throughout this analysis, we have seen that the root of the problem is the incompatibility between the absolute right of state sovereignty and the equally powerful cause of self-determination. When the nation and the state were made commensurate with one another, all the minority nationalisms were, in practice, reduced to an inferior status. Centralists saw their state power as historically justified because it was dedicated to the maintenance of the social fabric. In their mind, the choice was either national sovereignty or anarchy. They would not willingly give up their status as the dominant national entity.

For regionalists, this was simply an unsatisfactory state of affairs. They complained about political subjugation, economic inequality, social neglect, and psychological alienation. In its extreme form, they represented a stand which meant danger for the very existence of the state. The result was omnipresent tensions which disturbed the equilibrium of world society.

What are the prospects for the future? Most historians, as a matter of principle and in their acceptance of Ranke's dictum to stay with "*Was ist geschehen?*" decline to take on the mantle of Nostradamus. Those who risk prognosis see a dismal future. They say that integration of peoples requires statesmanship, patience, and delicacy of judgment, all of which are lacking in contemporary leaders. The problem, they feel, is without solution. Both the larger and smaller nationalisms remain psychologically motivated sentiments which do not lend themselves easily to rational argument. Accommodation, appeasement, devolution—all in the name of reason—have been tried and found wanting.

As in so many human affairs, decisions on nationalism are made by force. This may be regrettable, but it is, nevertheless, true. Throughout history, the expansion or shrinking of national borders has been determined, not by rational argument, but by might. The process is accompanied by heavy loss of life and property. Old grievances and old prides are satisfied only by the power principle. Tensions are certain to continue as long as nationalism remains a preferred mode of human behavior.

NOTES ————————————————————

Chapter 1 NATIONALISM AND ITS PERIPHERIES

1. On the general subject of nationalism, see C. J. H. Hayes, *Historical Evolution of Modern Nationalism* (1931), and *Nationalism: A Religion* (1960); H. Kohn, *The Idea of Nationalism* (1944, 1960), and *Nationalism: Its Meaning and History* (1955); B. C. Shafer, *Nationalism: Myth and Reality* (1955), and *Faces of Nationalism* (1972); and L. L. Snyder, *The New Nationalism* (1968), and *Varieties of Nationalism: A Comparative Study* (1976).

2. Walter Lippmann, quoted in *The New York Post*, Oct. 23, 1971.

3. For more detailed discussions of Soviet Russia's messianic nationalism, see Snyder, *The New Nationalism, op. cit.*, pp. 283–320, and *Varieties of Nationalism, op cit.*, pp. 211–27. For a treatment of the triumph of nationalism over communism, see E. Lengyel, *Nationalism: The Last Stage of Communism* (1970).

4. In 1964 *Isvestia* reported that more than a million applications had been received for membership in the newly founded All-Russian Society for the Preservation of Memorials of History and Culture.

5. The *Russity*, the new Russian nationalists, believe themselves to be the most disadvantaged of the more than 100 nationalities in the Soviet Union. Disappointed by the economic and human failures of communism after 60 years of Soviet power, they call for a strong Russia untainted by alien ideologies and with the old traditional values restored. They believe the Russians to be a chosen people who bear a higher truth. This type of nationalism is advocated by such exiles as Aleksandr I. Solzhenitsyn, who insists that his soul is still Russian. In a commencement address delivered at Harvard in June 1978, he also criticized corruption and materialism in the West and insisted that he would not be seduced by such false values.

6. D. Ronen, *The Quest for Self-Determination* (1979), pp. 25–26. For purposes of orientation, Ronen set up the following table:

The Five Manifestations of Self-Determination

Label Reference	Type	Dominant Period	Main Geographic Location
1. nationalism	national self-determination	1830s to 1880s	Europe
2. Marxism	class self-determination	mid-19th century	Europe plus

(continued)

257

The Five Manifestations of Self-Determination (*Continued*)

Label Reference	Type	Dominant Period	Main Geographic Location
3. Wilsonian self-determination	minorities' self-determination	1916 to 1920s	Eastern Europe
4. decolonization	racial self-determination	(1945) to 1960s	Africa and Asia
5. ethno-nationalism or sub-nationalism	ethnic self-determination	mid-1960s	Africa, Asia, Europe, North America, Far East

7. W. Connor, "The Politics of Ethnonationalism," *Journal of Educational Affairs*, XXVII, no. 1 (1973), p. 2.

8. There is an increasingly voluminous literature on ethnicity. Among recent publications are: C. Enloe, *Ethnic Conflict and Political Development* (1973); N. Glazer and D. P. Moynihan (eds.), *Ethnicity: Theory and Experience* (1975); and C. Young, *The Politics of Cultural Pluralism* (1976).

9. For more detailed examinations of the problems of race, see L. L. Snyder, *Race: A History of Modern Ethnic Theories* (1939), and *The Idea of Racialism* (1962). These studies examine the many illogical, irrational, and scientific fallacies concerning the meaning of race; project the idea that the term "race" should be restricted to its biological meaning; and reject the myth of "racial" purity and "racial" superiority.

10. See Baron de Montesquieu, *The Spirit of Laws* (1750).

11. See Voltaire, *Philosophical Dictionary* (1738).

12. See J. Locke, *An Essay Concerning Human Understanding* (1690).

13. See J. J. Rousseau, *The Social Contract or, Principles of Political Right* (1762).

14. *Ibid.*

15. This view was presented by Hans Kohn, in his *Prelude to Nation-States: The French and German Experience, 1789–1815* (1967), pp. 7 ff.

16. K. Deutsch, *Nationalism and Social Communication: An Inquiry into the Foundations of Nationality.* The first edition was published in 1953. The second edition appeared under the imprint of the MIT Press, Cambridge, Mass. (1966).

17. An excellent example of the use of the Deutsch formula in studies of nationalism is to be found in O. Dann and T. Schieder (eds.), *Nationale Bewegung und Socialze Organisation* (1978). Sponsored by Theodor Schieder's famed seminar at the University of Cologne, this volume contains comparative studies of national unification movements in 19th-century Europe. Peter Alter describes national organizations in Ireland, 1801–1921; Hans Henning Hahn treats the organizations of the Polish Great Emigration, 1931–1947; and Gerhard Brunn analyzes the organizations of the Catalan movement, 1859–1959. All three studies seek to strike a balance between economic, political, and social structures, but they place main emphasis on social aspects. This accent on social organization brings a new and important element to the study of nationalism. At the same time, the urge for quantification should not overshadow the fact that nationalism remains predominantly a political and psychological phenomenon.

Chapter 2   CHARACTERISTICS OF THE MINI-NATIONALISMS

1. *The New York Times,* May 20, 1978.

2. On the territorial imperative, see L. L. Snyder, "Nationalism and the Territorial Imperative," *Canadian Review of Studies in Nationalism,* III, no. 1 (Fall, 1975), pp. 1–21.

3. H. Seton-Watson, "Unsatisfied Nationalisms," *Journal of Contemporary History,* VI, no. 1 (1971), p. 3.

4. On the partitions of Poland, see R. H. Lord, *The Second Partition of Poland* (1915) and *Cambridge History of Poland* (1941–1950); A. Halecki, *A History of Poland* (1960); H. H. Kaplan, *The First Partition of Poland* (1962); and H. Roos, *A History of Modern Poland* (1966).

5. See Chapter 9.

6. At the age of 16, Menachem Begin, born in Brest Litovsk, Russia, on August 13, 1913, joined Betar, a youth organization representing the Revisionists, a militant Zionist group formed by V. Jabotinsky. In 1942 he went to Palestine, where he joined the activist Irgun underground. He engaged in terrorist activities, fighting British authority by violent means. Despite a price offered for his capture, he managed to avoid arrest. Later he served in the Knesset and in 1977 became Israeli Prime Minister.

7. On terrorism, see E. V. Walter, "Violence and the Process of Terror," *American Sociological Review,* XXIX, no. 2 (Spring, 1944), pp. 248–57. See also P. Wilkinson, *Political Terrorism* (1974).

8. P. Wilkinson, "Terrorist Movements," in Y. Alexander, D. Carlton, and P. Wilkinson, *Terrorism: Theory and Practice* (1979), p. 104.

9. For these categories I am indebted to Alexander *et al., Terrorism: Theory and Practice, op. cit.,* p. 104.

10. On European integration, see E. B. Haas, *The Unity of European Political, Social, and Economic Forces* (1958); B. A. Balassa, *The Theory of Economic Integration* (1961, 1962); L. N. Lindberg, *The Political Dynamics of European Integration* (1963); and U. W. Kitzinger, *The Politics and Economics of European Integration* (1963).

11. The original members of the Common Market were France, Belgium, Luxembourg, The Netherlands, Italy, and West Germany. In January 1973 the United Kingdom, Denmark, and Iceland became members. For a general treatment, see F. Jensen and W. Inge, *The Common Market: Economic Integration in Europe* (1965).

12. The seven countries of the EFTA, the Outer Seven, were Austria, Norway, Portugal, Sweden, Switzerland (original members in 1958), Finland (1961), and Iceland (1970).

13. Members in the ECSC included France, West Germany, Italy, Belgium, The Netherlands, and Luxembourg.

14. Members of Euratom are: Belgium, France, Luxembourg, The Netherlands, Italy, and West Germany. Its early intention was to establish a nuclear-energy industry on a European rather than on a national scale.

15. The founding states of the Council of Europe (May 5, 1943) were joined later by eight others. Greece withdrew in 1969.

16. The number increased to 435 in 1981, when Greece was scheduled to take part.

17. A historic milestone was reached in June 1979, when the first European election took place for seats in the European Parliament at Strasbourg. The Treaty of Rome in 1956, the charter for the Common Market, provided for such a parliament, as well as a court and bureaucracy, as basic European institutions for the proposed politically unified continent. The opposition was so strong, however, especially by President Charles de Gaulle of France, that the emphasis for integration remained on the economic and technological sides. Nevertheless, leaders of "Europe" went ahead with the long-delayed elections for the European Parliament as a measure to revive enthusiasm for European integration. (For accounts of the election, see *Europe: Magazine of the European Community* [July–August, 1979]. The issue is devoted to favorable reports on the elections.)

18. Even at its birth the European Parliament had to take into consideration the realistic issue of regional mini-nationalisms. National priorities played an important role in the elections. The French, concerned about the possibility of a weakened centralized state, insisted that a thoroughly "French" delegation be elected for its 81 seats out of a total of 410; they wanted to avoid "potential difficulties" by Bretons, Basques, Alsatians, and Corsicans. In Belgium there were indications of continuing linguistic problems: Flemings and Walloons were elected separately along their own national lines.

19. The elections revealed weaknesses. Each country worked out its own procedure, mostly proportional representation on the basis of regional districts (in France and The Netherlands, national districts). Each country made its own decision as to whether members of the national parliament could also represent voters in Europe. In addition, in most cases the elected candidates reserved the right to step down in order to concentrate on national, not European, politics.

In general, voters in most countries remained indifferent to the elections. Critics began to describe the European Parliament as "merely another piece of ineffective institutional scenery." A British poll showed that 35 percent of the public had never heard of the European Parliament. Popular interest in the proposed United Europe remained low. (See F. Lewis, in *International Herald-Tribune,* May 22, 1979.)

20. *International Herald-Tribune,* June 5, 1979.

21. For the entries under Asia and Africa, I am indebted to D. Ronen, *The Quest for Self-Determination* (1979), p. 43. Ronen's tentative listing is titled "Emergence of Ethnic Determination, 1966 to 1970." While Asian and African movements reveal characteristics of the mini-nationalisms, they should be judged as nascent mini-nationalisms not yet come of age. Some blocs of peoples have been relatively untouched by the quest for self-determination, notably the large populations of Latin America.

Chapter 3   BRITISH DEVOLUTION I: SCOTTISH NATIONALISM

1. On Scottish nationalism in general, see H. J. Hanham, *Scottish Nationalism* (1969); J. G. Kellas, *The Scottish Political System* (1973); and M. J. Esman, "Scottish Nationalism, North Sea Oil, and the British Response," in M. J. Esman (ed.), *Ethnic Conflict in the Western World* (1977).

2. Dov Ronen uses the term "functional aggregation" to describe a people's urge for activating a specific identity in a search for self-determination. See his treatment of the Scots in his *The Quest for Self-Determination* (1979), pp. 71–79.

3. *Ibid.*, p. 73.

4. Esman, *Ethnic Conflict in the Western World, op. cit.*, p. 281.

5. On the interplay of Scottish-English relations, see J. S. Blackie, *The Union of 1707 and Its Results* (1892); J. Mackinnon, *The Union of England and Scotland* (1896); P. H. Brown, *History of Scotland* (1902–1909); W. Notestein, *The Scot in History* (1946); A. M. MacKenzie, *Scotland in Modern Times* (1947); R. S. Rait and G. S. Pryde, *Scotland* (1954); *The Treaty of Union Between Scotland and England, 1707,* Secretariat No. 62 (1955); W. Ferguson, *Scotland, 1689 to the Present* (1968); and J. G. Kellas, *Modern Scotland* (1968).

6. Scots who still resent English control visit the battlefield at Bannockburn each year to keep alive the sentiment of independence. The inscription on the monument there reads:

WE FIGHT FOR GLORY NOT FOR
WEALTH NOR HONOUR, BUT ONLY
AND ALONE WE FIGHT FOR FREEDOM, WHICH
NO GOOD MAN SURRENDERS BUT WITH HIS LIFE

7. On the Scottish language, see W. A. Craigie, *Dictionary of the Older Scottish Tongue* (1931 ff.); W. Grant, *Scottish National Dictionary* (1934 ff.); J. Speirs, *The Scots Literary Tradition* (1940); A. McIntosh, *Introduction to a Survey of Scottish Dialect* (1963); and D. Daitsches, *Paradox of Scottish Culture* (1964).

8. According to the 1961 census, there were only 1,100 people who spoke Gaelic, most in the Hebrides and Glasgow. Fewer than 2 percent of all Scotsmen spoke both English and Gaelic.

9. Despite preference for English, there is intensive scholarly interest in Scottish linguistics, as indicated by two giant works, *Dictionary of the Older Scottish Tongue* and *Scottish National Dictionary*, both still being worked on at the University of Edinburgh. (See note 7 for citations.)

10. On Scottish culture, see I. Finley, *Scottish Crafts and Art in Scotland* (1948); S. Cursiter, *Scottish Art at the Close of the 19th Century* (1949); K. Wittig, *The Scottish Tradition in Literature* (1958); M. McLaren, *The Wisdom of the Scots* (1961); D. Craig, *Scottish Literature and the Scottish People, 1680–1830* (1961); and F. Collinson, *The Tradition and National Music of Scotland* (1966).

11. Hanham, *Scottish Nationalism, op. cit.*, p. 15.

12. On the economic history of Scotland, see W. H. Marwick, *Economic Development in Victorian Scotland* (1936); I. F. Grant, *The Economic History of Scotland* (1934); G. McCrone, *Scotland's Future: The Economics of Nationalism* (1969); and T. L. Johnston, N. K. Buston, and D. Mair, *Structure and Growth of the Scottish Economy* (1971).

13. On the Industrial Revolution in Scotland, see H. Hamilton, *The Industrial Revolution in Scotland* (1932); and I. F. Grant, *Economic History, op. cit.*, and W. H. Marwick, *Economic Development, op. cit.*

14. "It is an incorrect but generally held view that oil gave birth to a new Scottish drive for separation from England, but the perception of deprivation and hence the aggregation around an ethnic identity started before the oil crisis and persisted because of the prospects of economic wealth." (Ronen, *The Quest, op. cit.*,

p. 74). Ronen believes that it was not the discovery of oil that promoted the quest for Scottish ethnic self-determination, and that the current militant stance of ethnic self-determination is not a linear continuation of past demands but a new one.

15. On Scottish government and administration, see D. Milne, *The Scottish Office and Other Scottish Government Departments* (1958); C. Pryde, *Central and Local Government in Scotland Since 1707* (1968); J. G. Kellas, *Modern Scotland* (1968); and J. N. Rolfe (ed.), *Government and Nationalism in Scotland* (1969).

16. Scottish judicial and administrative headquarters remain in Edinburgh.

17. "This seeming inferiority of Scotland as well as the stifling domination of an alien Government, have in the past engendered a kind of national subservience in virtually the entire Scottish people—a race of political Milquetoasts. The national psyche has been permeated with the idea that Scotland is in a permanent and necessary state of dependence on England, from whom all law and wisdom flow." (R. Shirley, in *The New York Times,* June 12, 1974.)

18. On the Scottish Nationalist Party (SNP), see J. M. MacCormick, *The Flag in the Wind: The Story of the National Movement in Scotland* (1955); H. J. Paton, *The Claim of Scotland* (1968); J. N. Wolfeed, *Government and Nationalism in Scotland* (1969); and M. J. Esman (ed.), *Ethnic Conflict in the Western World* (1977). See also the publications of the Scottish National Party: *No Voice, No Entry* (1967); *SNP & You: Aim and Policy of the Scottish National Party* (1968); *Action Now: Coal and Power* (1968); and *Scotland's Future, A Manifesto* (1976).

19. *Scot Independent,* January, 1947.

20. D. Donnelly, "The Celtic Storm," *News of the World,* July 21, 1968.

21. The SNP argument: Scotland has a population of just over five million, which works out to 173 persons per square mile. England, grossly overpopulated, has approximately 910 persons per square mile. It followed that England, the exploiter, was economically unbalanced, but still controlled economically balanced Scotland. (Shirley, *The New York Times, op. cit.*)

22. Scone, a parish of Perthshire, Scotland, contained Old Scone, the site of a historic abbey and palace. The Stone of Destiny, on which the Celtic kings were crowned, was deposited in Scone, from which it was conveyed to Westminster Abbey by Edward I in 1296. Here it lay beneath the coronation chair. For a description of the episode, see I. R. Hamilton, *No Stone Unturned: The Story of the Stone of Destiny* (1952).

23. *Ibid.*

24. In recent years there has been a strong leftist movement in Scotland, including the Communists. But the Communist vote has remained negligible, and most leftists prefer to work inside the Labour Party.

25. From 1929 to 1970, the SNP had no seats in the British House of Commons.

26.
General Election Voting in Scotland 1929–1974
(in percentages)

Year	Conservative	Labour	Liberal	SNP
1929	35.6	41.5	18.1	0.1
1970	38.0	44.5	5.5	11.4
Feb. 1974	32.9	36.6	7.9	21.9
Oct. 1974	24.7	36.3	8.3	30.4

British Parliamentary Seats Won in General Elections, 1929-1974

Year	Conservative	Labour	Liberal	SNP
1929	22	36	14	—
1970	23	44	3	1
Feb. 1974	21	40	3	7
Oct. 1974	16	41	3	11

SOURCE: *Scotland's Future,* SNP Manifesto (1976).

27. *Ibid.*

28. There is much admiration in Scotland for the patriotism of such nationalist leaders as Margo MacDonald, vice-chairman of the SNP, who stated in an election campaign: "We are battling for the soul of the country. Everything for the next generation hangs on this." The admiration, however, is muted, and does not extend to the point where a majority of Scots would favor the dissolution of the United Kingdom.

29. The census of 1931 listed a population of 4,842,554 for Scotland; the census of 1951 gave a total of 5,096,415. Approximately a quarter of the entire population signed the resolution for home rule.

30. This meant a legal minimum of 1,498,844 votes.

31. On the referendum campaign, see *The New York Times,* Feb. 23, 1979. On its results, see *Time,* Mar. 12, 1979, p. 38.

32. Quoted in *The New York Times,* Sept. 18, 1980.

33. *The New York Times,* Oct. 16, 1980.

34. R. Reed, "Shetlanders Seek to Keep Their Distance from the Scots," *The New York Times,* Mar. 21, 1979.

35. *Ibid.*

36. There is an even smaller mini-nationalism in the Isle of Man, a self-governing dependency of the British Crown. Just to the west of central Britain, the island is 227 square miles in area, with a population of 49,300. The people of this tiny island have their own miniscule nationalism. In the summer of 1968, they attracted the attention of the British press when their Executive Council decreed that the Union Jack would not fly thereafter from public buildings on official occasions. Instead, they would display the Manx flag on royal birthdays. The British public, always fascinated by eccentric behavior, was amused.

Chapter 4   BRITISH DEVOLUTION II: THE RED DRAGON OF WALES

1. The Peterloo Massacre, also called the Manchester Massacre, took place on August 16, 1819. Public distress caused by war and taxation led to popular discontent with the parliamentary system of representation. Dissent was met by repression, culminating in the affair at Peterloo. On the appointed day, an immense crowd gathered at St. Peter's Field in Manchester to petition for a redress of grievances. The authorities feared an armed insurrection. A clerical magistrate read the Riot Act, but it was unheard by the crowd. Suddenly, drunken yeoman cavalry turned loose on unresisting spectators and used their sabers, killing six and wounding others. The magistrates received the thanks of the

Prince Regent and the ministry, but there was indignation throughout the country against this "un-English conduct." The Peterloo Massacre gave strong impetus to the British reform movement.

2. Karl Pearson demolished the idea of a "pure-blooded Englishman": "We are accustomed to think of a typical Englishman. For example, Charles Darwin, we think of his mind as a typical English mind, working in a typical English manner; yet when we study his pedigree we seek in vain for 'purity of race.' He is descended in four different lines from Irish kinglets; he is descended in as many lines from Scottish and Pictish kings. He has Manx blood. He claims descent from at least three lines from Alfred the Great, and so links up with Anglo-Saxon blood, but he links up also in several lines with Charlemagne and the Carlovingians. He sprang also from the Saxon emperors of Germany, as well as from Barbarossa and the Hohenstaufens. He had Norwegian blood and much Norman blood. He had descent from the Duke of Bavaria, of Saxony, of Flanders, the Prince of Savon, and Kings of Italy. He had the blood in his veins of Franks, Alamans, Merovingians, Burgundians, and Langobards. He sprang in direct descent from the Hun rulers of Hungary and the Greek Emperors of Constantinople. If I reckon rightly, Ivan the Terrible provides a Russian link. There is probably not one of the races of Europe concerned in folk-wanderings which has not had a share in the ancestry of Charles Darwin. If it has been possible in the case of one Englishman of this kind to show in a considerable number of lines how impure is his race, how can we venture to assert that if the like knowledge were possible of attainment, we could expect greater purity of blood in any of his countrymen?" (K. Pearson, "The Problems of Anthropology," *Scientific Monthly* [November, 1920], p. 455.)

This down-to-earth paragraph by an able anthropologist effectively demolishes the argument for "pure races" in mini-nationalisms anywhere.

3. On the ethnic background of Wales, see J. E. Lloyd, *A History of Wales from the Earliest Times to the Edwardian Conquest* (1939).

4. On the general history of Wales, see E. Lewis and P. Lewis, *The Land of Wales* (1937); J. E. Lloyd, *A History of Wales, op. cit.;* D. Williams, *A History of Modern Wales* (1950); and E. G. Bowen (ed.), *Wales: A Physical, Historical and Regional Geography* (1957). See also the *Blue Book, Report of the Royal Commission on Land in Wales* (1896).

5. According to an old English legend, Edward I attempted to appease his unruly Welsh subjects by promising them another prince who would be "born in Wales, could speak no English, and whose life and conversation nobody could stain." Welsh nationalists claim that this promise has never been fulfilled.

6. On the Welsh language, see J. Strachen, *Introduction to Early Welsh* (1909); and H. M. and H. E. Chadwick, *The Ancient Literatures of Europe* (1932). On Welsh literature, see W. J. Hughes, *Wales and the Welsh in English Literature from Shakespeare to Scott* (1924). See also the governmental report, *Report on the Welsh Language* (1963).

7. The census of 1938 showed the proportion of the population able to speak Welsh at 26.8 percent.

8. The organization known as *Urdu Gobaith Cymru* ("League of Youth") lists as one of its major objectives "protection of the native Welsh tongue."

9. On the special character of Welsh poetry, see H. I. Bell, *The Development of Welsh Poetry* (1936); and I. William, *Lectures on Early Welsh Poetry* (1944).

10. On the Welsh economy, see D. Williams, *History of Modern Wales, 1483 – 1939* (1950); A. H. John, *The Industrial Development of South Wales* (1951); A. H. Dodd, *The Industrial Revolution in North Wales* (1951); D. Williams, *The Rebecca Riots: A Study in Agrarian Discontent* (1955); T. M. Thomas, *The Mineral Wealth of Wales and Its Exploitation* (1961); and B. Thomas (ed.), *The Welsh Economy* (1962).

11. The South Wales coal fields, an area of about 1,000 square miles, covers most of Glamorganshire, Monmouthshire, and Carmarthenshire. The largest continuous coal field in Britain, it has valuable deposits of both bituminous and anthracite coal.

12. The "foreigners" included both English and Irish miners. Conditions worsened in the coal fields to a point where many Welshmen migrated to industrial areas in England or to the United States. The U.S. Census of 1890 lists more than 100,000 natives of Wales who had migrated to America because of unsatisfactory living conditions at home.

13. In the early 19th century, economic conditions in Wales were similar to those in Ireland. Economic distress was due in large part to exorbitant "rack-renting" by absentee landlords in London, extraction of tithes, and unreasonable tolls on turnpikes. The "Hungry Forties," culminating in the Great Irish Famine of 1848, hit Welshmen almost as hard as the Irish. The depressed economy led to Irish and Welsh emigration from the mid-century on. Nationalists in both Ireland and Wales blamed "London foreigners" for their economic predicament.

14. The eight new units were Cwyd, Dyfed, Gwent, Gwynedd, East Glamorgan, West Glamorgan, South Glamorgan, and Powys. The purpose of the new units was to ease administration and also to give a measure of more autonomy to satisfy Welsh nationalists.

15. The flag issue is considered to be of major significance in most mini-nationalisms. Natives of the tiny Isle of Man insist on displaying their own flag instead of the Union Jack on official occasions. According to the British Home Office, "there are no laws governing flying of flags." (See *The Times* [London], July 10, 1977. See also footnote 36, p. 263.)

16. *The New York Times*, May 17, 1977.

17. *The Times* [London], July 10, 1968.

18. For accounts of the investiture of the Prince of Wales, see *The New York Times*, June 30, 1969; and *Time*, July 14, 1969, pp. 26-27.

19. The British Government was careful to use the Prince of Wales in its appeasement of Welsh nationalism. In 1971 it created the Prince of Wales Committee for the Environment in Wales to promote safeguards for the Welsh mountains and coastline, as well as to improve Welsh living conditions.

20. *Time*, Mar. 12, 1979, p. 38.

21. See Chapter 3.

22. *The New York Times*, Nov. 6, 1979.

23. *Ibid.*, Apr. 5, 1980.

24. Associated Press, July 19, 1980.

Chapter 5   *NORTHERN IRELAND: THE WAY OF TERROR*

1. On the English-Irish confrontation, see J. O'Connor, *History of Ireland, 1796-1924* (1926); D. R. Gwynn, *The Irish Free State, 1922-1927* (1928); J. E. Pomfret, *The Struggle for Land in Ireland, 1800-1923* (1930); L. P. Dubois and T. P. Gill, *The Irish Struggle and Its Results* (1934); J. C. Beckett, *A Short History of Ireland* (1952); P. S. O'Hegarty, *A History of Ireland Under the Union, 1801-1922* (1952); T. Wilson (ed.), *Ulster Under Home Rule* (1955); T. B. Barry, *Guerrilla Days in Ireland, 1919-1941* (1956); and J. Meenan, *The Irish Economy Since 1922* (1970).

2. Cromwell was impelled by the belief that he was a servant of the Lord sent to purify the Irish and to root out "papacy and episcopacy" by any and all means. His butchery of the Irish was savagely pursued. "I am persuaded that this is a righteous judgment of God upon those barbarous wretches who have imbrued their hands in so much innocent blood." The Irish were infuriated by Cromwell's cruelty.

3. The Protestants in Ulster still celebrate the victory with a mammoth parade on July 12 each year. Protestants don their orange sashes and march through Belfast in honor of William of Orange's victory over England's last Catholic monarch, James II, at the Battle of the Boyne.

In the battle itself, William had an army of British and Dutch soldiers, with a regiment of Huguenot refugees. The army of James II, composed mostly of Irish with some English and French officers, was numerically inferior. After the battle, James fled to France, his hope of restoration to the English throne ended.

4. Pitt intended that the Act of Union be accompanied by a measure of Catholic emancipation, but George III insisted that his coronation oath forbade it. Rather than break what he regarded as a solemn pledge, Pitt resigned in 1801. With the Roman Catholic Emancipation Act (1829), Catholics could sit in the House of Commons.

5. For a dramatic account of the potato famine, see C. Woodham-Smith, *The Great Hunger* (1962).

6. Boycotting was a form of coercion consisting of a conspiracy to prevent all social, commercial, or other dealings with some person or persons. It was first used against a Captain C. C. Boycott, an English land agent in Ireland in 1880. Later, the boycott became more and more a form of international warfare against a whole people instead of an individual.

7. Also called the Wyndham Act.

8. *Newsweek,* Dec. 2, 1968, p. 45.

9. On the "Black and Tans," see W. A. Phillips, *The Revolution in Ireland, 1906-1923* (1923); and E. Holt, *Protest in Arms: The Irish Troubles, 1916-1923* (1961).

10. Ireland now assumed the title of "Republic of Ircland." In 1955 it joined the United Nations. In 1960 an Irishman, Frederick H. Boland, served as president of the General Assembly of the United Nations at a time when Soviet-bloc leaders referred to the Irish as "an oppressed colonial people which deserves to be liberated."

11. Executive authority in Ulster consists of a government representing the Crown and a cabinet of ministers responsible to a bicameral legislature. The

government administers its own affairs but not foreign policy. Northern Ireland sends approximately 13 representatives to sit in the House of Commons.

12. A British intelligence report estimated that about $145,000 a year went to the IRA from the United States. (*Time,* Nov. 26, 1979, p. 92.)

13. Prime Minister Jack Lynch urged Americans "to desist from giving support to these people. If Americans imagine that they are helping Ireland, they are wrong. They are doing just the opposite." (*Time,* Nov. 26, 1979, p. 92.) IRA guerrillas, he said, "have proved themselves to be the real enemies of our country. Anybody who supports them is also an enemy of our country." (*The New York Times,* Nov. 5, 1979.)

14. In the summer of 1979, 400 IRA inmates in Ulster's Maze Prison staged a campaign to win milder treatment as political prisoners rather than as common criminals. (*Newsweek,* July 23, 1979, p. 21.) There was also a serious hunger strike in December 1980.

15. *The New York Times,* Aug. 16, 1979.

16. *The New York Times,* Sept. 15, 1979.

17. *Newsweek,* July 23, 1979, p. 19.

18. *Ibid.*

19. *The New York Times,* Nov. 3, 1979.

20. See interview with Humphrey Atkin, Britain's new Secretary of State for Northern Ireland, in *Newsweek,* July 30, 1979, p. 11. "It's more policemen we need. We are trying to defeat terrorism through the law—bringing terrorists to court. We are not using detention, we are not shooting people."

21. See interview with Prime Minister Lynch, *Time,* Nov. 12, 1979, p. 75. "What kind of ideology they [IRA terrorists] have I do not know, but it is the antithesis of democracy. The church has no control over them."

Chapter 6   REGIONALISM IN FRANCE, SWITZERLAND, AND ITALY

1. Carlton J. H. Hayes, pioneer scholar of nationalism, titled his study of French nationalism *France: A Nation of Patriots* (1930).

2. For a satisfactory survey of French history, see G. Duby and R. Mandrou, *A History of French Civilization* (1964). On France in the Middle Ages, see *The Cambridge Medieval History,* vols. 6–8 (1929–1936).

3. On the Hundred Years' War, see E. Perroy, *The Hundred Years' War* (1951); and P. S. Lewis, *Later Medieval France: The Polity* (1968).

4. Outstanding studies of the French Revolution include: A. Mathiez, *The French Revolution,* 3 vols. (1956); G. Lefebvre, *The French Revolution,* 2 vols. (1962–1964); and L. Gershoy, *The French Revolution and Napoleon* (1933, 1964), and *Ten Years That Shook the World* (1957).

5. The most satisfactory treatment of Napoleon and the Napoleonic era is still G. Lefebvre, *Napoleon,* revised by A. Souboul, 2 vols. (1969). See also biographies by E. Tarle (1942); E. Tersen (1959); E. Ponteil (1966); and J. Godechot (1969).

6. See Hayes, *France: A Nation of Patriots, op. cit.*

7. Quoted in *Time,* Feb. 8, 1963, p. 23.

8. On regionalist, minority, and separatist problems in France, see P. Sérant, *La France des minorités* (1965); and T. Flory, *Le mouvement régionaliste français* (1966), and *La révolte des Basques* (1970).

9. Frankish invaders pushing westward were not able to overwhelm the Celts in France. Culturally, they came into contact and absorbed Breton *lais* (lays) about King Arthur and the Round Table. These *lais,* which became differentiated from epics, represented the essential virtues of medieval society. (See C. G. Crump and E. F. Jacob, *The Legacy of the Middle Ages* [1969], pp. 183–84.)

10. *The Cambridge Medieval History,* vol. 3 (1957), pp. 8–9.

11. *Ibid.,* p. 9.

12. American tourists traveling in the Nantes area in the summer of 1979 reported large inscriptions on walls painted by the *Front Libération Bretagne:*

NON À L'OCCUPATION FRANÇAISE—

F.L.B.

[NO TO FRENCH OCCUPATION—

BRETON LIBERATION FRONT]

13. See report of the damage in *Time,* July 10, 1978, p. 35.

14. *Ibid.*

15. Until December 1978, no deaths resulted from explosions set by Breton separatists. After the conviction of two Breton guerrillas on Dec. 2, 1978, a bomb exploded in a Paris department store killing a woman employee. Breton nationalists claimed responsibility for the attack.

16. *The New York Times,* Mar. 14, 1980.

17. The term "Basque" is derived from the Latin *Vascones* used in Roman and medieval times.

18. Manuel de Lecuona, in his *Literatura oral vasca* (1964), p. 8, estimated that there were 90,000 *Euskera*-speaking people in the French Basque provinces and 600,000 on the Spanish side. Later figures (1970) give 120,000 Basques in France and 750,000 in Spain. Virtually all who speak Basque are bilingual and are fluent in either French or Spanish, an indication of the strength of the assimilative process.

19. See P. S. Ormond, *The Basques and Their Country* (1925), which is concerned primarily with the French provinces.

20. See W. Rollo, *The Basque Dialect of Marquina* (1925). On the Basque language, see also A. Tovar, *The Basque Language* (1957), an abridged English version of *La langua vasca* (1954), and *The Ancient Languages of Spain and Portugal* (1961).

21. See Tovar, *The Ancient Languages* for a discussion of Basque among extinct languages.

22. Basque was given official status in Spain for a short time (1936–1937) during the Spanish Civil War under a newly created Basque autonomous government.

23. On the history of France's Basque provinces, see P. Veyrin, *Les Basques de Labourd, Soule et Basse-Navarre* (1955); G. Berniville *et al., Pays Basque* (1964); and M. Sack, *Bayonne et le pays Basque* (1968).

24. French Basques, as well as their Spanish compatriots, are distinguished by a deep sense of family pride and allegiance to Roman Catholicism.

25. S. G. Payne, *Basque Nationalism* (1975), p. 28.

26. *Ibid.,* p. 254.

27. *The New York Times*, Jan. 31, 1979. Paris police officials announced that the seven expelled Basque guerrillas did not have valid residence papers.

28. After World War II, many Basques went into exile, especially to the Americas. A Basque "national government" still exists in Paris.

29. The history of Alsace (German, *Elsass*) and that of Lorraine (German, *Lothringen*) have been intermingled, but the emphasis here is on Alsace because of the separatist movement there.

30. From the beginning of the war, Bismarck accepted the proposal of his military experts that the annexation of Alsace-Lorraine would give the new German state a strategic advantage. Equally important in his mind was the necessity of giving German national sentiment a common symbol of victory after a new conquest. Later, he was said to have regretted the annexation of Metz, but there is no historical evidence for this supposition. (See A. J. P. Taylor, *Bismarck: The Man and Statesman* [1955]; and W. Richter, *Bismarck* [1964].)

31. The victorious Germans classified Alsace-Lorraine as *Reichsland* ("imperial state"), undoubtedly because of their new national spirit. Alsace-Lorraine had no viable government until 1902. It was granted its own constitution in 1911.

32. This spirit of revenge was revealed by wreaths placed on the Strasbourg statue in the Place de la Concorde. Several legends read: "1870–1871: FORGET? NEVER!"

33. D. W. Brogan, *The Development of Modern France, 1870–1939*, rev. ed. (1967), p. 620.

34. *Ibid.*

35. Alsatian Catholics reacted strongly against the anti-clericalism of the *Cartel des Gauches*, the leftist coalition in power in the 1920s. Catholics in Alsace even joined in a curious political alliance with the Communists, a move which angered most politicians in Paris.

36. Alsatian autonomists were tried at Colmar in 1928, but the convicted men were speedily pardoned when they were elected to the Chamber of Deputies. Soon after the outbreak of World War II, one of the defendants in the 1928 trials was executed for espionage. (Brogan, *The Development, op. cit.*, p. 621.)

37. *Oc* is derived from the Latin *hoc; oïl*, or *oui*, from the Latin *hoc ille*. The Languedoc language is also referred to as Provençal, or Occitan. This Romance tongue is spoken by people in southern France. Occitan is derived from Occitania, the region which includes Languedoc, the old Aquitaine, and the southern French Alps. The language is closely related to Catalan, and while influenced by French, its grammar is more closely connected with Spanish than French. Modern Occitan dialects resemble the speech of medieval troubadors.

38. The Cathari were also called Albigensians because many of them came from the town of Albi.

39. Neo-Manichean dualism professed two principles—one good and the other evil. All matter was identified as evil. The Albigensians rejected much of the Old Testament and set up an elaborate mythology to replace it. They regarded Jesus only as an angel. Extremely ascetic, they were bound to absolute chastity and abstained from eating flesh in all its forms, including milk and cheese. They regarded suicide, preferably by starvation, as a good practice, for if

this life be evil, its end should be hastened. Enthusiastic and vigorous preachers, they excelled at proselytizing.

40. On Pope Innocent's role in the Albigensian Crusade, see A. Luchaire, *Innocent III,* 6 vols. (1906–1908); L. E. Benns, *Innocent III* (1941); and J. Clayton, *Innocent III and His Times* (1941).

41. On the Albigensian Crusade, see E. F. Jacob, in *The Cambridge Medieval History,* vol. 6 (1957), pp. 21–28.

42. Throughout the countryside of Languedoc, the visiting tourist today sees many slogans in Occitan written on trees, walls, and buildings, all calling for regional autonomy.

43. Corsica lies 50 miles west of Italy and 100 miles southeast of France.

44. On the history of Corsica, see P. Arrighi (ed.), *Histoire de la Corse* (1971), a collection of chapters by a team of experts.

45. One consequence of the transfer was the French citizenship of Napoleon, who was born at Ajaccio in 1769. The process of absorption into centralized France was accelerated during the era of Napoleon.

46. *International Herald-Tribune,* June 1, 1979.

47. Cologne *Express,* May 8, 1979.

48. *International Herald-Tribune,* June 1, 1979.

49. *Newsweek,* July 2, 1979, p. 14.

50. *Die Welt,* Nr. 160, July 12, 1979.

51. *Ibid.*

52. Brogan, *The Development, op. cit.,* p. 727.

53. *The New York Times,* Jan. 15, 1980.

54. *Newsweek,* July 2, 1979, p. 14.

55. See H. Kohn, *Nationalism and Liberty: The Swiss Example* (1956), in which high praise is accorded the Swiss system by a pioneer scholar of nationalism.

56. On the history of Switzerland, see: E. Bonjour, *Swiss Neutrality: Its History and Meaning* (1946); A. Siegfried, *Switzerland: A Democratic Way of Life* (1950); and E. Bonjour, H. S. Offler, and G. R. Potter, *A Short History of Switzerland* (1952).

57. C. Hughes, *Switzerland* (1975), pp. 136–37.

58. Cantonal governments keep the central government tightly reined: it cannot increase taxes without a constitutional amendment, which requires a national referendum.

59. The Swiss have $15,270 in their banks for every man, woman, and child, more than double the U.S. rate. There are 1,641 independent banks in the country, with deposits of at least $250 billion. The Swiss National Bank rigidly controls inflation by restricting the money supply.

60. J. C. Herold, *The Swiss Without Halos* (1948), p. 6.

61. *The New York Times,* May 6, 1968.

62. *Ibid.,* Oct. 20, 1968.

63. *Ibid.,* Nov. 15, 1968.

64. *Ibid.,* Nov. 20, 1968.

65. The protesters identified themselves as members of the Rams, the most radical group of the Jurassic separatist movement. (*The New York Times,* Dec. 12, 1968.)

66. See A. von Bossi Federigotti, *Andreas Hofer* (1935). By the Treaty of Schönbruun, Tyrol was again ceded to Bavaria. Once more Hofer took up arms but had to disband his followers and retire to the mountains. He was betrayed, captured, and shot.

67. H. F. Young, "South Tyrol: New Approaches to an Old Problem," *Canadian Review of Studies in Nationalism*, II, no. 1 (Autumn, 1974), p. 133.

68. When his troops attacked a folklorist process in Bolzano, Mussolini commented: "A thousand good Fascist boots are getting practice trampling on German skulls." (See C. Gatterer, *Kampf gegen Rom* [1968].)

69. The agreement was made in 1946 and granted by the republican constitution of 1947.

70. For the German case, see P. Herre, *Die Südtirole Frage* (1927); and O. Stolz, *Die Geschichte des Landes Tirol* (*1956*). U. Corsini, G. B. Emert, and H. Kramer, in *Alto Adige dall' Austria all'-Italia* (1969), attempt to bridge the differences. For a non-Italian or non-Germanic study, see A. E. Alcock, *The South Tyrol Question* (1970).

71. When Yale psychologist Leonard W. Doob investigated South Tyrolean assimilation into the Italian state, he was surprised to find that the German element, far from being assimilated, had retained its own sense of national consciousness. This became the theme for his *Patriotism and Nationalism: Their Psychological Foundations* (1964). Doob concluded that "patriotism reflected the belief of German-speaking South Tyroleans as dependent on the preservation or expansion of their own culture and society."

Chapter 7   THE LOW COUNTRIES AND DENMARK

1. In 1972 there were approximately 2,517,000 Bretons in an estimated French population of 51,487,000. In the 1970 census in Spain, there were 2,141,400 Basques in a population of 33,956,000. The four provinces of Britanny cover 10,486 square miles of a total national French area of 210,000 square miles. The four Basque provinces of Spain have an area of 6,824 square miles of a total national area of 504,750 square miles.

2. On the historical background of the Flemish-Walloon controversy, see H. Pirenne, *Histoire de Belgique*, 7 vols. (1900–1932); E. Cammaerts, *The Keystone of Europe* (1939); H. Schreiber, *Belgium* (1949); and E. Eyck, *The Benelux Countries: An Historical Survey*, rev. ed. (1968).

3. Léon Degrelle was born on June 15, 1906, in Bouillon. Failing three times to pass the final law examinations at the University of Louvain, he decided to enter politics. A dynamic orator, he attacked corruption by national leaders and in 1930 organized the Rexist movement with the purpose of "cleansing the Roman Catholic hierarchy of political contamination." At first a wing of the ruling Catholic Party, the Rexist movement went into opposition. During World War II, Degrelle and his followers collaborated with the German occupation authorities. In late 1944 he fled to Spain. A Belgian High Court sentenced him to death *in absentia* for treason. In 1946 he went to Argentina and then returned to Spain. Found living in a luxurious apartment in Madrid by a Dutch television team in April 1973, Degrelle praised Hitler as the greatest statesman of his age.

"I am only sorry I didn't succeed, but if I had the chance I would do it all again, but much more forcefully." (See C. d'Ydewalle, *Degrelle, ou La triple imposture* (1968).

4. In the order of battle of the *Waffen-SS,* the 27th unit was the *SS Freiwilligen-Grenadier-Division-Langemarck,* organized in 1945 and composed of Flemings and Belgians; the 28th unit was the *SS Freiwilligen-Grenadier-Division-Wallonie,* composed of Walloons/Belgians. Both units surrendered in 1945.

5. On linguistic distinctions between Flemings and Walloons, see C. Verlinden, *Les origines de la frontière linguistiques en Belgique et la colonisation franque* (1955); and Belgian Information and Documentation Institute, *The Language Problem in Belgium* (1967).

6. German and Dutch were regarded as separate languages until the 16th century. The early beginning of Dutch as a literary language centered in Flemish areas in the 13th century, and only in the 16th century did it shift toward Holland.

7. For the development of the Flemish movement, see A. Vermeylen, *Quelques aspects de la question les langues en Belgique* (1919); and S. B. Clough, *A History of the Flemish Movement* (1930).

8. Because of their increasing importance in the Belgian economy, Walloons expected political rights commensurate with their economic status. At the same time, industrial conflict in Wallonie led to the emergence of dissenting political forces. Walloon Belgium became a predominantly Socialist stronghold, while the northern Flemish area remained conservative. Such political rivalries were added to linguistic and economic differences between Flemings and Walloons.

9. Between 1956 and 1969, the sum of a billion dollars in foreign capital was invested in Belgium, about two-thirds of it by some 750 companies, many of them multi-nationals which set up affiliate branches in the country. Most of these firms were American-controlled, with headquarters in Brussels but plants in Flanders, to the distress of Walloons.

10. In *The Meaning of Nationalism* (1954), this author attempted to apply psychological techniques to help explain the meaning of nationalism. In recent years, the new discipline of psycho-history has emerged to bring a closer coordination between the two disciplines. In his presidential address at the annual dinner of the American Historical Association in New York City on December 29, 1957, William L. Langer of Harvard University spoke about the historian's next assignment: "I refer more specifically to the urgently needed deepening of our historical understanding through exploitation of the concepts and findings of modern psychology." (See W. L. Langer, "The Next Assignment," *The American Historical Review,* LXIII, no. 2 [January, 1958], pp. 283–304.) Langer referred not to classical or academic psychology but rather to psychoanalysis and its later developments and variations as included in the terms "dynamic" or "depth psychology."

Langer's view was limited, but other historians turned to the development of a new psycho-history. As with any new discipline, there was much floundering and elaborate guesswork. Among the more solid studies were those by David H. Donald, *Charles Sumner and the Coming of the Civil War* (1960); *The Politics of*

Reconstruction, 1863–1867 (1965); and *Charles Sumner and the Rights of Man* (1970). From the psychoanalytical side, the works of Erik H. Erikson have won much attention. Erikson sought to elicit from historical materials the motivations behind actions of great historical figures. In *Young Man Luther* (1958), he treated the historical, religious, and social context of the reformer's life.

11. See "National Character," in L. L. Snyder, *The Meaning of Nationalism, op. cit.*, pp. 162–87. Arguments both for and against the concept of national character are presented with a recommendation for the idea of limited validity.

12. *Newsweek*, June 21, 1968, p. 43.

13. *Ibid.*

14. *European Community* (November–December, 1978), p. 18.

15. By the linguistic frontier set up in 1963 by the Belgian Government, Louvain was placed seven miles inside Flanders, a decision that inflamed the already bitter language war.

16. For a discussion of the Louvain rioting, see *Time*, Feb. 16, 1968, p. 43.

17. *Newsweek*, June 24, 1968, p. 43. Vanden Boynants resigned in favor of Gaston Eyskens, a fellow Christian Democrat and a Fleming who taught political science at Louvain University.

18. *The New York Times*, Dec. 4, 1968.

19. As many as a third of Belgian marriages probably cross linguistic lines. Yet, paradoxically, language barriers survive in Belgian society.

20. *Daily Telegraph* [London], Aug. 23, 1963.

21. *The New York Times*, international edition, Dec. 20, 1965.

22. On the history of the Frisians, see C. Woelchen, *Das Land der Friesen und seine Geschichte* (1973).

23. The word "dream," for example, is the same in Frisian as in English. "Thin" is *tin* and "green" is *grien*. For a general treatment of Frisian and English cultural similarities, see H. Fenger, *Friesland und England in ihren kulturellen und wirtschaftlichen Beziehungen* (1935).

24. The line of the Frisians came to an end in 1890 with the death of William III.

25. The 11 provinces of the Netherlands are: North Holland, South Holland, Zeeland, Utrecht, Gelderland, Overijssel, Groningen, Drenthe, North Brabant, Limburg, and Friesland.

26. B. Burrows, "Frisian Spoken Here," in *Saturday Evening Post* (January–February, 1979), pp. 130–34.

27. In the midst of Leeuwarden, Friesland's largest and capital city, is a replica of a fat dairy cow set in the middle of the town square. The statue bears the affectionate name *Us Mem*, Frisian for "Our Mother." Friesland's most important contribution to agriculture was stock breeding of the famous black and white cattle which led to the Holstein. Frisians regard cows as playing a most important role in their success. Irreverent Dutchmen from the south claim that of the one million Frisians, one-half are cows. (See Burrows, "Frisian Spoken Here," *op. cit.*, p. 132.)

28. Frisians remain loyal to their native-born. When a movement was started to raise funds for a statue to Mata Hari, there was a loud protest by some

outraged citizens. But supporters of the celebrated courtesan won, and the statue was erected outside the gabled house where Margarethe Zelle had played as a child.

29. On the formation of the Dutch Empire in the East Indies, see E. S. de Klerch, *History of the Netherlands East Indies* (1938); B. H. M. Vlekke, *Nusantata: A History of the East Indies Archipelago* (1943); J. S. Mantz, *Indonesia* (1961); and L. H. Palmer, *Indonesia and the Dutch* (1962).

30. These ties were dissolved completely in 1954. The Dutch tried to hold on but finally gave up Netherlands New Guinea in 1963.

31. Sukarno set aside the Constitution, suspended the elected Parliament, and exercised complete control as President for Life. As elsewhere, independence was followed by authoritarianism with accompanying economic distress.

32. For an account of this commando strike, see *Time,* June 20, 1977, pp. 32–34.

33. *The New York Times,* June 15, 1977.

34. *Ibid.,* Sept. 9, 1977.

35. *Ibid.,* Sept. 11, 1977.

36. On the history and development of Greenland, see V. Stefansson, *Greenland* (1942); P. E. Victor, *Greenland* (1949); G. Williamson, *Changing Greenland* (1953); Danish Ministry for Foreign Affairs, *Greenland* (1956); M. E. B. Banks, *High Arctic* (1957); and S. Klitgaard, *Greenland* (1970).

37. The modernization process was stimulated from Denmark; the natives remained backward. Today there are only two native Greenland doctors, one dentist, and three lawyers.

38. Alcoholism was a special problem. The yearly consumption of alcohol in Greenland came to 21 quarts for every person on the island. One in 10 deaths was alcohol related. Up to 10 percent of the island's licensed automobile drivers were arrested for drunken driving in a single year. Venereal disease afflicted a third of all adults.

39. The new Parliament (*Landsting*) has 18–21 members. From three to five members of Parliament act on behalf of the *Landstyre* (local government). (See R. Dale, European editor of the London *Financial Times,* in *Europe* [March–April, 1979], p. 18.)

40. *Time,* May 14, 1979, p. 21.

Chapter 8   PLURINATIONAL SPAIN: BASQUE AND CATALAN SEPARATISM

1. Reported by James M. Markham in *The New York Times,* Oct. 9, 1979.

2. For the gist of this brief section on regionalism in Spanish history, I am indebted to S. G. Payne's excellent *Basque Nationalism* (1971), which shows how Basque nationalism was born out of the contradictions, imbalances, and frustrations in the organization of the modern polity, economy, and culture of Spain.

3. When Charles de Gaulle, who regarded himself as the standard-bearer of French nationalism, proclaimed in Canada: "*Vive le Québec libre!*" enthusiastic

French Basques displayed signs reading *"Vive Euzkadi libre!"* The message was clear: what was good enough for Quebec nationalism was good enough for Basque nationalism inside France. (See *Time*, Sept. 6, 1966, p. 40.)

4. See Chapter 6 for a discussion of Basque origins. On Basque history in general, see M. García Venero, *Historia del nacionalismo vasco, 1793–1936* (1945); Payne, *Basque Nationalism, op. cit.;* and K. Medhurst, *The Basques* (1972).

5. See Payne, *Basque Nationalism, op. cit.,* p. 9.

6. The Carlists were partisans of Don Carlos (1788–1855) and his successors, who claimed the Spanish throne under the Salic law of succession. In the civil war of the mid-19th century, most Spanish Basques, hoping for autonomy for their provinces, supported Don Carlos. In 1873, after the son of Don Carlos attempted another uprising, Basques were punished by loss of their traditional privileges. Revived Carlists supported the Insurgent cause in the Spanish Civil War of 1936–1939.

7. The little fishing village of Guernica in Vizcaya was a traditional Basque assembly place. In 1937 German planes sent to support the insurgents in the Spanish Civil War bombed Guernica and totally destroyed it. The event inspired Picasso's famous painting.

8. On the Basque language, see A. Tovar, *The Basque Language* (1957) and *The Ancient Language of France and Portugal* (1961). For an introduction, see R. Lafon, *"La langua vasca,"* in *Encyclopedia lingüística hispánica,* vol. 1 (1960).

9. Basques derive their name from *Euskaldunak* (*Euskera*), the native name for their language.

10. Basques contend that no foreigner has ever been able to master their language. They tell an old legend in which the devil himself visited the Basque country to learn the tongue and make disciples. He tried for weeks, but was defeated, and returned to Hell after having learned no more of the language than *bai* ("yes") and *ez* ("no"). (P. Dickson, "The Separate Land," *Saturday Review,* Sept. 7, 1968, p. 50.)

11. The Basque language is replete with Xs, Ks, and Zs and is most difficult to use in literary works. There are several dialects. There is no English-Basque dictionary. (See Dickson, "The Separate Land," *op. cit.,* footnote 10.)

12. About 12,000 Basques now live in and around Boise, Idaho.

13. A favorite Basque slogan indicates the affinity between Spanish and French Basques: "Three plus four equals one," meaning that the three French Basque provinces should be united with the four Spanish Basque provinces. (See *Time*, Sept. 6, 1968).

14. *Time*, Jan. 22, 1969.

15. At the time of the trial, ETA militants kidnapped a West German consul and threatened to kill him if any of their comrades in prison were executed.

16. *Washington Post*, Jan. 20, 1972. At the same time, students demonstrated in the heart of Madrid in remembrance of a fellow student who had lost his life two years earlier in a street demonstration.

17. *The New York Times*, Oct. 11, 1977.

18. *Daily Telegraph* [London], July 17, 1978.

19. *The New York Times*, Oct. 11, 1977.

20. United Press, Feb. 23, 1978.

21. On the July 1978 violence in Spain, see *Daily Telegraph* (London), July 15, 17, and 18, 1978, with reports from Michael Field in San Sebastian.

22. *Daily Telegraph* [London], July 15, 1978.

23 *Ibid.*, Sept. 1, 1978.

24. Associated Press, Nov. 16, 1978.

25. *The New York Times*, Dec. 6, 1978.

26. Associated Press, Nov. 16, 1978.

27. *Time*, Jan. 22, 1979.

28. *The New York Times*, Mar. 27, 1978.

29. *Die Welt* [Essen], July 5, 1979.

30. *The New York Times*, Sept. 24, 1972.

31. *Time*, Sept. 6, 1968.

32. *Newsweek*, May 26, 1969.

33. Even before he came to power, Franco was infuriated by the Basque clergy, which had committed itself to the Republican cause. During the Spanish Civil War (1936–1939), Franco's authorities executed 16 priests and monks. (*Newsweek*, May 26, 1969.) This kind of treatment led other Basque priests and monks to join the ranks of the ETA.

34. R. Eder, "Benedictine Abbey in Spain a Center of Basque Discontent," *The New York Times*, Nov. 4, 1968, p. 3.

35. On the history of the Catalans, see F. Soldevila Zubiburo, *Historia de Catalunya*, 3 vols. (1934–1935); M. García Venero, *Historia del nacionalismo catalán, 1793–1936* (1944); and R. d'Abadal e de Vinyals, *Els primers contes catalans* (1958).

36. *The New York Times*, Oct. 24, 1977.

37. *Newsweek*, July 18, 1977.

38. *Ibid.*

39. *Ibid.*

40. *The New York Times*, Oct. 24, 1977.

41. A. Burgess, "Homage to Barcelona," in *The New York Times Magazine*, Dec. 4, 1977, p. 84.

42. *The New York Times*, Dec. 11, 1977. On Dec. 8, 1977, thousands of Basque nationalists demonstrated in Pamplona for the integration of the Navarra provinces in the autonomous Basque province. They carried placards reading: "Navarra is Basque," demanded the dismissal of the Navarra provincial council chosen by Franco, and rejected integration with the three neighboring Basque provinces of Guipúzcoa, Vizcaya, and Alava. Leftists and rightists clashed during a right-wing rally opposing Navarra's absorption by the Basques. (*The New York Times*, Dec. 12, 1977.)

43. *The New York Times*, Nov. 28, 1980.

44. *Ibid.*

45. R. P. Clark, *The Basques: The Franco Years and Beyond* (1979), p. 380.

46. *The New York Times*, May 11, 1981.

47. Quoted in C. Sterling, *The Terror Network* (1981), p. 173.

Chapter 9   SEPARATISM IN THE BALKANS

1. The easternmost peninsula of southern Europe, the Balkans are bounded by the Black Sea and the Sea of Marmara in the east, the Aegean Sea in the southeast, the Mediterranean Sea in the south, the Ionian Sea in the southwest, and the Adriatic Sea in the west. The line of the Sava and Danube Rivers is generally considered to be the northern limit.

2. On the Hapsburg monarchy and the Austro-Hungarian Empire, see R. Kann, *The Multinational Empire, 1840–1918*, 2 vols. (1940, 1964), and his shorter *A History of the Hapsburg Empire, 1826–1918* (1974); A. J. May, *The Hapsburg Monarchy* (1951); and C. A. Macartney, *The Hapsburg Empire, 1790–1918* (1969).

3. The main linguistic difference was that Serbs and Bosnians use the Eastern Cyrillic alphabet, while the Croats and Slovenes use the Western, or Roman, alphabet.

4. On the history of Yugoslavia, see R. J. Kerner (ed.), *Yugoslavia* (1949); R. L. Wolff, *Yugoslavia* (1971); and M. Heppel and F. B. Singleton, *Yugoslavia* (1961). P. Auty (1965) and S. K. Pavlovich (1971) have written useful histories. See also Rebecca West's superb *Black Lamb and Grey Falcon* (1941).

5. Stephen Radić (1871–1928), of peasant background, organized the Croatian Peasant Party in 1904, with a platform stressing Croatian autonomy. He was imprisoned in 1919–1920 because of his disagreements with the Belgrade regime. In 1923, he went abroad to seek support for his projected Croatian Peasant Republic but returned disappointed a year later only to be imprisoned for another year. During a heated debate in the National Assembly on June 22, 1928, he was shot and mortally wounded.

6. Prince Paul, Alexander's cousin, was regent for Peter II, son of the assassinated king.

7. In 1941 Croatia declared war on the United States.

8. For details of the Tito-Mikhailovich feud, see L. S. Stavrianos, *The Balkans Since 1453* (1958).

9. In 1948 Yugoslavia was expelled from Stalin's Cominform for what became known as "Titoism" but was actually national communism.

10. On problems of Yugoslav nationalities, see J. C. Fisher, *Yugoslavia, A Multinational State* (1966); and F. W. Hondius, *The Yugoslav Community of Nations* (1968). The latter book emphasizes constitutional development.

11. For a discussion of recent thinking on territorial aspects of nationalism, see L. L. Snyder, "Nationalism and the Territorial Imperative," *Canadian Review of Studies in Nationalism,* III, no. 1 (Autumn, 1975), pp. 1–21.

12. For the life of Tito, see the official biography by V. Dedijer (1953); F. MacLean, *Disputed Barricades: The Life and Times of Josip Broz—Tito* (1957); and P. Auty, *Tito* (1970).

13. This remark, made in late 1968, expressed Tito's philosophy of national sovereignty from the first day of his rule. (Quoted in *Time,* Nov. 8, 1968, p. 34.)

14. In 1972 foreign-currency arrangements were liberalized for Croatia, which was now allowed to keep 20 percent of its exports instead of 7 percent, and

45 percent of tourist earnings instead of 40 percent. Even these favorable measures did not satisfy Croatian militants, whose calls for separation became even
more strident. (See J. Feron, in *The New York Times,* Jan. 25, 1972.)

15. In a letter dated January 24, 1973, to *The New York Times,* Bogden Denitch, senior staff associate of the Bureau of Applied Social Research, Columbia
University, wrote that the nationalist claim that Croatia had been exploited systematically by the federal government on behalf of the least developed areas is
generally refuted by the available data. He cited figures given in the English-
language edition of the *Economist,* published in Zagreb, the Croatian capital, in
1970 "during the height of the pronationalist euphoria." "If we examine the
fixed income per capita, taking 100 percent to be the national average, the
incomes for Croatia and Serbia, respectively, were 116 percent and 92 percent in
1957, a gap 24 percent in favor of Croatia." In the same period, in the least
developed area, Kosovo, income dropped from 53 percent of the national average to 38 percent. Denitch concluded that these figures provided hardly a case
for gross exploitation of more developed Croatia.

16. In the early 1970s, there were more than 300,000 university students in
Yugoslavia's 200 institutions of higher learning, 10 institutes of economics, and 3
nuclear-science institutes. There were more graduates than the economy could
absorb. More than 30,000 young Yugoslavs migrated to western Europe to find
work. In late December 1971, thousands of Croatian students went on strike.
Meeting in Republic Square in Zagreb, they chanted Croation slogans, called for
an end "to the colonial situation," and taunted the police. Many students were
injured in the subsequent fracas with the police.

17. For details of Croatian activism, see *Time,* Dec. 27, 1971, p. 32; and *Newsweek,* Jan. 17, 1972, pp. 34–35.

18. From a large advertisement headed "Yugoslavia Will Not Survive," in *The
New York Times,* Mar. 14, 1980. The advertisement was paid for by the Croatian
National Congress.

19. Among the dissenters were some whom Tito had regarded as loyal subor-
dinates. Croatian Communist chiefs were accused of secessionist activities. Although they claimed that they only wanted a democratic communism and recognition of legitimate Croatian political and economic demands, Tito looked upon
them as opponents who should have known better. The dictator installed Mrs.
Milka Planning as the new leader of Croatia's Communist Party, with instruc-
tions to strengthen the party in its struggle with Croatian nationalism.

20. *The New York Times,* Dec. 8, 1979.

21. U.S. federal and local authorities expressed concern about the violent and
unpredictable behavior of both Serbs and Croats in the Chicago area. In March
1978, six Serbs from Chicago were indicted for conspiracy to murder Tito on his
visit to Washington, D.C.

22. Croatian militants were active in Australia. In early September 1978, 18
Croatian separatists were caught in New South Wales with land mines and other
explosives and remanded on high bail. (*Daily Telegraph* [London], Sept. 5, 1978.)

23. *The New York Times,* June 15, 1977.

24. *Ibid.*

25. New York City police were infuriated when the bomb, which had been removed to a firing range, exploded and killed one officer and wounded three others. Four of the Croat hijackers were convicted and sentenced to long prison terms. Croatians both in the United States and Yugoslavia regarded these men as innocent martyrs.

26. *The New York Times,* June 15, 1977.

27. *The New York Times,* Nov. 7, 1977. Moderate Croatians in Chicago claimed that the letters had been sent by Yugoslav secret police to discredit the Croatian nationalist movement.

28. *Norddeutsche Zeitung,* Aug. 18, 1978.

29. *The New York Times,* Dec. 8, 1978. The German public was angered by what it regarded as irrational behavior on the part of Croatian separatists.

30. "National Problems in Yugoslavia," *The Times* [London], June 4, 1968.

31. Muslim nationalists in Bosnia could state their preference for the first time in 1971 in the first national census. According to the census, 39 percent declared themselves Muslims, 21 percent Croats, and 3 percent Serbs. Officials believed the Muslim percentage to be even higher. (*The New York Times,* Apr. 8, 1974.)

32. As early as November 1968, three Croatian leaders were found shot to death in their Munich office. Croatian exiles blamed Tito's secret service for the slayings. (*Time,* Nov. 8, 1968, p. 34.)

33. See K. Janics, "Czechoslovakia's Magyar Minority," trans. by T. Spiro, *Canadian Review of Studies in Nationalism,* III, no. 1 (Autumn, 1975), pp. 34-44.

34. On the history of Rumania, see R. W. Seton-Watson, *A History of the Roumanians from Roman Times to the Completion of Unity* (1931); and M. Ghilka, *A Documented Chronology of Roumanian History from Historic Times to the Present Day* (1941). On the Germans in Rumania, see T. Schieder, *Das Schicksal der Deutschen in Rumanien* (1957).

35. G. Castellan, "The Germans of Rumania," *Journal of Contemporary History* VI, no. 1 (1971), pp. 52-53.

36. Speech delivered on February 28, 1969. Quoted in Castellan, "The Germans of Rumania," *op. cit.,* p. 74.

Chapter 10   MINORITY NATIONALISMS IN THE SOVIET UNION

1. B. Russell, *Roads to Freedom* (1918).

2. On the triumph of nationalism over communism, see G. H. N. Seton-Watson, *Nationalism and Communism* (1946, 1953); R. V. Burks, *The Dynamism of Communism in Eastern Europe* (1964); and E. Lengyel, *Nationalism—The Last Stage of Communism* (1970).

3. The *Russity* equate Jews with Zionism and attack them as traitors. Much of current Soviet anti-Semitism is predicated on the assumption that any concessions allowing Jews to emigrate to Israel would be followed by increasing demands upon the part of other minorities for more autonomy.

4. On mid-19th-century Czarist governmental relations with the nationalities,

see Hugh Seton-Watson, *The Russian Empire, 1801–1917* (1967), in *The Oxford History of Modern Europe,* and *Decline of Imperial Russia, 1855–1914* (1952); and R. Pipes, *Russia Under the Old Regime* (1975).

5. On Polish national consciousness, see W. F. Reddaway (ed.), *The Cambridge History of Poland* (1941–1950); R. Dyboski, *Poland in World Civilization* (1950); and O. Halecki, *A History of Poland* (1961).

6. Rivalry between the Orthodox Church and Muslims at times took on political overtones. Both attempted to convert small national groups who spoke Finno-Ugrian. In the process, there were mutual recriminations.

7. In 1936 there were 11 Soviet republics; in 1940, the number was increased to 15. Nationality and numerical status in 1979:

S.S.R.'s	1979 Population
Russian	137,552,000
Ukrainian	49,757,000
Uzbek	15,391,000
Byelorussian (White Russian)	9,559,000
Kazakh	14,685,000
Azerbaijanian	6,028,000
Armenian	3,031,000
Georgian	5,016,000
Moldavian	3,948,000
Lithuanian	3,399,000
Tadzhik	3,801,000
Turkmen	2,759,000
Kirghiz	3,529,000
Latvian	2,521,000
Estonian	1,466,000
Total	262,442,000

8. In 1940, shortly after the outbreak of World War II, the Soviet Union took possession of territories which had been taken from the Russian Empire after World War I. These included the Baltic states of Latvia, Estonia, and Lithuania; Karelia from Poland; Bessarabia from Rumania; and areas of the Ukraine and White Russia from Poland. Moldavia, the three Baltic provinces, and Karelia were Sovietized and added to the USSR as republics on an equal status with the older ones. In 1956, the Karelo-Finnish Soviet Socialist Republic lost this status.

9. The other nationalities were small and isolated communities without the political consciousness deemed necessary for recognition as distinct nationalities. Many were in Asiatic Russia.

10. The Constitution of 1936 created an upper legislative house called the Council of Nationalities, to which each of the SSR's sent 25 delegates; each autonomous republic, 11 delegates; each autonomous region, 5; and each national district, 1.

11. In theory, Soviet federalism was supposed to be a democratic structure in which political rights were granted to all nationalities. In fact, the leadership of

the Communist Party was all-embracing. A guiding principle was to maintain the power of the overwhelming Slavic population.

12. Again, in theory, each constituent republic was supposed to conduct its own foreign policy, but in practice, the Kremlin reserved this right for itself. It was on the basis of the "sovereignty" of individual republics that the Soviet Union, on the formation of the United Nations in 1945, demanded 16 votes for its "sovereign" units. Three were admitted (USSR, Byelorussian SSR, and U-krainian SSR).

13. According to the geopolitical theories of Karl Haushofer, a general turned geographer and propagandist, and director of the *Institut für Geopolitik* in Munich before World War II, the Ukraine was one of the earth's "heartlands" because of its agricultural wealth. In Haushofer's view, if the Ukraine were combined with Germany's advanced industrial area, there would be wealth and prosperity for an expanding Germany. These theories undoubtedly contributed much to Hitler's strategy of conquest. (See A. Dorpalen, *The World of General Haushofer* [1942].)

14. On the history of the Ukraine, see M. Hrushevsky, *A History of the Ukraine* (1941); J. S. Reshetar, Jr., *The Ukrainian Revolution, 1917–1920* (1952); and R. S. Sullivan, *Soviet Politics in the Ukraine, 1917–1957* (1962). Hrushevsky's book, as well as his monumental *History of the Ukraine*, 10 vols. (1899–1937), is the work of a zealous Ukrainian nationalist and presents a strongly subjective case for separation from the Soviet Union. Hrushevsky repudiated the Russian nationalist tradition that traced the history of Russia from ancient Kiev. He was exiled from Kiev in 1930 by Russian authorities.

15. The first and most important collection of Shevchenko's poems was *Kobzar* (1840), English translation by A. J. Hunter (1925).

16. Nationalists inside the Ukraine called for a "national renaissance because national feeling lives in the soul of every human being." Outside the Ukraine, in European capitals and especially in the United States, Ukrainian exiles spoke of "deprived nationhood" and "the national Ukrainian organism." The Ukrainian separatist movement is the best organized of any similar group outside the Soviet Union.

17. In his *Gulag Archipelago,* Aleksandr Solzhenitsyn commented on Lenin's original support for Ukrainian autonomy. On November 2, 1917, the central *Rada* adopted a "Declaration of the Rights of the Peoples of Russia." Solzhenitsyn asks: "Was it a trick when they declared that the peoples of Russia did indeed have the right of self-determination, up to and including secession?"

Six months later, the Soviet Government requested the assistance of Germany to help Russia conclude peace and define its boundaries with the Ukraine. Lenin signed a treaty to this effect on June 14, 1918. "By doing so," writes Solzhenitsyn, "he showed himself fully reconciled to the detachment of the Ukraine—even if it became a monarchy as a result."

As soon as the Germans were defeated, Solzhenitsyn adds, "we immediately crossed the border which we had recognized and imposed our rule on our blood brothers . . . started hunting them down, torturing them, executing them, and dispatching them to the camps." (A. Solzhenitsyn, *Gulag Archipelago*, vol. 1, trans. by H. Willette [1976], pp. 44–45.)

18. After the overthrow of the Czarist regime and the proclamation of an independent Ukraine, Soviet troops entered the territory. Germans and Austrians then overran the Ukraine. The Treaty of Brest Litovsk (March 1918) required the Soviets to withdraw their troops. The Central Powers were then forced to withdraw in turn by the Armistice of 1918. In January 1919, Russian troops were back in the Ukraine. A four-cornered struggle took place between the Red Army, Poles, Ukrainians, and the counter-revolutionary army led by Gen. Anton Deniken. By late 1920, the Soviets were in control, and in 1922, they incorporated the Ukraine into the USSR.

19. In 1938 Nikita Khrushchev was made First Secretary of the Ukrainian Party, and in that capacity, he carried out Stalin's ruthless purge of its ranks. At the 20th All-Russian Party Congress in 1956, Khrushchev bitterly denounced the personality and actions of Stalin but did not dwell on his own role in the Ukrainian purge.

20. For accounts of recent Ukrainian separatism, see J. A. Armstrong, *Ukrainian Nationalism*, rev. ed. (1963). For its early history, see W. Chamberlin, *The Ukraine: A Submerged Nation* (1944), in which the author gives not only a history of the Ukrainian nation but also a full endorsement of the Ukrainian desire for independence. Chamberlin concluded that an independent Ukraine was "an indispensable element in a free Europe and in a free world."

21. See, especially, *The Ukrainian Bulletin*, published semi-monthly in New York by the Ukrainian Congress Committee of America. An organization calling itself Members of Americans of Ukrainian Descent holds annual meetings, confers Shevchenko Freedom Awards, supports the Organization of Captive Nations, and lobbies actively with appeals to U.S. legislators.

22. V. Chornovik, *The Chornovik Papers* (1968). Chornovik himself was arrested in 1967 and charged with possessing anti-Soviet documents. He was sentenced to 18 months' hard labor.

23. A. Solzhenitsyn, *The Cancer Ward* (1969), p. 607.

24. See note 17.

25. Bernard Levin, in *The Times* [London], July 25, 1974.

26. *Ibid.*

27. While serving on the first Central Committee of the Bolshevik Party in 1913, Stalin, then known as Joseph Vissarionovich Djugashvili, published at Lenin's suggestion what was regarded as an important article on Marxism and the national question. Appearing originally in the periodical *Prosveshchenie*, it was re-issued in English in 1935 under the title "Marxism and the National and Colonial Question." Throughout his career, Stalin regarded Soviet centralism as absolutely essential.

28. On the history of Georgia, see W. E. D. Allen, *The History of the Georgian People* (1932); Z. Avalishvili, *The Independence of Georgia in International Politics, 1918–1921* (1940); and D. M. Lang, *A Modern History of Soviet Georgia* (1962).

29. Bolsheviks and Mensheviks were two main branches of Russian socialism from 1903 until the consolidation of the Bolshevik dictatorship under Lenin in 1920. At the Second Congress of the Russian Social Democratic Labor Party held at Brussels and in London in 1903, Lenin's faction gained a majority (Bolsheviki means majority) over his opponents, the Mensheviki (minority). The Bolsheviks, however, soon lost their numerical superiority. In 1912 the two parties sepa-

rated. During the bitter infighting of the Russian Revolution of February 1917, Mensheviks participated in the Kerensky regime. In 1918 the Bolsheviks became the Russian Communist Party. The Mensheviks were suppressed in 1921. (See L. Schapiro, *The Communist Party of the Soviet Union* [1970].)

30. David K. Shipley, in *The New York Times,* May 18, 1976.

31. On the history of Armenia, see K. Ashlan, *Armenia and the Armenians* (1920); and V. M. Kurkjian, *A History of Armenia* (1959).

32. On Armenian literature, see Z. C. Boyajian (ed.), *Armenian Legends and Poems* (1959).

33. Armenians emigrated not only to Syria and Russia, but also to Iran, Iraq, Lebanon, several European countries, and the United States. There are about half a million Armenians in the United States, concentrated in Greater Boston, New York, southern New Jersey, Philadelphia, Detroit, Chicago, and San Francisco. Many are successful merchants, businessmen, educators, engineers, doctors, lawyers, and journalists. (See R. P. Jordan, "The Proud Armenians," *National Geographic* [June, 1978], pp. 846–73.)

34. David K. Shipley, in *The New York Times,* May 31, 1977.

35. Mount Ararat, supposed to be the resting place for Noah's Ark, is considered by Armenians to be a part of their homeland. It is often mentioned in Armenian national poetry.

36. Incorporation of all three Baltic states into the USSR was never recognized by the United States or other NATO countries.

37. When the Vilna soccer team won the national championship of Lithuania in the fall of 1977, thousands of Lithuanian fans surged through the streets shouting anti-Soviet and nationalist slogans. The demonstrators overturned automobiles, set fire to police cars, smashed windows, and expressed their opinion of Moscow's centralism by tearing down Soviet propaganda banners.

38. C. Robin Knight, in *U.S. News and World Report,* Sept. 25, 1978, p. 43. According to Knight, prosperity in the Baltic states, at least for now, outweighs the drawbacks of contemporary Kremlin control.

39. Among other mini-nationalisms in the Soviet Union are the Crimean Tatars, who were deported from their homeland on Stalin's orders in World War II. The dispossessed minority carried on a systematic campaign for its national rights. As a result, Crimean Tatars were subjected to arrest, expulsion from the Communist Party, prison sentences, and other forms of oppression.

40. Seventy-five-year-old Ukrainian nationalist Oksana Meshko had been active in the Ukrainian branch of the Helsinki human-rights group, an unauthorized organization which sought to monitor Soviet compliance with the Helsinki accords on human rights. She was taken to a mental hospital on Oct. 10, 1980. (United Press International, Oct. 28, 1980.)

41. *The Economist* [London], Aug. 30, 1980.

42. Zbigniew Brzezinski, in his foreword to *The Chornovik Papers* (1968).

Chapter 11   IRAN AND IRAQ

1. On the history of Iran, see P. M. Sykes, *A History of Persia* (1951); R. N. Frye, *Iran* (1955); H. H. Vreeland (ed.), *Iran* (1957); D. N. Wilber, *Iran: Past and Present* (1958); J. M. Upton, *History of Modern Iran* (1960); L. Binder, *Iran:*

Political Development in a Changing Society (1962); and J. Marlowe, *The Persian Gulf in the Twentieth Century* (1962).

2. Persians were converted to Islam after the Arab invasion in the 7th century. Today, 98 percent of Iranians are Muslims, 93 percent of them are of the Shi'ite sect, the rest are Sunnis.

3. Iranians later contended that the Shah was returned to his throne in August 1953 through the machinations of the American CIA, which helped arrange the supposedly elected government.

4. SAVAK was the acronym for *Sazeman-e Ettela' at va Amniyat-Keshvar* ("Information and Security Organization of the Country"). Established in 1957, it became the sole authority to guard the security of the country and "to prevent any kind of conspiracy detrimental to the public interests." It was accused of systematic mass arrest and torture of the Shah's enemies.

5. The Shah insisted that he was a victim of his own desire for progress of his country: "When I began a shock program which would enable Iran to make up in 25 years the backwardness of centuries, I realized that success would only be possible by mobilizing all its resources. . . . If a country is to be mobilized, it has to be driven, and, when it sets to work, it must be defended against those who would hinder the process. To have saboteurs to operate in freedom would certainly not have permitted realization of this program." (Quoted in *Time*, Dec. 17, 1979, p. 24.) In an earlier interview, the Shah was said to have admitted that "every country uses torture. . . . Show me the country that does not." (*The Observer* [London], Nov. 23, 1975.)

6. This is the theme of Boyd C. Shafer's *Faces of Nationalism* (1972), a superb inquiry into the rise of the modern nation-state. Nations, says Shafer, are constantly in the process of taking form out of unpredictable, often irrational, forces or circumstances.

7. In virtually all the standard textbooks on the history of the modern world, there is no mention of the Kurds.

8. Estimates of the Kurdish population vary considerably. In the Turkish population of 39,180,000 (Government estimate, 1975), there were approximately 3,200,000 Kurds. In Iraq, with a total population of 10,000,000 (estimated, 1977), the Kurdish minority was believed to be about 1,500,000. In Iran, with a population of 33,020,000 (Government estimate, 1975), the number of Kurds was given as 1,800,000.

9. The "mountain Turks" speak a debased form of Turkish, Persian, and Arabic. The Turks, who regard the Kurds as ignorant and backward, use "mountain Turks" as a term of derision.

10. Doctrinal differences arose early in the history of Islam. The Sunnite sect of Islam consisted of orthodox Muslims who accepted the first three caliphs as legitimate successors of Muhammad. The Shi'ites, the second great division of Islam, were followers of a Persian variation: they were partisans of Ali, Muhammad's cousin and son-in-law, and of Ali's two sons, Hasan and Husein. After the murder of Ali and the assassination of his two sons, all three were elevated to the status of sainted martyrs. Shi'ites regard the Caliphate as in the hands of usurpers. Deep hostility continues between the two sects. (See D. H. Donaldson, *The Shi'ite Religion* [1933]; H. A. R. Gibb, *Mohammedanism* [1949]; and A. S. Tritton, *Islam* [1951].)

11. C. J. Edmonds, "Kurdish Nationalism," *Journal of Contemporary History,* VI, no. 1 (1971), pp. 86–89.

12. On the history of the Kurds and Kurdistan, see A. M. Hamilton, *Road Through Kurdistan* (1943); B. Nikitine, *Les Kurds* (1956); and C. J. Edmonds, *Kurds, Turks, and Arabs* (1957).

13. The Assyrians were the first to give the Kurds the name of Kardo.

14. In his *Anabasis* (ca. 400 B.C.), Greek historian Xenophon tells of the luckless expedition of Cyrus the Younger from Sardis to the Euphrates and the retreat of the ten thousand Greek mercenaries who accompanied him. The epic retreat was made through hostile territory in Kurdistan, Armenia, and Georgia to the Black Sea. The Greeks incurred heavy casualties in their desperate struggle with fierce Kurdish tribesmen. (See H. Richards, *Xenophon and Others* [1967].)

15. Saladin won a reputation among Christian Crusaders not only for his skill as a warrior but also for his generosity and chivalry in victory. (See biographies by C. J. Tosebault [1930] and G. E. T. Slaughter [1955].)

16. Abdul Hamid II (1842–1918), who became Sultan in 1876, was deposed in 1909. Because of the Armenian atrocities from 1894 to 1896, he was given the title of "Great Assassin" by British Prime Minister William Ewart Gladstone. He lost his throne during the Young Turk revolution.

17. Kurdish cavalry was suppressed after the downfall of Abdul Hamid II in 1909.

18. Edmonds, "Kurdish Nationalism," *op. cit.,* p. 89.

19. Point 12 of President Wilson's Fourteen Points reads: "The Turkish portion of the present Ottoman Empire should be assured a secure sovereignty, but the other nationalities which are now under Turkish rule should be assured an undoubted security of life and an absolutely unmolested opportunity of autonomous development, and the Dardanelles should be permanently opened as a free passage to the ships and commerce of all nations under international guarantee." (From the text in *Congressional Record,* vol. LVI [1918], part I, pp. 680–81.)

20. A "vilayet" is one of the chief administrative units of Turkey.

21. Edmonds, "Kurdish Nationalism," *op. cit.,* p. 91.

22. See note 8 for population figures.

23. Edmonds, "Kurdish Nationalism," *op. cit.,* p. 94.

24. *Ibid.*

25. Mustafa Barzani used the religious title of Mullah, a teacher and expounder of the laws of Islam. He was a brother of Sheik Ahmad, religious head of the northern district of Barzan.

26. This time Barzani went to the United States to seek treatment for lung cancer as well as for asylum. He settled in northern Virginia in 1976 and died in Washington, D.C., on Mar. 1, 1979.

27. See note 10.

28. Barzani was supported by the Shah until the latter closed Iran's borders to the guerrillas in 1975 in a deal with Iraq. To some Kurds, Barzani was regarded as a traitor because he had dealt with the Shah. (See Nicholas Gage, in *The New York Times,* Mar. 1, 1979.)

29. See Jonathan C. Randal in the *Washington Post,* Nov. 22, 1979.

30. Conservative Kurds suspected the Kurdish Democratic Party of being

influenced by Iraq's ruling Marxist party, the Baathists. Another leftist group was formed by Sayad Mohammed Nexani, an educator. Still another leftist guerrilla unit, led by Jelal Telebani, operated on the Iraq border. (Gage, *The New York Times,* Mar. 1, 1979, *op. cit.,* footnote 28.)

31. The Shah launched his "revolution from the throne" in 1961, in which he called for the end of serfdom, land distribution, and electoral reform. He was opposed adamantly, however, to give more than token autonomy to Kurds and other Iranian minorities.

32. Khomeini gave himself the new title of *Oloamr,* in Koranic terms, a religious leader competent to judge all matters and whose orders it was a religious task to obey. In secular terms, this was a euphemism for a religious dictatorship.

33. *The New York Post,* Feb. 22, 1979 (UPI dispatch).

34. Quoted in *The New York Times,* Mar. 1, 1978.

35. *Newsweek,* Apr. 2, 1979, p. 47.

36. *Ibid.*

37. Quoted in *The New York Times,* Mar. 23, 1979.

38. *Ibid.,* Apr. 23, 1979.

39. *International Herald-Tribune,* July 20, 1979.

40. Associated Press, Aug. 16, 1979.

41. *The New York Times,* Aug. 22, 1979.

42. *Ibid.*

43. *Ibid.,* Aug. 24, 1979.

44. *Ibid.,* Sept. 6, 1979.

45. When Revolutionary Guards in and around the former rebel stronghold of Saqqi issued an ultimatum that all handguns be turned in within 24 hours, Kurds paid no attention. After the five-day amnesty ran out, only six weapons were collected. (*The New York Times,* Sept. 7, 1979.)

46. The Khomeini regime came into a major confrontation with the United States in late 1979, when revolutionary students took over the American Embassy in Teheran and held some 75 of the diplomatic personnel as hostages. The students insisted that they would not release the hostages until the United States returned billions in frozen Iranian funds as well as the personal fortune of the deceased Shah. The last 52 Americans were released on January 21, 1981.

47. *Washington Post,* Nov. 23, 1975.

48. Edmonds, "Kurdish Nationalism," *op. cit.,* p. 107.

49. Kurdish students living abroad set up "national" headquarters in Paris, West Berlin, Vienna, London, Belgrade, Amsterdam, and Uppsala.

50. Azerbaijan's Turks played a very important role in Iran's economy. The nation's middle class, they dominated the bazaars of Teheran, provided about two-thirds of the army officers, and included many of the country's intellectuals, writers, and teachers.

51. *Newsweek,* Jan. 14, 1980, p. 35.

52. *Time,* Dec. 24, 1979, p. 15.

53. *The New York Times,* Dec. 21, 1979.

54. *Ibid.,* Jan. 8, 1980.

55. *Ibid.,* Dec. 27, 1979.

56. *Ibid.,* May 6, 1980.

57. *Ibid.*, May 1, 1980.
58. *Time*, Oct. 27, 1980, p. 35.
59. *The New York Times*, Oct. 24, 1980.
60. *U.S. News and World Report*, Oct. 27, 1980, p. 18.

Chapter 12   PLO, ISRAEL, AND LEBANON

1. The word "Palestine" is derived from Philistine, an inhabitant of ancient Philistia. In the Bible, Palestine is called "Canaan" before the invasion of Joshua. In Hebrew, the name is "Eretz Israel" ("Land of Israel"), land promised by God to the Jews. The term "Philistine" took on the meaning of a person antagonistic to anyone of artistic or poetic temperament.

2. On the history of Palestine, see J. C. Hurewitz, *The Struggle for Palestine* (1950); A. M. Hyamson. *Palestine Under the Mandate, 1926–1948* (1951); H. F. Frischwasser-Ra'anan, *The Frontiers of a Nation* (1955); B. Tuchman, *Bible and Sword* (1956); E. W. Bethmann, *Decisive Years in Palestine, 1918–1948* (1957); O. Janowsky, *Foundations of Israel* (1959); E. Anati, *Palestine Before the Hebrews* (1963); and K. S. Salibi, *Crossroads to Civil War* (1976).

3. On Jewish immigration to the United States, see M. Kraus, *Immigration: The American Mosaic* (1979).

4. On Zionism and Israel, see I. Cohen, *The Zionist Movement* (1945); M. Buber, *Israel and Palestine: The History of an Idea* (1952); and B. Halpern, *The Idea of the Jewish State* (1961).

5. The text of the Balfour Declaration:

> Foreign Office,
> November 2, 1917

Dear Lord Rothschild:

I have much pleasure in conveying to you, on behalf of His Majesty's Government, the following declaration of sympathy with Jewish Zionist aspirations which has been submitted to, and supported by the Cabinet.

> His Majesty's Government view with favour the establishment in Palestine of a National Home for the Jewish people, and will use their best endeavours to facilitate the achievement of this object, it being clearly understood that nothing shall be done which may prejudice the civil and religious rights of existing non-Jewish communities in Palestine, or the rights and political status enjoyed by Jews in any other country.

I should be grateful if you would bring this declaration to the knowledge of the Zionist Federation.

> *Yours sincerely,*
> Arthur James Balfour

(Text in I. Stein, *Zionism* [1925].)

6. For a discussion of the confrontation between Arabs and Jews, see D. Ben-Gurion, *Rebirth and Destiny of Israel*, trans. by M. Nurock (1964). These essays, written from 1915 to 1952, concentrate on the war for independence and reveal the unfolding views of Israel's first Prime Minister.

7. The Wailing Wall, about 60 feet high, is a portion of the wall which formerly surrounded the Temple in ancient Israel. The Jews regard it as their most sacred shrine and insist that they have worshipped there for centuries before Islam came into existence. They claim a prescriptive right of 19 centuries' duration. Muslims, on the other hand, claim that the Wall and its adjoining pavement are an integral part of the shrine, ranking next to Mecca and Medina in holiness.

8. In 1933, Jewish immigration to Palestine rose to 30,032, including 5,392 from Nazi Germany and 13,125 from Poland. In 1934, there were 42,358 authorized Jewish immigrants; in 1935, 61,854. By 1939, the influx of settlers raised the Jewish population of Palestine to more than half a million.

9. On the emergence of Israel, see Royal Institute of International Affairs, *Great Britain and Palestine, 1915–1945* (1946); M. Davis (ed.), *Israel: Its Role in Civilization* (1956); W. Eytan, *The First Ten Years: A Diplomatic History of Israel* (1956); H. B. Ellis, *Israel and the Middle East* (1957); W. Frank, *Bridgehead: The Dream of Israel* (1961); and Z. Vilnay, *The Guide to Israel* (1968).

10. On the Arab-Israeli disputes after 1948, see S. Rosenne, *Israel's Armistice Agreements with the Arab States* (1951); E. H. Hutchinson, *Violent Truce* (1956); D. Peretz, *Israel and the Palestinian Arabs* (1958); and N. D. Benwich, *Israel Insurgent* (1960).

11. For a biography of Arafat, see Y. T. Kiernan, *Arafat: The Man and the Myth* (1976). For a brief biography, see *The New York Times*, Sept. 26, 1970.

12. The name Al Fatah is an acronym for the organization's full name, *Harakat al Tahrir al-Falaston*, Arabic for "Movement for the Liberation of Palestine." The initials HFT form the Arabic word for "death"; the reversed initials FTH spell *Fath*, the Arabic word for "conquest." Al Fatah was at first only one of many similar organizations, but it soon became known for its fierce militancy. It pledged allegiance to no one Arab government but took aid from all. Arafat assumed leadership of Al Assifa ("The Storm"), the military arm of Al Fatah.

13. *The New York Times*, Sept. 26, 1970.

14. For a defense of the Palestinian cause, see E. E. Said, *The Question of Palestine* (1979).

15. Nearly four million Palestinians were distributed as follows:

Jordan	1,150,000
West Bank	700,000
Israel	500,000
Gaza Strip	450,000
Lebanon	400,000
Syria	250,000
Kuwait	250,000
Saudi Arabia	125,000

The remainder were refugees in other Arab nations, in Europe, and in the Americas.

16. Mohammed Milhem, mayor of Halhul on the West Bank, quoted in *Newsweek*, July 8, 1979, p. 24.

17. Quoted in *Time*, Apr. 14, 1980, p. 49.

18. *Ibid.*

19. *Time,* May 21, 1979, p. 54.

20. In early December 1979, there occurred a split between Arafat and the Libyan leader, Col. Muammar el-Qaddafi, when the PLO appealed to Libya to end a siege of its office in Tripoli. The Libyan action was apparently part of a campaign to make the PLO follow a more radical policy toward Israel and President Anwar Sadat of Egypt, regarded as a traitor to the Arab cause because of his negotiations with Israel. (See *The New York Times,* Dec. 10 and 12, 1979.)

21. In July 1979, much to the consternation of Israeli officials, Austrian Chancellor Bruno Kreisky, a non-practicing Jew himself, greeted Arafat with an official reception in Vienna. Israel made a formal protest. (See *Time,* July 23, 1979, p. 28.)

22. The Italian Government granted official political recognition; in Paris, PLO representatives were guests of honor at a French Diplomatic Press Association dinner; and in Brussels, PLO members were received by Common Market officials and Belgian ministers. (See *The New York Times,* Oct. 30, 1979.)

23. On the history of Lebanon, see P. K. Hitti, *Lebanon in History* (1957); R. Patai, *The Republic of Lebanon* (1957); L. M. T. Meo, *Lebanon: An Improbable Nation* (1965); E. Salem, *Contemporary Lebanon* (1971); and K. S. Salibi, *Crossroads to Civil War: Lebanon, 1958–1976* (1976).

24. An Eastern Catholic sect, the Maronites took their name from patron saint Marun, an ascetic monk who died in the wilderness in 410. Maronites wandered into Lebanon from Syria in the 5th century to escape persecution.

25. *Washington Post,* Aug. 26, 1979.

26. *The New York Times,* Nov. 5, 1979. The serpentine nature of Lebanese politics was revealed by clashes between Christian clans which resulted in scores of killings.

27. In the early 1970s, an attempt was made to satisfy religious differences by parceling out governmental posts among varied sects. The President was to be a Christian; the Prime Minister, a Sunnite Muslim; and the President of the National Assembly, a Shi'ite Muslim. The proposed solution proved to be unworkable.

Chapter 13   *CANADIAN QUANDARY: FRANCOPHONES VERSUS ANGLOPHONES*

1. G. Spry, "Canada: Notes on Two Ideas of Nation in Confrontation," *Journal of Contemporary History,* VI, no. 1 (1971), p. 181.

2. The ten provinces of Canada and the dates on which they entered the Confederation are: Alberta (1905); British Columbia (1871); Nova Scotia (1867); Manitoba (1870); New Brunswick (1867); Newfoundland (1949); Ontario (1867); Prince Edward Island (1873); Quebec (1867); and Saskatchewan (1905).

3. On the general history of Canada, see J. H. Rose (ed.), *The Cambridge History of the British Empire,* vol. 6 (Canada) (1930); C. F. Wittke, *A History of Canada* (1941); M. H. Long, *A History of the Canadian People* (1942); D. C. Creighton, *Dominion of the North* (1944); A. R. M. Lower, *Colony to Nation* (1946); E. McInnis, *Canada: A Political and Social History* (1949); G. W. Brown, *Canada*

(1950); D. C. Masters, *A Short History of Canada* (1958); J. B. Brebner, *Canada* (1960); R. Jones, *Community in Crisis: French-Canadian Nationalism in Perspective* (1966); and R. Cook (ed.), *French-Canadian Nationalism: An Anthology* (1969).

4. About 47 percent of Canada's approximately 23 million people are of British origin; 20 percent, of French background; 13 percent, of other European origins; and the remainder, of either North American Indian or Eskimo origins.

5. In his *Report* (1839), Lord Durham stated that he found in Canada "two nations warring in the bosom of a single state." (See also notes 9 and 10.)

6. Recent evidence claims that for centuries preceding the Age of Exploration, Vikings reached Newfoundland and Canada's eastern coastline. If the "we-got-there-first" argument is to be validated, Scandinavians, too, have a claim to Canadian territory. (See H. R. Holand, *Explorations in America before Columbus* [1956]; and J. Bronsted, *The Vikings* [1960].)

7. Early explorers of Canada were both French and English. Added to the Cabots, Cartier, and Champlain were Henry Hudson, who entered Hudson and James Bays in 1610; Pierre Esprit Radisson, who explored territory west of the Great Lakes from 1654 to 1660; and Pierre de la Verendrye, who set out from Montreal in 1731 and in the next decade built a chain of fur-trading posts in the western Canadian prairies.

8. In debates in the British Parliament on the Quebec Act, Lord North spoke strongly for the rights of French Canadians: "Giving the Canadians their old system of laws would be the only means of making them a happy people." (*The History, Debates and Proceedings of the British House of Parliament of Great Britain, 1743–1774*, vol. 7 [1792], pp. 289, 321–22.)

9. *Report on the Affairs of British North America from the Earl of Durham. . . . Presented by Her Majesty's Command, Ordered to be Printed 11th February,* 1839.

10. Although the *Report* was well received by the English Canadian community, much of its phraseology angered Quebeckers. In a special section titled "Inferiority of the French," Lord Durham wrote in terms that infuriated French Canadians: "I know of no national distinctions marking and continuing a more hopeless inferiority. The language, the laws, the character of the North American Continent are English; and every race but the English (I apply this to all who speak the English language) appears there in a condition of inferiority. . . . The great mass of the French Canadians are doomed, in some measure, to occupy an inferior position, and to be dependent on the English for employment. . . . They are a people with no history and no literature. . . . I believe that tranquillity can be restored by subjecting the province to the vigorous rule of an English majority; and that the only efficacious government would be that formed by a legislative union." (Section C.) This publicized conclusion did much to aggravate French Canadian resentment.

11. For the full text of the British North America Act of 1867, see 30 and 31 Victoria, C. 3, printed in *British North America Act and Selected Statutes* (1948).

12. French is spoken on two levels in Canada, reflecting class and social differences. The upper class and the French Canadian literary world use a purist French, which they hold up to their compatriots as a model. By far the largest majority of Francophones speak *joual,* a kind of degraded French, distinct from the language spoken in Paris. They take pride, nevertheless, in their colloquial French as a symbol of their distinctiveness from the Anglophones. (See R. M.

Chadbourne, "Three Expressions of Nationalism in Modern Quebec Litera-ture," *Canadian Review of Studies in Nationalism,* IV, no. 1 [Fall, 1976], pp. 47–48.)

13. Government estimate, January, 1976.

14. *Ibid.*

15. *The New York Times,* Jan. 25, 1979.

16. For details of Bill 101, see *Time,* Feb. 13, 1978, p. 35.

17. *The New York Times,* Sept. 4, 1977.

18. The linguistic problem in Quebec was aggravated by the religious issue. The school system was based on two major religions, with Catholic and Protes-tant schools roughly corresponding to French-speaking and English-speaking groups of the population.

19. In January 1978 a Quebec judge ruled that a part of Bill 101 was uncon-stitutional. He found that French could not be the only language in the provin-cial legislature or provincial courts because usage of English was guaranteed by Canada's Constitution. Quebec's Anglophone community was jubilant over what it regarded as a great legal victory. The Quebec Government saw the judgment as a setback and appealed it. (*The New York Times,* Jan. 28, 1978.)

20. On Canadian culture in general, see J. Park (ed.), *The Culture of Contempo-rary Canada* (1957); and C. F. Klimck and others (eds.), *Literary History of Canada* (1965). On French Canadian culture, see A. Roy, *Les Sciences et les Arts au Canada sous la Régime Française* (1930); G. Frégault, *La Civilisation de la Nouvelle France, 1713–1744* (1944); and G. Tougas, *History of French Canadian Literature* (1966).

21. Among the leading personalities were the historian François-Xavier Gar-neau (1809–1866), the romantic poet Joseph Octave Crémazie (1827–1879), and the novelist Antoine Gérin-Lajoie (1824–1882). These authors, angered by Lord Durham's estimate of French culture in Canada, aimed to prove him wrong. (See Masters, *A Short History of Canada, op. cit.,* pp. 50–51.)

22. Chadbourne, "Three Expressions of Nationalism," *op. cit.,* p. 39.

23. R. Jones, *Community in Crisis, op. cit.,* p. 11.

24. This idea of differing positions is the theme of R. Cook (ed.), *French Canadian Nationalism, op. cit.*

25. The novel tells the story of Minaud, an old widowed logger, who is humil-iated by having to work for a lumber company controlled by Anglo-Canadian and American interests. In the opening scene, he listens to passages from a novel by a Breton writer: "We came hundreds of years ago and we have remained. . . . Strangers came and surrounded us, took almost all our wealth, but in Quebec nothing has changed." (Quoted by Chadbourne, "Three Expressions of Nation-alism," *op. cit.,* p. 46.)

26. Aquin also expressed a political position in his *Pointe de Fuite* (1971).

27. *The New York Times,* Apr. 2, 1978.

28. In his poem "*Octobre,*" Miron referred to nationalist violence in October 1970, which was suppressed by armed force and mass arrests.

29. *Time,* Feb. 13, 1978, p. 35.

30. For an account of the current status of McGill University in Montreal, see A. H. Malcolm, in *The New York Times,* Sept. 10, 1979.

31. On the Canadian economy in general, see H. A. Innis and A. F. Plumptre, *The Canadian Economy and Its Problems* (1934); R. E. Caves and R. H. Holton, *The Canadian Economy: Prospect and Retrospect* (1959); W. T. Easterbrook and C. J.

Aitkin, *Canadian Economic History* (1965); and G. Teeple (ed.), *Capitalism and the National Question in Canada* (1972).

32. *U.S. News and World Report,* Nov. 28, 1977, p. 46.

33. René Lévesque, Quebec's Premier, saw the flight of business from his province as a promising trend: "You have to go through breaking some eggs before the omelet appears." At the same time, he expressed his bitterness as a Quebec nationalist: "As long as we're under the present setup, we are exposed to blackmail by those bastards, and we're exposed to destabilizing intentions." (Quoted in *Time,* Feb. 13, 1978, p. 36.)

34. In a speech delivered at Quebec on June 24, 1885, Laurier said: "We are French Canadians, but our country is not confined to the territory over-shadowed by the citadel of Quebec: our country is Canada, it is the whole of that covered by the British flag on the American continent.... I am a Canadian.... I do not want French Canadians to domineer over anyone, nor anyone to domineer over them. Equal justice; equal rights.... Cannot we believe that in the supreme battle here on the Plains of Abraham, when the fate of arms turned against us, cannot we believe that it entered into the designs of Providence that the two races, enemies up to that time, should henceforth live in peace and harmony? Such is the inspiring cause of Confederation." (Quoted in M. Wade, *The French Canadians, 1760–1945* [1955], pp. 427–28.)

35. In a speech delivered on June 24, 1889, Mercier said: "The province of Quebec is Catholic and French, and it will remain Catholic and French.... While desiring to live in the most perfect harmony [with other peoples and religions] in the shadow of England's flag and under the protection of a sovereign dear to all, we solemnly declare that we shall never renounce the rights which are guaranteed to us by the treaties, the law, and the constitution.... 'We die Catholic and French.' That will be our last testament, ... the supreme last will of an heroic people, transmitted from father to son, from generation to generation, until the end of time." (Quoted in Wade, *The French Canadians, op. cit.,* p. 426.)

36. Opposition to British imperialism was promoted by the imperialist wing of the Canada First movement, organized in 1868, and also by the formation of branches of the Imperial Federation League between 1885 and 1888. (Masters, *A Short History of Canada, op. cit.,* p. 55.)

37. Because of increasing difficulties with voluntary recruiting, the Canadian Government in 1917 called for compulsory military service, or conscription, for all Canadians. Francophones were unalterably opposed. The issue led to a widening breach between Francophones and Anglophones.

38. Trudeau sent into Quebec 10,000 troops under orders to hunt out terrorists and suppress the FLQ. In mid-1971 two FLQ members were tried and convicted of the Laporte murder. (See *Time,* Feb. 13, 1978, p. 34.)

39. The *Parti Québécois* slipped into power with only 21 percent of the vote. Four other parties split the rest.

40. At this time, French Canadians held 12 out of 33 seats in the Federal Cabinet at Ottawa. Anglophones deplored this situation as uncalled-for appeasement. They complained that the policy of giving in by inches had led inevitably to demands for the proverbial mile.

41. G. Radwanski, *Trudeau* (1978), p. 311.

42. See *ibid.* for a recent biography of Trudeau.

43. Trudeau was succeeded in May 1979 by Joe Clark, leader of the Progressive Conservative Party. At 39, Clark was Canada's youngest Prime Minister. Trudeau was returned to power in late 1979, when Clark's government fell on the issue of energy.

44. For an account of Trudeau's administration, see R. Butler and J. G. Carrier, *The Trudeau Decade* (1979).

45. Radwanski, *Trudeau, op. cit.,* p. 311.

46. See interview with A. de Borchgrave, in *Newsweek*, Dec. 5, 1977, p. 53.

47. Radwanski, *Trudeau, op. cit.,* p. 343.

48. *Time*, Feb. 13, 1978, p. 37.

49. Interview with K. M. Kyrsley, in *U.S. News and World Report,* Sept. 20, 1977, pp. 70–72.

50. *Newsweek*, Dec. 9, 1977, p. 55.

51. For an account of de Gaulle's highly emotional nationalism, see L. L. Snyder, *Varieties of Nationalism* (1976), pp. 140–43.

52. H. Giniger in *The New York Times*, Nov. 2, 1977. Although most Frenchmen seemed to know a little about Quebec, there was some confusion. A member of the guard of honor furnished by the 403rd Artillery from nearby Chaumont thought he was honoring the Prime Minister of Canada.

53. *Newsweek*, Dec. 5, 1977, p. 55.

54. *The New York Times*, May 18, 1980.

55. The official English text of the referendum appeared in *The New York Times*, May 21, 1980.

56. For a report of the referendum results, see *The New York Times*, May 21, 1980.

57. *Newsweek*, June 2, 1980, p. 54.

58. Spry, "Canada: Notes on Two Ideas," *op. cit.,* p. 196.

59. Quoted in an editorial in *The New York Times*, May 22, 1980.

60. *Time*, Nov. 10, 1980, p. 60.

61. *Ibid.*

62. J. Jacobs, *Quebec and the Struggle over Sovereignty: The Question of Separatism* (New York, 1980), p. 4.

Chapter 14   THE AMERICAN MOSAIC

1. On American nationalism in general, see M. Curti, *The Roots of American Loyalty* (1946); H. S. Commager, *The American Mind* (1950); M. Savelle, *The Seeds of Liberty: The Genesis of American Politics* (1953); and H. Kohn, *American Nationalism* (1957).

2. Kohn, *American Nationalism, op. cit.,* pp. 99–100.

3. On immigration to the United States, see M. Kraus, *Immigration: The American Mosaic* (1979).

4. American pride in broad diversity was demonstrated in World War I on a popular war poster by Howard Chandler Christy, which depicted a young girl appealing to Americans to buy Liberty Bonds. She was shown pointing proudly

to a list of names, saying, "Americans all!: Du Bois, Smith, O'Brien, Knutson, Cejka, Haucke, Pappandeikopolous, Gonzales, Andrassi, Villoto, Levy, Turovich, Kowalski, Chiczanevica." Racialist Madison Grant was appalled by this poster, which he attributed to "some misguided enthusiast" in the U.S. Treasury Department. He was annoyed especially by Christy's depiction of a girl "of pure Nordic type." "The one native American," he complained, "is hidden under the sobriquet of Smith, and there is an implied suggestion that the very beautiful lady is a product of this melting pot." (M. Grant, "The Racial Transformation of America," *North American Review,* CCXIX [March, 1924], p. 343.) Grant's point of view was highly unpopular; most Americans were proud of their intermingled nation as an expression of the American dream.

5. See Chapter 13.

6. See Chapter 10.

7. D. Ronen, *The Quest for Self-Determination* (1979), pp. 65–66.

8. On the history of the American Indian, see C. Wissler, *Indians of the United States* (1946); R. H. Lowie, *Indians of the Plains* (1954); W. T. Hagen, *American Indians* (1961); D. McNickle, *The Indian Tribes of the United States* (1962); E. M. Spicer, *A Short History of the Indians of the United States* (1969); H. C. Dennis, *The American Indian* (1971); and W. H. Oswatt, *The Land Was Theirs* (1973).

9. The Dawes Severalty Act (February 8, 1887) provided for the dissolution of Indian tribes as legal entities and the division of tribal lands among individual members. Each head of family was to have 160 acres and each adult single person 80 acres. The right to sell was withheld for 25 years, after which the Indian was to become complete owner of his land.

10. On the Custer massacre, see E. I. Stewart, *Custer's Luck* (1955).

11. For an account of the decision, see *The New York Times,* July 1, 1980. See also *Newsweek,* July 14, 1980, p. 25.

12. *Ibid.*

13. *The New York Times,* July 14, 1980.

14. For an excellent treatment of Indian nationalism, see Spicer, *A Short History, op. cit.,* pp. 142–46.

15. National Congress of American Indians brochure (1957).

16. American Indians resented especially their depiction as helpless drunks. In 1965 the executive director of the National Congress of American Indians strongly criticized a whiskey advertisement headed: "If the Sioux had had soft whiskey they would never have called it firewater." It was a bitter complaint: "Your people have found in 300 years that a drunken Indian is much easier to make treaties with." The advertisement was withdrawn. (See *Indian Voices* [March, 1965], pp. 18–19.)

17. American Indian Chicago Conference (June 13–20, 1961).

18. *Ibid.,* p. 20.

19. United Press International, Oct. 11, 1980.

20. American Indian Chicago Conference (June 13–20, 1961).

21. Use of the term "American black" here reflects an interesting development in linguistic evolution and social mores. From the early 17th century until the last decade, the word "Negro" was used by both the public and by historians (George Washington Carver, "the Negro scientist"), or "colored" (the National

Association for the Advancement of Colored People—NAACP). As recently as 1970, the scholar Rayford W. Logan titled his 2-volume Anvil Book, *The Negro in the United States.* The use of "negro" in lower case was resented by black Americans as a racial slur. With the rise of pride in color, a new tendency emerged, with the rejection of the word "Negro" in favor of "black."

22. For a treatment of the Soviet point of view, see M. Rywkin, "Black Americans: A Race or Nationality? Some Communist Viewpoints," *Canadian Review of Studies in Nationalism,* III, no. 1 (Fall, 1975), pp. 89–96.

23. See R. E. Kanet, "The Comintern and the Negro Question," *Survey* (London), no. 4 (1973).

24. The term "nationalitarianism" is often used to describe the process of nation-building in the Third World. Soviet intellectuals use the designation also to describe the status of American blacks, who, they say, have become the most unassimilable element in the American melting pot. They point out that American blacks have no common territory but do live in urban ghettos and segregated city blocks. Such a people, they say, are entitled to self-determination even as any other minority of the same size living in a homogeneous territory. Psychologically, they say, American blacks have shared experiences in historic slavery, inequality, and oppression, a major step in the nationalitarianism leading to nation-building.

25. See R. S. Browne, "The Case for Separatism," *Chronicles of Black Protest* (1969), p. 225.

26. For example, the U.S. Supreme Court on May 17, 1954, by decisions on *Brown* v. *Board of Education* and three other public-school cases unanimously reversed a previous decision and declared that "in the field of public education the doctrine of 'separate but equal' has no place."

27. On the history of American blacks, see C. C. Woodson, *The Negro in Our History* (1947); R. Ottley, *Black Odyssey* (1948); E. F. Frazier, *The Negro in the United States* (1957); J. H. Franklin, *From Slavery to Freedom* (1967); and R. W. Logan and M. R. Winston, *The Negro in the United States* (1970).

28. In 1517 Spanish colonizers were allowed to import 12 slaves each. By 1540 more than 10,000 were being imported into the Spanish West Indies annually. By the end of the century, Barbados had a slave population of over 80,000.

29. In the Virginia code at the end of the 17th century, no slave was allowed to leave the plantation without his master's permission. Robbery was punished by whipping, maiming, or branding. Slaves found guilty of murder or rape were hanged.

30. By Article 1, Section 2 of the U.S. Constitution, three-fifths of a state's slaves counted toward its portion of representation in Congress. There was to be a public obligation to return fugitive slaves (Article 3, Section 2). However, the Constitution provided for prohibition of trade in "Persons" after 1808 (Article 1, Section 9). The Constitution carefully avoided use of the words "slave," "slavery," or "slave trade."

31. From the text of Booker T. Washington's speech, printed in C. G. Woodson (ed.), *Negro Orators and Their Orations* (1925), pp. 580–83. This speech won for Booker T. Washington a reputation as leader of his people.

32. Sec. 163, US 737 (1896).

33. H. H. Turner, *Voices of Missions* (1900).

34. In August 1906, President Theodore Roosevelt dishonorably discharged three companies of the Twenty-fifth Infantry for allegedly precipitating a riot in which a number of white citizens of Brownsville, Texas, were killed. Black leaders were shocked and grieved by this action.

35. The group met on the Canadian side of Niagara Falls because its members could not obtain accommodations on the American side.

36. Harper's Ferry, West Virginia, was the scene of the abortive revolt led by John Brown in 1859 in a vain effort to liberate slaves.

37. Quoted in Logan, *The Negro in the United States*, vol. 1, p. 64.

38. From A. A. Anderson, *Prophetic Liberator of the Colored Race of the United States of America: Command to His People* (1913), *passim*.

39. Most of the 404,348 black troops, including 1,353 commissioned officers, 9 field clerks, and 15 Army nurses, were in the Services of Supply. About 100,000 went overseas in these units. Blacks also participated in major American offensives and won many decorations. (See Logan, *The Negro, op. cit.*, vol. 1, pp. 76–77.)

40. A protest meeting by blacks in Philadelphia against the Liberian venture turned into a national demonstration when 3,000 delegates passed resolutions declaring it their right and intention to remain in the United States.

41. Quoted in Logan and Winston, *The Negro, op. cit.*, vol. 2, pp. 72–73.

42. For a sketch of Garvey's life, see R. Ottley, *New World A-Coming* (1943), pp. 68–81. For his ideology, see A. Jacques-Garvey (ed.), *Philosophy and Opinions of Marcus Garvey*, 2 vols. (1923–1935).

43. From a tract written by Garvey while in Tombs Prison, New York, on April 30, 1923. Quoted in A. Jacques-Garvey, *Philosophy and Opinions, op. cit.*, vol. 1, p. 37.

44. Quoted in Ottley, *New World, op. cit.*, p. 71.

45. Shares in the Black Star Line were sold to investors for five dollars each. Some 40,000 stockholders lost their investments. Garvey purchased a steamer which he christened the *Frederick Douglass*. Moored in the Hudson River, the ship was visited by thousands who paid admission of half a dollar to shake hand with the black crew. Loaded down with a cargo of whiskey on its maiden voyage to Cuba, the ship foundered a few miles off Newport News. Garvey denounced the crew for drunkenness and playing dice, and charged the black captain with being in the pay of white enemies. The Black Line was an utter fiasco.

46. According to Roi Ottley, the UNIA had 2 million active dues-paying members and 4 million sympathizers throughout the world. (Ottley, *New World, op. cit.*, p. 77.)

47. Logan, *The Negro, op. cit.*, vol. 1, p. 81.

48. See L. L. Snyder, *Varieties of Nationalism* (1976), pp. 242–43, for an account of Du Bois's version of embryonic Pan-Africanism.

49. Ottley, *New World, op. cit.*, p. 88.

50. E. S. Cox, a leader of the Ku Klux Klan, spoke several times from the platform of Liberty Hall and praised Garvey's Back-to-Africa Movement. Defending himself against criticism, Garvey maintained that, in reality, the Ku Klux Klan was a better friend of blacks than hypocritical whites.

51. Between 1919 and 1921, the UNIA took in a total of $10 million. In its investigation of the Black Star Line, the government could find no tangible assets. There was a deficit of $700,000.

52. Logan, *The Negro, op. cit.*, vol. 1, p. 81.

53. Logan and Winston, *The Negro, op. cit.*, vol. 2, p. 74.

54. The resolution is reprinted in B. Chambers (ed.), *Chronicles of Negro Protest* (1968), pp. 281-82. Among its main points were: systematic oppression of blacks; little prospect for an end to prejudice; opposition to segregation; the clash of black and white interests in America; the psychological handicap of no black national homeland; and violence to the self-image of the black man.

55. E. Muhammad, "The Muslim Program," in *Muhammad Speaks* (1962).

56. *Ibid.*

57. *Ibid.*

58. It was common practice among Black Muslims to renounce their parents' name because it was given by slaveholders of their parents. Later, Black Muslims gave themselves full African or Arabic names as testimony to their "decolonization."

59. See Malcolm X, *The Autobiography of Malcolm X* (1965). The tremendous sale of this book helped establish Malcolm X as a symbol of black nationalism.

60. See Malcolm X's enunciation of his Muslim program in *Muhammad Speaks* (1960), pp. 20-22.

61. Stokely Carmichael headed the Student Non-Violent Coordinating Committee from 1966 to 1967. H. Rap Brown became its chairman from 1967 to 1968. In July 1979, the word "National" was substituted for "Non-Violent" in the title of the organization, an indication of growing militancy.

62. From a speech by Stokely Carmichael on July 28, 1966. See S. Carmichael, *Notes and Comments* (1966).

63. The black panther was taken as a symbol because white segregationists in Alabama had a white rooster as the emblem for their party lists. In the news media, Black Panthers were portrayed as unprovoked users of force.

64. E. Cleaver's *Soul on Ice* (1967) was a best-seller in the United States and abroad. Serving as Minister of Information for the Black Panthers, Cleaver was accused of violating parole. He skipped bail, fled abroad, and became a hero of the black revolutionary movement.

65. On the history of Puerto Rico, see B. W. Diffie and J. W. Diffie, *Puerto Rico: A Broken Pledge* (1931); R. Tugwell, *The Stricken Land* (1947); J. W. Pratt, *America's Colonial Experiment* (1950); M. Hansen and H. Wells (eds.), *Puerto Rico: A Study in Democratic Development* (1953); H. Wells, *The Modernization of Puerto Rico* (1969); and C. A. Haubera, *Puerto Rico and Puerto Ricans* (1975). On Puerto Rican migrants to the United States, see C. Rand, *The Puerto Ricans* (1958); E. Padilla, *Up From Puerto Rico* (1958); O. Handlin, *The Newcomers* (1959); and O. Lewis, *La Vida: A Puerto Rican Family in the Culture of Poverty* (1966).

66. M. D. Fenyo, "Puerto Rican Nationalism—'A Moderate Revolution'," *Canadian Review of Studies in Nationalism*, I, no. 1 (Fall, 1973), p. 121.

67. Muñoz was reelected by large majorities in 1952 and again in 1956 and 1960.

68. In 1952 a popular vote ratified a constitution similar to that of the United

States. On July 3, 1952, a U.S. Congressional resolution approved the new constitution, elevating Puerto Rico to the status of a free commonwealth in association with the United States.

69. All five nationalists were sentenced to prison. In 1977 President Jimmy
Carter freed Cordero, who was dying of cancer. In early September 1979, the
four remaining prisoners were given clemency for "humane considerations."

70. *Newsweek,* Dec. 17, 1979, p. 55.

71. Independence support fell off from 19 percent—its highest total—in 1952
to 6 percent in 1976. More than 94 percent of Puerto Ricans preferred their
American citizenship to independence.

72. *Time,* Apr. 21, 1980, p. 25.

73. Credit for the attack was claimed by three terrorist groups favoring independence: the Volunteers for the Puerto Rican Revolution, the Boricuan
Popular Army, and the Armed Forces of National Liberation. Despite the high-
sounding names, all were tiny splinter groups favoring a revolutionary nationalism. (See *Time,* Dec. 11, 1979, p. 30.)

74. The New York *Post,* Jan. 13, 1981.

75. Clyde Haberman, in *The New York Times,* Dec. 5, 1979. The established
leaders of the independence movement—the Puerto Rican Independence Party,
a moderate Socialist group, and the Marxist Puerto Rican Socialist Party—
together drew only 6 percent of the vote in the last six elections before 1980.

Chapter 15   FRAGMENTATION IN AFRICA

1. Comparatively few Europeans, other than those who acted as agents for
entrepreneurs, came to Africa, but a minority of about 2 percent in a total
population of nearly 200,000,000 controlled the continent. In 1915 there were
only four independent states—Egypt, Liberia, South Africa, and Ethiopia.

2. For the process of decolonization, see L. L. Snyder, *The New Nationalism*
(1968), pp. 104 ff.

3. H. Kohn and W. Sokolsky, *African Nationalism* (1965), p. 16.

4. T. W. Wallbank, *Contemporary Africa: Continent in Transition* (1964), p. 11.

5. J. Hatch, *Africa Emergent* (1964), p. 35.

6. E. Huxley, "Clues to the African Personality," *The New York Times Magazine,*
May 31, 1964, pp. 18, 34.

7. W. H. Bascom, "Tribalism, Nationalism, and Pan-Africanism," *Annals of the
American Academy of Political and Social Science,* CCCLIX (July, 1962), pp. 21–29.

8. Hatch, *Africa Emergent, op. cit.,* p. 35.

9. On the history of Nigeria, see A. C. Burns, *A History of Nigeria* (1956); J. S.
Coleman, *Nigeria: Background to Nationality* (1958); M. Crowder, *A Short History of
Nigeria* (1962); and G. Arnold, *Modern Nigeria* (1977).

10. The Muslim north, with approximately half of Nigeria's population, had a
larger share in the colonial Federal Parliament. Other tribes, which regarded
northerners as backward, refused to accept the political arrangement.

11. D. Ronen, *The Quest for Self-Determination* (1979), p. 81.

12. *Ibid.*

13. More than a million Biafrans succumbed to starvation despite the efforts

of the Red Cross and other charitable organizations to airlift food and medical supplies.

14. Hatch, *Africa Emergent, op. cit.,* p. 41.

15. *Ibid.,* p. 37.

16. The largest tribal group was the Baoulés, with about 700,000 members, forming part of the Agnis-Ashantis-Baoulés combination of tribes extending into Ghana. Others included the Kwakwa, Krunen, Madingo, Senufo, Dan, and Gouro. Although some tribes adapted to either Islam or Christianity, most pre-ferred to retain their animism.

17. The Ivory Coast is the world's third largest producer of coffee and the fourth largest producer of cocoa. Coffee-growing was first established under French rule. In the 1960s the Ivory Coast was in a favorable position to take advantage of the world boom in instant coffee.

18. Bascom, "Tribalism," *op. cit.,* p. 26.

19. See Snyder, *The New Nationalism, op. cit.,* p. 114.

20. Quoted in *Newsweek,* International edition, Aug. 9, 1965, pp. 36–37.

21. W. H. Vatcher, Jr., *White Laager: The Rise of South Afrikaner Nationalism* (1965), p. 35.

22. On the history of South Africa, see M. Ballinger, *From Union to Apartheid* (1969); P. Mason, *Pattern of Dominance* (1970); A. Keppel-Jones, *South Africa: A Short History* (1975); P. L. van den Berghe, *South Africa: A Study in Conflict* (1975); and G. M. Carter, *The Politics of Inequality: South Africa Since 1958* (1977).

23. In a current population of more than 20 million, government-estimated racial groupings are: Bantu, 17.7 million; white, 4.1 million; colored (mixed), 2.4 million; and Asians, 700,000. The Bantu, in turn, are divided into Zulu, 4 mil-lion; Xhosa, 3.9 million; Tawana, 1.7 million; and Sotho, 3.3 million. The overall racial division includes: Europeans (or Afrikans and English-speaking whites), blacks, coloreds, and Asians.

24. Although many South African whites, mainly those of British extraction, vaguely favored a modification of *apartheid,* they, too, supported it as a means of assuring white control.

25. Of the white population, 60 percent speak Afrikaans, 40 percent speak English.

26. In 1959 the government provided for the eventual creation of several Bantu nations on 12 percent of the country's land area, a decision opposed by most Bantu leaders. In 1963 the Transkei in the southeast became the first of these partly self-governing territories. By 1974 there were ten of these "home-lands."

27. Ronen, *The Quest, op. cit.,* p. 92.

28. In 1966 the UN General Assembly adopted a resolution holding that South Africa had forfeited its right to mandated territory. In 1969 the UN Security Council condemned South Africa for its refusal to allow the United Nations to take control of South-West Africa following termination of a League of Nations mandate.

29. In 1953 the Kabaka King Mutesa II was deposed and exiled to London. He was restored to the throne by the British as a constitutional monarch. After independence, he was elected president by Parliament, only to be deposed by A. Milton Obote in 1966.

30. It is believed that more than 90,000 of Amin's opponents were slaughtered after 1971. In 1972 he expelled almost all of Uganda's 45,000 Asians (Indians and Pakistani), who formed the business and professional classes of the country. Amin himself was later deposed and fled in exile to Libya.

Chapter 16   CENTRIFUGAL FACTIONALISM IN ASIA

1. J. Kennedy, *Asian Nationalism in the Twentieth Century* (1968), p. 101.

2. Quoted in M. N. Roy, "Asian Nationalism," *Yale Review*, XLII (September, 1952), p. 99.

3. W. L. Holland (ed.), *Asian Nationalism and the West* (1953), pp. 4–5.

4. "The bulk of the people throughout Asia are steeped in ignorance, which keeps them welded to medieval prejudices. The teleological view of life, the most outstanding feature of the medieval religious culture, creates an authoritarian mentality—the psychological predisposition to cultivate submission as a virtue and to accept authority as providentially ordained. With the ignorant multitude, the cultural tradition takes the form of fatalism, it makes the politically-minded minority regard dictatorship of paternalism as more desirable than democracy." (M. N. Roy, "Democracy and Nationalism in Asia," *Pacific Affairs*, XXV, no. 2, p. 141.)

5. On religious feuds in Asia, see L. S. S. O'Malley, *Popular Hinduism, The Religion of the Masses* (1935); W. C. Smith, *Modern Islam in India* (1947); A. P. Wright, *Buddhism in Chinese History* (1959); E. Zürcher, *Buddhism* (1962); F. R. J. Verboeven, *Islam* (1962); C. N. E. Eliot, *Hinduism and Buddhism* (1962); E. Conze, *Buddhist Thought in India* (1962); L. Rahman, *Islam* (1964); R. H. Robinson, *The Buddhist Religion* (1970); and *Cambridge History of Islam* (1970).

6. Quoted in D. Ronen, *The Quest for Self-Determination* (1979), pp. 128–29.

7. Kennedy, *Asian Nationalism, op. cit.,* p. 106.

8. M. Kaufman, in *The New York Times,* Aug. 9, 1980.

9. On the caste system, see A. M. Hocart, *Caste: A Comparative Study* (1950); J. M. Hutton, *Caste in India* (1951); M. Marriott (ed.), *Village India* (1955); G. S. Churge, *Caste, Class, and Occupation in India* (1961); L. Dumont, *Homo Hierarchichus* (1970); and C. Bougle, *Essays on the Caste System* (1971).

10. On the history of India, see T. G. P. Spear, *India: A Modern History* (1973); D. N. Majumdar, *Races and Cultures of India* (1973); *Cambridge History of India* (1973); and D. Hiro, *Inside India Today* (1978).

11. On the Sepoy Rebellion, see R. Collier, *The Great India Mutiny* (1964); and C. Hibbert, *The Great Mutiny* (1978).

12. Under British sponsorship, some 56 million acres were reclaimed through irrigation. British engineers also supervised construction of the great Ganges and Jumna canals, with 1,200 miles of main channels and 6,500 miles of distributaries.

13. H. Kohn, *Nationalism: Its Meaning and History* (1965), p. 86.

14. In World War I, Indian princes and masses remained loyal to Britain and furnished more than a million fighting men for the Allied cause.

15. See M. K. Gandhi, *Hindu Swaraj, or Indian Home Rule* (1938), pp. 131–36.

16. See J. Nehru, *The Discovery of India* (1959).

17. It is estimated that more than 11 million refugees crossed borders in this

mass transferral in India in 1947. More than 200,000 were killed in communal fighting.

18. On the background of the Kashmir question, see J. Korbel, *Danger in Kashmir* (1954); and Lord Birdwood, *Two Nations and Kashmir* (1956).

19. *The New York Times*, Aug. 9, 1980.

20. *Ibid.* Aug. 18, 1980. Several days later, the issue was inflamed again when Islamic militants took to the streets to press the cause of secession and seek to force the issue into international forums. In August 1980 more than 80 people died in the Indian city of Morabadad in fighting between Hindus and Muslims. Although there was an economic boom promoted by India in Kashmir, religious revivalism promoted a strong separatist feeling among Islamic Kashmirs. (See M. T. Kaufman, in *The New York Times*, Aug. 22, 1980.)

21. On the history of Pakistan, see K. I. Sayeed, *Pakistan: The Formative Phase* (1961); W. A. Wilcox, *Pakistan: The Consolidation of a Nation* (1963); D. P. Singhal, *Pakistan* (1972); and Keesing Research Report, *Pakistan from 1947 to the Creation of Bangladesh* (1973).

22. On the emergence of Bangladesh, see P. Sviraitava, *The Discovery of Bangladesh* (1972); K. Subrahmanyam, *The Liberation War* (1972); and S. R. Choudbury, *The Genesis of Bangladesh* (1972).

23. The annual per-capita income of a Bengalese at the time was about $24.

24. The Security Council of the United Nations was unable to intervene because of Soviet Russia's veto. The General Assembly then called for a cease-fire by a vote of 104–11. Representatives of India paid no attention. The Soviet Union also turned down the appeal for peace.

25. Bangladesh joined the Commonwealth in 1972 and the United Nations in 1974.

26. The people of Chittigong were especially angered by the construction of the Kaptai Dam, which created a 250-square-mile lake flooding tribal settlements.

27. On the history of Ceylon, see A. J. Tressidor, *Ceylon* (1960); E. P. C. Ludowyk, *The Modern History of Ceylon* (1966); and R. Beny, *Island Ceylon* (1971).

28. On Tamil culture, see R. F. Nyrop *et al.*, *Tamil Culture in Ceylon* (1971).

29. H. Kamm, in *The New York Times*, Aug. 18, 1980.

30. For an excellent treatment of the Bougainville secession movement, see P. P. Premdas, "Ethnonationalism, Copper, and Secession in Bougainville," *Canadian Review of Studies in Nationalism* (Spring, 1977), no. 2, pp. 247–65.

31. See also L. Hannett, "Down Kieta Way: Independence for Bougainville," *New Guinea Quarterly* (March/April, 1969).

32. Bougainville leaders pointed out that they had only four seats in the Central Parliament of 100 members.

33. Premdas, "Ethnonationalism," *op. cit.*, pp. 255–56.

34. The taxes derived from the copper mine operation yielded from 50 to 100 million dollars annually, depending on the price of copper in the world market. This income formed more than half the central government's internal revenue. (*Ibid.*, p. 252.)

35. New Zealand rates next to Australia as the world's largest exporter of meat, mostly lamb.

36. *The New York Times*, Nov. 4, 1980.

37. *Ibid.*, Jan. 15, 1980.

38. The accord was to be ratified in a plebiscite by the islanders and by the President and Congress of the United States. It set a pattern for similar settlements proposed for other states of the Trust Territory—the Federated States of Micronesia and the Palau Islands in the western Pacific. The Northern Mariana Islands had already elected to become a commonwealth of the United States, like Puerto Rico.

39. *The New York Times,* Jan. 15, 1980.

40. The proposed agreement encountered obstacles within a few months. The Federated States of Micronesia balked at a U.S. proposal that the draft compact giving the islands semi-independence be changed to include a permanent ban on the military presence of any third power without Washington's consent. Ratification of the agreement was delayed by the protest. (*The New York Times,* Oct. 6, 1980).

BIBLIOGRAPHY ─────────────

Books

Alba, V. *Catalonia.* London, 1965.
Alcock, A. E. *The History of the South Tyrol Question.* London, 1971.
Allworth, E. (ed.). *Soviet Nationality Problems.* New York, 1971.
Ammende, E. *Die Nationalitäten in der Staaten Europas.* Wien, 1931.
Antonius, G. *The Arab Awakening: The Story of the Arab National Movement.* Philadelphia, 1965.
Ardagh, J. *The New France: A Society in Transition, 1945–1977.* London, 1977.
Armstrong, J. A. *Ukrainian Nationalism.* New York, 1963.
Bendix, R. *Nation-Building and Citizenship of our Changing Social Order.* New York, 1964.
Bilinsky, Y. *The Second Soviet Republic: The Ukraine After World War II.* New Brunswick, N.J., 1961.
Bogdanor, V. *Devolution.* New York, 1979.
Borkenau, F. *Socialism, National or International.* London, 1942.
Bracey, J. H., Jr., Meier, A., and Rudwick, E. (eds.). *Black Nationalism in America.* New York, 1970.
Brecher, M. *The New States of Asia.* London, 1963.
Browne, M. (ed.). *Ferment in the Ukraine.* Woodhaven, N.Y., 1973.
Browne, R. S. *The Case for Separation.* New York, 1969.
Brugmans, H. *L'Idée Européen, 1918–1966.* Bruges, 1966.
Buchanan, W., and Cantril, H. *How Nations See Each Other.* Urbana, Ill., 1953.
Buchheit, L. C. *Secession: The Legitimacy of Self-Determination.* New Haven, Conn., 1978.
Burns, R. E. (ed.). *One Country or Two.* Montreal, 1971.
Caerlon, R. *La Revolution Bretonne Permanente.* n. p., 1969.
Cameron, D. *Nationalism, Self-Determination, and the Quebec Question.* Toronto, 1974.
Carlisle, R. *The Roots of Black Nationalism.* New York, 1975.
Carter, G. (ed.). *National Unity and Regionalism in Eight African States.* Ithaca, N.Y., 1969.
Clark, R. P. *The Basques: The Franco Years and Beyond.* Reno, Nev., 1979.
Cobban, A. *The Nation-State and Self-Determination.* New York, 1969.
Coleman, J. *Nigeria: Background to Nationalism.* Berkeley, Calif., 1965.
Collier, J. *Indians of the Americas.* New York, 1947.
Cook, R. *Canada and the French-Canadian Question.* Toronto, 1970.
Cornford, J. (ed.). *The Failure of the State.* London, 1975.
Cottan, R. W. *Nationalism in Iran.* Pittsburgh, 1964.

Coupland, R. *Welsh and Scottish Nationalism.* London, 1954.
Curti, M. *The Roots of American Loyalty.* New York, 1965.
Dann, O. *Nationalismus und Sozialer Wandel.* Hamburg, 1978.
Dean, D. M. *Defenders of the Race.* Boston, 1979.
Desbarais, P. *René, A Canadian in Search of a Country.* Toronto, 1971.
Deutsch, K. *Nationalism and Social Communication, An Inquiry into the Foundations of Nationality.* Cambridge, Mass., 1966.
Deutsch, K., and Foltz, W. J. (eds.). *Nation-Building.* New York, 1963.
Dmytryshyn, B. *Moscow and the Ukraine, 1918–1953: A Study of Russian Bolshevik Nationality.* New York, 1956.
Doob, L. *Patriotism and Nationalism: Their Psychological Foundations.* New Haven, Conn., 1964.
Driedger, L. (ed.). *The Canadian Ethnic Mosaic.* Toronto, 1978.
Dzyuba, I. *Internationalism or Russification.* London, 1968.
Edwards, O. D., *et al. Celtic Nationalism.* New York, 1968.
Ellis, P. B. *Wales: A Nation Again.* London, 1968.
Emerson, R. *From Empire to Nation: The Rise to Self-Assertion of Asian and African Peoples.* Cambridge, Mass., 1960.
————. *Self-Determination in the Era of Decolonization.* Cambridge, Mass., 1963.
Enloe, C. H. *Ethnic Conflict and Political Development.* Boston, 1973.
Esman, M. J. (ed.). *Ethnic Conflict in the Western World.* Ithaca, N.Y., 1977.
Essien Udom, E.U. *Black Nationalism: A Search for Identity.* Chicago, 1962.
Ethnic Pressures in the Soviet Union. Conflict Studies. London, 1972.
Fey, H. E., and McNickle, D. A. *Indians and Other Americans.* New York, 1959.
Fishman, J. *Advances in the Sociology of Language.* The Hague, 1972.
Fishman, J., *et al. Language Loyalty in the U.S.* The Hague, 1966.
Frank, T. M. (ed.). *Why Federations Fail.* New York, 1968.
Geertz, C. (ed.). *Old Societies and New States: The Quest for Modernity in Asia and Africa.* Glencoe, Ill., 1963.
Glazer, N., and Moynihan, D. P. *Ethnicity: Theory and Experience.* Cambridge, Mass, 1975.
Goldhagen, E. (ed.). *Ethnic Minorities in the Soviet Union.* New York, 1968.
Gordon, D. C. *Self-Determination and History in the Third World.* Princeton, N.J., 1971.
Gordon, M. M. *Assimilation in American Life: The Role of Race, Religion, and National Origin.* New York, 1964.
Grant, R. W., and Wellhofer, E. S. *Ethnic Nationalism, Multinational Corporations, and the Modern State.* Denver, 1979.
Haim, S. (ed.). *Arab Nationalism.* Berkeley, Calif., 1962.
Hanham, H. J. *Scottish Nationalism.* Cambridge, Mass., 1969.
Harvis, C. *Scotland and Nationalism.* London, 1977.
Hatch, J. *Africa Emergent.* Chicago, 1974.
Havannisian, R. G. *Armenia on the Road to Independence.* Los Angeles, 1967.
Hayes, C. J. H. *Essays on Nationalism.* New York, 1926.
————. *The Historical Evolution of Modern Nationalism.* New York, 1931.
————. *Nationalism: A Religion.* New York, 1960.

Hechter, M. *Internal Colonisation: The Celtic Fringe in British National Development.* Berkeley, Calif., 1975.

Heimsath, C. H. *Indian Nationalism and Hindu Social Reform.* Princeton, N.J., 1964.

Herbert, J. *The Black Dilemma.* New York, n.d.

Hodgkin, T. *Nationalism in Colonial Africa.* London, 1956.

Huter, F. *Suedtirol: Eine Frage des Europäischen Gewissen.* Wien, 1965.

Innis, H. A. *Essays in Canadian Economic History.* Toronto, 1956.

Isaacs, H. *Idols of the Tribe: Group Identity and Political Change.* New York, 1975.

Jaarsveld, F. A. *The Awakening of Afrikaner Nationalism, 1868–1881.* Cape Town, 1961.

Jacobs, J. *The Question of Separatism: Quebec and the Struggle over Sovereignty.* New York, 1980.

Jesperson, O. *Mankind, National and Individual from a Linguistic Point of View.* Oslo, 1925.

John, H. *American Nationalism.* New York, 1957.

Jones, M. *American Immigration.* Chicago, 1960.

Jones, R. *Community in Crisis: French-Canadian Nationalism in Perspective.* Toronto, 1976.

Joy, R. *Languages in Conflict.* Toronto, 1971.

Kahin, G. M. *Nationalism and Revolution in Indonesia.* Ithaca, N.Y., 1952.

Kann, R. A. *The Multinational Empire: Nationalism and National Reform in the Hapsburg Monarchy, 1848–1918.* New York, 1950, 1964.

Kautsky, J. H. (ed.). *Political Change in Underdeveloped Countries: Nationalism and Communism.* New York, 1962.

Kedourie, E. (ed.). *Nationalism in Asia and Africa.* New York, 1970.

———. *Nationalism.* New York, 1971.

Kimball, S. *Czech Nationalism.* Urbana, Ill., 1964.

Kohn, H. *The Idea of Nationalism.* New York, 1944.

———. *Nationalism: Its Meaning and History.* Princeton, N.J., 1955.

———. *Prelude to Nation-States.* Princeton, N.J., 1967.

Kohr, L. *The Breakdown of Nations.* London, 1957.

Kraus, M. *Immigration: The American Mosaic.* New York, 1979.

Lambert, R. D. (ed.). *Ethnic Conflict in the World Today.* Philadelphia, 1977.

Lang, D. M. *The Georgians.* New York, 1966.

Langlet, J. A. *Pan-Africanism and Nationalism in West Africa, 1900–1945.* London, 1973.

Laqueur, W. *A Continent Astray: Europe 1970–1978.* New York, 1979.

Le Dantec, J. P. *Bretagne.* Paris, 1974.

Leland, W. G. (ed.). *Nationalism.* Bloomington, Ind., 1934.

Lember, E. *Nationalismus.* Reinbek-bei-Hamburg, 1964.

Lévesque, R. *My Québec.* Toronto, 1979.

Lloyd, D. M. *Plaid Cymru.* Cardiff, Wales, 1949.

Logan, R. W. *The Negro in the United States: A History to 1945.* New York, 1970.

Logan, R. W., and Winston, M. R. *The Negro in the United States: The Ordeal of Democracy.* New York, 1970.

Lonsdale, J. M. *The Emergence of African Nations.* Nairobi, Kenya, 1968.

McCaffrey, L. J. *Ireland: From Colony to Nation-State.* Englewood Cliffs, N.J., 1979.

McCrone, G. *Scotland's Future: The Economics of Nationalism.* London, 1969.

Machray, R. *The Problem of Upper Silesia.* London, 1945.

McNickle, D. *The Indian Tribes of the United States: Ethnic and Cultural Survival.* New York, 1962.

Magnago, S. *30 Jahre Pariser Vertrag.* Bozen, 1976.

Malik, H. *Moslem Nationalism in India and Pakistan.* London, 1963.

Mayo, P. E. *The Roots of Identity.* Plymouth, England, 1974.

Medhurst, K. *The Basques.* London, 1972.

Merry del Val, M. *The Spanish Basques and Separatism.* London, 1939.

Michael, P. H., and Taylor, G. E. *The Far East and the Modern World.* London, 1956.

Miller, F. J. *The Search for a Black Nationality.* Urbana, Ill., 1975.

Minogue, K. R. *Nationalism.* New York, 1967.

Mogui, J. P. *La Révolte des Basques.* Paris, 1970.

Morgan, W. J. (ed.). *The Welsh Dilemma: Some Essays on Nationalism in Wales.* Swansea, Wales, 1973.

Moses, W. J. *The Golden Age of Black Nationalism.* Hamden, Conn., 1979.

Motyl, A. J. *The Turn to the Right: The Ideological Origins and Development of Ukrainian Nationalism, 1919–1929.* New York, 1980.

Munger, E. S. *Afrikaner and African Nationalism.* London, 1967.

Murdock, G. P. *Africa: It Peoples and Their Cultural History.* New York, 1959.

Nairn, T. *The Breakup of Britain.* London, 1977.

Nisbet, T. A. *The Quest for Community: A Study of the Ethics of Order and Freedom.* New York, 1953.

Nordlinger, E. A. *Conflict Regulation in Divided Societies.* Cambridge, Mass., 1972.

Nuseibeh, R. Z. *The Idea of Arab Nationalism.* Ithaca, N.Y., 1956.

Ottenberg, S. *Cultures and Societies of Africa.* New York, 1960.

Padelford, N. J., and Goodrich, L. M. (eds.). *The United Nations in the Balance.* New York, 1965.

Page, S. W. *The Foundations of the Baltic States.* New York, 1970.

Pan, C. *Südtirol als Völkisches Problem.* Wien, 1971.

Parker, G. *The Logic of Unity.* London, 1975.

Payne, S. G. *Basque Nationalism.* Reno, Nev., 1975.

Philippneau, M. *Debout Bretagne.* St. Brienne, 1970.

Poliakov, L. *A History of Racist and Nationalist Ideas in Europe.* New York, 1974.

Pollock, N. C. *Studies in Emerging Africa.* London, 1971.

Preston, P. (ed.). *Spain in Crisis.* London, 1976.

Quinn, H. F. *The Union Nationale: Quebec Nationalism from Duplessis to Lévesque.* Toronto, 1979.

Reece, J. E. *The Bretons Against France.* Chapel Hill, N.C., 1977.

Reisner, E. H. *Nationalism and Education Since 1789.* New York, 1922.

Reports of the Commission into the Position of the French Language in Quebec. Quebec, 1972.

Reports of the Royal Commission on Bilingualism and Biculturalism. Quebec, 1972.

Reshetar, J. S. *The Ukrainian Revolution, 1917–1920: A Study in Nationalism.* Princeton, N.J., 1952.

Richards, A. *The Multi-Cultural Status of East Africa.* London, 1970.

Rigo Dueda, A. *The Evolution of the Right to Self-Determination.* Leiden, 1973.

Rogel, C. *The Slovenes and Yugoslavism.* Boulder, Colo., 1977.

Romein, J. *The Asian Century: A History of Modern Nationalism in Asia.* New York, 1962.

Ronen, D. *The Quest for Self-Determination.* New Haven, Conn., 1979.

Rose, R. *Northern Ireland.* London, 1976.

Rossinyol, J. *Le Problème National Catalan.* Paris, 1974.

Rotberg, R. I. *The Rise of Nationalism in Central Africa.* Cambridge, Mass., 1965.

Rotberg, R. I., and Mazrui, A. A. (eds.). *Protest and Power in Black Africa.* New York, 1970.

Roucek, J. S. "Regionalism and Separatism." In F. Gross (ed.), *European Ideologies.* New York, 1948, 1979.

Rundle, S. *Language as a Social and Economic Factor in Europe.* London, 1946.

Sabaliunas, L. *Lithuania in Crisis: Nationalism to Communism, 1939–1940.* Bloomington, Ind., 1970.

Salvi, S. *La Nazione Prohiti.* Florence, 1973.

Schieder, T., and Dann, O. *Nationale Bewegung und soziale Organisation.* Wien, 1978.

Schneider, H., and Wessels, W. *Auf dem Wege zur Europäischen Union.* Bonn, 1977.

Scott, P. R., and Oliver, M. *Quebec States Her Case.* Toronto, 1969.

Seal, A. *The Emergence of Indian Nationalism.* London, 1968.

Sehn, H. (ed.). *Die Behauptung Tirols.* Innsbruck, 1973.

Seton-Watson, R. W. *The Rise of Nationality in the Balkans.* London, 1966.

Shafer, B.C. *Nationalism: Myth and Reality.* New York, 1955.

———. *Nationalism: Interpretation and Interpreters.* Washington, D.C., 1966.

———. *Faces of Nationalism.* New York, 1972.

Sierra Bustamente, R. *Euzkadi.* San Sebastian, Spain, 1941.

Sigmund, P. E., Jr. (ed.). *The Ideologies of the Developing Nations.* New York, 1963.

Silvert, K. H. (ed.). *Expectant Peoples: Nationalism and Development.* New York, 1963.

Sithole, N. *African Nationalism.* London, 1968.

Smith, A. *Nationalism in the Twentieth Century.* New York, 1979.

Smith, A. D. *Theories of Nationalism.* London, 1971.

Snyder, L. L. *The Meaning of Nationalism.* New Brunswick, N.J., 1954.

——— (ed.). *The Dynamics of Nationalism.* Princeton, N.J., 1964.

———. *The New Nationalism.* Ithaca, N.Y., 1968.

———. *Varieties of Nationalism.* New York, 1976.

———. *Roots of German Nationalism.* Bloomington, Ind., 1978.

Spicer, R. H. *A Short History of the Indians of the United States.* New York, 1969.

Stalin, J. *Marxism and the National Question.* New York, 1942.

Sterling, C. *The Terror Network.* New York, 1981.

Stevenson, G. *Unfulfilled Union.* Toronto, 1979.

Sugar, P. F., and Lederer, I. J. *Nationalism in Eastern Europe*. Seattle, Wash., 1969.
Sullivant, R. S. *Soviet Politics and the Ukraine, 1917–1957*. New York, 1962.
Symmons-Symonolewicz. *Nationalist Movements: A Comparative View*. Meadville, Pa., 1970.
Talmon, J. L. *Political Messianism: The Romantic Phase*. New York, 1961.
Tarrow, S., Katzenstein, P. J., and Graziano, L. (eds.). *Territorial Politics in Industrial Nations*. New York, 1978.
Taylor, P. *Distant Magnet*. New York, 1972.
Tillett, L. *The Great Friendship: Historians on the Non-Russian Nationalities*. Chapel Hill, N.C., 1969.
Touval, S. *Somali Nationalism*. Cambridge, Mass., 1963.
Tovar, A. *The Basque Language*. Philadelphia, 1957.
Trudeau, P. *Federalism and the French-Canadian*. Toronto, 1968.
Tudjman, F. *Nationalism in Contemporary Europe*. New York, 1981.
Tütsch, H. E. *Facets of Arab Nationalism*. Detroit, Mich., 1965.
Umonozurike, U. G. *Self-Determination in International Law*. Hamden, Conn., 1972.
Vilar, S. *Protagonistas de la España Democratica*. Paris, 1968.
Wambaugh, S. *Plebiscites Since the World War*. Washington, D.C., 1933.
Ward, B. *Nationalism and Ideology*. New York, 1966.
Webb, M. *The Growth of Nationalism in Scotland*. Glasgow, 1977.
Williams, D. *A History of Modern Wales*. London, 1969.
Wishy, B. *Loyalty in America*. Berkeley, Calif., 1957.
Wittke, C. *We Who Built America*. Cleveland, Ohio, 1967.
Wolpert, S. *Tilak and Gokhale: Revolution and Reform in the Making of Modern India*. Berkeley, Calif., 1962.
Young, C. *The Politics of Cultural Pluralism*. New York, 1976.
Ziedonis, A., Jr., *et al. Problems of Minorities: Baltic Perspectives*. San Jose, Calif., 1973.
Znaniecki, F. *Modern Nationalities: A Sociological Study*. Urbana, Ill., 1952.

Periodicals

Agnew, J. A. "Political Regionalism and Scottish Nationalism in Gaelic Scotland." *Canadian Review of Studies in Nationalism*, VIII, no. 1 (Spring, 1981).
Appel, K. E. "Nationalism and Sovereignty: A Psychiatric View." *Journal of Abnormal and Social Psychology*, XL (1945).
Attwater, D. "Welsh Nationalism." *Commonweal* (Jan. 27, 1939).
Baker, R. K. "The Emergence of Biafra: Balkanization of Nation Building." *Orbis*, XII, no. 1 (Spring, 1968).
Berghe, P. L. van der, and Brass, P. "Ethnicity and Nationalism in World Perspective." *Ethnicity*, III (1976).
———. "Ethnic Pluralism in Industrial Societies." *Ethnicity*, III (1976).
Birch, A. H. "Minority Nationalist Movements and Theories of Political Integration." *World Politics*, XXX, no. 1 (1978).

Birch, J. "The Ukrainian Nationalist Movement in the USSR Since 1956." *The Ukrainian Review*, XVII, no. 4 (1970).

Breton, A. "The Economics of Nationalism." *Journal of Political Economy*, LXXII (1964).

Bukowski, J. "Yugoslavism and the Croatian National Party in 1867." *Canadian Review of Studies in Nationalism*, III, no. 1 (Autumn, 1975).

Chadborne, R. M. "Three Expressions of Nationalism in Modern Quebec Literature." *Canadian Review of Studies in Nationalism*, IV, no. 1 (Fall, 1976).

Cole, D. (ed.). "Anglo-Canadian Nationalism and Social Communication." *Canadian Review of Studies in Nationalism*, VII, no. 1 (Spring, 1980).

Connor, W. "Nation-Building or Nation-Destroying." *World Politics*, XXIV, no. 3 (1972).

————. "The Politics of Ethnonationalism." *Journal of International Affairs*, XXVII, no. 1 (1973).

Corbett, P. E. "The Future of Nationalism and the National State." *Annals of the American Academy of Political and Social Science*, CCXVIII (1941).

Curtin, P. D. "Nationalism in Africa, 1945–1965." *Review of Politics*, XXVIII (1966).

Dawn, C. E. "The Rise of Arabism in Syria." *Middle East Journal*, XVI (1962).

Deutsch, K. W. "The Trend of European Nationalism: The Language Aspect." *American Political Science Review*, XXXVI (1942).

Doob, L. W. "South Tyrol: An Introduction to the Psychological Syndrome of Nationalism." *Public Opinion Quarterly*, XXXVI (1962).

Dyke, van V. "Self-Determination and Minority Rights." *International Studies Quarterly*, XIII, no. 3 (1969).

Emerson, R. "Paradoxes of Asian Nationalism." *Far Eastern Quarterly*, XIII, no. 2 (1954).

Fenyo, M. D. "Puerto Rican Nationalism, A Moderate Revolution." *Canadian Review of Studies in Nationalism*, I, no. 1 (Fall, 1973).

Frendo, H. J. "Language and Nationality in an Island Colony: Malta." *Canadian Review of Studies in Nationalism*, III, no. 1 (Autumn, 1975).

Gillin, J. "National and Regional Values in the United States." *Social Forces*, XXXIV (December, 1955).

Gourevich, P. A. "The Reemergence of Peripheral Nationalism." *Comparative Studies in Society and History*, XXI, no. 3 (1979).

Hannett, L. "Down Kieta Way: Independence for Bougainville?" *New Guinea Quarterly* (Spring, 1975).

Horak, S. "Studies on Non-Russian Nationalities of the USSR in the United States: An Appraisal." *Canadian Review of Studies in Nationalism*, II, no. 1 (Autumn, 1974).

Horowitz, D. "Three Dimensions of Ethnic Politics." *World Politics*, XXIII, no. 2 (January, 1971).

Humphreys, E. M. "Welsh Nationalism and Its Background." *Fortnightly*, CL (August, 1938).

Irele, A. "Negritude, or Black Cultural Nationalism." *Journal of Modern African Studies*, III (October, 1965).

Isaacs, H. "Nationalism Revisited, Group Identity and Political Change." *Survey* (October, 1968).

Isajiw, W. "Definitions of Ethnicity." *Ethnicity,* I (1974).

Jahoda, G. "Development of Scottish Children's Ideas and Attitudes About Other Countries." *Journal of Social Psychology,* LVIII (1962).

Janica, K. "Czechoslovakia's Magyar Minority: An Example of Diaspora Nationalism." *Canadian Review of Studies in Nationalism,* III, no. 1 (Autumn, 1975).

Jelavic, J. "Serbian Nationalism and the Question of Union with Croatia in the Nineteenth Century." *Balkan Studies,* III (1962).

Jelinek, Y. "Between Nationalism and Communism: The Slovak Question." *Canadian Review of Studies in Nationalism,* II, no. 2 (Spring, 1975).

Jorgensen-Dahl, A. "Forces of Fragmentation in the International System: The Case of Ethnonationalism." *Orbis,* XIX (Summer, 1975).

Keech, W. R. "Linguistic Diversity and Political Conflict." *Comparative Politics* (April, 1972).

Kilson, M. L., Jr. "The Analysis of African Nationalism." *World Politics,* X (1957–1958).

Knopff, R. "Language and Culture in the Canadian Debate." *Canadian Review of Studies in Nationalism,* IV, no. 1 (Spring, 1979).

Layton, J. "Nationalism and the Canadian Bourgeoisie: Contradictions of Dependence." *Canadian Review of Studies in Nationalism,* III, no. 2 (Spring, 1976).

Levine, M. "The Basques." *Natural History,* LXXVI, no. 4 (April, 1967).

Levitt, J. "Race and Nation in Canadian Anglophone Historiography." *Canadian Review of Studies in Nationalism,* VIII, no. 1 (Spring, 1981).

Lonsdale, J. "Emergence of African Nationalism." *African Affairs,* LXVII (1968).

McKown, R. E. "National Integration in Africa: Measurements and Correlates in Ghana and Kenya." *Canadian Review of Studies in Nationalism,* III, no. 1 (Autumn, 1975).

Majumdar, R. C. "The Growth of Nationalism in Asia." *Indo-Asian Culture,* X (1961).

Marchak, P. "Nationalism and Regionalism in Canada." *Canadian Review of Studies in Nationalism,* VII, no. 1 (Spring, 1980).

Mayer, K. "Cultural Pluralism and Linguistic Equilibrium in Switzerland." *American Sociological Review,* XVI (1951).

Miller, P. "The Shaping of the American Character." *New England Quarterly,* XVIII (1955).

Moore, M. F. "Nationalisme et contre-culture au Québec." *Canadian Review of Studies in Nationalism,* V, no. 2 (Autumn, 1978).

Morgan, K. O. "Welsh Nationalism." *Journal of Contemporary History,* VI (1971).

Nye, J. S. "Multinational Enterprises and Prospects for Regional and Global Political Integration." *Annals of the American Academy of Political and Social Science,* CCLVIII (1972).

Payne, S. G. "Catalan and Basque Nationalism." *Journal of Contemporary History,* VI (1971).

Popielovsky, D. "Nationalism as a Factor of Dissent in the Contemporary Soviet Union." *Canadian Review of Studies in Nationalism,* II, no. 1 (Fall, 1974).

Premdas, R. R. "Ethnonationalism, Copper, and Secession in Bougainville." *Canadian Review of Studies in Nationalism,* IV, no. 2 (Spring, 1977).

Qualey, C. C. "American Ethnic Nationalism." *Canadian Review of Studies in Nationalism,* IV, no. 1 (Spring, 1979).

Rogger, H. "Nationalism and the State: A Russian Dilemma." *Comparative Attitudes in Society and History,* IV (1962).

Roheim, G. "The Psychology of Nationalism." *American Image,* III (1959).

Ronen, D. "Alternative Patterns of Integration in African States." *Journal of Modern African Studies,* XIV, no. 4 (1976).

Rose, R. "The Options for Constitutional Unity in Great Britain Today." *Rowntree Devolution Conference Papers* (May, 1976).

Rosenthal, H. "National Self-Determination: The Example of Upper Silesia." *Journal of Contemporary History,* VII (1972).

Rotberg, R. I. "The Rise of African Nationalism, The Case of East and Central Africa." *World Politics,* XV (1962–1963).

Rothschild, D. S. "The Politics of African Separatism." *Journal of International Affairs,* XV (1961).

Roucek, J. S. "Nationalismus und Partikularismus Junger Staaten." *Archiv,* XXII (March, 1967).

———. 'Russia's Brand of Nationalism." *Annali di Sociologis,* IV (1967).

———. "The Rise of Black Power in the United States." *Contemporary Review,* CCXII (January, 1968).

———. "The Explosion of Mini-Nationalism." *Queensborough Community Scholar,* II (1968).

Roy, J. L. "Dynamique du Nationalisme Québécois, 1945–1970." *Canadian Review of Studies in Nationalism,* I, no. 1 (Fall, 1973).

———. "Le Nationalisme Québécois," *Canadian Review of Studies in Nationalism,* V, no. 2 (Autumn, 1978).

Rywkin, M. "Black Americans: Race or Nationality." *Canadian Review of Studies in Nationalism,* III, no. 1 (Autumn, 1975).

Seton-Watson, H. "Unsatisfied Nationalisms." *Journal of Contemporary History,* VI (1971).

Skendi, S. "Beginnings of Albanian Nationalism and Autonomous Trends." *American Slavic and East European Review,* XII (1953).

Smart, N. "Nationalism, Identity, and a More Secure World Order." *Worldview,* XII, no. 6 (June, 1979).

Symmons-Symonolewicz. "Ethnicity and Nationalism." *Canadian Review of Studies in Nationalism,* IV, no. 1 (Spring, 1979).

Taylor, A. H. "The Electoral Geography of Welsh and Scottish Nationalism." *Scottish Geographical Magazine,* XXVIX (1973).

Thompson, L. M. "Afrikaner National Historiography and the Policy of Apartheid." *Journal of African History,* V (1963).

Warburto, T. R. "The Rise of Nationalism in Switzerland." *Canadian Review of Studies in Nationalism,* VII, no. 2 (Fall, 1980).

Wilhelm, B. "Un Autre Pays Sans Litterature Nationale: L'Exemple Suisse." *Canadian Review of Studies in Nationalism,* IV, no. 1 (Spring, 1979).

Williams, C. H. "Cultural Nationalism in Wales." *Canadian Review of Studies in Nationalism,* IV, no. 1 (Fall, 1976).

Windmiller, M. "Linguistic Regionalism in India." *Pacific Affairs,* XXVII (1954).

Wynar, L. R. "Ukrainian-Russian Confrontation in Historiography." *Ukrainian Quarterly,* XXX, no. 1 (1974).

Young, H. F. "South Tyrol: New Approaches to an Old Problem." *Canadian Review of Studies in Nationalism,* II, no. 1 (Fall, 1974).

Zernato, G. "Nation: The History of a Word." *Review of Politics,* VI (1944).

INDEX

About the Author

LOUIS L. SNYDER is Professor of History, Emeritus, The City College of The City University of New York. One of the world's authorities on German history and nationalism, he has published fifty-eight earlier books.